Eagle Day

Richard Collier was born in Croydon, London. He joined the RAF in 1942 and became War Associate Editor of Lord Mountbatten's Phoenix Magazine for the Forces. After the war, he joined the *Daily Mail* as a feature writer and wrote fifteen major works of military history.

RICHARD COLLIER

EAGLE DAY

CANELOHISTORY

First published in Great Britain in 1966 by Hodder & Stoughton

This edition published in the United Kingdom in 2021 by

Canelo
Unit 9, 5th Floor
Cargo Works, 1–2 Hatfields
London, SE1 9PG
United Kingdom

A CIP catalogue record for this book is available from the British Library.

Print ISBN 978 1 80032 589 0
Ebook ISBN 978 1 80032 588 3

Look for more great books at www.canelo.co

Printed and bound in Great Britain by Clays Ltd, Elcograf S.p.A.

To the unknown pilot

Chapter One

"My God, Life Wouldn't Seem Right..."

August 6–7

At sunrise the house named Karinhall was silent. It sprawled, as still as a slumbering animal, a vast unwieldy pile of hewn stone, forty miles north-east of Berlin, amid the sandy plain called the Schorfheide. Yet the silence was deceptive: on this hazy August morning of 1940, eyes were watching everywhere at Karinhall. Through the dark forests beyond the terrace wound fences inset with photo-electric cells, set to sound instant alarm in guardrooms along the boundary. In these razor-edged days, the house's 120-strong security force, under General Karl Bodenschatz, could take no chances.

But this morning, there were few overt signs of trouble; the overlord of this feudal complex, forty-seven-year-old Reichs-marschall Hermann Goring, Commander-in-Chief of the Luftwaffe, was in benevolent mood. As Goring towelled after an icy shower, before donning an ornate silk robe, his valet, Robert Kropp, knew just the gramophone music to choose for his master's serenade this morning – lively excerpts from Auber's *Fra Diavolo* or even *Arabella*. For today, Tuesday, August 6, 1940, all the omens were good.

It was just nine weeks since Dunkirk, six since the Fall of France – yet still there was no indication that Great Britain would realise the true hopelessness of her position and sue for peace. Three weeks back, even before Winston Churchill's outright rejections of a peace offer, made through the King of Sweden, Hitler, angered by the stalemate, had issued his famous Directive No. 16: since England seemed unwilling to compromise, he would prepare for, if need be carry out, a full-scale thirteen-division invasion of the island on a 225-mile front – from Ramsgate on the Kentish coast to west of the Isle of Wight. The code-name for what Hitler styled "this exceptionally daring undertaking" was "Sea-Lion".

But, the directive stressed, prior to any such landing, "The British Air Force must be eliminated to such an extent that it will be incapable of putting up any substantial opposition to the invading troops."

To Goring, sipping breakfast coffee, this seemed no insuperable task. The French collapse had given his Luftwaffe fully fifty bases in northern France and Holland; even the short-range planes that accounted for half of the 2,550 machines immediately available – Messerschmitt 109 fighters, Junkers 87 (Stuka) dive-bombers – were now within twenty-five minutes striking distance of the English Channel coast. Since July's end, no British convoy had dared to run this formidable gauntlet – and as Goring had warned the world through a July 28 interview with a U.S. journalist, Karl von Weygand, to date the Luftwaffe's strikes had been child's play, "armed reconnaissance only".

And to the top commanders whom he'd this day summoned to mull over final details, men such as Generalfeldmarschall Erhard Milch, the Luftwaffe's Inspector-General, and Generaloberst Hans-Jurgen Stumpff, commanding Air Fleet Five in Norway, it seemed that Goring hadn't a care in the world. Both Air Fleet Two's Generalfeldmarschall Albert Kesselring, and Generalfeldmarschall Hugo Sperrle, chief of Air Fleet Three, whose 300-pound bulk earned him the nickname "The Monocled Elephant", found him benign, even cocky. To Goring, following the whirlwind Polish and French campaigns, to step up aircraft production beyond the 1939 level of 460 planes a month now seemed pointless – and bombers, the proven spearhead of these campaigns, still had priority above fighters.

So this morning, as some present later recalled, it was as much a social occasion as a rehearsal for battle. Resplendent in his sky-blue uniform, Goring seemed more eager to show off the Renoirs in his art-gallery than to discuss tactics – and as aides in smartly cut uniforms hovered with brandy and cigars, Kesselring and Sperrle exchanged meaningful glances. Now, with each week that passed, Goring, like any new-rich millionaire, grew more steadfast in fantasy – and today his whole strange world, lying at the end of a two-mile avenue flanked by marble lions, would surely be displayed to them anew... the silk and silver hangings and the crystal chandeliers... the gold-plated baths... the private cinema and the bowling alley... the model beer-cellar... even canary cages shaped like dive-bombers.

Later, if time allowed, the party might pay a visit to what was virtually a private shrine: the tomb of Goring's beloved first wife Karin, on whom in life he'd lavished a hundred red roses at a time. Six years earlier, with the full approval of Emmy, his second wife, Goring had not only built this mighty hunting-lodge, naming it after Karin, but had re-interred her here in a sunken vault deep beneath the Schorfheide's sandy soil.

Pacing the tapestry-hung corridors in Goring's wake, neither Kesselring, Sperrle, nor the other members of the party were much taken aback by these diversions; by now the Reichsmarschall's way of running an air war was too well known. Though a stream of memoranda countersigned by Goring flooded almost daily from Karinhall, the brunt of planning aerial missions in detail rested as squarely as always on the Air Fleet chiefs and their staffs. As a thrusting Minister of Aviation whose drive, from 1934 on, had wrought the Luftwaffe into the world's most powerful air-arm, Goring's disdain of technical detail had still been such that he met his inspector-general, Erhard Milch, just once every three months.

It wasn't that his Air Fleet commanders didn't raise objections over the forthcoming battle – but Goring, in euphoric mood, brushed them cheerfully aside. To Sperrle, the target selection seemed faulty; if Britain was 100 per cent dependent on seaborne traffic, shouldn't ports be the main target? But Kesselring just couldn't see it. One swamping attack on a key target – say London – was almost always the answer.

As things stood now, the main attack plan – *Adlerangriff*, or attack of the Eagles, to come into force on receipt of the codeword *Adler Tag* (Eagle Day) – was scattered along the whole invasion front: airfields, ports, even aircraft factories. Following hard on this, more mass-attacks – code-named *Lichtmeer* (Sea of Light) – were slated to wipe out all the R.A.F's night operational bases between the Thames and the Wash.

Poring over a map, the three men did check over key targets... the radio direction finding (later called radar) stations on England's south coast, for a start, though their true function was still something of a mystery... the coastal airfields, naturally, Manston, Hawkinge and Warmwell in Dorset... the major airfields such as Biggin Hill, lying inland, eighteen miles south of London.

As yet no final date could be fixed – from August 5 onwards, meteorologists predicted a high-pressure zone moving slowly towards the Channel from north-west England – but on one score Goring was adamant. By the yardstick of the Polish and French campaigns, the Royal Air Force should be out of the picture in four days flat.

Hie decision made, Goring led his guests towards the showpiece he'd all along had in store for them: the vast model railway that snaked beneath Karinhall's rafters, past miniature farms and forests, under papier-mache mountains six feet high. A shade bemused, the field-marshals watched as their host pressed a button and a glinting squadron of toy bombers glided on taut wires from the eaves to shower their bombs on a model of the French Blue Train. Toy signal lights changed from red to green, from green to red, and Goring relaxed, content.

He had just set the most powerful air force in the world the toughest task they'd ever been commanded to carry out.

Across the English Channel, where twenty-three R.A.F. fighter squadrons were defending a 250-mile front against odds of three to one, the people waited for the worst that could happen.

Most yearned for a break in the monotony. At Biggin Hill airfield in Kent, Corporal Elspeth Henderson had pined for action for eight long months – yet though experts warned that the field was on the direct bomber route to London from the southeast, life at the 450-acre hilltop site called "Biggin-on-the-Bump", as uneventful as pre-war Edinburgh, where Elspeth, a Scottish law professor's daughter, had passed her childhood days.

Aged twenty-six, a petite, determined redhead, Elspeth had swiftly rebelled against the stifling routine of life as a volunteer nurse; she yearned for action, to be in the thick of things. Within three months of war's outbreak, armed with little more than a suitcase containing two evening dresses, she had set off from Edinburgh, to join the W.A.A.F.

Now eight months later, she knew every corner of Biggin Hill's Operations Room, which controlled four fighter squadrons over a crucial 2,800 square-mile sector, as intimately as once she'd known her father's library, crammed with its leather-bound volumes of Dickens and Scott. As a trainee plotter she'd worked with the long-handled magnetic plotting rods, tracing suspected German raiders on the big glass screen that showed Biggin Hill's operational area; on night watches, she'd even slept beneath the operations table, stirring and sneezing lustily as the straw in her palliasse worked loose.

Yet for three long months, while Biggin's runways were constructed, there hadn't even been a squadron to control – and for the most part Elspeth and her friends Barbara Lecky and Yvonne Simmons could only spread their knitting patterns on the table and gossip. The operations officers whiled away tedium with a card game called "Up the River" for penny stakes. And during the hot sultry nights, penned behind the black-out curtains, not one solitary German bomber showed up to enliven the watch – only moths and cockchafers battering against the electric lights, to fall writhing on the controller's dais, the maps, the telephone keys.

So often, as much for encouragement as anything, Elspeth would re-read the notice that Group Captain Richard Grice, the Station Commander, had posted everywhere, the words of the Prime Minister to the nation as long ago as June 18: "What General Weygand called The Battle of France is over. I expect The Battle of Britain is about to begin. Upon this battle depends the survival of Christian civilisation."

At this same hour on August 6 – while Goring was still finalising last-minute details with Kesselring and Sperrle – the author of those words, Winston Spencer Churchill, was touring the defences of England's east coast with No. 257 Hurricane Squadron. Today, The Old Man seemed as indomitable as ever – yet his bodyguard, Detective-Inspector Walter Thompson was worried sick. Now that invasion was an ever-present possibility, Thompson felt burdened in more ways than one. On trips like this he not only had to carry his own gas-mask and steel helmet but Churchill's as well, to say nothing of Churchill's Colt .45 and his own .32 Webley – so how could any man thus laden hope to be quick on the draw?

Himself a dead shot, who still found time for target practice on the drive at Chequers, the Prime Minister's official country residence, Churchill pooh-poohed such anxieties, but Thompson was less ebullient. Only recently the French Underground had come up with disquieting news: not only did Churchill stand in imminent danger of assassination but German intelligence were well aware of his bodyguard's identity.

"When we are ready," warned one German news-sheet, "all the Thompsons in England won't prevent us."

Though Churchill found nothing but exhilaration in the prospect – "If they do come, Thompson," he chuckled, "I can

6

always take a few of them with me" – Thompson wasn't reassured at all. Never could he remember times so grave: though every post brought cheese, eggs, even chickens to 10 Downing Street, tokens from Churchill's loyal admirers, security now decreed that every gift – even fine Havana cigars – ended up in Scotland Yard's furnace.

Much of Churchill's do-or-die spirit infused the pilots of the Royal Air Force: as yet, many were still unblooded and they ached to prove themselves in action. At Kenley airfield, outside London, Squadron Leader Aeneas MacDonell, commanding No. 64 Squadron, summed up the spirit of many such outfits. "It's like holding in a team of wild horses to keep them in formation when there are Germans near."

A few, more seasoned, took a graver view: How long before one saw death as in a mirror? At Tangmere, on the Sussex coast, Hurricane pilot Tom Hubbard likened it to a game of roulette: "It's like backing black all the time. Our luck can't come up forever." Pilot Officer George Bennions, a fiery Yorkshireman, felt differently; it seemed that life had never offered more. In the officer's washroom at Hornchurch, Essex, he burst out to Harry "Butch" Baker: "My God, life wouldn't seem right if you didn't go up to have one scrap in the morning and another in the afternoon."

Most were light-hearted – uncertain of how they'd stand the strain, it seemed safer to play it cool. At Warmwell airfield, Dorset, Pilot Officer Eugene "Red" Tobin joined in the private joke of No. 609 Spitfire Squadron: the lull of these first August days was easily explained. Goring had given the Luftwaffe a whole week's rest, before facing the R.A.F.

Posted to 609 only four days earlier, along with his friends Andy Mamedoff and "Shorty" Keough, Red Tobin could rarely resist a wisecrack. And to Red, in any case, the fact that three native-born Americans should be here in England fighting with an R.A.F. squadron had an especially humorous slant. Just six months earlier, at Mines Field, near Inglewood, California, an agent had been busy signing up both Red and Andy Mamedoff as fighter pilots for the war in Finland. The bait: all their expenses to Helsinki and a hundred dollars a month while they lasted.

A twenty-three-year-old real estate operator's son from Los Angeles, with blue eyes and flaming red hair, Tobin had assented cheerfully – undeterred by the fact he'd never flown a fighter in his life. Unlike Andy Mamedoff, who scratched a living barnstorming with his own plane, Red had stuck prudently to his job as an M.G.M. studio messenger, running errands for stars such as Humphrey Bogart and Charles Boyer. His sole flying experience was 200 hours on antiquated Cubs and Luscombs.

Yet ever since his first flip as an eight-year-old at Rogers' Field, Los Angeles, flying and engines had made up Red Tobin's world – so much so that in all his years at Hollywood High he'd never once brought home a good report card. Somehow stripping down abandoned cars, making friends with the pilots at Burbank Field, had taken up all the time he had to spare.

Thus, neither Red nor Andy had turned a hair when the war in Finland folded before they'd even left Los Angeles. As Red put it reasonably, "If you go looking for a fight, you can always find one." Ten days later, as embryo pilots of the French Armee de l'Air, they'd boarded a freighter in Halifax, Nova Scotia, along with Brooklyn-born Vernon "Shorty" Keough, a professional parachute-jumper they'd met along the way, bound for the French port of St. Nazaire.

But hard as they looked, the Americans found no fighting in France. All the way from Paris through Tours to Bordeaux they stayed just one jump ahead of the German advance, living on unsweetened coffee and potato soup, bedding down on piles of damp hay, unable even to cadge a combat flight in an antiquated Potez 63. At noon on June 22, Armistice day, they reached St. Jean de Luz on the Spanish frontier to tumble aboard the *Baron Nairn*, the last ship to leave occupied France. Two days later, still seeking that fight, Red Tobin and his friends disembarked at Plymouth.

Now, thanks to a chance contact with a friendly Member of Parliament, they were on the point of finding it; after four weeks brief indoctrination at No. 7 Operational Training Unit, Hawarden, Cheshire, they'd adopted the sky-blue silk scarves of 609 Squadron and were ready for action. Already, they found, their fellow pilots held them in some awe; to gloss over his inexperience, Red had generously credited himself with 5,000 flying hours.

But it wasn't just flying hours that had 609 intrigued; to them Red and the others seemed as colourful a trio as ever enlisted to fight an air war. Six feet tall in his stockinged feet, flight charts always poking from his flying boots, Red, with his rye and ginger ale and the lurid Turkey carpet on which he shot craps, was like the traditional hero of a Western film – and his sidekicks were as unique. An incorrigible gambler from Miami, who'd cheerfully cut a deck for a pound, Andy Mamedoff swore solemnly that he'd come to fight the Luftwaffe solely to uphold the honour of all the White Russians. At four foot ten-and-a-half inches, Vernon Keough, in his size five flying boots, was the shortest man who'd ever passed into the R.A.F.; only two air cushions and his parachute enabled him even to peer over a Spitfire's windscreen. Yet, as a veteran of 480 parachute jumps, he'd time and again risked his life for a meagre twenty-seven cents whip-round.

Yet never once did the Americans seem conscious that in a space of months they'd seen more action than any other squadron member. Most often Red Tobin would shrug off such exploits as their hair-raising ride to Bordeaux on an ammunition train with his favourite wisecrack: "We had a million laughs."

One man was in no mood to laugh; he and all his squadron were filled with cold implacable hatred. At thirty-six, Major Zdzislaw Krasnodebski, joint-commander of the newly-formed 303 Polish Squadron, had seen his world turned upside down; since that September day in 1939, when he took off from Zielonka airfield to see the German warplanes raining bombs on Warsaw, Krasnodebski had known the end was predictable in days. Shot down in flames on his first day of combat, he and his men had soon travelled as tortuous a road as Red Tobin's – to Bucharest, where the Rumanians impounded their planes – to Italy, via Belgrade – at last to France, to find all the heart for fighting gone. Each day as the German bombers circled Tours and Lille unmolested, French pilots relaxed in the bar, sipping their vermouth, ignoring the brand-new Curtis fighters parked on the tarmac outside.

Now that this world was past, Krasnodebski was like every Pole who'd elected to continue the fight from English soil – a man living on memories. They flooded back to him this August morning as he stood in the bar at Northolt airfield, ten miles west of Hyde Park Corner, toying moodily with a whisky... the rolling acres of his father's vast estate at Wola Osowinski... the sleek Arabs he'd ridden as a young nobleman destined for the cavalry... the time when he was nine years old and looked up to see his first Russian plane circling low on manoeuvres, and his sudden boyish decision, triumphantly fulfilled: "Flying will be my life."

Above all, he thought of his wife, Wanda, whom he'd been forced to leave behind with relatives in Warsaw. Was she even now alive there – or a German prisoner? Was she still working as a nurse – or more deeply involved than ever in the Polish Resistance? Sometimes, not often, a brief stereotyped letter would reach him via Lisbon – "I am well and working hard and in good health": the language of love made barren by censorship.

A spare dark disciplinarian, Krasnodebski was, in one way, supremely lucky: the years had taught him needed patience. For the eager young Poles he commanded, thirsting for combat, their reception at Northolt had come as a bitter blow. No doubt the Hurricane fighters were fine planes, superior by far to the obsolescent P.11s they'd flown in Poland – but who'd ever heard of planes with retractable undercarriages? The airspeed indicators registered miles, not kilometres – and the altimeters showed only feet. Some of the British officers assigned to them, such as Squadron Leader Ronald Kellett, the joint-commander, had fluent French – but the Operations Rooms officers spoke only unfamiliar English.

As training mishaps mounted steeply, Group Captain Stanley Vincent, Northolt's station commander, laid down a flat ultimatum: "Until this squadron understands English, it's grounded. I'm not having people crashing round the sky until they understand what they're told to do." Then to a junior officer, in a rueful aside, "Their spirit's magnificent – I think they hate my guts now more than they hate the Germans."

And at lunchtime on this August Tuesday, Krasnodebski knew it was all too true. It wasn't easy for pilots with 2,000 hours flying behind them to cool their heels in the mess ante-room, thumbing through 2,000 *Simple Words in English*. These men resented even the sunshine, to them bird-song was a mockery; at each Sunday church service, ending with the National Anthem, "*Boze Cos Polske*" (God That Hast Poland), they prayed for nothing but the chance of combat. Yet before they killed, they must sit dutifully like schoolboys, studying their English grammars.

That they'd kill with deadly efficiency, given the chance, Krasnodebski never doubted. Even the brief savagery of the Polish campaign had cost the Germans more than 600 planes. And some of their getaways had involved phenomenal flying skill like Wojciech Janusewicz, who, fleeing southern France, glided the last thirty miles across the Mediterranean without fuel, before crash-landing on a beach near Algiers.

As he drank up his whisky and strode in to lunch, Krasnodebski was sure of one thing. When they did become operational the Germans – and the British – would see exactly what a Polish squadron could do.

The mood wasn't universal; in these last hours before the battle, some men were racked by doubts. At Hawkinge airfield,

Kent, within sight of the blue-grey Channel waters, Pilot Officer Geoffrey Page, sprawled on the grass, exchanging banter with the pilots of No. 56 Squadron, didn't seem to have a care in the world – yet a small hard core of fear was lodged within his mind. Only recently, as his Hurricane closed in on a Stuka over Dover Harbour, Page had felt a sudden frightening shock of exultation as he thumbed the firing button. At once yellow flame had whooshed from the Stuka's wing-roots – yet as it plunged like a comet towards the sea, Page was still firing, appalled yet knowing he'd enjoyed this kill.

A sensitive, fair-haired twenty-year-old, Page gave few outward signs of his inner secret: all his life had been a battle against fear. Page, a pupil of the R.A.F. College at Cranwell before the war had told himself time and again that a fighter pilot's was the one career worth the winning. How could an ace such as Captain Albert Ball, the World War One fighter V.C., whose portrait seemed to dominate the college's art gallery, ever have known the doubts and insecurity that tortured *him*?

Rarely free from such doubts after a sheltered childhood in his mother's home, Page had seen a life modelled after Ball's as the only answer. Nothing had dashed his hopes more when the college's top brass flatly disagreed: though he had a great future as a flying instructor, he just didn't possess a fighter pilot's temperament.

Overnight, Hitler's invasion of the Low Countries had reversed his luck: trained fighter pilots were needed, and fast. Now after three months with 56 Squadron, Page, by August 1940 standards was virtually a veteran – and daily, in secret triumph, he noted each victory over the inner self that cared and doubted. The moment when a Hurricane on a training flight crashed before his eyes at North Weald airfield – unmoved by the stink of charred flesh and smoking metal, he'd told himself: They can't shock me – I'm immune. The magic discovery, too, that alcohol would blunt most pain, and that he could hold his liquor with any of them – his flight commander, the bulky Flight Lieutenant "Jumbo" Grade, or even Flight Sergeant "Taffy" Higginson, the squadron's veteran at twenty-seven.

Now, frightened that he'd reached a point where only killing had power to stir him, Page was fighting to brush the fear aside. Defiantly he told himself: This is what they call drinking the red wine of youth – so enjoy it while it lasts. The battle hasn't started yet – it can't last long.

In the fields bordering Hawkinge, where Geoffrey Page chatted with the others, the old immemorial round went on almost as if Goring and his Luftwaffe had never existed to challenge the RAF.

At Ladwood Farm, forty-year-old Robert Bailey was doing what he did every day soon after mid-day: scrubbing down the dropping boards of the poultry house where some of his 1,500 hens were kept. His farm, cupped in a shelving green valley flanked by tall groves of beech trees, lay only two miles north-west of Hawkinge airfield – a priority target for the Luftwaffe when they came.

The Luftwaffe *would* come, perhaps even the invasion forces: at long last, Bailey accepted this. For months after the war began he had steadfastly refused to admit that it could come to anything, and he had said – because he wanted to believe it – that peace would be made by Christmas. But Dunkirk had changed all that.

Robert Bailey would never forget the shock of staring across the Channel to the blue haze-shrouded coastline of France and knowing that this was now German territory and that shells, bombs and even paratroops might soon be singling out Ladwood Farm.

It was then, for the first time, that he realised that a farmer was as much a part of this war as any soldier, and he told his wife Vera: "We ought to stay. Even if they come and occupy us, like in France, we ought to stay."

Even now, it wasn't easy to accept. On this sultry August day, Ladwood's hundred acres, where the loudest sounds were the sheep in the fold and the soft scolding of wood pigeons, were outwardly as peaceful as that other August morning in 1914, when fourteen-year-old Robert came from stacking wheat sheaves in his father's barn to watch his two elder brothers march off to fight the Kaiser, with brass bands to cheer them on their way.

But there were still small signs about the farm that added up to disaster. Those long black poles, placed to repel glider landings, jutting from the ripening wheat in Raikes Hole field – and though a tractor-driver, Earl Knight, was working steadily on with the new Fordson tractor, a galvanised iron canopy was rigged above his head now to screen him from falling shrapnel.

Robert Bailey knew all about those anti-invasion poles. Before gangs of workmen had descended on every farm to set them up, Bailey himself, as local secretary of the National Farmers' Union had hared round the district in his old Ford 8, urging each farmer to set up makeshift obstructions – hay elevators, waggons, even sheep huts – on every stretch of level ground. Many were as unwilling to accept the worst as Bailey himself had been – yet when it came to the pinch, few could resist the urgency of this gentle blue-eyed man who'd farmed Ladwood all his life and had taught their children in Sunday school for as long as most could remember.

Like hundreds of farmers across southern England, Bailey was carrying on in the heat of the driest summer for seven years. Rations were low, and would be lower yet – two ounces of tea a week, four of butter, one and tenpence worth of Argentine meat – but determination didn't waver. The girls of Britain's 80,000-strong Women's Land Army bent to stooking the last of the harvest. The London Cockneys who garnered most of the hops for British brewers were back in Kent as usual – and wearing steel helmets as they picked.

Yet each day hundreds more left the coastal zone. Five miles from Ladwood Farm, in the Kentish port of Folke-stone, removal vans bulked in every street; in Margate's deserted shopping centre, Northdown Road, grass sprouted from the kerbside. House after house stood as empty as a ghost town's, often with beds unmade and ham and eggs congealing on the stove.

Westwards, from low-lying Romney Marsh, 100,000 prize sheep had been evacuated. The children had gone, too, with Mickey Mouse gas-masks for the toddlers to make it all seem a game.

Others just wouldn't budge. At Folkestone, eighteen-year-old Betty Turner, garbed in swimsuit and steel helmet, still wormed through a chink in the beach's barbed wire for her morning bathe. Nearby, in George Lane, Mr. Pink's grocery store carried on with just eight customers – seventeen fewer than the official qualifying number, but eighty-year-old William Pink had personally convinced the Minister of Food, Lord Woolton, that a grocer had a duty to those he dealt with. And somehow Robert Bailey's neighbours on Firs Farm, Arthur and Mary Castle, still took thirty gallons of milk to market daily – in an old Morris Oxford topped with straw bales to ward off shrapnel.

Ministry of Information lecturers, touring the coast, had finite instructions – "Hitler is irrevocably committed to invasion" – but it wasn't easy to convince the public when domestic concerns loomed larger. To the G.B.S.'s Ed Murrow, touring Kent, the talk was all of the heavy oat crop, the glut of strawberries at tenpence a pound. If a few feared incendiary bombs on ripe corn, more grumbled over beer at sevenpence a pint... the shortage of chicken wire... the new order against rearing cockerels.

When it came to adversity, most perversely looked on the bright side. At Wateringbury, Kent, when blast from a stray bomb stripped an entire apple orchard the farmer exulted – it was the quickest picking he'd ever known. At Hayling Island, Portsmouth, families still took picnics to the beach; it was nice to say they'd seen the barbed wire. If petrol was short, one

Romney Marsh farmer, John Hacking, still squired his wife Anne weekly to dances – in a horse-drawn cart. For Mrs Martha Henning and her friends, a shopping trip to Dover was always good for a laugh; sometimes a uniformed provost checked your identity card over morning coffee.

To Robert Bailey, still conscious of his new-made decision, life wasn't all humour; his love for Ladwood, with its leaded windows, the red Kentish brick that had endured for two centuries, its black oak beams, went too deep for that. Somehow it all added up to a heritage he must stay on and cherish. Bending again to the dropping boards, he reflected wryly: Thanks to the war, farming Ladwood was profitable again after twenty years' penury – and now 2,500 German planes were massed just twenty-five minutes' flying time away.

–

In northern France, the Germans were in relaxed mood, too. With the sun dazzling on the Channel waters, the weather seemed too wonderful for war – and despite Hitler's Directive No. 16, the prospects of invasion seemed remote. Hadn't Oberst Werner Junck, regional fighter commander for Air Fleet Three, told his pilots the British must sue for peace? His source seemed impeccable, too: the former German Ambassador to Britain, Joachim von Ribbentrop.

It wasn't that any German pilot doubted ultimate victory; when one of his fliers sought leave of absence to marry, the fighter ace Werner Molders, twenty-five victories to his credit, counselled: "Why marry now, when only England's left? Marry later to celebrate the victory." For by noon on August 7, twenty-four hours after Goring's crucial Karinhall conference, it was nine days since a destroyer, let alone a coastal convoy, had moved in the English Channel.

Even at Karinhall, the prospects of action had seemed so remote that only recently, irked by the lotus-eating life of the

Stuka pilots on the coast, Goring had snapped: "Well, what *can* we do with them? They can't just sea-bathe all summer."

Few would have shared the Reichsmarschall's Spartan view. After the rigours of the French campaign – often eight sorties a day – most were content to take life as it came. Major Hennig Strumpell's pilots were taking time off to brush up their tennis... Major Martin Mettig's 54th Fighter Group were almost a fixture on Boulogne's Berck beach... and any day now, grouse shooting would be in season.

Many had brought pets to divert them on the Channel coast – often just a dog, to add the home-from-home touch, such as Hauptmann Rolf Pingel's dachshund, Raudel, who'd even flown on reconnaissance flights to England. Others had fauna strange enough to stock Stuttgart's famous zoo: the 3rd Fighter Group with their owl, their tame hawk, and Oberleutnant Franz von Werra's lion cub, Simba... Major Hennig Strumpell's group, at Beaumont-le-Roger, Normandy, tended a menagerie of ravens, goats, parrots, even donkeys. Some units had their own pet bear – such as "Petz", the 27th Fighter Group's shaggy black mascot, who'd recently disgraced himself by playfully nibbling the thigh of a visiting concert party soubrette.

And to many those homely touches seemed needed; with most airfields little more than landing strips, conditions were as primitive as might be. Oberleutnant Victor Bauer's outfit, No. 3 Wing, 3rd Fighter Group, were shakily operational from a former football pitch. At Guines, near Calais, Oberleutnant Hans Ekkehard Bob's unit had a pasture so furrowed with sheep-tracks that tyros almost always came to grief at the moment of take-off. At Desvres, near Boulogne, Leutnant Erich Hohagen's men first had to harvest an entire wheatfield, then roll it level.

As with the fields, so with the billets. At Beaumont-le-Roger, Hauptmann "Assi" Hahn slept with a loaded revolver beneath his pillow; each night the deserted villa they'd taken over came alive with sleek grey rats. Even the top brass had few mess privileges. Generalmajor the Baron von Richthofen, head of the 8th Flying Corps at Cherbourg, still thought ruefully of the fine lobster pool in his former Deauville Headquarters, while the 2nd Corps' General Bruno Lorzer made do with a flea-ridden farmhouse near Calais, with plumbing that was better left unplumbed.

In this first week of August, the German pilots, much like the British, were living from day to day and relishing such creature comforts as came their way. At Crepon in Normandy, Hauptmann Werner Andres, heading No. 2 Wing, 27th Fighter Group, had welcome news; tomorrow, August 8, his unit was on twenty-four-hour stand-down, one whole day's freedom from the cramped gipsy caravan that served him as billet. Hans-Joachim Jabs, a twenty-two-year-old ME 110 pilot, was checking over his laundry; if combat threatened, he always liked a clean white shirt to fly against England.

Yet, over pre-dinner drinks, he'd still join his comrades in their unvarying toast: "God preserve for us the ground fog and our flying pay." It wasn't all jest, either; an unmarried pilot could draw up to 220 marks – about £18 a month.

One man was bent on action – a welcome relief after weeks of sitting cooped in the-stuffy omnibus that was his headquarters at Cap Blanc Nez, near Wissant, dwarfed, ironically, by the memorial to Louis Bleriot, the first-ever cross-Channel flier. After days of fiddling paper work, the stocky, smiling fifty-year-old Oberst Johannes Fink, newly-appointed *Kanalkampfführer*, or Channel Battle Leader, knew just what he had to do.

Since *kanal*, in German, can be translated as either "Channel" or "drain", colleagues had light-heartedly dubbed him "Chief Sewage Worker" – and though Fink enjoyed the joke as keenly as any, he wasn't, by nature, a flippant man. A dedicated safety-first expert, who deplored the Luftwaffe's dispensing with priests, Fink saw himself as almost a proxy chaplain to the bomber crews he commanded – and for their part they accorded him a respect they gave few others.

Before each mission, Fink would tell his crews, "Each sortie is a dedication – you must put all your past life behind you" – advice that angered the irreligious Goring beyond all reason. Yet none could deny Fink's mastery of his job. Posted to the Channel one month earlier, with orders to win and keep air superiority over the Straits of Dover, Fink had fulfilled that task in twenty-seven days flat.

Today, Wednesday, August 7, he was tense and excited; returning post-haste from the Karinhall conference, Generalfeldmarschall Albert Kesselring had called a top-level conference at his headquarters nearby. Straight from the shoulder, Kesselring had told them: "Things are going to be different from now on. We're going to attack the airfields."

Chapter Two

"This Is What You Asked For — How Do You Like It?"

August 8–12

Hauptmann Werner Andres saw the waters of the English Channel racing to meet him, faster and faster now at over 300 miles an hour: he tensed himself for the shock. Already he'd thrown back the cockpit hood and released his parachute harness; with white steam pluming furiously from the shattered radiator of his Messerschmitt 109, it would all be over in seconds.

Then a wash of grey water swamped the tailplane and Andres was scrambling; as he dived he felt the icy-cold knife through the blue-grey gabardine trousers the pilots called "Channel pants". Striking out, away from the wreckage, he saw the fighter's nose tilt steeply. Within sixty seconds it had wallowed from sight.

Swimming steadily, Andres fumbled for the kilo packet of fluorescine strapped to his belt above the right knee. He ripped it open, and the yellow-green patch of marker dye spread sluggishly outwards, like ripples from a tossed stone — a sure guide for the rescue planes that would be cruising even here, thirty miles northwest of Cherbourg. Now his thoughts furled rapidly back over the day just past, one of the most disastrous he could ever remember — a day that had cost Goring's Luftwaffe thirteen planes for a loss of twenty-two British ships.

First, his unit had been cheated of their rest-day, after all; from first light his hopes of escaping from his billet in the cramped gipsy caravan had dwindled to zero. For in the small hours of this day, August 8, had come the astonishing news that the British were daring once again to force the Channel passage – twenty-five merchant ships under aimed escort steaming from the Thames Estuary towards Falmouth in Cornwall. At once, from his Cherbourg headquarters, the 8th Flying Corps' Generalmajor the Baron von Richthofen had sent positive orders: "This convoy must be wiped out."

A trigger-tempered disciplinarian who would reprimand a pilot for loosening his collar in a heat wave, von Richthofen invariably expected 100 per cent success from each sortie – and today had been no exception. By noon, 300 planes – the 8th Flying Corps' Stuka dive-bombers, escorted by fighters of Major Max Ibel's 27th Group – had wiped out close on 70,000 tons of shipping; all the way from Dover to St. Catherine's Point, the Channel bobbed with rafts, hatch-covers, life-jackets, the empty shells of abandoned ships glowing red-hot.

Still von Richthofen wasn't satisfied; despite the first two all-out attacks, observation planes reported that six ships still remained defiantly afloat. In the early afternoon of August 8, he ordered yet a third strike.

Though head of the 27th Fighter Group's 2nd Wing, Werner Andres hadn't flown on those first sorties; his machine had been stripped down for overhaul. Now came final orders; overhaul or no, the mechanics must reassemble his plane and his wing must fly with the rest. It was small wonder Andres blazed: "Are they mad – or must the German public have good news every day of the week? However stupid the English are, they'll have guessed our target by this time."

And by 3 p.m., on August 8, cruising with the Stukas across the drifting waste of jetsam, Andres knew he'd been right; he never even saw the plane that hit him. Fighters spun and stalled everywhere, too fast to know whether they were German or British, and then Andres was diving for his life, barely twenty feet above the choppy water. To protect the Stukas was beyond his power now, and every man in his wing faced this same problem.

Lacking diving brakes, a 109 just couldn't avoid over-shooting the dive-bombers, screaming for the sea at 375 miles an hour; the Stukas, swooping like black gulls for the convoy's shattered remnants, had air-brakes that throttled them back to less than half this speed. And time and again, as they flattened out at the end of their dive, the R.A.F. had struck with deadly accuracy.

As he swam on, lucky enough to attract a rescue plane after four bone-chilling hours, Andres reflected that twenty-two craft crippled or sunk was a heavy price to pay for the day's losses. Suddenly, an incongruous thought struck him: the marker dye, soaking through his fur-lined jacket and blue-grey shirt, had stained his wallet bright yellow. Cut into thin strips that would make some very fancy sandal straps for Frau Andres.

–

At Headquarters, Fighter Command, twelve miles north of London on the Hertfordshire border, Air Chief Marshal Sir Hugh Dowding was soon to feel the same perturbation. As he paced his high Georgian office facing south towards the spire of Harrow Church he knew the losses of August 8 – nineteen planes – were higher than Fighter Command had ever been called upon to bear.

And Dowding cared deeply because Fighter Command was his life. At fifty-eight, nineteen years a widower, the pale, austere man they nicknamed "Stuffy" was still a mystery to his officers; never once, in four years at Headquarters, had he been known to enter the mess. Instead, his punishing routine never varied... four hours desk-work until 1 p.m.... lunch at "Montrose", the rambling gabled house in nearby Cordon Avenue, where his sister Hilde kept house for him... more paper work and home again for a quick dinner at 7.30 p.m.... then back to his desk until it was time to set out for a small-hours visit to one of the new night-fighter stations, still grappling with the unsolved problem of intercepting the night-bomber.

It was no new role for Dowding; even the 1,434 pilots, the 708 fighters, that were this day available to him – two-thirds of them Hurricanes, which Luftwaffe fighters saw as easy meat – had involved a hard-fought battle. As far back as early May, Dowding had warned Squadron Leader Theodore McEvoy, of Air Ministry's Directorate of Operations: "I tell you, McEvoy, every Hurricane we send to France is a nail in our coffin" – nor had his protests stopped short there. On May 15, standing alone before the entire War Cabinet, Dowding had rammed home the worst: to date the French campaign had cost him nearly 300 trained. Further to weaken fighter defences at home by despatching yet more squadrons to France would be fatal.

As he spoke, he flung down his pencil – so forcefully that the Minister of Aircraft Production, Lord Beaverbrook, was convinced he had only resignation in mind. In fact, Dowding hadn't; the attention-getting gesture was designed to show Winston Churchill that he meant business. Now, passing along the ranks of Cabinet Ministers to set a graph squarely in front of Churchill, he told him: "If the rate of wastage shown here continues for another fortnight, we shan't have a single Hurricane left in France *or* in this country."

It was enough; the ten Hurricane squadrons France's Prime Minister Paul Reynaud had demanded to stem the German breakthrough were never forthcoming. But even those machines still available had needed vital modifications; to convert every Hurricane and Spitfire in Fighter Command from two-pitch to constant-speed (variable-pitch) propellers, ensuring maximum take-off and flight speed, mechanics were even now working all night in blacked-out hangars, making do on ten-minute coffee-breaks.

No man to mince words, Dowding was constantly at odds with authority; the Air Staff looked askance at a man whose sole reply to a prosy five-page minute was, "Gosh!" Yet despite all opposition, Dowding, in four years flat, had built the formidable machine that was Fighter Command... pressing for all-weather runways on six airfields, which now had them... urging for one whole year that only the dispersal of planes on airfields could safeguard squadrons against low- or high-level attacks... even pioneering bullet-proof windscreens for fighter planes. Since May he had known a valued ally in Lord Beaverbrook, whose get-up-and-go had now pushed fighter production to an all-time high of 496 machines a month – yet so often did the Air Staff still threaten to retire Dowding, he confessed: "I feel like an unsatisfactory housemaid under notice."

And now, with the Luftwaffe's arrival on the Channel coast, his whole defence system was in some ways outmoded; to intercept German formations approaching at more than 200 miles an hour, R.A.F. fighters, which needed close on twenty minutes to reach operational height, would have to climb from coastal airfields laid down when the Rhine was the frontier. Only recently Dowding had gone on record: "The Germans could lay large areas of our big towns in ruins at any time they choose to do so" – and how his pilots would fare now he did not know, if the losses of August 8 were a harbinger of what was to come.

As "Stuffy" Dowding studied the flimsy green combat reports the pilots had scrawled at day's end, the carnage was plain. From Hornchurch in the east to Middle Wallop in the west, the six Sector Controllers who manoeuvred the squadrons into battle over southern England had scrambled them too late and too low.

Just one unit – Squadron Leader John Peel's No. 145 Hurricane Squadron – had had the lucky height. At 9 a.m., on August 8, patrolling 16,000 feet above the haze-shrouded waters off St. Catherine's Point, the Isle of Wight's southernmost tip, they'd seen the Stukas streaking like furies for the packed black mass of shipping. Appropriately, breaking radio silence, John Peel now gave the fighter pilot's war cry: "Tally ho!"

At once, as if on cue, twelve hump-backed Hurricanes altered course – heading not for the shattered convoy but for the brassy orb of the sun that swam above them. If they dived from the sun, Peel knew, the Germans' vision would be dazzled from the start.

Eighteen-thousand feet above the water now and again Peel's voice rasped through the intercom – "Come on, chaps, down we go!" – and suddenly, as the Hurricanes swooped, ninety-six .303 Browning machine-guns were chattering as one, marking the first-ever shots fired in the Battle of Britain.

It was a breath-taking sight… a tanker splitting clean in two with a mighty mushroom of smoke… everywhere parachutes blossoming white, rocking in the slipstream of hard-diving 109s… barrage balloons dripping flame towards the shining water… the pale fire of Very lights bursting red against the sun.

And, despite individual setbacks, the squadron had luck on their side. Days earlier, slipping on wet rocks at a beach party, Flight Lieutenant Roy Dutton had broken a carpal bone in his right hand, an injury so painful he could barely press the starter button; even changing into coarse pitch was now a left-handed action. Suddenly with a 109 rock-steady in his sights, his engine, overheated, cut out altogether. Still Dutton wasn't unduly worried. He had height and position enough to tackle a slow-moving Stuka.

And fortune favoured him. Diving fast on the rearmost Stuka of a group, he jabbed the firing button for four long seconds; as the bomber's nose dipped, it spun like a spent bullet towards the sea. Relieved in more ways than one, Dutton realised that dive had cooled off the engine; all at once it had coughed into life.

Below him, another Stuka was poised for the dive; as swift as a darting shark, Dutton was on it Another burst – but as the bomber struck the water in a soaring geyser of foam, he knew a chill of disquiet. He was now fifteen miles out to sea – and with that second dive his engine had cut out for good and all.

To Dutton, it seemed an eternity before he could coax the crippled craft as high as 1,000 feet above the sandy Sussex coastline, to set her down somehow at Tangmere airfield. For six months thereafter, Dutton's right hand was encased in plaster.

And for every pilot of 145 it seemed a field-day all the way; even a novice such as nineteen-year-old James Storrar, whose cheery take-off cry was "Fuel and noise – let's go!" felt himself a world-beater. Opening fire on a Stuka, Storrar didn't even know he'd hit it, until its rear machine-gun canted crazily skywards: the gunner was lolling dead. Then, as he watched, what seemed "like liquid fire" rippled along one wing and down the leg of the Stuka's undercarriage.

Flying level, only yards distant, Storrar could see the German pilot clearly now – watching, with almost clinical detachment, as the wrapping orange flame engulfed his own wing. Without warning, the Stuka nose-dived, spreading blow-torch fire across the sea.

Convinced they'd knocked down twenty-one German planes single-handed, the squadron that night threw an all-ranks party to end them all – as Storrar recalls it: "The floor literally swam in beer." Quietly confident, John Peel inscribed one swastika in his log-book. To 145, it seemed the battle was almost over.

But while this one squadron had gained needed height, most, thanks to raw controlling, hadn't come within an ace of it.

Though Air Chief Marshal Dowding's twenty-odd radar stations, stretching from the Isle of Wight to the Orkneys, could pick up a German formation's course, even gauge its strength, their estimation of height was almost always unreliable. Then, too, the Germans timed each sortie to strike with the dazzling sun behind them – yet the Sector Ops Rooms didn't even plot the sun's position on the board.

As yet few Sector Controllers even realised that height, above all, was what their squadrons needed – and that the tried-and-true slogan of World War One's fighter pilots, "Beware of the Hun in the sun", had never applied more forcibly.

But scores of pilots, on August 8, never-saw "the Hun in the sun". One Spitfire pilot, Edward Hogg, never forgot this day: twisting and weaving above the foundering convoy, he was time and again forced to break from combat without firing a shot. However high he climbed, there were always ME 109s still higher – and always the sun struck at his eyes like white fire.

To most of Dowding's pilots, it seemed the Luftwaffe held the sky as never before. Even at mid-afternoon – about the time Hauptmann Werner Andres was ditching his 109 in the Channel – 43 Hurricane Squadron, from Tangmere, saw a sight to turn them cold: von Richthofen's third and last sortie, an umbrella of German planes filling the sky all the way to Cherbourg.

To Pilot Officer Frank Carey, it was "a raid so terrible and inexorable it was like trying to stop a steam-roller" – and the simile had its points. Within minutes 43 Squadron, two wounded, two injured, were out of the combat.

Lacking the height that might have saved them, men took desperate evasive action. Tony Woods-Scawen, of 43 Squadron, flew clean through a cloud of Stukas, firing as he went; if they retaliated, they'd surely hit each other. Undaunted, the Stukas hosed him with fire; he escaped by a hair's-breadth. Sergeant John Whelan, breaking from a head-on attack at 24,000 feet, spun his Spitfire off a high-speed stall and didn't recover level flight until 16,000 feet. Back at Hawkinge, Squadron Leader Aeneas MacDonell reproved him, deadpan: "Don't do that again – they'll claim they shot you down."

The day's losses weren't surprising. Though the War Cabinet had yielded to Dowding, withholding his precious squadrons from France, recently they'd hampered his efforts in another way. As early as July 10, urged by Professor Frederick Lindemann (later Lord Cherwell), Winston Churchill's scientific adviser, they'd drastically reduced the pilots' operational training – from six months to four scant weeks. Faced with a dearth of trained pilots, a glut of operational machines, they'd seen no other solution.

Confident that the monthly output of pilots could be boosted from 560 to 890 per month, Lindemann challenged: "Are not our standards of training too high? The final polish should be given in the squadrons."

Westwards, over the shattered convoy, more and more, on August 8, acquired that "final polish" – through a cruel baptism of fire. One Hurricane squadron, No. 238, operating from Middle Wallop airfield, Hampshire, had been formed so quickly that they'd never done a training flight together; sighting the Germans over the Channel they opened fire half a mile out of range. Pilot Officer Vernon Simmonds, as green as any, didn't even realise battle had commenced until empty cartridge cases showered him like hail. Then he realised.

When two of his pilots were reported missing in the Channel, Squadron Leader Harold Fenton flew gamely off to search for them – only to find himself outduelled and shot down by a German observation plane. Hauled aboard the trawler H.M.S. *Bassett*, Fenton spent a damp unhappy afternoon drying out in the boiler-room – along with a German pilot so confident he'd flown over England with nothing more lethal than a Very pistol and a packet of prophylactics.

Hence Air Chief Marshal Dowding's unease, for as he leafed through the combat reports, it was plain that 145 Squadron's success was as much due to luck as judgment – and soon many squadrons, down to half-strength after the debacle of Dunkirk and costly convoy patrols, must be pulled out to rest and reform.

Within days, 238 Squadron, minus Squadron Leader Fenton and two flight commanders, went west to Cornwall... at Hornchurch in the east, the under-strength 41 Squadron were this day moving out to Catterick, Yorkshire... and as Squadron Leader John Peel's outfit left the front-line for Scotland on August 14, one pilot from the relieving unit hailed another: "Come and meet 145 Squadron. Nice chaps – all two of them!"

So if Reichsmarschall Goring stepped up the pressure, what could Dowding do? In southern England, he had just twenty-three squadrons and he couldn't afford to strip northern England of the fighter units guarding the vital industrial areas of the Tyne and Clydeside. If Fighter Command's losses could be assessed at a steady drain of twenty per day, could even Lord Beaverbrook's Ministry of Aircraft Production keep pace?

For so many thousands, as yet, the battle had barely started – and Dowding couldn't know.

–

Pilot Officer Geoffrey Page awoke with a start; for a second he couldn't even recall where he was. Then, abruptly, it came back to him; along with ten other young pilots of No. 56 Squadron he was jammed into Flight Sergeant "Taffy" Higginson's ancient rattletrap called "Esmeralda", returning from a night on the town. It was not long before dawn on August 12. Soon the main guardroom of North Weald airfield, on the fringe of Epping Forest, would loom from the milky dawn mist.

Now, as the old car wheezed towards the airfield's main gates, the sentry's dutiful challenge rang out, "Halt, who goes there?" and eleven pilots roused themselves, to salute him as one: "Santa Claus, eight reindeer, and a couple of other silly buggers!" They heard the sentry chuckle dryly: "Pass, friends."

Hazily, Geoffrey Page reviewed the night gone past – one of many such nights when the squadron had lived it up to the hilt in the smoky London night club called The Bag O'Nails. The band had seemed as bored as ever, but at least, Page thought gratefully, the dance floor had been packed. He and the dark slinky hostess in the scarlet evening dress hadn't been able to do much more than crush-dance – so his limitations as a dancer hadn't been too painfully apparent.

How much liquor they'd consumed between them he could scarcely guess; bottles had seemed to come and vanish at amazing speed. Already, within hours, the night was just a series of blurred impressions… the way they'd all split their sides when the hostess tweaked "Taffy" Higginson's bushy moustache… the bawdy choruses they'd sung on the way to the garage where Esmeralda was parked… how they'd escaped in the nick of time when Sergeant George Smythe, who couldn't resist tinkering with gadgets, dismantled the headlight of a customer's car.

As Esmeralda gathered speed up the ramp, outdistancing the angry garage attendant pursuing them, they'd hauled the puffing Smythe aboard head first; in fist-shaking fury, the attendant had given up.

Stretched out on his cot at dispersal, his head throbbing gently, Page hardly hoped for sleep in the few hours before combat. And now the party was over, he'd welcome combat, to distract the mind from follies such as regret or pity. It was only a game, and death was bound to win, but wasn't the very act of cheating him a little longer, even in the warm murky twilight of The Bag O'Nails, the most exciting game a youngster could play?

Suddenly because the tension was unbearable, Page sat bolt upright in bed. By the light of a torch, he tried to set down all he felt in a letter to an old Staff College friend, Michael Maw: "I sometimes wonder … if the whole war isn't a ghastly nightmare from which we'll wake up soon. I know all of this sounds nonsense, but I'm slightly tight, and it's only an hour to dawn… To me, it will mean just another day of butchery… it makes me feel sick. Where are we going and how will it all end?"

Most felt this sense of expectancy they couldn't quite define – though, as always, there were exceptions. From Tangmere airfield, Flying Officer William Clyde, 601 Squadron, flew north for the first day's grouse shooting: on principle, he wouldn't let Goring interfere with the "Glorious Twelfth". Others felt something big would break at any minute; on the previous day, the R.A.F. had lost an all-time high of thirty-two planes.

Twenty-five minutes flying time away, the Germans were awake early, and with reason. This morning, following days of frustration, the battle would move away from the Channel and over England itself. On August 9, everything had seemed set fair for the following day, but by nightfall the big strike was off again – bad weather might set in. Now, at least, the meteorologists had so far unbent as to make a positive prognosis. On the morrow, there would be fine clear weather over the United Kingdom.

Alerted by Goring's headquarters, O.K.L. *(Oberkommando der Luftwaffe)*, Air Fleets Two and Three had been ordered to clear the decks. The all-out attack, the Sunday punch – Eagle Day – was timed for 7 a.m., on Tuesday August 13.

They were leaving nothing to chance. Those giant aerials, towering 350 feet above the Kent and Sussex coastlines and clearly visible by telescope from France, must first be neutralised. Constant monitoring of British radio had made plain to General Wolfgang Martini, the Luftwaffe signals chief, that R.A.F. fighters kept in touch with their bases by ultra-short-wave transmissions. And these coastal aerials must somehow link up with this – and the fact that Fighter Command always knew when German formations were approaching.

Martini didn't quite know how, but he'd pounced on one salient fact: these detector stations virtually ruled out any chance of a surprise attack. As early as August 3, his appeal to Generaloberst Hans Jeschonnek, Chief of Staff to the Luftwaffe, had borne fruit. Then Jeschonnek had ruled: "Identified British detector stations are to be attacked in force and put out of action early on."

Only one man, Oberst Paul Deichmann, the 2nd Flying Corps' Chief of Staff, voiced a minority view. Surely the whole aim of Eagle Day was to destroy the British fighter force? In that case, wasn't it better this system *should* warn them, so that they came up to be destroyed in the air?

Among the pilots, reactions varied, but none saw the struggle ahead as a walk-over; the British would prove formidable adversaries. Over a man-sized breakfast — sausages, eggs, hot crisp rolls — in his billet at Desvres, Leutnant Erich Hohagen was recounting a typical tangle with a lone Spitfire over Dungeness, Kent. Surprised by four of Hohagen's outfit, the pilot had still, at 30,000 feet, battled on for five homicidal minutes.

With ungrudging admiration, Hohagen wound up: "He was solid as a rock."

The other grunted assent — and in all of their minds lurked the thought that they must contend not only with the British. Von Richthofen's ruthless handling of pilots in the big convoy attack showed just how hard the top brass might drive them.

At Beaumont-le-Roger airfield, Major Hennig Strumpell was debating this same point with his adjutant, Oberleutnant Paul Temme. The previous day, August 11, both had flown escort duty for a heavy attack on the British naval base at Portland — and to both the orders of the day had seemed suicidal. The ruling: regardless of the odds, every German fighter must stay in combat for twenty-five uneasy minutes.

A few had blind faith; at Cherbourg-West, Oberleutnant Ludwig Franzisket, of the 27th Fighter Group's 1st Wing, thought it only a matter of time. Officially he'd heard that the British had only fifty Spitfires left, and the top brass should know. Others, lacking inside knowledge, still had the uncanny hunch that Hitler saw "Operation Sea-Lion" as little more than a study plan. Oberleutnant Victor Bauer and his friends agreed: "If he didn't invade after Dunkirk, he can't really mean business."

It troubled the enthusiasts, too. Fearful that the war might peter out before they'd had their share of glory, many German pilots pinned their faith ironically in Winston Churchill's fighting spirit: surely this man would never give in? At Caffiers, near Calais, a Spitfire pilot making a forced landing was almost mobbed by well-wishers led by Leutnant Gerhard Muller-Duhe; who enquired solicitously: "And how is Churchill?" Gently the British pilot rebuked than: "Mr. Churchill, please."

If morale was at peak, most were resigned to a long hard struggle ahead. Hauptmann Walter Kienzle, newly arrived on the coast, had it straight from Oberst "Uncle Theo" Osterkamp, the regional fighter commander for Air Fleet Two. An Anglophile, to whom the British were always "the lords", Osterkamp warned: "Now we're going to fight 'the lords', and that's something else again. They're hard fighters and they're good fighters – even though our machines are better."

A few were spurred by private ambitions. At forty-seven the bald, eagle-faced Oberstleutnant Hassel von Wedel had found his eyes playing too many tricks for operational flying – but when Hermann Goring, his old World War One comrade, appointed him official Luftwaffe historian he'd stubbornly resisted relegation to a desk in the German Air Ministry. He must serve with a frontline unit and see for himself how things went.

Though most groups had tried to wriggle out of it – a myopic middle-aged war-reporter on the strength meant diverting four good pilots to protect him – you couldn't disregard an order from Goring. This morning, at Samer, near Boulogne, Oberstleutnant von Wedel was officially attached to the 3rd Fighter Group, eager to record the next brisk chapter in the saga.

Hauptmann Herbert Kaminski had more martial ambitions. A chunky, fair-headed perfectionist of thirty-one, Kaminski jokingly styled himself "The Last of the Prussians": heaven help the man who fell down on a job if Kaminski was the overseer. Despite an unhealed wound in his right shoulder, a legacy of the French campaign, Kaminski still flew his ME 110, making do without harness straps, but close friends gibed that what really ailed him was "throat-ache" – the ambition to see the Knight's Cross, the coveted Luftwaffe award, hanging on a black ribbon round his neck.

Kaminski, who was far from denying it, now warned Unteroffizier Strauch, his long-suffering gunner: "There's nothing doing just now – but there may be soon. Make sure you understand all the procedure of inflating and boarding the dinghy – just in case."

At group commander level, there were reservations; victory might be assured, but they still distrusted the high command's airy optimism. After one full-dress conference, when Kesselring reiterated Goring's belief in a four-day victory, thirty-four-year-old Major Hans Trubenbach, commanding the 52nd Fighter Group at Coquelles, summed up what many felt: "I'm too old a one to be caught by nonsense like that."

Like many commanders, Trubenbach felt that Goring, weak in logic, pinned his faith in the wrong planes – above all, the twin-engined ME 110. Christened the *Zerstorer* (destroyer) the twin-seater fighter, meeting only token opposition, had first won easy laurels in the French campaign – yet all through July, as Oberst Fink's units triumphantly swept the Channel skies, its losses had mounted steeply.

A long-range escort fighter, designed to clear the way for mass bomber attacks, the 110 looked foolproof on the drawing-board; against the ME 109's maximum cruising range, 412 miles, the 110 could clock up 680 miles. Yet, loaded, the 110s outweighed the streamlined 109s by almost 10,000 pounds. Their lack of manoeuvrability and speed were a byword with every pilot.

In combat, their stock tactic was what the R.A.F. called "the circle of death" – a defensive gambit that had the machines circling warily, each guarding the other's tailplane, perilous to friend and foe alike. Only recently Major Hennig Strumpell had found himself in one such circle dog-fighting with a Spitfire – while 110s blasted tracer at both of them impartially.

Yet to all arguments, Goring was obdurate: "If the fighters are the sword of the Luftwaffe, the ME 110 *Zerstorer* is the point of that sword."

Goring's unswerving belief in the Stuka troubled his commanders, too. Unrivalled in precision-bombing and close infantry support when the Luftwaffe held the sky, they now made up one-third of the Luftwaffe's bomber force – for maximum success at minimum cost of material the Reichsmarschall saw them as unbeatable. Yet to most, the heavy losses of August 8 presaged the shape of things to come.

One man was quietly confident; with luck, the element of surprise would come to his aid today, just as it had done yesterday. At thirty, Hauptmann Walter Rubensdorffer, a tall, dynamic Swiss with an infectious sense of humour, knew that he held a unique command in the Luftwaffe; as leader of Test Group 210, a task force of twenty-eight hand-picked pilots, he had spent long weeks of trial and error at the Luftwaffe's experimental station at Rechlin on the Baltic, proving that fighters could not only carry bombs but could hit their targets.

Many Luftwaffe chiefs – Kesselring among them – had scoffed at the notion of 109s and 110s with bombs beneath their fuselage, but Rubensdorffer, a former Stuka ace whose brainchild this was, had seen his perseverance pay off. Only yesterday, swooping on a British convoy, code-named "Booty", fifteen miles south-east of Harwich, his unit had met only desultory ack-ack: what harm could fighter planes do to shipping?

But Test Group 210, loosing salvoes of 250-kilo bombs, had scored mortal hits on two large ships – and then, as the R.A.F.'s 74 Squadron zoomed to engage, had once again resumed their role as fighters. From the whirling catherine-wheel of planes, 100 feet above the water, two British fighters had failed to return. As he drank his breakfast coffee at Calais-Marck airfield, Rubensdorffer was confident, yet tense. By now, Test Group 210 were Kesselring's most cherished unit – often the Feldmarschall arrived on a visit armed with a jeroboam of champagne – and this morning their mission was the most crucial yet: to knock out four key radar stations on the Kent and Sussex coast. On this mission might hinge the whole success of the battle – for if Rubensdorffer succeeded, and the R.A.F. lacked all radar warning, the way would lie wide open for Oberst Johannes Fink's massed airfield attacks, the onset of Eagle Day.

The targets were vital indeed. Set down amid the Kentish apple orchards and the flat salt marshes, the brick-built radar stations, girdled by barbed wire, were a mystery to all except the screened personnel who lived and worked there. And the sinister latticework of steel aerials rearing 350 feet above them lent colour to that mystery – some country folk swore they housed powerful rays, which could cut out the engine of a hostile aircraft at one flick of a switch.

But the truth, if more mundane, spelt equal danger to the Germans: once the echo of approaching aircraft showed as a V-shaped blip of light on the convex glass screen in the station's Receiver Block, the news flashed like wildfire... from detector station to Fighter Command's Filter Room... from Filter Room to Air Vice-Marshal Keith Park's H.Q. 11 Fighter Group, controlling southern England... from 11 Group to the sector stations directing the fighter squadrons.

The whole intricate structure of Dowding's Fighter Command must stand or fall by this high-pressure plotting, which from the first blip on a screen to a squadron racing for its planes had a time-lapse of just six minutes.

So this morning every coastal radar station was gripped by tension: no units in Fighter Command could predict their own danger more surely. At Rye, near the old Kentish seaport, Corporal Daphne Griffiths, one of the morning watch of four, had just taken over the screen in the flimsy wooden Ops hut from her friend Helen McCormick, a pretty New Zealander. Now, as Daphne mechanically intoned plots to Fighter Command's Filter Room at Stanmore, Corporal Brenda Hackett, stood by to keep record of every one – its time, range, bearing and grid reference.

At 9.25 a.m., Daphne was alerted: a V-shaped blip of light had registered suddenly off northern France. Calmly she reported: "Hullo, Stanmore, I've a new track at thirty miles.

Only three aircraft – I'll give you a plot." Seconds later, the thought struck her: were other stations plotting these same planes? But the Filter Room reassured her. She alone had registered them – and could they please have a height?

As Daphne Griffiths reported back – "Height, 18,000" – she noted that the range was fast decreasing, too. Was there any identification? The Stanmore plotter's voice was metallic in her headphones: "No, there's nothing on it yet." By now, Daphne was perturbed: two more plots had made it clear that if the planes continued on course they would pass clean overhead. Again she queried: "Stanmore, is this track still unidentified?" The Filter Room seemed unruffled: they had that moment marked the plot with an x, which signified doubtful, to be watched and investigated.

There was less doubt on the coast. Behind Daphne Griffiths, the station adjutant, Flying Officer Smith, one of several officers who'd drifted in to watch, recalled that the Ops hut was protected only by a small rampart of sandbags. He told Corporal Sydney Hempson, the N.C.O. in charge: "I think it would be a good idea if we had our tin hats."

At that moment the voice of Troop Sergeant Major Johnny Mason, whose Bofors guns defended the six-acre site, seemed to explode in their headsets: "Three dive-bombers coming out of the sun – duck!"

It was split-second timing. All along the coast, Test Group 210, split now into squadrons of four, came hurtling from the watery sunlight… Oberleutnant Wilhelm Roessiger's pilots making for the aerials at Rye… Oberleutnant Martin Lutz and his men streaking for Pevensey, by Eastbourne… Oberleutnant Otto Hintze barely a thousand metres above the Dover radar station, flying for the tall steel masts head-on in a vain effort to pinpoint them… Rubensdorffer himself going full throttle for the masts at Dunkirk, near Canterbury.

In the Ops hut at Rye, the snarling whine of Roessiger's engines seemed to drown out all sound – until Daphne Griffiths, still glued to the set, heard a faint, faraway voice in her headphones: "Rye, what's happening? Why don't you answer me?" With a nineteen-year-old's conscious dignity, she reproved them: "Your *X* raid is bombing *us*, Stanmore, and it's no wonder you can't hear me – we can't hear ourselves either."

Now the whole hut shuddered, and glass and wooden shutters were toppling; clods of earth founted 400 feet high to splatter the steel aerials. Prone beneath the table, the W.A.A.F. crews saw chairs and tables spiral in the air like a juggler's fast-flying balls – and everywhere the sites were under fire. At Pevensey, tons of gravel swamped the office of the C.O., Flight Lieutenant Marcus Scroggie, only minutes after he'd left it; at Dover, a bomb sheared past recumbent operators to bury itself six feet beneath the sick quarters. All along the coast the tall towers trembled, and black smoke was rising to blot out the sun.

Inland, they shared the tension, too; in Fighter Command's Filter Room, Pilot Officer Robert Wright cut in on a frenzied running commentary from an N.C.O. at Ventnor Detector Station on the Isle of Wight, simultaneously under fire by fifteen Junkers 88 dive-bombers. Flames were spreading like a curtain across the site, the Fire Brigade, pumping up water through 560 yards, just couldn't cope, and a W.A.A.F. called "Blondie" was missing.

It was all so stirring that Wright, a pre-war screenplay writer, seized a microphone to shatter the Filter Room's cathedral calm, yelling: "Well, where are the rest of you?" When a colleague threw out disdainfully, "Don't get *too* Hollywood," Wright was so furious he forgot whose side he was on. He blazed back: "You English make me sick."

On the coast they were less excited: the suddenness of the attacks had them dazed. At Rye, Assistant Section Officer Violet Hime, the W.A.A.F. administrative officer, groped shakily from the floor of the Ops hut, eyes and nostrils choked with grit – to find Corporal June Alderson, a stunning blonde, diffidently proffering a cigarette. Corporal June promised: "I'll light it for you, too, if my hand isn't shaking too much."

As a yellow blade of flame spurted in the blackness, Violet Hime knew a moment of quiet triumph – there wasn't even a tremor in June Alderson's hand. Days earlier, the camp's flight sergeant had enquired casually of Violet Hime just when R.A.F. operators would be replacing the W.A.A.F.: if invasion was imminent, he didn't want morale affected by a pack of hysterical airwomen. Now, within hours of the raid – which showered Rye with forty bombs in four minutes flat – he was back to offer abject apologies.

And every site could tell the same story. At Dunkirk, Kent, where one of Rubensdorffer's thousand-pounders had literally shifted the concrete transmitting block by inches, the W.A.A.F.s registered a formal complaint with the C.O.: from now on they wanted more salads and garden-fresh vegetables, all this bread and meat was producing unsightly blackheads. Somehow no one thought to mention the bombing.

Back at Calais-Marck, Rubensdorffer had reasons for elation: each squadron in his group had scored triumphantly. Already, Pevensey was reported silent: eight of Oberleutnant Lutz's 500-kilo bombs had found their target, with one slicing clean through the main electric cable. Over Rye, Roessiger had reported ten hits – only later did he realise that these were empty barracks and that the main installations had gone unscathed. At Dover, Hintze had seen the aerial towers sway palpably, and many buildings were a total write-off.

But by mid-afternoon, General Wolfgang Martini, as Luftwaffe signals chief, knew bitter disappointment: operating with standby diesels, every station except Ventnor – a write-off for three long weeks – was reported back on the air. To Martini, it didn't seem now as if radar stations could be silenced for more than a few hours at a time.

They had been crucial hours, even so. At noon, with the radar stations still inoperative, the coastal airfields had lain open to the worst the Luftwaffe could do – and they had lost no time. Already at 12.50 p.m., Rubensdorffer's Test Group 210 were back over Kent's east coast: twenty bomb-laden ME 109s and 110s, diving at 375 miles an hour on Manston, the 530-acre forward base code-named Charlie Three, pitting it with 100-plus craters.

That Manston was caught unawares was almost symbolic. An all-grass field, lacking runways, its largely civilian staff still viewed daily life in terms of peace, not war. Hard-pressed flight mechanics, lacking a spanner, found that main stores did things by the book: emergency or no, only the right form, duly countersigned, worked the oracle.

Operational pilots could rarely rustle up so much as a snack – and even transport from dispersal to mess involved completing a Form 658 one day in advance.

One squadron, No. 65, was caught at the second of take-off: from 3,000 feet Oberleutnant Otto Hintze glimpsed their Spitfires clearly, lined up in neat V-shaped formations of three, engines turning over. Then Rubensdorffer had peeled off, a hangar went skywards in a spawning cloud of rubble, and the planes were lost to view, taxi-ing blindly through choking smoke. Bombs rained, and blast sucked at Flying Officer Wigg's Spitfire, stopping his airscrew dead. Only one pilot, Flight Lieutenant Jeffrey Quill, was airborne amid the bombs – too late to exact revenge from the fast-retreating Test Group 210.

Another Spitfire squadron, No. 54, saw it all from first to last: only sheer misfortune stopped Flight Lieutenant Al Deere, this day leading the squadron, from a classic intercept. A chunky, eupeptic New Zealander of twenty-one, whose split-second bale-outs were legendary, Deere was at 20,000 feet when he saw Rubensdorffer's planes streaking from Manston. At once, breaking radio silence, he hailed Pilot Officer Colin Gray, a fellow New Zealander leading Blue Section: "Do you see them?" As Gray exulted, "Too bloody right," Deere knew they were all set.

Then suddenly, as 54 loomed within striking distance of the raiders, everything was wrong. Despairing, Deere saw

Gray's section was no longer with him; only now did he realise that Gray, instead, had sighted a second formation, approaching Dover, and was already in combat. Vainly, Deere yelled, "Where the hell are you?" then saw a vast white cloud of what looked like pumice pressing slowly upwards from Manston. Fastening on to the tail of a swift-diving 109, he didn't realise it was chalk dust, whirling from scores of craters; he thought Manston was on fire. Flying Officer Duncan Smith, 600 Squadron, returning from leave in an old Tiger Moth biplane, was even more taken aback; he didn't know Manston had been attacked. As he circled the drome and saw the white seething patches he thought: Who's been spreading fertiliser?

Below, the airfield was a thundering horde of blue-clad men seeking shelter. Planes passed like black shadows, and Corporal Francis De Vroome, priding himself on his cunning, leapt for a brand-new bomb-crater: they wouldn't strike twice in the same place. Within seconds, he'd clawed his frantic way out; the walls of the crater were glowing red-hot. Manston's medical officer, Squadron Leader John Dales, racing for the main camp in his staff car, slewed suddenly on screaming tyres; the car's right window had burst across his arm. Later he found that nineteen bullets from a low-level dog-fight had ricocheted from the road.

Inland, at Biggin Hill, the pilots of 32 Hurricane Squadron heard of Manston's ordeal over lunch at dispersal – with one spontaneous unsympathetic guffaw: "Let's hope that bloody cook had to run for it." In recent weeks, with bitter experience of Manston's by-the-book routine, the squadron had taken the law into their own hands. Denied transport to the mess, they'd first commandeered a tractor at revolver point and driven there in style. When a smug steward explained the chef had gone home and dinner was over, Squadron Leader John Worrall blasted the lock from the larder door – and his pilots ate.

At Fighter Command, Dowding's staff officers heard the news more gravely: the airfield attacks had barely started, yet Manston's morale was in doubt. Whether or not the cook had run for it, hundreds had – to the deep chalk shelters that wound like catacombs beneath the airfield – and here many, despite their officers' exhortations, would stay for days on end, contracting out of the battle for good and all.

At Rochford airfield in Essex, the old Southend Flying Club, now a satellite aerodrome for Sector Station North Weald, news of Manston's plight hadn't yet reached Geoffrey Page and the pilots of 56 Squadron. Stretched out on the cool grass at dispersal, in the aerodrome's farthest corner, Page, his eyes closed, was more conscious of the bird-song than of the muttered conversation of his friends. For four hours now they'd vainly awaited action; still bone-tired after the night's party, Page was within inches of drifting off to sleep.

Then the screeching brake drums of the tea waggon snapped him back to consciousness; through half-closed eyelids he saw "Jumbo" Gracie and the others unloading heavy Thermos flasks of tea, hunks of cut bread-and-butter, a jar of strawberry jam. As Page struggled upright, they were already piling the Thermoses and plates of food round the field telephone. At Rochford, chairs and tables were unknown luxuries; except for a large bell-tent, the field-telephone, linked to North Weald Ops room, was their sole item of furniture.

Staring fixedly at the telephone, the young pilot felt an overwhelming desire to retch: one ring of that hated bell and all their lives could change within minutes, as so many lives had been already changed. Suddenly, alarmingly, he knew his nerves had reached the pitch where only fatigue checked him from lunging forward to rip the leads from their terminals.

Now as always when fear strove for mastery, Page sought relief in action: there was a plague of wasps that summer, and the jam jar was suddenly the target for a horde of yellow-striped raiders. Leaning forward, he plunged a spoon into the sticky red mass – then, with a mound of strawberry jam poised eighteen inches above a crawling wasp, he let fly.

As Pilot Officer Michael Constable-Maxwell and Flight Sergeant "Taffy" Higginson watched intrigued, Page explained:

"They're the ground targets – the jam's the bomb-load." As the others warmed to the schoolboy game, Constable-Maxwell ribbed him unthinkingly: "You'll come to a sticky end, Geoffrey, like those wasps."

But Page, jam-spoon at the ready, barely heeded him; with a war-whoop of "Bang, bang! Jolly good", he'd just put the tenth striped raider out of action. He was manoeuvring the spoon above number eleven when the telephone rang.

As "Jumbo" Gracie grabbed for the receiver, Page's hand trembled violently; he saw the jam spill wide. He told himself: Watch it, Page, my boy, you're getting the twitch. Already Gracie was on his feet: "Scramble... seventy-plus approaching Mans-ton... angels one-five."

In the fighter pilots' jargon, "angels" signified "height per thousand feet", so the message was plain to all: more than seventy German aircraft were approaching Manston at 15,000 feet. It was just 5.20 p.m. on Tuesday, August 12.

There was no time for further reflection. As he pelted the fifty yards to his waiting Hurricane, Page felt the sickness drain from his stomach: the suspense was banished now and his mind was clear and alert, with only physical action to preoccupy him. Right foot into the stirrup step, left foot on the port wing... one short step along... right foot on the step inset in the fuselage... into the cockpit. Deftly his rigger was passing parachute straps across his shoulders, then the Sutton harness straps... pin through and tighten the adjusting pieces... mask clipped across and oxygen on.

He had primed the engine, adjusting the switches, and now his thumb went up in signal to the mechanics. The chocks slipped away, the Rolls-Royce Merlin engines roared into life, flattening the dancing grass with their slipstream, and Page was taxi-ing out behind "Jumbo" Gracie.

Then the Hurricanes were climbing steeply, gaining height at more than 2,000 feet per minute, and Page, sweltering in the cockpit's greenhouse heat, slid back the hood, allowing the wind to cool his sweat-soaked body. Momentarily he noticed he'd forgotten to don his flying gloves, then shrugged it off. Many old hands dispensed with them now, claiming their touch was surer on the control column.

The voice of Wing Commander John Cherry, North Weald Controller, filled their earphones, calling "Jumbo" Gracie: "Hello, Yorker Blue Leader, Lumba Calling. Seventy-plus bandits approaching Charlie Three, angels one-five." Then Grade's high-pitched voice, acknowledging: "Hallo, Lumba, Yorker Blue Leader answering. Your message received and understood. Over."

Now one of the squadron's pilots chipped in: lack of oil pressure was sending him home. Again Gracie acknowledged: ten Hurricanes swept on to intercept seventy German aircraft Page thought idly, Odds of seven to one – no better nor worse than usual. They were following the serrated coastline of north Kent now; his altimeter showed 10,000 feet.

Suddenly, what looked like a swarm of midges was dancing in the top half of his bullet-proof windscreen. But Page, craning closer, knew better. They were several thousand feet higher than the Hurricanes, and more deadly than any insect – thirty Dornier 215 bombers escorted by forty Messerschmitt 109s.

Incongruously, Page thought: Not unlike wasps at a distance – how bloody stupid if our guns fired strawberry jam at them.

He heard "Jumbo" Grade call, "Echelon starboard – go," and saw Constable-Maxwell's Hurricane slide beneath Gracie's. Cheerfully, Page thumbed his nose at Constable-Maxwell, then took up position slightly to the right and astern. Habit prompted him to lock his sliding hood in the open position – for a hurried exit, if need be.

On the ground, hundreds saw the bombers and held their breath. At Ladwood Farm, Robert Bailey was standing waist-deep amid the shimmering gold of the wheat in Raikes Hole field; the sky was mottled with broken cloud and at first, despite the deep intense drumming of the engines, he could see nothing. Then he saw them – the mightiest armada he'd ever seen, now black, then silver, against the sunlight, winging unopposed across the sky, like a giant flock of wild geese.

Now, though his determination to cling to Ladwood was still unflinching, Bailey told young Stuart Swaffer, whose family occupied part of the farmhouse: "It's time we built a dug-out, lad Things are getting serious." And he elaborated: to shelter Bailey and his wife, Vera, the farm-hands and the Swaffer family, they'd need a sizeable one, as deep as a bear-trap, behind the farmhouse. They'd cover it with poles and galvanised iron and on top of these would lie a foot or so of rammed earth.

It was a timely decision. Scarcely had Robert Bailey spoken than the whole earth seemed to tremble; two miles south, a cloud of Junkers 88 dive-bombers were pounding Hawkinge airfield, scoring it with twenty-eight craters, closing it down for the rest of that day. Hangars split apart like matchwood, and above Raikes Hole field the skyline trembled with leaping orange fire. At a resolute jog-trot, Bailey started back for the farmhouse. That trench would have begun to take shape before ever he took a bite of his evening meal.

Despite the odds, the R.A.F. weren't giving up. The Dorniers that Geoffrey Page had sighted were turning north now, setting course over the sea, but the Hurricanes were gaining on them, banking in pursuit; minute by minute, the distance between the fighters and the slim pencil-shaped bombers was closing. Now, as they gained equal height, Page saw to his surprise that Gracie planned to attack the leading aircraft in the bomber formation. It was a strange decision: to reach it they'd run a gauntlet of fire from almost thirty Dornier rear-gunners lying between the spearhead and the Hurricanes.

Closer now, and faster. To Geoffrey Page, it was suddenly like an express overhauling a freight train: there was time for bomber and fighter pilots to exchange silent glances as the Hurricanes forged on for the bomber leader. Swiftly, Page glanced behind and aloft, but no – the ME logs weren't pouncing yet.

At 600 yards, too far away to register, Page opened fire on one of the leading machines, then abruptly stopped short. One moment there had been clear sky between himself and thirty Dormers. Now the air was criss-crossed with a fusillade of glinting white tracer – cannon shells converging on the Hurricanes.

He saw Grade's machine peel from the attack; the distance between Page and the leading bombers was only thirty yards now. Strikes from his machine-gun fire flashed in winking daggers of light from a Domier's port engine; it was suddenly a desperate race to destroy before he himself was destroyed.

As a thunderclap explosion tore at his eardrums, Page's first reaction was: I can't have been hit. It could happen to other people, but not to me. Then all at once fear was surging again: an ugly ragged hole gaped in his starboard wing.

At that moment, the petrol tank behind the engine, sited on a level with his chest, blew up like a bomb; flames seared through the cockpit like a prairie fire, clawing greedily towards the draught from the open hood. A voice Page barely recognised was screaming in mortal terror: "Dear God, save me – save me, dear God."

Desperately he grappled with the Sutton harness, head reared back as if in rictus from the licking flames, seeing with horror the bare skin of his hands on the control column shrivelling like burnt parchment in the blast-furnace of heat Struggling, he screamed and screamed again, and all along the south coast the sky blossomed white with parachutes as men baled out.

Among them, at this same moment was Pilot Officer Art Donahue, a likeable twenty-year-old farm boy from St. Charles, Minnesota, who'd joined the R.A.F. soon after Dunkirk and was in his first week of combat. To him, this first-ever bale-out seemed a milestone moment and one that called for apt comment.

Aloud, as he drifted across the sky, he voiced the question hundreds on either side had yet to ask themselves; "Well, this is what you asked for – how do you like it?"

Chapter Three

"Ah, a Very Early Guest…"

August 13

Oberst Johannes Fink was as puzzled as any conscientious commander could be at dawn on Tuesday, August 13. At first, as eighty-four bomb-laden Dorniers gained height over airfields ringing Arras, everything had seemed set fair for the long-awaited Eagle Day. Already, Fink knew, the bomber crews had breakfasted, and breakfasted well; before a mission, his wing commanders must fix reveille early enough for each man to get his fill of coffee and rolls.

And no man would be saddled with the burden of a hangover – if a raid was scheduled, unit messes, on Fink's orders, closed up their bars by midnight at the latest. The Luftwaffe's former chief accident investigator, Fink insisted on every precaution that could widen the safety margin.

Minutes earlier, like any chaplain, he'd given them all his accustomed pre-flight blessing, concluding as always: "Even if this sortie ends in dismal failure, it is an experience that you must assimilate into your souls." Yet as the Dorniers droned towards the rendezvous with their *Zerstorer* escort, failure didn't seem really in the cards. All reports suggested the previous day's softening-up attacks by Rubensdorffer's Test Group 210 had gone according to plan.

Yet now Fink was both puzzled and angry. Over Cap Blanc Nez, a cold marrow-damp bank of cloud was rolling in over the Channel – something the weathermen had never predicted. Worse, there was no sign at all of the fighter escort.

Suddenly the ME 110 of the fighter group commander, the wooden-legged Oberstleutnant Joachim Huth, loomed dead ahead of them. For a second now Fink wondered whether Huth had taken leave of his senses – for the Messerschmitt, instead of setting course for England, swept clean past the Dornier's nose in a series of jinking dives, then curved steeply away towards the ground.

Outraged, Fink couldn't make head or tail of it. Why choose such a dangerous and unconventional way of letting him know that the raid was on?

Then, abruptly, he shrugged it off. The cloud was now so dense the fighters had vanished completely, but Huth's weird aerobatics at least proved they'd kept the rendezvous. Now, as leader of the attack and navigator of his own plane, Fink set course for Eastchurch airfield, Kent, the first of many Eagle Day targets.

At 5.30 a.m., on August 13, Johannes Fink had no way of knowing that through a freakish chain of mishaps only three units were, in fact, launching Eagle Day. Early forecasts routed to Goring's headquarters, O.K.L., revealed that overnight the weather had changed; across the English Channel, at any height between two and four thousand feet, the cloud had thickened to ten-tenths. Accordingly, Goring had postponed the strikes until 2 p.m.

Incredibly, this message had reached only the fighters – and since no radio link existed between fighters and bombers, Oberstleutnant Huth's antics had been a last vain attempt to tell Fink that Eagle Day was off. Nor did Fink even realise the long-range radio in his plane wasn't functioning; the frantic "*Angriff beschranken*" (attack cancelled) sent out by Kesselring's headquarters went unheeded. Only one radioman, on the plane flown by Major Paul Weitkus, 2nd Wing leader, picked it up, and again the unit's luck was out. Muzzy with 'flu and a high temperature, the Radio Op logged the message as "*AA*" – *Angriff ausfuhren*, or carry on.

Other crews, aside from Fink's, were perturbed; they'd seen Huth's strange manoeuvres then, suddenly, no more fighters. Pilot Heinz Schlegel of the 2nd Wing, still recalls: "There was a lot of radio chatter from plane to plane, then Weitkus ordered 'Go ahead'."

Innocent of all fighter cover, Fink's *Kampfgeschwader* (bomber unit) 2 droned on through fleecy cloud towards east Kent. Briefly, as Margate loomed below, the cloudbank parted; for an instant they glimpsed the Channel, white-flecked and restless in the dawn light. Then Margate was lost to view, and Fink, ever mindful of safety precautions, decided to loosen the formation; a descent through cloud so thick could step up the risk of collision. The order passed from plane to plane: "*Ausschwarmen*" (spread out).

Peering to right and left, Fink was keeping a wary eye open for stragglers. In weather like this, his prime concern was always for the inexperienced few who might lose contact – what he called his "straying sheep"; at fifty, one of the oldest Luftwaffe officers still operational, Fink took pride that his unit had come through the French campaign with lower losses than any. And thanks to Fink's paternalism, his Dorniers boasted more do-it-yourself modifications than any bomber unit: extra machine guns, armour-plated shields behind the pilot, steel helmets specially moulded by a blacksmith to clamp over the rear-gunner's flying helmet and save him from injury.

Suddenly all anxiety left him; he couldn't believe his luck. Abruptly, the clouds had parted, and there, 10,000 feet below and three miles ahead, lay Eastchurch airfield, planes lined up in neat rows, wing-tip to wing-tip, almost inviting a bombing raid. As one, eighty-four bomb-aimers, prone on their stomachs, began setting the five complex readings of the bomb sight; Oberleutnant Karl Kessel, of the 1st Wing, was only one of many to warn his crew: "In three minutes, down go the bombs."

To achieve the maximum effect from carpet bombing, Fink insisted every bomb-aimer must pinpoint his own target.

It was just then, Oberleutnant Heinz Schlegel always remembered, that the sun blazed through the piled clouds, blinding the gunners of the rearmost formation – and without warning the Spitfires of 74 Squadron pounced. But more than fifty Domiers sped on for Eastchurch.

Thanks to the vagaries of the weather, the airfield was still unalerted. Though the radar stations had charted Fink's progress, his destination was still in doubt – and the low-lying cloud had given local Observer Corps posts no chance of a visual check. At 6.57 a.m., Bromley's Observer Corps Controller Brian Binyon had asked Fighter Command's liaison officer: "Have we a large number of aircraft near Rochford?" But the answer was prompt and disconcerting: "No."

Within minutes – at 7.02 a.m. – Controller Binyon had brought them up to date: "Raid 45 is bombing Eastchurch drome."

On the airfield, men could scarcely take it in. The station commander, Group Captain Frank Hopps, awoke in bed to the telephone's strident jangle, to find H.Q. 16 Group, Coastal Command, on the line: "We think there may be some bandits bound for you." Barely had Hopps pulled on his flying boots and dived for a slit trench outside than from 9,000 feet the bombs came screaming. As plaster dust seethed like fog across the airfield, Hopps could only think despairingly: My God, the station's worth millions – some accountant's got a job to do writing off this lot.

It was the same at all levels. In the N.C.O.s' mess, Sergeant Reginald Gretton, a young Spitfire pilot, was still in pyjamas at his bedroom window, savouring the dawn peace and the memory of last night's supper – a mouth-watering shepherd's pie of minced meat, potato and onion to rival anything Mother had ever made. As the distant specks of Fink's Dorniers grew ominously larger, Gretton couldn't credit it: he'd thought of life at Eastchurch in terms of good home-cooking. He cried shrilly, like a thwarted child: "They're dropping bombs. They're dropping bombs on *us*."

They were indeed, and 250 of them were hurtling almost as one... writing off five Bristol Blenheim fighters and all 266 Squadron's Spitfires... killing twelve and wounding twenty-six... smashing the Ops Block... cutting off all electricity and telephone links... destroying vital petrol supplies.

As the aerodrome quaked with the force of the bombing, instinct drove men to strange feats of self-preservation. Pilot Officer Robbie Roach and five others scrabbled like climbing-boys up the enormous chimney of the mess ante-room; they emerged caked in greasy soot to find all the water mains severed. Sergeant David Cox, a seconded Spitfire pilot, was hustled bodily into a urinal by an elderly flight sergeant, who warned him: "Son, this is no time to be squeamish." With that, both men hit the deck face down.

Minutes later, Cox staggered out to fall almost headlong over the bloody remains of an airman on the concrete path outside. As he recoiled, his stomach heaving, a senior officer contemptuously turned the body over with his boot: "Haven't you ever seen a dead man before?"

In a bungalow on the airfield's perimeter, Mrs Eva Seabright, an Army wife newly arrived to join her husband, complained tearfully above the bombardment: "I haven't even unpacked yet – and you said this was a quiet area." Concern for her safety drove all thoughts of tact from Private Reg Seabright's mind: "It was, ducks, until you came here."

No one had yet grasped that quiet areas were a thing of the past: from this moment on, civilians were in the front-line, too.

But Oberst Fink's advantage was fleeting; within minutes of the raid passing, *Kampfgeschwader* 2 was in trouble. The sun that had earlier troubled Oberleutnant Heinz Schlegel and the pilots of the rearmost formation now proved a godsend to the pilots of Squadron Leader John Thompson's 111 Squadron. Soon after 7 a.m., patrolling the coastline above Folkestone, Thompson had had word from Squadron Leader Ronald Adam, Hornchurch Sector Controller: "Hullo, Hydro Leader, this is Tartan. Vector three-four-zero, look out for bandits returning from the Isle of Sheppey."

Then, from high in the sun, Thompson saw them: ten of Fink's Dorniers, lacking all fighter cover, speeding for the mouth of the Thames Estuary and the open sea. At once Thompson's Hurricanes were diving in an all-out, head-on attack; ten more Dorniers, coming up from astern, ran into the same wall of fire. Under the scything shower of tracer, engine cowlings exploded like shrapnel; their bombers that hadn't found their target now jettisoned them to gain height and speed. The rout was over within minutes. By 7.40 a.m., claiming five of Fink's Dorniers, 111 Squadron were breakfasting at Croydon airport, feeling the day had begun well.

To Oberst Johannes Fink it seemed, by contrast, that the High Command had wantonly sacrificed his crew's lives; as the returning raiders touched down in the fields circling Arras, he was so shaken by anger he could scarcely speak. All along he'd striven to minimise the risks for his men, yet now, only six days after Generalfeldmarschall Albert Kesselring's ebullient pep-talk on the coast, criminal negligence had cost him five crews, twenty experienced men – dead or taken prisoner, he couldn't know. Hastening to a phone, he demanded a priority link-up with Kesselring's Cap Blanc Nez H.Q., an underground dug-out the staff called "The Holy Mountain".

Now, as Kesselring came on the line, the devout soft-spoken Fink forgot he was talking to a field-marshal; anger and grief for those who'd gone swept all discretion aside. Dimly, he heard Kesselring trying to interject, and each time, blind with passion, he shouted: "Where the hell were those damned fighters, then? Just tell me that." Patiently, Kesselring sought to mollify him, explaining the details of the last-minute cancellation, and Fink grew angrier still.

He raged: "Well, I don't understand this any more than the other thing – a major attack can just be cancelled then, can it, at one moment's notice? Has anybody down there ever taken the trouble to estimate how long it takes my *Kampfgeschwader* to get across?"

An aching silence, then Kesselring said strainedly: "Well, let's leave it for now. I'll come over and see you."

In fact, Kesselring was as good as his word – but as Fink listened in silence to his chief's halting apologies, it was plain that Eagle Day had started as badly as could be. The sudden thick cloud... the amazing speed of the radar stations in setting up stand-bys... the Luftwaffe's inexperience of promoting large-scale co-ordinated aerial missions without reference to Army needs... these factors had cost the High Command, all too many men.

It wasn't only Kesselring and Fink who were dismayed: in many places on this day, German pilots abruptly found their worlds turned upside down. Oberleutnant Heinz Schlegel, of Fink's rear-guard formation, had seen Eastchurch looming ahead without loosing one single bomb; those Spitfires of 74 Squadron had swooped from the sun too swiftly. There was a rending clatter, and the starboard engine spluttered and died; the Dornier was yawing violently to the left. A hot yellow light flashed before his eyes, and now the port engine was in trouble, too.

Breaking for cloud cover, Schlegel fought to keep the Dornier airborne, steering what he hoped was due south. Then the clouds parted and his spirits rose exultantly, only to sink; land loomed beneath them but it wasn't familiar terrain. Cautiously, Oberleutnant Gerhardt Oszwald the navigator, voiced what all of them felt: "I don't think *this* is France. Shall we make it?"

His mouth spittle-dry, Schlegel could only mutter: "Let's wait and see."

But in minutes he realised that they wouldn't. Both the gunner and the radioman, in the rear turret, had suffered arm wounds – how bad Schlegel didn't know. Briefly, he thought: If I give the order to jump, will they make it in time? But in fairness he couldn't risk it. Grimly, he set the Dornier careening for the flat English pastures, seeing too late that the one unobstructed field for which he'd aimed was scored by a deep trench – but there was no time to pull up and seek a fresh landing place. Swaying from side to side like a truck out of control, the bomber ripped like a juggernaut across the meadowland, then, with a sickening half-swing, wrapping its starboard wing round a tree, smashed to a halt.

To the crew's astonishment, they had barely had time to crawl from the plane before ten British soldiers came storming through the grass to disarm them, whooping like Comanches on the warpath, exclaiming excitedly over their fine new Mausers. By degrees, it dawned on Schlegel that the men wouldn't harm them – but as Dunkirk veterans they'd returned to England without even a rifle. If invasion was imminent, it was politic to make sure of a weapon.

Bewildered, Schlegel next found himself a captive at an outpost of the London Scottish Regiment, near Barham, Kent, confined in a small office adjoining the unit canteen. At a counter, a long line of men was queuing unhurriedly to buy regimental cap-badges and tartan stocking tabs; from somewhere he heard the far keening of bagpipes. Still dazed from the shock of the forced landing, Schlegel puzzled: If England's due to be conquered in three days, how can they take time off for this?

Oberleutnant Paul Temme felt the same: was life in England always as leisurely as this? At Beaumont-le-Roger in Normandy, no news of Eagle Day's postponement had reached the pilots of No. 1 Wing, 2nd Fighter Group; at dawn, along with eleven others, Temme, the unit's adjutant, had set off on what the Luftwaffe called a "free hunt" – a cross-Channel fighter-sweep, independent of bombers, designed to bring the R.A.F. up off the ground to fight.

Over Shoreham airfield, near Brighton, Temme's outfit found little enough doing until they turned for home – then, as his oil pressure reached danger point, two Spitfires were on Temme's tail. One hail of bullets and he knew his radiator cooling system was out, too – and now the Spitfires were hareing for the coast, both pilots waving farewell. Sadly, Temme acknowledged the truth: he hadn't seen the last of England.

Close by Shoreham airfield he hit an acre of potatoes in a splintering, rending crash-landing, ripping off both wings and the tailplane, grinding to a halt suspended upside down in the cockpit, only the soft dangerous tick of petrol dripping on a red-hot engine to break the silence. But as he released his harness, tumbling to the soft earth, gunners from an ack-ack site were already doubling towards him, rifles at the ready and seeming in the mood for trouble.

Suddenly, Temme felt an overwhelming desire to relieve the needs of nature, using the fuselage of the wrecked plane as a focal point. It was the unaffected gesture that was needed: as one the rifles were lowered, the gunners relaxed.

And it seemed that relaxation was the order of the day. In his dug-out on Shoreham airfield, the station commander was still shaving; as Temme was led in, he greeted him nonchalantly, in perfect German: "*Oh, ein sehr fruher gast*" (Ah, a very early guest). Apologising for his incomplete toilet, he was at once solicitous: by now, surely, Temme must be ready for breakfast?

Politely, Temme shook his head – he'd breakfasted already. Though it was a white lie, he couldn't be an extra mouth at an adversary's table. Then a steward appeared with piled plates – ham and eggs, crisp toast, China tea – and his resolution crumpled. When, between mouthfuls, the C.O. confessed, "I'm not really sure what I'm supposed to do with you," Temme, a fellow administrator, could appreciate his dilemma. Buttering a fresh round of toast, he sympathised: "I know how it is. Had the regulations in my own desk all along – somehow never got around to reading them."

To Shoreham's C.O. it seemed an Army matter; breakfast done, he ordered his staff car and drove Temme to the Royal Artillery mess at Brighton nearby. The Army, busy with the morning papers in the mess, had only one immediate solution: Temme must join them for breakfast. As he settled to more ham and eggs, Temme confided: "I'd no idea you had such protocol between your different services."

But the Army's decision wasn't helpful: whoever's responsibility Temme might be, he wasn't theirs. By 9.30 a.m., a gunner escort had delivered him back to the R.A.F., this time fifty miles away at Farnborough, Hampshire. Though Junkers 88s of the 54th Bomber Group, unaware that Eagle Day was off, had strafed it only hours earlier, the airmen seemed to bear no malice. After one sharp interchange with an Army interrogator, Temme was handed back to an R.A.F. officer, who consoled him: "Take no notice of him, he isn't a pilot – and now, what about some breakfast?"

It was all so tranquil and civilised there might never have been a war at all – and by the time Temme arrived at the London District Prisoner-of-War Cage, Kensington Palace Gardens, it was long past midnight. Here the final shock awaited him: his hosts' unbelted hospitality had cost him one week's prisoner-of-war pay. At midnight they'd closed the books.

But by noon on August 13, it was plain that Eagle Day had gone awry all over. To the west, the 54th Bomber Group, slated for a second sortie, against the naval base at Portland, got word the main strike was delayed and didn't fly – but their fighter escort, the vulnerable ME 110s of *Zerstorer* Group 2, had no such message. Forging on for Portland, vainly seeking the bombers, they lost five planes in as many minutes – among them Unteroffizier Kurt Schumacher, who was harried to the end by three Spitfires.

To Schumacher's chagrin, the odds and the sudden shock proved all too much for his gunner, young Obergefreiter Otto Giglhuber; hunched over his machine-gun, the boy could only weep brokenly. All at once there was a sound as if a giant paper sack had been blown up and burst behind their ears. The ME 110 shook all over, and there was a noise like hail striking a tin roof. Sick at heart, Schumacher ordered: "Bale out."

From the clifftops, above the shining waters of Kimmeridge Bay, Dorset, scores had a grandstand view. It was just past noon when Mrs Ivy Marshall, a lobster fisherman's wife, riveted at the door of her whitewashed cottage, saw the crippled Messerschmitt pass overhead "like a black bird shedding feathers". As it dropped from sight, plunging out of control towards Swalland Farm, close by, twin parachutes flowered like giant chrysanthemums over the water.

As Kurt Schumacher drifted towards the water, he was surprised and relieved to see a motor boat puttering its way towards him. Mrs Marshall's husband, Anthony, tending his lobster pots on Portland Roads, a mile and a half from the shore, had watched the descent, too; at once he veered his boat, *The Miss Ivy*, in the German's direction. Once Schumacher had handed over his pistol, Marshall hauled him aboard, directing him to sit in the bows.

The rescue was so unexpected and the day had gone so badly that Schumacher, whose English was fluent, felt the aching need to talk. As they curved to come alongside the gunner, he told Marshall: "He was too young, you know – just a frightened boy." Dripping and gasping, Giglhuber was hauled aboard. Again, eager for human contact, Schumacher said: "I could have coped with one Spitfire, but not three." He made a sudden resolve: when they landed, he'd give this fisherman his inflatable yellow life-jacket as a souvenir.

Marshall set course for the shore. From his seat in the bows, Schumacher could see the shelving cliffs of Goulter's Gap, where the Marshalls' cottage lay, the cliff paths alive with scrambling troops and farm-workers. Eagle Day was five hours old, and for him the war was over. Looking at Giglhuber he said again, with no tinge of emotion: "He was too young – too young."

In one way, Kurt Schumacher was supremely lucky. Day by day, as the air battle mounted, the English Channel, its tides sometimes reaching a rate of seven knots, would claim victim after victim. Within days of Schumacher's rescue, Air Chief Marshal Dowding, pressed for accurate figures by Winston Churchill, reported the worst: 60 per cent of all fatal air battles were taking place over the sea.

In such an event, whether any man was rescued or not lay in the lap of the gods.

It was a shameful record. Despite soaring casualties – 220 killed or missing over the sea in three July weeks – the Air Ministry had provided only eighteen high-speed rescue launches to cover Great Britain's entire coastline, just two craft more than the 1936 establishment. Pilots such as Flying Officer Guy Branch, 145 Squadron, literally drowned within sight of the Dorset shore; the only rescue craft on hand, the Poole lifeboat, just hadn't the turn of speed to reach him. At Warmwell airfield, nearby, Squadron Leader Peter Devitt's 152 Squadron counted every casualty except one in terms of death by drowning.

Pilot after pilot could tell the same alarming story. Baling out over St. Margaret's Bay, Kent, Flying Officer Paul Le Rougetel was saved by the merest fluke; still drifting as night fell, the tiny luminous dial of his wrist watch caught the eye of Margate lifeboat's Coxswain "Sinbad" Price in the instant the pilot heeled over, unconscious. And Sergeant Peter Hillwood escaped as narrowly; after battling the waves for two-and-a-half miles without seeing one rescue craft, he was near collapse when two keen-eyed ack-ack gunners from a coastal battery stripped off their clothes and toiled out to save him.

It was small wonder that some men took action on their own account. Appalled by the needless loss of life, Flying Officer Russell Aitken, a young New Zealander, borrowed a Walrus floatplane from the Fleet Air Arm and set up his own private rescue service off the Isle of Wight – often waiting patiently on the water only a quarter of a mile from a Heinkel 59 rescue plane.

Chivalry decreed that neither opened fire on the other – and that each, as the battle raged, rescued Britons and Germans impartially.

As he lay in a cool white room at Margate General Hospital, the fear of death by drowning still lingered in the mind of Pilot Officer Geoffrey Page. Twenty-four hours back, as he saw the dark rushing shape of the Hurricane vanish from beneath his legs, his chances of rescue seemed one in a million; despite the cool and blessed air striking his livid face, he was falling like a stone, powerless to stop. Frantically, as the crazy kaleidoscope of sky and sea tumbled before him, his brain had commanded: *Pull – pull the ripcord* – but each time the mutilated fingers touched the chromium ring, they jerked from the agony of contact.

Then the searoads loomed closer, overlaid by a golden patina of sunlight, and swiftly one fear supplanted another; better one second of agony than to hit the water like a thrown rock at 200 miles an hour. *Never mind the pain – pull the ripcord*.

Pain lanced from his fingers, then his shoulders jerked violently; with a snapping crack the silk canopy had opened. Now, swaying soberly at eleven miles an hour, the sensitive Page's nostrils wrinkled fastidiously – never in his life had he smelt such an evil sick-sweet stench. Then it hit him: it was the smell of his own burnt flesh. With everything he knew, he fought back the desire to vomit.

It was as well; there hadn't even been time for the luxury of self-disgust. Despite the puffy flesh about his eyes, Page could mark his position clearly. A long way off – he thought perhaps ten miles – lay Margate and the coastline. Ten-thousand feet below crawled the empty sea – not a ship, not even a seagull in sight. Worse, he'd known that shock was fast taking hold of him. Spasms of shivering shook him like an ague; his teeth chattered violently.

In the same instant, Page felt another fear rack him. If he didn't get rid of his parachute within seconds, it would entrap him there, beneath the water, as surely as the tentacles of an octopus.

For most pilots, the procedure was simple: a small metal release box, fitting over the stomach, clasped the four ends of the parachute harness after they had passed down over the shoulders and up from the groin. A small metal disc on the box, when turned through an angle of ninety degrees and banged, released the parachute.

It was then Page had discovered that, try as he might, his blackened, blistered fingers just weren't equal to it. Still struggling, he hit the water feet first. Kicking out madly he came to the surface, arms fearsomely entwined in the parachute's wrapping shrouds.

Then Geoffrey Page had battled literally for his life. Flesh was flaking from his fingers, blood poured from the raw tissues, but still, spewing mouthfuls of salt water, he fought on. If he didn't master the disc, and soon, the water-logged chute would tug him inexorably towards the sea-bed.

Suddenly, with a jerk, he felt the disc give; he was free. Sobbing with relief, he thrashed blindly away from that nightmare patch of water. The next stage, he knew, was to inflate his "Mae West" life-jacket – yet even then the chances of rescue seemed remote, unless the tide carried him nearer the coast.

It was the least of his problems, as Page soon knew. Unscrewing the valve with his teeth, he clamped his lips round the long rubber tube that inflated the "Mae West" – then saw a mocking string of bubbles stream from the jacket's hem. Fire had scorched a gaping hole through the rubber bladder.

Now Page made a desperate decision: if air-sea rescue was non-existent, he could only keep swimming for the shore until his strength gave out.

It was a brave resolution – brave because every measured stroke sent pain coursing like liquid fire through his body. The salt was fast drying on the weeping tissue of his face; the strap of his flying helmet, contracting too, cut like a thong into his chin. Flames had welded buckle and leather into one solid mass; he couldn't even wrench it off.

Then, close to his last gasp, he remembered the brandy – a slim silver flask-full, a present from his mother, conserved in his tunic's breast pocket. Often, when a bartender called "Time", he'd come close to battle royal with his fellow pilots, who insisted this "state of emergency" was excuse to pass round the flask. But Page would have none of it, guarding it jealously for just such a moment.

Again, as his fingers inched beneath the useless Mae West, he suffered the tortures of the damned, holding his breath to bursting-point to withstand each wave of pain, legs still paddling feebly. At last, when he found the flask, his fingers could take no more; gingerly, using his wrists as a clamp, he brought it to the water's surface. Grasping the screw-stopper between his teeth, head tugging backwards, he felt it give, the hot tang of the spirit tormenting his nostrils.

Suddenly the flask slipped between his wet wrists, vanishing for ever beneath the water.

And then Page was weeping, as uncontrollably as a child; he knew that everything was against him now; he didn't stand a chance. He was cold and exhausted, the flesh so swollen about his eyes he could no longer see the sun to steer by. When the black smoke-trail from a friendly merchant ship hove into view, Geoffrey Page had resigned himself to die.

All that followed seemed unreal now, like a half-remembered dream. There'd been the merchant ship's motor launch, circling cautiously and asking if he was a German, until Page cut loose with a hysterical barrage of oaths. "We knew you were an R.A.F. officer," one of the crew explained with unconscious humour, "the minute you swore." Dimly he recalled they'd stripped off his sodden clothing, swaddling him in blankets… the skipper had fashioned fingerless gloves for his ravaged hands with large squares of pink lint... then the Margate lifeboat had taken charge... recumbent on the stretcher, Page had been relieved to see an ambulance waiting at the quayside... and flabbergasted to see a dozen-strong reception committee, led by Margate's top-hatted mayor, waiting, too.

Now, like any youngster on the threshold of life, Page was beset by one anxiety: what had the fire done to his face? Why wouldn't they tell him? Were they afraid? Was he so marked that all his life he'd be set apart from other men?

Twice he'd asked to see a mirror, as casually, he hoped, as possible – and twice the doctors had hastily switched to other topics.

To Page, on this August Tuesday, that eagerness to know the truth overcame most considerations – though his ears told him one more life-and-death battle had been joined in the sky above. The fiendish shriek of Stukas, the thunder of ack-ack rattling Margate Hospital's windows almost drowned out conscious thought.

Geoffrey Page could hardly know it, but by noon on Eagle Day, the eyes of the world were on this stretch of coastline. The broad sweep of Dover's Shakespeare Cliff, with its fluttering clouds of white chalk butterflies, was now an amphitheatre packed with newsmen, squatting amid ripening red-currant bushes, eyes straining upwards. To the east they saw the main waves of Kesselring's Air Fleet Two streaming towards Rochester... towards Detling airfield near Maidstone... over Lympne airfield... Ramsgate Harbour. To young Ben Robertson, of New York's *P.M.*, the Spitfires of 65 Squadron, battling for height with the 109s, "seemed to mark the sky as skaters mark ice".

And he reflected: an air war swooping down on you was as strange as death itself, yet even war was not as terrible as the fear of war had been.

For days now, the free world's press had crowded out the little grey port, twenty-three miles south of Margate, ready to record the greatest air battle in history. Queuing impatiently to file their despatches from the Grand Hotel's phone booths were men and women whose bylines were known to millions… C.B.S.'s Ed Murrow… Virginia Cowles of the North American Newspaper Alliance and U.P.'s Ed Beattie… the London *Daily Herald's* Reg Foster, so scoop-minded he even took his camera to the bathroom… Hilde Marchant of the *Daily Express*… the Pulitzer Prize-winning Ray Sprigle of the *Pittsburgh Post Gazette*, colourful with his Stetson and corncob pipe.

Now the war had moved from the port, where the sirens had often shrilled twenty times each day, and to the arc of sky above the cliffs. Beyond the barrage balloons, tethered like flocks of grazing sheep, the newsmen saw thin streamers of smoke staining the sky, moving in deadly concert with the whirling, snarling ballet of planes. A current joke at the local Hippodrome Music Hall gained new point: "Dover is a nice little town near Germany."

To some, thoughts of a historic last stand came inevitably. Young Ben Robertson thought of Daniel Boone's Kentucky stockade – the Indians were coming and the settlers had manned the ramparts. Then the frontier had been the West; now England's frontier was the sky. Best-seller Vincent Sheean recalled Dolores La Pasionara's stirring speech at Madrid in the Spanish Civil War: "*Camaradas, no podremos perder mas territorio*" (My friends, we can lose no more territory). To Sheean, this was the point the British had reached.

Calmest man of all was *March of Time* cameraman Art Menken; between each reel of film he took time off to help a clifftop allotment holder harvest his early potatoes.

Few correspondents perched on the cliff saw more than brief snatched cameos – yet the Luftwaffe reverses they witnessed this day could be laid squarely at Hermann Goring's door. For the brunt of this two-pronged assault was borne, despite its extreme vulnerability, by the JU 87 Stuka dive-bomber – for no better reason than its resounding success in France and Poland. Along with fighter escort that couldn't hope to protect the unwieldy planes, no fewer than fifty-two Stukas were briefed to attack airfields in the Portland area – while another eighty-six attacked Detling airfield in Kent.

It was a dire decision. At Detling, shrieking from thick cloud cover soon after 4 p.m., the Stukas achieved the measure of surprise they needed: many airmen were taking tea in the canteen as the first bombs came tumbling... wrecking every runway... firing the hangars... destroying twenty aircraft on the ground. As the Ops Room vanished in one nightmare detonation, the C.O., Group Captain Edward Davis, a former Wimbledon tennis champion, fell dead, a dagger of concrete driving clean through his skull – and others died as precipitately. Casualty Clearing Officer Wallace Beale, a Maidstone undertaker, sped to the shattered aerodrome to find a death roll topping fifty – though many needed only the five-foot coffins reserved for unidentified remains.

But for every Stuka over Portland, one crew in five had bought a one-way ticket. Weighed down by a 1,000-kilo bombload, it had taken Major Graf Schonborn's Stuka Group 77 a full hour to climb to 16,500 feet – ample time for any radar station to register their approach. And over the coast, baulked by thick clouds, the Stukas couldn't even locate their targets – though this, to the High Command, wasn't the first requisite. As the group commanders had explained at that afternoon's briefing: primarily the Stukas were a decoy, designed to lure up the R.A.F. fighters as prey for the 109s. Clambering into his plane at Dinard airfield, Stuka wing commander Major Paul Hozzel joked wryly: "Just like showing a dog a sausage."

But once over Portland, humour was at a premium. With height and sun in their favour, seventy Hurricanes and Spitfires came peeling from the sun – a battle so frenzied that Pilot Officer Red Tobin, chafing back at Warmwell airfield, heard the details of the thirteen-minute combat with something akin to despair. Until Red, Andy Mamedoff and Shorty Keough had mastered every technicality of the Spitfire, Squadron Leader Horace Darley, commanding 609 Squadron, was confining them to routine ferrying jobs – yet now, it seemed, they'd missed out on one of the squadron's bloodiest actions.

As thirteen Spitfires touched down at Warmwell, it was plain each man had seen hard fighting; on the wings of every plane, long black streaks showed where the fabric covering the gun ports had been blasted away by the first shots of the battle. Glumly the three Americans heard the lucky combatants excitedly gabbling out their story: in thirteen minutes thirteen Spitfires had accounted for thirteen Stukas.

In fact, the Germans had lost only five Stukas, but in the flaring heat of combat such over-claims were invariable. Flushed with victory, Flight Lieutenant David Crook announced excitedly: never again would he distrust number thirteen. Flying Officer Ostazewski, a Polish ace, had actually seen the cockpit door of a 109 hurtle into space like a giant tea-tray as the pilot baled out. Flying Officer Harry Goodwin, so carried away he'd forgotten he was out of ammo, had chased a fighter thirty miles to Yeovil in Somerset – only to find it was a British Blenheim.

Now Red Tobin and his friends exchanged rueful glances: maybe, someday, somebody would realise they'd come to England seeking some action, too.

Unbeknown to 609 Squadron, V.I.P.s had watched their battle royal. From the cliffs above Portland, Winston Churchill, along with Lieutenant-General Alan Brooke, C.-in-C., Home Forces, Claude Auchinleck, G.O.C.-in-C., Southern Command, and the 5th Corps' Major-General Bernard Montgomery, had broken off a survey of coastal defences from Exmouth to Weymouth to marvel at the spectacle – a brief diversion from grave issues now confronting them.

Already the Admiralty had picked up rumours that German divisions had embarked from Norway on the night of August 11; the invasion of northern England could be only a matter of days.

Other reports hinted at a strike from the south – with Austrian mountain divisions arriving in the Pas de Calais, equipped with mules to scale the Kentish cliffs.

To the Stuka crews in the sky above them, invasion, even air supremacy, seemed as far away as the mountains of the moon. Dry-mouthed with horror, Major Paul Hozzel saw planes transformed into fantastic fiery rockets as they blew up with their bombs still on board. Breaking for base, he loosed his own bombs on any coastal target he could see, then skimmed back across the water for Dinard. As angry as Oberst Johannes Fink had been that morning, Major Walter Enneccerus, another wing commander, got back, too, to lay it on the line to the top brass: "They ripped our backs open right up to the collar."

And the men who'd flown with him saw his anger as fully justified. Many planes in the fighter escort had been unwieldy ME 110s – Goring's beloved *Zerstorer* – and most had been too caught up in a free-for-all with three Spitfire squadrons to offer protection to the Stukas. Those 110s that got back did it by a hair's-breadth – Obersdeutnant Friedrich Vollbracht curving so fast away the thrust of G blacked out his gunner; Oberleutnant Schafer calling in mounting agitation to a gunner so riddled with bullets he would never hear again. Feldwebel Johannes Lutter still recalls: "If you survived three trips like that one, you were lucky."

As the last skirmishes of Eagle Day drew to a close, one of the most formidable adversaries the British would ever know was over Dover with his wing, flying as escort to German rescue planes, and mentally giving the British their due. To Major Adolf Galland, one thing was plain: if this day's combat was any guide, no easy task lay ahead for his unit, the 26th Fighter Group's 3rd Wing. What he had seen only confirmed his opinion of the British ever since those first Channel battles of July.

These men who would fight on with their engines smoking, often when their planes were too near the earth to risk baling out, won his unbounded admiration. Their courage and discipline were equal to anything he had ever seen.

And Adolf Galland, for the most part, was a man grudging with praise; a tall, moody twenty-eight-year-old, whose swarthy good looks bespoke his Huguenot descent, he'd seen action enough to justify his own high standards. As a Condor Legion pilot in the Spanish Civil War, he'd seemed a man born to command from the first, even quelling a mutiny on the stinking tramp steamer that took the volunteers from Hamburg to El Ferrol by strapping the ringleader to the mast. The veteran of 280 Spanish missions, Galland had gone on to fly eighty-seven missions in Poland – and only three times had seen the Polish fighters up.

The son of a well-to-do bailiff, flight had obsessed Galland for as long as he could remember: as a glider-mad schoolboy, his hobby had eaten into so much study time his parents, desperate, had promised him his own glider – if only he'd pass his Abitur, Germany's high school graduation. Cannily, Galland had chosen gliding as the subject of his prize composition; within weeks he'd won not only his glider but a regional record for endurance.

And twelve days back, on August 1, after seventeen confirmed victories, Galland's status as an ace had been confirmed, as Generalfeldmarschall Albert Kesselring pinned the coveted Knight's Cross to his breast at Cap Gris Nez. Suddenly, high overhead, two British fighters passed that Kesselring couldn't identify, so the hawk-eyed Galland had enlightened him: they were Spitfires. At once Kesselring chuckled heartily: "The first to congratulate you."

Already Galland was something of a legend in the Luftwaffe, and the knowledge didn't displease him. Beyond a point, few men could probe his restless, complex mind – yet everything about the man somehow set him apart. To the fury of the ascetic Hitler, Galland not only smoked twenty black Brazilian cigars a day; he'd coolly installed a special ashtray and lighter in the cockpit of his ME 109. Up to 9,000 feet, when the oxygen mask went on, he could puff contentedly away.

A ruthless logician, Galland had seen one factor as plain: the Luftwaffe's recent attempts to attain air supremacy as a tactical fighter-force just couldn't pan out. To set the fighter pilots a task beyond their strength could do nothing but discourage them. But at last, as his plane winged its way towards Caffiers airfield at Calais, Galland saw fresh hope: the bomber attacks that were now building up could prove to be the answer they'd sought.

Now, at long last, the R.A.F. would be forced to leave their airfields – and come up and fight to the last man.

Chapter Four

"Don't Speak to Me – I Have Never Been So Moved"

August 14–15

Air Chief Marshal Sir Hugh Dowding could have wept with sheer relief. Pacing his office at 10 a.m., on Tuesday, August 14, thumbs, as always, hooked in his tunic belt, Dowding's normally pallid cheeks were flushed with excitement. To Lieutenant-General Sir Frederick Pile, Chief of Anti-Aircraft Command, who set this hour apart each morning to hear his old friend's troubles, the architect of Fighter Command was more animated than he'd ever known him.

Now steering a waste-paper-basket with his foot, to simulate a German bomber formation, next swooping on it with his folded spectacles to demonstrate the fighter attacks of Eagle Day, Dowding burst out, "Pile, it's a miracle."

And for the R.A.F., Eagle Day had indeed proved a miracle. Though Fighter Command's initial claim – sixty-nine German planes shot down – was swiftly scaled down to thirty-four, the R.A.F. had lost only thirteen Hurricanes and Spitfires, losses easily made good. And while the Luftwaffe had flown an impressive 1,485 sorties, successfully strafing nine airfields, all too many strikes had been launched at bases outside Dowding's command.

Both Detling and Eastchurch had paid a heavy price – but these were bases of Coastal Command, whose prime function was look-out patrols against German naval raiders. Andover, an

Army Co-operation Command field, had been pounded too. Though Oberstleutnant Josef "Beppo" Schmid, the Luftwaffe Intelligence Chief, for the most part knew where British fighters were located, the overall O.K.L. plan inexplicably laid little enough stress on priorities. The primary aim of the Eagle Attacks was to vanquish Fighter Command – yet time and again German bomber units were sent to blitz the wrong bases.

Hence Dowding's jubilation, for if no worse attacks than these developed, the R.A.F. had little to fear.

Only one factor nagged Fighter Command's chief: how would his pilots stand up to still harder pounding? But on August 14, at least, it seemed that the front would stay quiet: at 2,000 feet, cotton-wool clouds still blanketed the English Channel. Those Germans who attempted a sortie would have all their work cut out.

It was true – yet some were determined to try it. At 4.30 that afternoon, a lone Junkers 88 dive-bomber of Oberst Alfred Bulowius' *Lehrgeschwader* (Training Unit) 1 passed high over the Hampshire coastline, heading for the Army Co-op Command base at Upavon. By chance the crew sighted instead a plum target seventeen miles east: Middle Wallop airfield, sector control station and home base for two day fighter squadrons. One was 609 Squadron, of which Pilot Officer Eugene "Red" Tobin was still a reluctantly non-combatant officer.

Only that morning, Red, Andy Mamedoff and "Shorty" Keough had again pressed Squadron Leader Horace Darley for an operational flight – and again he'd told them: "No matter how good your flying is, you must know how to protect yourself under actual combat conditions. Good flying isn't enough." Reluctantly, Red and his friends had acknowledged the wisdom of this, and the cautious Andy, as always, had added: "Well, time will tell."

So this afternoon, at 609's dispersal, Red Tobin saw no prospect of immediate action; even if a scramble sounded he'd be left behind, as usual. Above all he was thinking of his fiancée,

Anne Haring, the dark and lovely girl he'd left behind in Los Angeles, and of how desperately he missed her; somehow, despite the wisecracks of the others, he'd never been able to look at another girl in all these months. Fingering the lucky St. Christopher medal he always wore, Tobin wondered just how long it would be before her next letter reached him – then abruptly the squadron's adjutant, Flying Officer Dick Anderson, hailed him: "Hey, Red, if you hop down to Hangar Five, there's a Spit to deliver to Hamble."

Since Hamble, close by Southampton, was the main Spitfire repair base, able to rehabilitate 140 Spitfires at one time, Red knew this was just one more ferrying job, but he wasn't displeased. To him, no aircraft had ever sung a blither tune than the Spitfire's thousand horse-power – "the sweetest little ship I've ever flown," as he'd written home.

On his way to the hangar, as a matter of routine, he checked with Ops Room, and was puzzled when a duty officer warned him: "Watch it, there's a bomber overhead." The stealthy advance of the lone raider hadn't escaped Middle Wallop.

Then, at 4.45 p.m., on August 14, death, for the first time, seemed to lay its hand upon Red Tobin. He was within eighty yards of Hangar Five when fear charged him like an electric current: a blue-bellied Junkers 88 dive-bomber, its twin Jumo engines bulking enormously, was 1,500 feet above the hangar, gliding like a giant bat. As the first stick burst from its bomb bay, Red, moving faster than he'd ever done, dived headlong for the earth.

Whoever the pilot was, he didn't lack courage; he lived a bare thirty seconds to enjoy his triumph. Now the Spitfires of 609 Squadron were airborne; as Red Tobin pressed his face to the dirt, debris and broken glass showering all round him, Sergeant Alan Feary, already on base patrol, was only 350 yards behind the steeply climbing bomber, slugging tracer home at its belly. For one moment it hung like a torch in the sky, then tore with unimaginable violence into a tree eighteen miles away.

Shakily, his head ringing with concussion, Red Tobin clambered to his feet; his flying overalls, even his dark-red hair, were as white with dust as a miller's smock. Then he was pelting for Hangar Five with all the strength his legs could muster, but already it was too late. The hangar entrance was like a charnel house... one airman's foot had been blown off... another's arm had been torn off at the shoulder... and three lay dead beneath the thirteen-ton steel hangar door they had been struggling to close when the bomb fell.

Sickened to his stomach, Red Tobin thought: This is war at its worst. Then, for the first time, the implacable calm of the British came home to him. There wasn't a trace of panic, scarcely a man in sight was even running; in the Ops Room, a democratic flight sergeant, picking himself from the floor, was just then remarking to the C.O., Wing Commander David Roberts: "This is where we're all on the same level, sir." Limping back to dispersal, Red Tobin reminded himself that in Britain stiff upper lips were mandatory. As a lusty cheer greeted his dishevelment, Red shrugged it off: "I had a million laughs."

At Manston airfield, two squadrons of Hauptmann Walter Rubensdorffer's Test Group 210 had met with the same unexpected tenacity. As Oberleutnant Wilhelm Roessiger dived with his sixteen ME 110s in the second all-out attack launched on Manston, a withering curtain of fire from the site named Charlie Three came rising to meet them.

Angered that hundreds, ignoring their officers' example, had remained rooted below ground in the deep chalk shelters since the bombing of August 12, the officers and men of No. 600 Squadron had been working overtime. A Bristol Blenheim night fighter squadron, grounded by day, they'd weighed in, regardless of rank, to fill the gap left by the defecting ground crews – refuelling, and re-arming those day fighters that were operational in a creditable twelve minutes flat. And they'd even contrived some station defence on their own account: "The Sheep Dipper", a spare set of Browning machine-guns rigged on a pole, and "The Armadillo", a truck converted through concrete sides to a primitive armoured car, a machine-gun fixed amidships.

Crouched on an improvised fire-step of trestles, Pilot Officer Henry Jacobs was one of six squadron air-gunners who were out to show the Germans; as Roessiger's 110s shrank to slim pencils in their sights, fire from their dismantled Brownings went hammering up the sloping roof of 600 Squadron's crew room. Then the 500-pounders came whistling, blast tore all six gunners from the trestle in a blasphemous tangle of arms and legs, but Manston's massed fire-power was paying off. At 600 feet, a Bofors forty-millimetre shell blasted Unteroffizier Hans Steding's tailplane clean away; its engines screaming in an uncontrolled dive, the plane cartwheeled across the aerodrome, smashing into the ground upside down.

As it struck, astonished onlookers saw that Steding's gunner, Gefreiter Ewald Schank, had baled out at 500 feet, barely 100 feet above the lowest safety height, his chute dragging him across the concrete outside 600 Squadron's hangar.

Miraculously, Schank was still alive; peeping from the sand-bagged slit trenches, men of 600 Squadron saw him staggering in crazy circles, one hand clapped to his head, while bombs from his own unit's planes tore the ground about him like shell-fire. Without hesitation, Flight Lieutenant Charles Pritchard sprinted from the trench to his rescue, dragging him shocked and bleeding to safety.

But though Pritchard and the others tried gently to question him, it was useless. Half-delirious, the wounded gunner had only scant English – though it was plain he was urging with all his might to be moved forthwith. "The big lick," he muttered, over and over like an incantation, "very soon, the big lick."

In silence, the men in the trench exchanged significant glances: "the big lick". The implication of the phrase seemed plain enough – but just how long before "the big lick" came?

At mid-morning on Thursday, August 15, Oberst Paul Deichmann could scarcely believe his eyes. No major sorties against
England were scheduled on this day – that much he knew.
Angered by the reverses of August 13, Goring had summoned
every top commander – Kesselring, Sperrle, even Deichmann's
own chief, General Bruno Lorzer, the head of No. 2 Flying
Corps – to justify their failures to him at Karinhall. It had
seemed as good a day as any – again the weathermen had
forecast only impenetrable cloud.

Yet now, staring from the rat-haunted farmhouse at
Bonningues, near Calais, which was 2nd Flying Corps H.Q.,
Deichmann, the Chief of Staff, saw only blue sky and brilliant
sunshine. The wind was zephyr-calm, direction west–north-
west at little more than two miles an hour and cloud was
negligible, a scattered front around 3,000 feet. It was perfect
weather for what Gunner Schank had styled "the big lick".

The abortive Eagle Day sorties had in fact been part of a
complex blueprint, applicable for any time the weather held
good – and on airfields all down the coast, Deichmann knew,
more than 1,000 fighters and 800 bombers of the 2nd Flying
Corps, which was scheduled to lead the attacks, were already
fuelled up, alert for take-off once the signal was given. "Well,"
Deichmann recalls thinking, "here we go."

Reaching for the phone, Deichmann gave crisp orders. A
dozen Stukas under Hauptmann von Brauchitsch, airborne
from Tramecourt, were to form the spearhead of the attack,
bound for Hawkinge; two dozen more under Hauptmann
Keil, loaded with 500-kilo and 250-kilo bombs, must head
for Lympne. Twenty-five Dorniers of Oberst Chamier-
Glisczinski's 3rd Bomber Group should work over Eastchurch
yet again… another wing of the same group, over Rochester
airfield, were to use both delayed-action and incendiaries…
while Rubensdorffer's Test Group 210 tried their skill against
Martlesham Heath, on the Suffolk coast.

His orders acknowledged, Deichmann drove hard for "The Holy Mountain", Kesselring's bomb-proof underground H.Q. at Cap Blanc Nez. Today, with the field-marshal at Karinhall, his staff could relax for the first time in weeks. Long before the battle was a reality, Kesselring had installed himself here, along with fourteen officers manning a battery of telephones, forty steps below ground, resolved on checking the triumph or failure of every plane that took off.

No man to delegate even trifling decisions, Kesselring was rapidly driving himself and his staff beyond endurance. Conferences, even dinner parties, were confined to this fetid dug-out, its entry so low-slung that each time the stalwart Kesselring ventured out he invariably bumped his head. Even today the interior was so gloomy, lit only by a flickering oil-lamp, Deichmann had to crane to see Major Hans-Jurgen Rieckhoff, Kesselring's Operations Officer.

"Oh, Herr Oberst," Rieckhoff greeted him, "I expect you've heard. The attacks have been called off because of bad weather."

"My dear Rieckhoff," Deichmann said, "are you mad? It's a glorious day – come up and take a look."

Together the two men picked their way up rough-hewn steps to Kesselring's private look-out post, a sand-bagged, breast-high parapet jutting from the Channel cliffs. But Rieckhoff, though dazzled by the glaring light, still hung back; only that morning Goring had reiterated that no mass attacks should take place; as Kesselring's deputy, he couldn't really assume responsibility… as yet he hadn't fully grasped the extent of Deichmann's spur-of-the-moment decision. Assuming the planes had been ordered to a state of readiness, he decided to countermand it. He reached for the bunker phone and Deichmann's hand clamped down upon his wrist.

"It would be madness," Deichmann said, "and besides it's too late – they've already taken off."

They stood silent, deafened, as the planes roared overhead, wave after glinting wave; black, hump-winged Stukas, silver shark-nosed logs. The sky was suddenly a sounding-board, giving back the thunder of their engines, and even as the Germans watched they could see the tiny specks of bombs falling over Hawkinge airfield, the black smudges of ack-ack.

Alarmed, Rieckhoff rang Kesselring, a personal call to Karinhall, but he couldn't make connection beyond the duty operations officer. Kesselring was in the Reichsmarschall's conference and not to be disturbed – was there some message they could pass to him later? By this time, Deichmann thought, Rieckhoff seemed almost resigned. "Orders or no orders – they are flying just the same."

-

At the precise moment that Major Rieckhoff was trying to raise Kesselring at Karinhall, Robert Bailey, twenty-seven miles away, was among the winter oats at Densole Farm, Hawkinge, two miles south of his own farm, Ladwood. Months earlier, Bailey had managed to buy a second-hand self-binder, and since then requests from neighbours for a helping hand had flooded in from all over the district – requests that it just wasn't in Bailey to refuse. Bailey prized nothing in war more dearly than this heightened camaraderie, with neighbour gladly helping out neighbour as the need arose.

This morning was no exception: Bailey and his tractor driver, Earl Knight, weren't the only two who'd come to help Harry Greenstreet, Densole Farm's owner, with his winter oats. Old Walt Fagg and Sid Wood were there, too – old-time tenant farmers of the kind who still used binder twine to hitch up their corduroys, they'd been a part of the scene for as long as Robert Bailey could remember. Now, as Bailey worked to repair a minor breakdown in the binder, Walt and Sid were patiently standing up the sheaves.

Suddenly, from above in the sun, there came a strange sharp-edged whining, followed by the snarl of engines – and with no more warning the Stukas of Hauptmann von Brauchitsch's 4th Wing *Lehrgeschwader* I fell like falcons from the sky.

The quiet sunlit farms were suddenly a devil's chorus of sound… the metallic panging of the airfield's Bofors guns… the high-pitched scream of the diving Stukas… the pandemonium of exploding hangars as the bombers made their mark. Suddenly the farmers felt nakedly exposed, marooned in the centre of the eight-acre field; as one they were running, pell-mell, for the shelter of a distant elm grove. It was now that Robert Bailey, bringing up the rear, became conscious of a pulsating sense of excitement. He was under fire, and Bailey, who'd never before sought any greater stimulus than the changing seasons of the year, suspected he was secretly enjoying it.

Abruptly he was choking with laughter, because old Walt Fagg, bent on warding off stray bullets, was running altogether blind, his jacket sheathing his head. Somehow, by sheer instinct, the old man found the five-barred gate at the far end of the field – then, a countryman to the last, still navigating blind, he swung and slammed the gate shut. It was one move Bailey wasn't expecting; with bone-jarring force he cannoned head-on into it.

All unknowing, the farmers had just witnessed the first bombs of Eagle Day proper. The time was 11.35 a.m. (to the Germans on the Continent, keeping middle European time, 12.35 p.m.) Thursday, August 15.

Though Bailey and his mates took this to be an all-out assault on Hawkinge, this was far from the truth. Between now and 8 p.m. approximately 2,119 German planes of all types would be unleashed in a pile-driving effort to bring the R.A.F. fighters into the air and smash Fighter Command once and for all.

The trouble was that Oberst Paul Deichmann's plans succeeded beyond his wildest dreams. In the next crucial hours, fully twenty-six squadrons – almost 300 fighters of Dowding's force – would be airborne to face the worst the Luftwaffe could do.

And though Goring's plan committed less than half the Luftwaffe's total bomber force to the battle, the targets allotted to them ranged more than 125 miles of the south coast of England alone... Kesselring's Air Fleet Two, striking once more across the Straits of Dover, heading for the Short Brothers aircraft factory at Rochester, Kent... yet again to the radar stations of Dover and Rye... while to the west the units of Sperrle's Air Fleet Three were to launch feint attacks to bring up the fighters over Portland naval base, the airfields at Odiham and Middle Wallop.

One formation was doomed from the start: the sixty-three Heinkels of Oberstleutnant Fuchs' 26th Bomber Group, called "The Lion *Geschwader*", just then winging its way towards Newcastle-on-Tyne, 274 miles north. Their sole escort was twenty-one ME 110s of the 1st Wing, 76th *Zerstorer* Group, led by Hauptmann Werner Restemeyer. Pitifully vulnerable as they were, the 110 was the sole fighter with the range to do the job.

In a daring attempt at a flank attack, only recently sanctioned, the Heinkels, part of Generaloberst Hans-Jurgen Stumpff's Air Fleet Five, had flown more than 400 miles from Stavanger, Norway – confident that Dowding's fighter squadrons in the south would be too tied up to oppose a northern thrust.

It was a vain hope. Already in Fighter Command's Filter Room, Dowding, steel-helmeted, was watching absorbed; forty minutes distant from the coastline, the radar stations had picked up tracks of a sortie approaching northern England. Unerringly the W.A.A.F. plotters showed the raid building up, the long handled magnetic plotting rods indicating the track... the news passing to the Sector Ops Rooms of No. 13 Group at Newcastle-on-Tyne... to 12 Group at Watnall, near Nottingham.

More to himself, the C.-in-C.'s aide-de-camp, Pilot Officer Robert Wright, murmured "My God, they're plotting well" –

and was startled when "Stuffy" Dowding rejoined quietly, "But they always do."

And Dowding knew a moment of quiet triumph. His determination, despite all pressures, not to strip northern England of fighter squadrons was vindicated now. This morning, thanks to this decision, at least nine squadrons would be ready to intercept – among them the Hurricanes of 605 Squadron, milling expectantly over the Tyne River. Fifteen miles north of them, from Acklington airfield, near Morpeth, the Spitfires of No. 72 Squadron were already airborne and closing in – forty miles out to sea off the Northumberland coast, 25,000 feet above the rocky blur of the Farne Islands.

In truth, both Wright and Dowding had paid too generous a tribute. The tracks the Filter Room were plotting and passing weren't those of the Heinkels at all – merely a diversion raid of seaplanes heading for the Firth of Forth. Yet so bad was the bombers' navigation, that they too were following this diversionary course – fully seventy-five miles south of their assigned targets, the airfields of Dishforth, Usworth and Linton-upon-Ouse.

What followed was stark slaughter. As fighter-leader, Werner Restemeyer had planned that his ME 110 should function as a kind of flying Ops Room from which he directed the battle – but barely had he seen the Spitfires, 4,000 feet above, then his radiotelephone crackled into chaos. "Red Indians on the left" – "Red Indians from the stun" – a score of fighter pilots yelling the Luftwaffe's code – alert for British planes. Simultaneously, in 72 Squadron's formation, someone hailed Flight Lieutenant Ted Graham, the leader, "Have you seen them?" and Graham, who stuttered badly, replied: "Of course I've seen the b–b–b–b–astards – I'm t–t–t–rying to w–w–w–ork out what–what–to–d–do."

But already the attack was on. As Graham hurtled in on the starboard flank, reefing through the gap between bombers and fighters, every man was picking his own target. Awed, Pilot Officer Robert Deacon-Elliott saw the mass formation split, and the Heinkels were jettisoning their loads: the grey swell of the North Sea churned white with bombs, as if a colony of whales were spouting. Before he could even co-ordinate the defences, Restemeyer was dead; a soft yellow gasp of flame and his Messerschmitt was lost to view.

And others fared as badly. At the tail-end of the fighters, Unteroffizier Karl Richter, out cold with a glancing head-wound, swooned forward over the control column; his 110 spun without check towards the sea. To his radioman-gunner, Unteroffizier Geisechker, it seemed that all was lost; he baled out. In the nick of time, Richter came groggily to; half-blinded by blood he still fought his plane back across the North Sea for a crash-landing at Esbjerg, Norway. Oberfeldwebel Lothar Linke made it, too, limping back to Jever, North Germany, with only the power of the port engine. Others, such as Oberleutnant Gordon Gollob, fought like furies and somehow made it to base – at a fearsome cost of six fighters, eight bombers.

From Aalborg, Denmark, the 30th Bomber Group did better; unescorted, their fifty Junkers 88s still broke through the defences above Flamborough Head to ravage the aerodrome at Driffield, Yorkshire, destroying twelve Whitley bombers on the ground for a cost of five JU 88s. Yet this again was a Bomber Command airfield, independent of Dowding's defences; the one ill-planned sortie had cost Air Fleet Five twenty of the 154 planes available. The Fighter Command squadrons that had risen like angry hornets to the defence had only damage that could be repaired at base.

From this moment on, Air Fleet Five was out of the dayfighting altogether – and the battle had barely started.

Three hundred miles south, between Dover and Southampton, it seemed to most that the battle had never stopped – this whole August Thursday was given over to the fearful martial music of the bombardment. To widowed Mrs Joanna Thompson, crouched inside her garden shelter with her small son, Roger, the sky seemed to rain blazing planes, parachutes, even flying boots; shrapnel was crashing and bouncing like thunderbolts on the shelter's tin roof. At St. Mary Cray, near Biggin Hill airfield, Mrs Mary Simcox darted for her mother's shelter nearby, a dustbin lid serving as a steel helmet – but even underground, with three thick topcoats wound round her head, she couldn't shut out the noise.

In the stifling darkness she felt her mother's left hand clutched in hers while her right hand told her rosary: there was no other way to communicate.

The noise troubled others in the strangest ways. At Abbotsbury, Dorset, swanherd Fred Lexster, who'd worked at the unique 1,200-strong swannery for twenty-five years, even showing off his charges to Pavlova, was perplexed and disturbed: the cacophony so outraged his birds they refused to hatch their eggs. And Flight Lieutenant Geoffrey Hovenden, Hawkinge airfield medical officer, was puzzled, too – by an entire sick parade of station defence troops troubled by wax in their ears. With an auriscope Hovenden corrected their diagnosis: the non-stop percussion of their pom-pom guns had blocked their ears with blood clots, rendering them temporarily stone deaf.

Wherever battle was joined, there was no escaping its impact. In an orchard at Higham, near Maidstone, Land Girl Liz Bradburne watched alarmed as ripe red apples, lashed by shrapnel, fell like cannonballs; hastily she and her co-workers fell face down with wicker baskets shielding their heads. By West Malling airfield, eighteen-year-old Brenda Hancock, picking apples to help the war effort, proved more adventurous. With every dogfight she ventured higher and yet higher up the ladder – a thing she'd never deign to do when only apples were involved.

To the *Daily Express's* Hilde Marchant, watching from Dover's Shakespeare Cliff, the thundering phalanxes of planes seemed "to make an aluminium ceiling to the sky".

It was a heart-stopping sight – yet everywhere along the southern coast hundreds who'd never been under fire resolutely summoned courage, almost as if conscious it was now the fashionable thing to be a front-liner. At Dover's Grand Hotel, one luncheon guest complained bitterly of shrapnel in his soup, but headwaiter George Garland coaxed him to rise above it, and greeted newcomers to the dining room: "Good morning, sir! A nice table here, sir, away from the broken glass…"

A few miles down the coast, at Folkestone, it was the same. As Mrs Mary Castle queued outside a pastrycook's, shrapnel and machine-gun bullets spattered the pavement. At once, without more ado, two airmen queuing in the shop's doorway, ahead of her, stepped politely back, raising their forage caps, enabling her to pass inside.

Whatever the inconvenience, people were careful to shrug it off. At Homefield, Kent, ancestral home of the wealthy Smithers family, William, the butler, did the rounds of the velvety lawn after each dog-fight, sweeping up spent machine-gun bullets as deftly as ever he'd brushed crumbs from a damask tablecloth. Fifty miles south-west, at Worthing, Sussex, Miss Vera Arlett's maid was equally matter-of-fact: "Shall we have plums and custard for dessert – oh, and they're machine-gunning the back garden."

Later, on a bus bound for nearby Shoreham, Miss Arlett marvelled. The conductor, craning from the step, was keeping toll of the battle overhead like an umpire, scribbling the score on a scrap of paper tacked by the door – something he'd done all the forty miles from Portsmouth.

To Dowding's pilots, the score was still in doubt. By the early afternoon of August 15, British radar stations monitored track after confusing track over northern France. Minute by minute the numbers increased… sixty-plus Ostend… 120-plus Calais… the range still constant though the heights escalated steadily… 8,000 feet… 10,000 feet… 18,000 feet… 20,000 feet. On a sudden, in the Receiver Block at Rye Radar Station, Corporal Daphne Griffiths heard one of the duty watch shatter the mounting tension: "They're under starter's orders – they're off!"

Now Rye's cathode ray tube, like every other, was a truly amazing sight. So massive were the German formations that there wasn't even the ghost of a trace for forty miles – and as the planes broke and spread over the Channel, to plot or distinguish individual tracks was well-nigh impossible. Already eleven British fighter squadrons – 130 Spitfires and Hurricanes – were airborne, yet every Sector Controller, confused as to the ultimate target, was forced to improvise.

Airborne from Martlesham Heath, Suffolk, No. 17 Hurricane Squadron were twenty miles out to sea, at 12,000 feet, steering seventy degrees magnetic to cut off the Germans' Raid 22 – twenty-four aircraft at that same height. Now came baffling instructions: they must steer forty-five degrees magnetic instead. From Debden, No. 19 Spitfire Squadron, steering the same course, were also seeking the elusive Raid 22.

Unopposed, Raid 22, Rubensdorffer's top scoring Test Croup 210, accepting Oberst Deichmann's challenge, swept down on Martlesham Heath airfield, loosing salvo after salvo for five long minutes.

Though Rubensdorffer's report that Martlesham was "a heap of smoking rubble" was optimistic, it took officers and men, working full pitch, one whole day to clear the debris.

Now, on a score of airfields, Air Chief Marshal Dowding's pilots were as hard-pressed as any men alive. At least 100 of them had been at readiness – at their dispersal points, life-jackets already adjusted – since dawn: others, more sorely tried, had been on stand-by – strapped in their cockpits, facing the wind, engines ready to turn over. Only the fortunate few had drawn available – in the mess and ready to take off within twenty minutes. Garbed in flying overalls or rolltop sweaters, with silk scarves for comfort, they had lolled on the grass or on canvas cots, the thump-thump of the petrol bowsers' delivery pumps dinning in their ears, lucky enough to breakfast off luke-warm baked beans and tepid tea.

And still, ten hours later, the pressure was stepping up: at North Weald, Essex, the pilots of 56 Squadron, starting lunch soon after noon, were scrambled so often they didn't reach dessert until 3.30 p.m. At Hawkinge, the station defence officer warned others clustered in the mess: "Don't take too long over that sherry. I've only sounded the all-clear so that we can get some lunch." For many, food, even a bed, was a luxury. At Rochford, 151 Squadrons pilots bedded down in their cockpits; the airfield's dew-soaked grass was the one alternative. It was the same for 32 Squadron at Biggin Hill; on call since 3 a.m., Squadron Leader John Worrall's men had slept beneath their Hurricanes, using parachutes for pillows.

Grimly the pilots kept going, because they were the kind of men who would – freebooters who were often frightened sick, but men who lived for the moment. Lean, handsome Robert Stanford Tuck, who affected monogrammed silk handkerchiefs and long cigarette holders, had shot down eleven planes already and could start up a Spitfire blindfolded... explosive pipe-puffing Douglas Bader, whose tin legs, the result of a pre-war crash, were a legend even with the Luftwaffe... often, playing squash, Bader disconcerted an opponent by "breaking" a leg and fitting on a spare... Adolph "Sailor" Malan, late Third Officer of the Union Castle Line, soon styled "The Greatest Fighter Ace of all Time".

Not all were aces, but the backgrounds they hailed from, the way they lived now, marked them down as different... Warrant Officer Edward Mayne, Royal Flying Corps veteran, at forty the oldest man to fly as a regular combatant in the battle... young Hugh Percy, an undergraduate from Cambridge University, who kept his log-book in Greek... New Zealander Mindy Blake, Doctor of Mathematics, who approached each combat like a quadratic equation... The Nizam of Hyderabad's former personal pilot, Derek Boitel-Gill... Randy Matheson, ex-Argentine gaucho and Johnny Bryson, a former Canadian Mountie... Squadron Leader Aeneas MacDonell, official head of the Glengarry clan… Red Tobin from Los Angeles with the barnstormers, Andy and Shorty.

Some had fought across the world: Rodolphe, Comte de Grune, Belgian nobleman and veteran Condor Legion pilot with fourteen victories in the Spanish Civil War, now with No. 32 Hurricane Squadron, pitting his wits against his former allies. Some hadn't fought at all: at Northolt airfield, No. 1 Squadron, Royal Canadian Air Force, wealthy Canadian blue-bloods, had acquired a 1911 Rolls-Royce and a liveried British chauffeur, Sebastian, but as yet, no battle honours. Some had fought, and thirsted for the chance to fight again, such as Squadron Leader Zdzislaw Krasnodebski's Poles – joined now by Sergeant Josef Frantisek, twenty-eight, a lone-wolf Czech, soon to claim a German victim for every year of his life.

At least a third were auxiliaries, wealthy weekend fliers of pre-war days, enlisted by regions – and they did things their own way. At Tangmere, No. 601 Squadron enlivened their powder-blue uniforms with scarlet linings, sported blue ties because the R.A.F.'s black depressed them; when the pilots sat down to poker, the game was mostly £100 a stake. Too recently formed to boast World War One traditions, the auxiliaries had started a few of their own; when "Big Jim" McComb's 611 Squadron approached an airfield they flew, perversely, in perfect swastika formation. Edinburgh-based 603 Squadron boasted their own pipe-band to play "Lament for Flodden"; their ground crews wore thistles and white heather. For the Durham-recruited 607 Squadron, known as "The Bloody Coal Miners", standard white flying overalls were out; all wore mauve, the County Palatine colour.

The legends that adorned their warplanes showed their don't-give-a-damn spirit – the regulars as much as the auxiliaries. Many were Disney-minded. "Big Jim" McComb's Spitfire had Snow White on the fuselage; other 611 men, according to temperament, were "Grumpy", "Sneezy" or "Dopey". Hurricane pilot Ian Gleed showed Figaro, with the little cat swatting a swastika as blithely as a mouse, Polish ace Jan Zumbach, of Krasnodebski's outfit, had Donald Duck at his jauntiest.

Most were irreverent – Leslie Charteris's The Saint, or Canadian Norrie Hart's design of swastikas showering into a chamber pot. Calgary's Willie McKnight had a sharp-edged scythe dripping blood, to symbolise death, the grim reaper; after one nightmare combat, McKnight touched down to find the emblem blotted out by the splattered remains of his German adversary. Others had to show just where they stood on things: Dublin-born Bryan Considine's *Erin Go Bragh* (Ireland For Ever), with a pot of Guinness and a shamrock leaf... John Bisdee's family coat of arms, a medieval fleur-de-lis with a mural crown... Sub-Lieutenant Jimmie Gardner's "England Expects", spelt out in flags, its designer one of sixty-eight Fleet Air Arm pilots on loan to the R.A.F., slow to discard the Navy's starched white collars.

None set the keynote better than New Zealand's Flying Officer D. H. Ward of 87 Squadron – a coat of arms mocked up from a figure 13, a broken mirror, a man under a ladder and three on a match, captioned, "So what the hell?"

And to back the pilots at this critical hour, there were still station commanders who saw things their way – men who would turn the blindest of eyes to protocol and red tape. At Biggin Hill, Group Captain Richard Grice laid on crates of beer for all returning pilots, invited W.A.A.F.S hauled up for breaches of discipline to sit down and have a cigarette. Wing Commander Cecil Bouchier, Hornchurch's peppery C.O., handed out candy as often as rebukes – and kept station morale at peak with non-stop running commentaries on the Ops Room's tannoy loudspeaker. At North Weald, Victor Beamish, a fire-eating Irishman, would leap clean through his open office window sooner than miss a scramble – and Northolt's Group Captain Stanley Vincent, World War One fighter ace, felt the same. His Station Defence Flight – one lone Hurricane – was formed to get him airborne whenever possible.

The pilots proved worthy of such backing. Outnumbered as they were on August 15, they were still suicidally valiant in their efforts. Canada's Flight Lieutenant Mark Brown, sighting Rubensdorffer's Test Group 210, twenty-four strong, returning from the attack on Martlesham, thought the east coast port of Harwich, lying below, might soon be in trouble. Single-handed, he climbed to divert them, then a 109 harassed him with fire; he had to bale out. Though Brown had drifted five miles out to sea before a trawler sighted him, Harwich wasn't touched.

And others were as resolute. Over the Channel, Flight Sergeant "Gilly" Gilbert felt a bullet fracture his radiator's coolant system; one rending explosion and his Spitfire was enveloped in clouds of blinding glycol steam. Still with 109s on his tail, Gilbert unfastened his safety straps, raised himself in the cockpit, then, peering over the top of the windscreen like a fogbound motorist, steered his plane back to Hawkinge. Even in defeat, they did things in style; at the controls of a blazing Hurricane over Folkestone, New Zealand's Flying Officer John Axel Gibson saw no need for indecent hurry. Slipping off a brand-new pair of handmade shoes, he lobbed them into space; he didn't want them spoiled by sea-water. Next, he set course for the open sea – that way he couldn't endanger life or property. Finally, at 1,000 feet, he baled out.

To Gibson, the immediate award of the D.F.C. for his courage was almost as puzzling as another antic factor: a thoughtful civilian, retrieving his shoes, had posted them, on the off-chance, back to Hawkinge airfield.

Despite all such efforts, the bombers of *Kampfgeschwader* 3, forging westwards over Kent with a strong fighter escort, reached their targets unscathed. As Hauptmann Rathmann's 3rd Wing showered Eastchurch airfield with bombs, thirty Dorniers of the 2nd Wing were over the Short Brothers aircraft factory at Rochester, jubilantly reporting one direct hit after another – with ugly black palls of smoke burgeoning skywards.

Yet though the factory's final assembly line, building Britain's first four-engined bomber, the Stirling, was gutted by fire, stalling production for many months, fighters, not bombers, had first priority in Lord Beaverbrook's schedule – and Eastchurch was a Coastal Command airfield. The Luftwaffe had yet to destroy Fighter Command.

To the German fighter pilots, high in the sun, it was something of a miracle to have got the bombers through at all. This afternoon, Major Martin Mettig, the 54th Fighter Group's commander, had adhered to all the precepts that to date had ensured him minimal losses... one fighter group flying as direct protection, covering the bombers on every flank, right through to the target... a second batch moving in to relieve them, escorting the bombers from the target back to the Channel... a third group on "free hunt", combing the sky for British fighters... yet a fourth taking over at the Channel, shepherding the fighters back to France.

Yet Mettig, as fighter-leader, had flown the whole length of this formation, and now he wondered: How long before the system breaks down, for how can 120 fighters protect a bomber formation forty miles long?

The ME 109's tactical flying time was eight minutes and its operational radius 125 miles – which left just ten scant minutes, if the R.A.F. were in the mood for combat, to fight and break away.

It was a vital factor – and today, when Oberst Deichmann's snap decision had caught some units unawares, more vital than ever before. Despite the need for split-second timing, many of Sperrle's bomber units, assigned to the western feint, missed their rendezvous with their escorts altogether – or were as late as if time had lost all meaning.

Orbiting the Cherbourg peninsula at 15,000 feet, two escort pilots of the 53rd Fighter Wing, Leutnant Erich Bodendiek and Oberleutnant Hans Ohly, were, just before 5 p.m., on August 15, checking their stop-watches with growing alarm. Already the bombers they were assigned to protect were twenty minutes late for the rendezvous – and each minute was costing the fighters precious fuel.

Checking his watch yet again, Ohly groaned, "How in hell do we protect them *and* get back?"

It was a pertinent question – for with the attacks jumping spottily from target to target, Goring's units were losing all technical advantage. Given luck, Dowding's squadrons would find the chance to land, re-fuel and re-arm – and, given time, the detector stations would signal the Germans' approach.

As things turned out, all the fighters' fears were justified. As the 53rd Fighter Group, under Major Hans-Jurgen Cramon-Taubadel, cruised aimlessly in circles, along with two other escort squadrons, the radar stations were plotting their height and range to perfection. By 6 p.m., as the dive-bomber unit *Lehrgeschwader* 1, with two Stuka wings, plus their anxious escort, neared the English coast, they were known for what they were, a formation of 200-plus – and 170 British fighters were waiting.

Oberst Deichmann's plan to bring the fighters up had succeeded triumphantly – but not quite as he had planned.

Now came the worst part of this day's assault on southern England. To Hauptmann Joachim Helbig, leading the 1st Training Group's 4th Wing, it seemed he had barely sighted the coastline when eighty Spitfires were howling at him from 23,000 feet – a fire-power of 600-plus machine-guns matched against Helbig's one rear-gunner, Oberfeldwebel Franz Schlund. All the time the quiet, placid Schlund kept up a steady flow of injunctions, like a driving instructor on a summer highway: "Red Indians on your right, 1,300 feet… 1,200 feet… hold it… 1,000 feet."

For Helbig, it was only Schlund's iron nerve that saved the day. In the moment the lone machine-gun erupted, dealing death to at least one Spitfire, Helbig heeled sharply to port, a turn so sheer the Spitfires over-shot, then jinked to a lower altitude. His Junkers 88 sieved with 130 bullets, he soared due south for Orleans airfield – with five of his wing already lost to the British fighters.

It was the same in every outfit. From the 2nd Wing, only three dive-bombers out of fifteen reached their target, the naval base at Worthy Down, Southampton; the remainder jettisoned as one. Hauptmann Wilhelm Kern, heading the 1st Wing, did better; as Middle Wallop raced towards them, he trumpeted, "All Dora aircraft, all Dora aircraft – when I drop, you all drop," and together twelve 1,000-kilo bombs spilled towards the aerodrome, a ruse so startling the flak stayed silent. Before 609 Squadron below were even airborne, Kern and his crews were speeding south.

But for one bomber that made the target, three more were in trouble; their leisurely run-up to the rendezvous had cost them many lives. Frantically they looked to the fighters for protection, but most were lost to view in the vast egg-shaped swarm wheeling and stalling above the Hampshire coast. And already every German fighter was watching his fuel gauge, knowing the moment to break for base must be reckoned in seconds now.

Typical were the last desperate moments of young Josef Birndorfer, an ME 110 pilot, seeking vainly to shake 609 Squadron's implacable Flying Officer Ostazewski off his tail. Diving steeply for the ground in a series of S-turns, Birndorfer found himself curving, at 300 miles an hour, round a church spire… snaking perilously through the steel cables of Southampton's balloon barrage, cheating the grey, motionless sixty-foot-long porpoise-shapes by a hair's-breadth… now at hedgetop level, a dark speeding shadow across the lavender shadows of evening… onwards over the Solent's laden waters, with Ostazewski closing relentlessly from 300 yards. Then the Pole was down to a hundred yards, still firing, and white stars were winking and dancing along the *Zerstorer*'s fuselage. At Ashley Down, on the Isle of Wight, it struck a metalled road head-on, and suddenly it was a plane no longer but a fiery, skidding projectile ripping itself apart.

And still the Germans were coming: Oberst Deichmann's onslaught had reached juggernaut pitch by now. At 6.28 p.m., the Spitfire pilots of 54 Squadron, slumped on the grass at Manston airfield, were dreaming wistfully of beer and supper at their home base, Hornchurch, when the telephone's jangle sent their hopes plunging. Another seventy-plus German aircraft were in mid-Channel, surging for a landfall between Dover and Dungeness.

In truth, with several of Dowding's squadrons grounded after the hard day's fighting, this was the moment to have launched a saturation blitz. But on this day, known always to the Luftwaffe pilots as "Black Thursday", they had already lost close on fifty machines – and none of these, unlike the British planes, would be salvageable for further use.

Of all who had narrow squeaks this day, none came closer to bidding their comrades a long farewell than 54 Squadron's Flight Lieutenant Al Deere, who had so nearly missed forestalling Rubensdorffer's first raid on Manston. A rugged twenty-one-year-old from Wanganui, New Zealand, with a cheery grin and a broken nose, Deere's appetite for danger was as limitless as his hunger for solid protein. The survivor of a Dunkirk bale-out and two forced landings, he was notoriously first to the table in Hornchurch mess, ready to wolf the breakfast eggs of any pilot feeling off-colour.

Now, at 20,000 feet over Dungeness, Deere was in trouble once more; as 54 Squadron swept on towards the arrowhead German formation, one ME 109 broke from the chain, heading precipitately for France. At once Deere was away in pursuit, careful to stay just below the German's height, in the blind spot formed by the Messerschmitt's tail unit. If the log spotted him, he knew he would lose it in the dive. Outfitted with fuel injector pumps, a 109, unlike a Spitfire or a Hurricane, could dive steeply without its engine cutting out.

At 5,000 feet, almost in range to fire, Deere cursed softly; the 109 was suddenly swallowed by a thin curtain of cloud. Then he was flying in clear sky once more, and his jaw dropped stupidly; no longer flying level, the 109 was steepening its dive towards an airfield lying to starboard. The stalk had so absorbed the stocky little pilot he'd never even realised they had crossed the Channel – or that the 109 was preparing to land on its home base, Calais–Marck airfield. There wasn't time to wait longer. Still out of range, Deere thumbed the firing button.

In that second, all hell broke loose. As if galvanised, the German fighter went for Calais–Marck like a rocket. But below the airfield circuit was a beehive of 109s, and two were now streaking for the water to cut Deere off. Throttle wide open, he broke for Dover's white cliffs at sea level, the 109s screaming in pursuit.

Twice, as they pounced, Deere swung the Spitfire's nose viciously outwards, forcing them to break away, but soon the violent manoeuvres tired him, and in this moment they struck. Bullets riddled the instrument panel and the Perspex canopy, ripping the inner casing of his wrist watch from his left hand; the engine stuttered loudly. Thick heavy spurts of liquid bathed his cowling like rain – the oil tank had been hit.

At 1,500 feet over Ashford, Kent, with the 109s long departed, writhing flames took the Spitfire's engine, and Deere, releasing his Sutton harness, rolled the aircraft on its back, pushing hard on the stick. But as he catapulted from his seat, his parachute snagged on some part of the cockpit, and though he clawed and grappled to climb back in, the Spitfire was beyond control, tilting ever forward onto its nose, and the terrible airflow clamped him like a limpet to its fuselage.

Then, as the ground reared up to meet him, he broke loose, the blazing aircraft nearly vertical now, striking his wrist a savage welt against the tailplane. But the chute responded to the tug of the ripcord, and seconds later, with only a fractured wrist as souvenir, Deere was floating, miraculously alive, over silent woods, landing only 100 yards from where his Spitfire was exploding in blast after blast.

For the fourth time in ten weeks he had cheekily thumbed his nose at death – and when a passing ambulance took him to

East Grinstead Hospital, the nearest they could locate, its chief, Archibald McIndoe, the famous plastic surgeon, rang Wing Commander Bouchier, Hornchurch's station commander, to announce Deere's safe arrival.

With the mingled anger and love of a sorely taxed father, Bouchier roared: "Well, keep the little bugger there – he's costing us too many Spitfires."

Already, like many station commanders, Bouchier had a shrewd inkling that this day's losses were the heaviest yet; nor was his judgment misplaced. The R.A.F. had lost thirty-four fighters, with many others so badly mauled they would take time to replace, and how much loss the Germans had suffered by comparison was anybody's guess.

Meanwhile the Observer Corps H.Q. at Bromley, Kent, were puzzled. At 6.37 p.m., the very moment that Deere's squadron had dived to intercept the incoming raid over Dungeness, the formation had scattered and split. Within five minutes, the seething mass had dissolved into eight distinct formations, and the last of these, tagged as Raid 8 by the reporting chain, had mysteriously altered course. First heading north over Orpington and Bexley Heath, fifty miles inland, it had suddenly swerved and was dodging south.

Craning from their sandbagged posts, binoculars sweeping the evening sky, the observers could not realise that these twenty-three planes of Test Group 210, led on the last sortie of the day by their chief, Hauptmann Walter Rubensdorffer, had lost not only their way but their escort, the 52nd Fighter Group.

In the vanguard of the third squadron, made up of bomb-laden ME 109s, Oberleutnant Otto Hintze wrinkled his eyes against the evening sun. For a moment now they were flying due west, still seeking their target, the fighter airfield at Kenley, Surrey, but the summer heat-haze lay like gauze across the fields and hills. Hintze heard Walter Rubensdorffer ask quizzically: "Are we over land or over sea?" But no man could answer with certainty, so Rubensdorffer decided: "I'm going down."

So twenty-three planes were sweeping lower, down to 9,500 feet, but still the mottled clouds baulked their view. Then, in the same instant, two things happened. Rubensdorffer's voice, shorn of reproach or bitterness, was quiet in their headphones: "The fighter protection has withdrawn." And they saw what they took to be Kenley: the sprawling, solid, red-brick huddle of a peacetime fighter station.

So now it was too late. They fanned out for the attack.

Neither Rubensdorffer or any of his detachment realised that this was not Kenley, but its satellite, four miles north, the old peacetime airport of Croydon, only ten miles from central London. On Hitler's express orders – for the Fuhrer still hoped for a negotiated peace – Croydon and all London targets were forbidden, and any man attacking them was booked for a court-martial if he came back alive.

And now, as Rubensdorffer, the first to go in, pushed his nose down into a forty-degree dive, fear was like a small hard fist in his belly. Alongside him, planes were diving in concert, and these planes were not his own. In fact, they were the Hurricanes of Squadron Leader John Thompson's 111 Squadron, nine strong, all that could be mustered after seven hours' combat, patiently patrolling their base for the last seven minutes, knowing that Rubensdorffer would come.

On the ground there was no time to think, only to act. All over Croydon airfield the tannoy loudspeaker blurted into life, "Attack Alarm!" "Attack Alarm!" and Sergeant Frank Freeman, of the Middlesex Regiment was doubling from pill-box to pill-box, checking that every crew stood by to man the aerodrome's sole defences, twelve Vickers machine-guns. Then, high in the sky, he saw the wings of Rubensdorffer's 110 waggle convulsively, the signal for attack. At the pitch of his lungs he roared, "Look out, here they come!"

Then the machine-guns' coughing chatter was blotted out, the screaming engines of Test Group 210 seemed to burst through the solid concrete of the pill-boxes, and all the earth trembled with the shock waves. Coughing and retching through a fine rain of chalk dust, Freeman thought the situation still called for a soldierly demeanour: crawling angrily towards one man, who was calling on all the saints to preserve him, he shook him into slack-jawed silence.

The tragedy was that, unnerved by the sudden descent of Thompson's Hurricanes, many of Test Group 210 couldn't pinpoint their targets; bomb after bomb was over-shooting. The armoury... the Control Tower... three hangars... all were written off, but many single-storey factories on the airfield periphery suffered worst. The N.S.F. light engineering factory... the Bourjois scent factory... the Rollason aircraft company... partially converted to war production, all were working night shifts and none of their workers had been alerted.

Curiously, though the airfield had been alerted by 6.29 p.m., no air-raid warning had sounded for the general public. Not until 7.16 – seventeen minutes after the first bombs had dropped – did the cry of the siren rise and fall over Croydon's streets.

In the red-brick streets radiating from the airfield, bystanders watched aghast – then reacted as their backgrounds prompted them. From the door of his Duppa's Hill Lane office, 600 yards away, Commandant John Robert Smith, an on-the-ball civil defence chief, saw the first bombs fall, and bellowed: "One, one and one." Within minutes a stretcher party, an ambulance and a sitting-case car for walking-wounded had ground away from the depot. At Headcorn Road, Thornton Heath, Miss Lillian Bride asked her father fearfully, "Dad, what will it mean? You've seen through a few wars," and the eighty-four-year-old ex-soldier pondered: "Well, we don't know, but we've got to keep a stout heart." Roy Owen Barnes, an authentic fifteen-year-old, saw it differently. At his third-storey bedroom window he was riffling through his aircraft recognition booklets, trying clinically to identify the first Luftwaffe planes he had ever seen.

In the circular gallery of Fighter Command's Ops Room, Winston Churchill watched in silence as the W.A.A.F.s below him charted the raid, plying their long-handled plotting rods as deftly as croupiers. That very afternoon he'd told Parliament that despite heavy attacks the Germans couldn't penetrate to London – yet now the blast of Rubensdorffer's bombs was rattling the House of Commons' windows. Besides him, Air Chief Marshal Dowding, General Sir Hastings (later Lord) Ismay, and Lord Beaverbrook, grave-faced in a crinkled blue serge suit, were silent, too. No man to shirk an issue, Churchill had taxed Dowding bluntly: "You realise that serious doubts have been cast on your pilots' claims?" and Dowding had countered laconically: "If the German claims were correct, they would be in England now." But now Ismay saw Churchill freeze into total absorption: along the base of the wall display-panel, glowing red bulbs showed that every squadron in southern England was engaged or out of action. Ismay had to confess it: at this instant he felt "sick with fear".

Twenty-two miles south, above Croydon, Rubensdorffer's unit were fighting for their lives. To Oberleutnant Otto Hintze, in the last wave of all, the attack had suddenly assumed an unreal nightmare quality; planes zoomed and dived like spectres in the haze, then were lost to view. As he levelled out above the airfield's billowing dust, the R.A.F. fighters seemed everywhere, looming in his windscreen. Hintze didn't know it but III Squadron had been reinforced now by Squadron Leader John Worrall's 32 Squadron from Biggin Hill.

Overhead he saw Oberleutnant Martin Lutz's ME IIOs rotating steadily in the circle of death: flying white-hot tracer criss-crossed the sky, as the R.A.F. sought to penetrate their defences, and then Hintze was climbing steeply to join them, knowing that only an unbroken front against the British could hope to see them through. As he soared, orange flashes winking from the nose of his IO9, he saw a IIO break from the circle, hotly pursued by a lone Hurricane. Hauptmann Walter Rubensdorffer had seen that his fuel was getting tight.

Whoever pursued him, it wasn't Squadron Leader Thompson. Minutes earlier, seeing a IIO climbing near-vertically above him, he had launched his Hurricane high into the heavens, firing until the *Zerstorer*'s starboard engine had caught and the plane blew up like a dustbin emptying in his face. Then, to his amazement, he saw below him a 109, almost at ground level, holding to the shining ribbon of Purley Way, roaring upon the rooftops at 350 miles an hour. Then Thompson was above it and astern, in a paralysing battle below chimneypot height, until slates leaping from the ridged roofs struck a warning note: he might endanger civilian lives.

Breaking from combat, he thought incongruously: In peace-time I could have been court-martialled for that.

Somewhere beyond the airfield, a British plane plunged blazing; on a red double decker bus travelling Croydon's Brighton Road, passengers sprang cheering to their feet, certain the victim was a German. Only the bus conductress had seen it for a Hurricane; tears streaming down her face, she made the sign of the cross.

Below the combat, the airfield's surroundings were a scene of horror. To Sergeant Frank Freeman, of the Middlesex Regiment, one of the first on the scene at the shattered Bourjois scent factory, the mingled reek of blood and a perfume called "Evening in Paris" seemed to lodge in his stomach. Commandant John Robert Smith, following up his light rescue units, was appalled to see soldiers grope through writhing smoke bowed down by white naked torsos. It was a moment before he recognised them for what they were: huge white lengths of Army shaving soap, still unprocessed.

From an inferno of dust and licking flames, an incident officer's blue lantern glowed dimly; close by, a warden totting up the appalling casualty roll, sixty-two fatalities, 164 injured, stood calmly on one of the dead, a man stamped almost below ground level by hundreds of trampling feet.

At H.Q. Fighter Command, the wall display-panel showed more and more of Dowding's squadrons landing to re-fuel; the last waves of German raiders were receding towards the coast.

With scarcely a word, Winston Churchill left the gallery, head bent in ferocious thought, shoulders squared, moving at speed. As his Humber staff car took the road for Chequers, Ismay made to comment, but Churchill, almost savagely, cut him short, "Don't speak to me. I have never been so moved."

Five minutes passed, then Churchill, leaning forward, his voice shaken with emotion, said: "Never in the field of human conflict was so much owed by so many to so few." But Ismay could say nothing: he sat silent, the immortal words that were to echo round the world seeming to burn into his brain.

Far to the south, over Limpsfield in Surrey, Hauptmann Walter Rubensdorffer's 110 sank lower and lower towards the white, shocked corn, seeking a landing place; behind him his gunner, Feldwebel Richard Eherkecher, was still firing doggedly, but the Hurricane on their tail that had followed them all the way from Croydon would give them no peace. They veered south over Crockham Hill in Kent, the deadly Hurricane still closing, still firing. On the hillside below, a garage mechanic, Harry Bonwick, picknicking with his wife, saw the planes flying so low he thought paratroops were landing; pelting for his A.J.S. motor cycle he immobilised it, just as the printed police circulars had instructed.

Cartridge cases, twigs and shredded green leaves showered him while he worked, as bullets lashed the branches.

Then Edenbridge was past, and Chiddingstone, and now as Rubensdorffer raced south, blazing petrol from his punctured fuel tanks was rippling along his wings and fuselage. Only one of his unit, twenty-one-year-old Leutnant Horst Marx, was still valiantly keeping up; over the radio-telephone he'd heard his chief cry, "I've been hit," and he wouldn't break for home.

Then more Hurricanes were in view, singling out Marx's 109; over an apple orchard at Frant in Sussex, he baled out hastily, and Rubensdorffer was left alone, easing back his stick to gain height, needing all the "courageous leadership" for which Kesselring had officially paid him tribute, for this last lap of the journey. Then his starboard engine stopped dead.

At 7.30 p.m., Rubensdorffer's luck ran abruptly out: the tall, smiling Swiss, who had pioneered his unique fighter-bombing attacks as meticulously as he had left instructions for his own cremation, could hold up the plane no longer. As it passed over Denis Fishenden's smallholding, at Rotherfield, Sussex, molten fragments were already dripping from its wings.

A few hundred yards south, jobbing gardener Charles Wemban, stooping over the white waxy rows of his potato harvest, beheld a hair-raising sight: a blazing German plane, swooping clean over the roof of his tiny cottage, was coming for him head-on. Then, as Wemban fell prostrate, Rubensdorffer, with one last effort, lifted the plane, and it fell, trailing a great banner of flame, into the valley beyond, where it smashed with awful force into a tree-studded bank. At once the pent-up fuel burst violently outwards, ammunition splintered and rained like fire-crackers, and pigs ran squealing through the blazing wreckage.

From 10,000 feet up, to the last men still airborne, the blaze was barely more noticeable than a farmer's bonfire. To the civilians on the sidelines of the combat, lone, flickering fires, yellow-green dye patches splodging the sea, contrails graven in the sky above the apple orchards, remained to show that scores had fallen in a battle still undecided.

Above all, it was the aching silence after the bombardment that struck home most vividly – as the hours went by, it seemed to stretch and tauten. In her garden shelter at Borough Road, Folkestone, widowed Mrs Joanna Thompson had bedded down her little boy, Roger, but she herself couldn't sleep; it was suddenly like the silence before a storm. In all the street the only sound was an aged, half-blind woman, a few doors away, peering from her shelter, the old voice eerie in the night: "Are they up there? Are they up there?"

But for a few hours, they no longer were; at last it was quiet in Borough Road.

Chapter Five

"England's No Island Any More"

August 16–18

Reichsmarschall Hermann Goring had just one resolve as his conference re-assembled soon after breakfast on Friday, August 16. Whatever happened, his Luftwaffe would win the battle, or he'd know the reason why. Polished knee-length boots straddling his desk, arms folded, his face puckered in an unrelenting scowl, he told his staff bluntly: "England's no island any more – remember that."

Right from the start of the previous day's post-mortem, which had gone on all through the mass onslaught sparked off by Oberst Paul Deichmann, Kesselring, Sperrle and their chiefs of staff had known that Goring was in no mood for contradiction or compromise. The conference had been convened not in the big banqueting hall, its walls festooned with Goring's hunting trophies – antlers, boars' heads, tusks – but in a smaller room close by, an infallible sign the Reichsmarschall didn't feel expansive. And from the first, Goring had kept fiddling with an unlit Virginia cigarette – another sign of trouble.

And despite the patent hospitality – stewards circulating with trays of sherry, schnapps and Havana cigars – Goring had been in no mood to brook argument. To him, the lessons of the convoy attack and of the first abortive Eagle sortie were plain enough: if the Stukas had twice taken a beating over Portland, this was no good reason to abandon them. The reason they'd fared so badly had been lack of fighter protection.

And Goring delivered his ukase: from now on each Stuka wing should have three fighter wings – 120 planes, an entire group – to protect it. One wing to fly level with the Stukas – and dive with them in the same instant. A second to zoom at low level over the target, ahead of the rest, to intercept any R.A.F. planes poised to catch the bombers after their dive. The third wing would oversee the whole operation from above.

No technician, Goring ignored the one lesson the convoy attack had driven home – that since the ME 109 had no air-brakes it was bound to over-shoot the Stukas once it dived. And when the Stukas pulled out from their bombing attack, twice that many fighters would find themselves hard put to it to protect them.

More coffee and cigars, more blanket decisions. The ME 110 *Zerstorer* was troubling Goring, too. Though technically fighters, their losses were mounting steeply: at least one group leader, Oberstleutnant Friedrich Vollbracht, was to lose three wing commanders in as many weeks. But though the span of the plane alone – fifty-three feet as against the 109's thirty-two feet – invariably led the R.A.F. to single it out, Goring still had faith it could do the job.

Yet plainly they weren't a match for skilfully handled British planes, so in future every ME 110 unit in action must be guarded by an escort of 109s; a fighter in the ludicrous position of itself needing fighter protection.

Now Oberst Werner Junck, regional fighter commander for Air Fleet Three, jumped bravely in. If so many extra burdens were to be thrown on the 109, wouldn't the Reichsmarschall give serious thought to stepping up fighter production? Even in July, German aircraft factories had produced only 220 ME 109s – fewer than half Lord Beaverbrook's total output – and by the end of August, the figures would have slumped again, to 173.

Mock-solicitous, Goring stretched out his hand. "I must take your pulse to see if you are all right physically – it seems you have lost your senses."

It wasn't the first time Goring had heard such an argument from his production experts – and as summarily rejected it. Others had stressed that at the present rate of attrition, the Luftwaffe would need to shoot down four British fighters for every one they lost – yet even so, the ME 109 factories at Regensburg and Augsburg often worked a minimum six-hour day against the ten or twelve needed.

Only recently when General Thomas, Goring's production co-ordination chief, raised this point, Goring had crimsoned with rage: any such move would be fatal to home-front morale.

And this morning, despite the startling losses of August 15, Goring wasn't changing his tune. In the balmy make-believe world of Karinhall, surrounded by his inner circle of military sycophants, it was all too easy to believe just what he wanted to. As for the radar stations, it seemed pointless to continue strafing them – to date not one mast had been hit, and it might take weeks of saturation bombing before any vital equipment suffered damage.

Generalfeldmarschall Kesselring might complain bitterly, "We've been outsmarted," but the man the Luftwaffe knew as *Der Dicke* (The Fat One) didn't think so. As the meeting broke up, Goring hadn't a doubt in the world; the R.A.F. couldn't have more than 300 serviceable planes left to them. Properly protected, the Stukas and *Zerstorers* would finish the job.

–

Gently, Pilot Officer Robert Wright closed the door leading from his outer office to Air Chief Marshal Dowding's high Georgian room – then sadly shook his head. A loyal aide-decamp, he felt for Dowding deeply, and, this morning, seeing his chief come somewhere close to breaking point was more than Wright could bear. It was weeks now since The Old Man had dipped into a volume of his favourite Surtees or taken time off for his one main relaxation – a brisk Saturday morning's ice-skating at London's Queen's Club.

And today, when Dowding had arrived as late as 9.30 a.m., it was plain to Wright he'd overslept after one more gruelling small-hours vigil at a night-fighter interceptor station. Sensing his chief's terrible lassitude, Wright had come up with an offer: wouldn't it help if he too came along at nights to take notes and relieve the burden? Replying, Dowding's wintry smile was gentle: "A very nice suggestion, Wright, but you know somebody's got to be here first thing in the morning."

Now, minutes earlier, Dowding's buzzer had sounded again – and Wright, hastening in, had found his chief rooted to the floor, spectacles lodged on the bridge of his nose, staring trance-like into space. At length, rousing himself, he gestured: "All right, Wright, I'll ring for you again" – and his aide-de-camp, gently closing the door, knew that whatever was on Dowding's mind had been anaesthetised by fatigue in the seconds it had taken to cross the threshold.

Contrary to Reichsmarschall Goring's belief, the shortage of fighter planes was the last thing on Dowding's mind this day. Within the week, Lord Beaverbrook's Ministry of Aircraft Production was to achieve its highest-ever total during the battle – a record 440 fighters. It was trained pilots to fly those planes Dowding lacked above all – a need so dire that this day he was 209 pilots below strength. And though Dowding had time and again pressed the Air Ministry to divert Fairey Battle pilots to fill the gap, the Air Staff were still wavering. A large-scale withdrawal from the day-bomber squadrons could seriously jeopardise Britain's striking power come invasion day.

Haggard, scarcely ever able to snatch more than three hours' sleep a night, it was this problem that plagued the bone-tired Dowding above all.

It was no idle concern. The mounting losses now decreed that a pilot's expectation of life was no more than eighty-seven flying hours – and many were so near collapse their reactions were a long way off the medical board's touchstone: one-fifth of a second quicker than average. At Hawkinge, some pilots no sooner taxied in their planes than they slumped forward in the cockpit, as dead to the world as men under morphia, often close to coma for twenty-four hours. Young Pilot Officer Peter Hairs, a Hurricane pilot operating from Hawkinge, was typical of many. After the day's eighth sortie, he'd stare at his log-book, unable to record a thing except the times of take-off and landing. His mind blurred and seemed to take hold on nothing, and all night long he writhed and moaned, dreaming of blazing planes.

Sometimes one brief and bloody action tipped the scales. One pilot of 32 Squadron, breaking from combat over Dover, formated, as he thought, on a flight of Hurricanes bound for Biggin Hill – too weary to realise he'd tagged onto a flight of ME 109s.

Then the great fear that was to corrode his courage came on him, for the 109s were in sportive mood, taking leisurely turns to blast shining chunks of aluminium from his fuselage. And all the way back to Biggin Hill, the man's fear was a mounting frenzy as the 109s holed his airscrew blades, his starboard wing, his tailplane, even his wireless aerial. From then on, the pilot was an instructor, for he announced white-faced: "Nothing on earth will ever get me up there again."

Many cushioned their fear with liquor: 32 Squadron's C.O., Squadron Leader John Worrall, still recalls: "If you weren't in the air, you were plastered." At Andover's Square Club, where Middle Wallop fliers thronged, near-lethal mixtures were commonplace-vodka and apricot brandy, even brandy and port. At Wallop's forward base, Warmwell, the canny station doctor, Flight Lieutenant Monty Bieber, was for ever fixing up "harm-less" pink drinks to quieten morning-after stomachs – in reality, near-neat alcohol, which kept pilots grounded for safety's sake.

Some couldn't drink at all. At Northolt, Canadian Roland Dibnah, no teetotaller, found the tension so great even one jigger of liquor drove him vomiting to the washroom. His friend, Peter Boot, felt the same; after one nightmare force-landing amid sharp-pointed anti-invasion stakes, Boot was so angry when he met the defence expert who'd sited them that his fingers itched for a loaded revolver. Already their squadron, No. 1 R.A.F., felt that all the strikes were against them: though they'd lost their gear in France, Air Ministry was still quibbling over the £60 kit replacement allowance due to each man.

Twenty-five years later Boot recalls: "We were so wrought up there wasn't a pilot who didn't see it as deliberate – if they held out long enough we'd all be chopped and they'd save money."

To every man in those razor-edged days, the sense of doom impending took on a different guise. At Tangmere airfield, it was the thin black line in the mess ledger recording each pilot's mealtimes, ruled beneath name after name. Mess Steward Joseph Lauderdale, at Middle Wallop, had his own yardstick: often his pilots died too soon to qualify for a change of sheets. Day by day, a North Weald flight mechanic, George Perry, saw boys come back men after one eighty-minute sortie, their faces grey, a yellow froth about their mouths.

The ground staffs took infinite forethought. At mealtimes in Hornchurch officers' mess, Old Sam, the chef, with his tall white cap, kept up his soothing flow of patter: "Don't say you can't touch a bite, sir... just a shaving of the roast beef now... some of the underdone." Most, after his coaxing, rose from the table new men, replete with rare roast beef, bread and cheese and celery. For evening meals, Wing Commander Cecil Bouchier cut off the electricity altogether, importing candles from Harrod's department store. Few even realised Bouchier wasn't out to save fuel – or that the soft light was kind to the taut, strained boyish faces.

The more a squadron's losses mounted now, the more superstition held sway. At the Square Club, Andover, most gave "Terry" the dark svelte girl, her black belt studded with regimental badges, a wide berth: surely she spelt trouble? Two 238 Squadron pilots, the Tasmanian Stewart Walsh and young Frank Cawse, had known her, and both of them had died on one sortie. At Tangmere at least two pilots wouldn't fly without their magic scarves – pink-and-blue-checkered silk squares, which South African Caesar Hull had brought to 43 Squadron. Pilot Officer Tony Woods-Scawen, of the same outfit, clung doggedly to his "lucky" parachute. He knew it worked: he'd baled out four times already and had come back to talk about it.

Known to all the novices coming on the scene was the unvarnished truth: they would learn the art of survival the hard way, and to live through your first three sorties was to achieve a tenuous hold on immortality.

Few understood this better than Pilot Officer Red Tobin and his friends Andy Mamedoff and Shorty Keough. This morning, August 16, stretched out on the grass at Warmwell airfield, they were counted fully operational for the first time – each of them attached to a section of three as "weavers". As Squadron Leader Darley had explained: Though the numbers one and two men flew absolutely straight, the weaver's job, as "Arse End Charlie" was to fly on a twisting snake-like course behind them to protect their rear.

A straight-from-the shoulder commander, Darley warned them tartly: "If you want to go chasing D.F.C.s all over the deck, go somewhere else. We go up as twelve and we come down as twelve – if we lose even two, the odds are shortened immediately."

Red and his friends blenched. If things were tight as that they – and the British – would need all the luck in the world to pull through.

It was chilling advice – yet one hour of air combat taught Red Tobin it was true. For novice no less than veteran, the pre-flight tension was an ordeal in itself. Already, since dawn, he'd gone over his Spitfire for every fault conceivable – scanning the petrol gauges, checking the compressed air pressure for the gun system, switching on the reflector sights – and had seen Andy and Shorty do the same. In the seconds before he was airborne, there were more than forty checks a fighter pilot must make – and all three recalled Darley's steely warning: "Better go up and face the Germans than come down and face me if your oil pressure goes wrong or your oxygen packs up."

Then the telephone shrilled, and twelve men were springing as one for their parked Spitfires, and Red Tobin, elated, whooped, to his four-strong ground crew: "Saddle her up, I'm riding!" As the twenty-four-cylinder Merlin engines roared into life, a sirocco of dust whirled about the tailplanes, and Red, eyes alert, saw his section leader, Frank Howell, taxi to his take-off point and turn into the wind.

The squadron was airborne: twelve pilots, 15,000 horse-power, ninety-six machine guns with a total fire-power of 120,000 rounds a minute.

The radio telephone crackled into life; this was Squadron Leader Gavin Anderson, Middle Wallop's Sector Controller: "Hullo, Sorbo Leader, this is Bandy. Patrol Portland angels twenty. Many, many bandits."

Coolly, Red Tobin noted he still wasn't scared; there was too much to do. His mind was a catalogue of swiftly posed queries: Is the manifold pressure too high? Will the guns work? Is the oil pressure dropping? If a combat started and the answers were wrong, his gold cuff-links, along with a carefully phrased note, would soon be en route to his father in Los Angeles.

The squadron was at 18,000 feet now, levelled off, each man flying by throttle, opening and closing it to keep in correct formation position. At this moment, Red heard his section leader, Flight Lieutenant Frank Howell: "O.K. Charlie, weave."

Then, Red Tobin was as alert for trouble as he'd ever been: an order to weave meant something was about to break. So as Frank Howell and young Geoffrey Gaunt, the number two, flew resolutely on, Red was rocking the Spitfire's three tons of streamlined metal back and forth at 300 miles an hour, his blue eyes probing the bright morning sky.

He saw nothing – yet he smelt danger as acutely as he had done on his first-ever forced-landing, flying the owner of an old open-cockpit W.A.C.O. 6 and his girl friend on a round trip to San Diego. On the way back, fog had closed in and Red had landed, shakily but unharmed, in the mire of a ploughed field. Undeterred Red had the plane hauled to firmer ground and took off once more – this time alone. The landing – and the discovery Red held no licence – had so jolted his passengers they'd finished the trip by bus.

Tobin's headphones crackled again: "Many, many bandits three o'clock"; momentarily he relaxed. Using the clock system to spot planes in the air, the pilot saw himself in the centre of an imaginary dial – and three o'clock meant directly to starboard. He could see them now – more than fifty milling gnat-shapes – but he didn't worry. Time and again the veterans had told him, "You don't worry about the ones you can see."

Then a whispery voice, but packing a jolt like a high-tension cable: "Many, many bandits at six o'clock and 5,000 above."

And now Red knew a moment of sweating horror, for his task was to protect the two men ahead, yet he had seen not one single German plane 5,000 feet above. And the thought struck him: in this rigid display formation the R.A.F. still flew, made up of tight Y-shaped formations of three, there was no one to protect "Arse End Charlie" – except Charlie himself. As a caustic Canadian had summed up: "You're either promoted from this spot – or buried."

Eyes dilated, his neck muscles standing out like pencils, he craned frantically, then saw them, about a mile back, knowing he was safe for three more seconds.

Now Frank Howell's voice once more, edged with tension: "O.K., Charlie. Come on in."

Red knew the import: he was to stop weaving and rejoin his original formation of line astern. They were going to attack the bombers below – so fast that they'd be out and away before the German fighters aloft had time to dive on them.

Then everything happened so fast that later Red was hard put to it to sift his mind for the reasoned details a combat report needed. He saw Howell peel away, then Gaunt followed, and he too was howling down behind them, but in seconds he had lost them and he saw no bomber, only an ME 110 that went into a tight climbing turn to shake him. Then Tobin was firing, the glittering paper-chain of tracer telling him his shots were going as wide as the German rear-gunner's, and he told himself: Nose up, pull your nose up. Get him in front.

But he jerked up the Spitfire's nose too fast, nearly blacking out; a grey veil swam before his eyes, and he had time only for one long burst before the 110 was gone. Momentarily he was lost; the air seemed to split apart with screaming, diving planes, but he had no idea where Howell or the others had gone. Then there was that strange loneliness that seems always to follow an air battle, when men who have seen the sky choked with planes find dazedly that all have gone and they set course eagerly for home, because between the earth and the stratosphere theirs seems the only plane.

Back at Warmwell, Red Tobin was dumbfounded to find that in little more than an hour he'd used up eighty gallons of 100-octane fuel and fired 2,000 rounds, but the flurry of the morning's combat soon faded in the bleak news that greeted 609's return.

Already Middle Wallop Sector Station was barely operational, alive with unexploded bombs – and despite 609's efforts, this morning's raid had succeeded as never before. Smashing through the R.A.F.'s defences by sheer force, bombers of Air Fleet Three had struck the vital sector station of Tangmere, Sussex, with appalling accuracy.

All lighting, power and water were cut off—and almost every building on the aerodrome had suffered crucial damage. Hangars and workshops had been gutted to ground level – and fourteen planes destroyed or damaged on the field.

It wasn't the Luftwaffe's only triumph of the day. Across the Solent, on the Isle of Wight, five Stuka dive-bombers had worked over Ventnor Radar Station yet again for six merciless minutes, negating all the work that hard-pressed technicians had put in since August 12. At Gosport, across Portsmouth Harbour, Junkers 88s had struck a devastating blow at the anti-aircraft co-operation station. Eastwards, near Maidstone, Dorniers of the 76th Bomber Group had put West Malling airfield out of action for four long days.

By mid-afternoon on August 16, it looked as if all Goring's faith had been justified, and that the Luftwaffe would triumph after all.

Dowding's pilots were doing their best, but it was bitter uphill work; many had never flown a fighter sortie until this very day. Young Ellis Aries, flying for the first time with 602 Squadron, was bursting to acquit himself; he hoped the older pilots had really believed his tale of how a jealous girl friend, pinning his hand with a knife to the bedside table, had caused that polished scar. The prosaic truth – a childhood nurse had clumsily dropped hot sealing-wax on it – seemed to make him walk less tall.

Suddenly, as the squadron orbited the Sussex coastline at 15,000 feet, Aries saw them: his first-ever German planes, ninety-plus, boring for the shore. What looked like white glinting metal rods were stretching very slowly from them, describing a wide curve – away from him, then accelerating towards him. It was as well that Aries broke radio silence to ask, "Why are they dangling little wires at me?" In the nick of time, a veteran screamed a warning: "Break, you bloody fool! It's tracer!"

Pilot after pilot was as green. One Spitfire pilot Dudley Williams, reefing above a swarm of ME 110s over Portland, fired at one in the edge of his sights, saw the white chips showering, and almost crowed with joy. Hastily, realising more 110s were on his tail, he broke away with a roll – glowingly conscious he was at last operational.

Though Williams had twice before been allowed to fire his eight Browning machine-guns into the sea for practice, this was the very first time he had ever fired them in anger.

Incredibly, Williams was no lone example. Of all Air Chief Marshal Dowding's pilots, barely ten per cent had undergone more stringent gunnery practice. From the first to last, their training had stressed disciplined air-display flying in the V-shaped formations that had so puzzled Red Tobin – so tight-packed it wasn't uncommon for planes to return after mid-air collision with airscrews as snarled as metal tentacles. Until a formation broke up in dog-fights, no man had scope to weave or look about him; to keep station, wing-tip five feet from wing-tip, needed all the attention he could muster.

Predictably, most, unaccustomed to sighting their guns, opened fire at 600 yards – then at 200 yards, a surer range, broke from combat. In theory, each squadron had cine-guns, cameras synchronised with the guns, to correct this fault – but most were in the same plight as No. 266 Squadron at Hornchurch. Twelve planes had just two camera-guns between them – and both were liable to jam with the first burst of fire.

Almost as frustrating were the four standard Fighter Command attacks on bomber formations. Based on the pre-war theory that German bombers would fly in a straight line, without rear gun-turrets, unescorted by hovering fighters, the attacks still, incredibly, won favour with the Air Staff even now. In the pre-battle lull, most pilots spent hours daily perfecting the No. 1 Attack, where fighters swung into line behind their leader, queued to deliver a three-second burst, then swung away – their underbellies a sure target for a German gunner.

A few tyros felt they couldn't miss – but twenty-year-old Robert Doe, a pilot of No. 234 Spitfire Squadron, was convinced he could. Now, in his first anguished hour of combat over Swanage, Dorset, he knew nothing could save him from the pain and ignominy of being shot down. Fifty raiders were approaching Swanage at 11,000 feet – and Doe, who had barely scraped through his Wings exam, had never as yet peered through his reflector gunsights, or even touched the red-painted firing button at the apex of his control-column.

Now, as an ME 110 swam in the centre gap between the two horizontal lines of the sight, Doe, for the first time, squeezed the firing button. At a battering 1,260 rounds a minute, a firepower equal to a five-ton truck hitting a brick wall at sixty miles an hour blasted the Messerschmitt. Though Doe's heavy flying helmet muffled the sound, he felt the Spitfire shudder all over; the pungent reek of cordite drifted along the wings.

The only advice his flight commander, the Australian Pat Hughes, had ever offered came abruptly back to him – "Get as close as you can and you can't miss" – and in this moment he barely gave a thought to his adversary, the rear-gunner, hosing back fire until he baled out, only 1,000 feet above the water. Instead, he felt "suddenly invincible".

If he was, others were far from it; even the leaders had gone short of gunnery practice. South of Middle Wallop, Squadron Leader Eric King, 249 Squadron, pumped fully 2,400 rounds at a Junkers 88, and never once hit it; range was a closed book to him. By contrast, Squadron Leader "Tubby" Badger's German adversary understood it to perfection. The leader of 43 Squadron made it back to Tangmere with bullets riddling his glycol pipe, his hood, his airscrews, both his wings, his ignition leads, even the sole of his shoe.

If Dowding's pilots lacked experience they compensated, on August 16, with courage – and sometimes with sheer blind valour. At 1.45 p.m., while the shroud of brick-dust was still rising over Tangmere, Flight Lieutenant James Nicolson, 249 Squadron, was at 17,000 feet over Romsey, Hampshire, the enamelled blue of Southampton Water glinting nine miles off his Hurricane's port wing. A toothy, mop-headed twenty-three-year-old, six feet four inches tall, Nicolson was best known to the squadron as a youngster grudging with words, a man whose riposte to a wisecrack was, more often than not, a self-conscious grin.

This afternoon, his thoughts lay mostly with the baby his wife Muriel was expecting back in Yorkshire, but when three

Junkers 88 dive-bombers crossed his section's bows, Nicolson, who'd never come within shooting range of a German, didn't hesitate. Promptly he dived to investigate – then, cursing, swung back to rejoin the squadron. Twelve Spitfires, conjured from nowhere, were already attacking the bombers.

But Nicolson wasn't destined to make it. Unsuspected, an ME 110 was on his tail, and suddenly with shattering echoes, his entire Hurricane seemed to fall apart. A cannon shell tore through the Perspex hood, and splinters peppered his left eye, blinding him with blood. A second shell struck his reserve petrol tank; in one searing moment the plane took fire. More shots sledgehammered – tearing away his trouser leg, disabling his left heel.

As Nicolson reefed his plane blindly to starboard, away from the deadly shells, he saw the 110 had over-shot and was now 200 yards ahead, diving at 400 miles an hour. Beneath the blowtorch assault of the flames, his instrument panel was "dripping like treacle", but a deadly resolution took hold of him: the man who had subjected him to these terrors should be his first victim. The 110 was steady in his gunsights and, as he streaked in pursuit, the pent-up anger burst in him and he screamed: "I'll teach you manners, you Hun." His right thumb on the firing button, his left hand on the throttle, were boiling into white blisters in the furnace of heat.

Then Nicolson fired until the pain passed all tolerance level, his feet bundled up on his seat beneath the parachute, and he saw the 110 fall smoking for the sea. Lurching, he struck his head on the closed hood, then fought with his mutilated fingers to disentangle the harness straps, before diving head first, flames lapping at his overalls. For 5,000 feet he fell sheer, and when he found strength to pull the ripcord he saw blood was dripping from the lace-holes of his boots.

Forty feet from earth, above the village of Millbrook, Hampshire, he saw a trigger-happy Home Guard open fire from his front-garden, and then Nicolson was down, ignominiously wounded in the buttocks, his chute tugging painfully across rough pasture.

Through his one good eye, he saw that heat had melted the glass of his wrist watch, the strap hanging by a charred thread, but the watch was ticking merrily. It was still ticking three months later, when Nicolson, for an action that typified the whole last-ditch endeavour of the battle, became the first fighter pilot of World War Two to win the V.C.

—

The uniformed driver let in the clutch and the Horch staff car slid smoothly away from the ramp at Staaken airport, Berlin. From the back seat, Major Adolf Galland, erect bearing belying the bloodshot fatigue in his eyes, moodily surveyed the crowded sidewalks as the car purred steadily through the city towards Goring's Karinhall headquarters.

Now, soon after noon on Sunday, August 18, ten days since the battle commenced, Galland could hardly credit what he saw. The open-air cafes on Berlin's swanky Kurfurstendamm were bursting with family groups, chatting animatedly over foaming steins of beer. Already the first queues were forming outside the cinemas; on the Unter den Linden, soldiers, arm in arm with their girls, strolled as if they hadn't a care in the world. Try as Galland might, he could find no hint Germany was at war.

Suddenly he felt an aching surge of loneliness and disquiet: didn't the German people care?

Though Galland and the pilots of No. 3 Wing, 26th Fighter Group, had no true insight into the ramifications of strategy, they were dimly aware that their cross-Channel battle was decisive to Germany's future. Yet, here, there seemed such total indifference to war Galland's heart sank. Absurdly, in some ways, he felt closer to his British adversaries than to these complacent, slow-strolling crowds.

Since July 20, when Galland's outfit arrived on the coast, they had led a life as disciplined as anchorites. Soon after dawn, along with his friend Gerhard Schopfel and a few others, Galland took breakfast in the small middle-class villa at Guines, near Calais, where they were billeted. Galland could see it now – the chairs upholstered in sage-green plush, the net curtains edged with bobbles – and smell the fresh waxy smell of linseed polish. Breakfast over, they drove hard for Caffiers airfield.

Nourished on Thermoses of hot strong coffee and crusty French bread, they'd literally built this primitive aerodrome with their bare hands – starting in tents, their telecom sited in a bunker, before erecting every hut themselves. Even the temporary hangars – mats supported on tent poles, piled with sandbags against splinter blast, then plastered on top with grass and branches to resemble copses – were their own work. This superbly camouflaged airfield, which observation planes couldn't spot from 1,000 feet, they'd affectionately christened *Teufelsdorf* (Devil's Village), Galland County.

Moody, self-analytical, given to alternate flashes of gloom and gaiety, Galland found himself increasingly drawn to the pilots he commanded – and for their part they accorded him a trust they gave few others. True, he could be flamboyant – as a twenty-three-year-old air cadet at Doberitz, near Berlin, he'd early affected a leather jerkin and peaked cap while the others made do with regulation blue shirts and knickerbockers. If the pupils joked, "Here comes the great fighter ace," it didn't displease him – and even now, the gleaming silver Mercedes he'd bought from movie star Jan Kiepura, the yellow riding boots and long yellow falconer's gloves he sometimes wore strolling on Dusseldorf's Konigsallee, marked him as a showman.

But unlike some fighter aces, who sought only personal glory, Galland looked after the younger pilots in his outfit, so that whenever he strode into view, his long-haired, black-and-brown setter, *Schweinebauch* (Fig's Belly), trotting at his heels, men felt their spirits suddenly lifted.

In combat he was no easy man to keep up with: his penchant for long vertical dives and tight pull-outs made it hard for his wingman to follow him. Nor could every man keep pace with him on the ground; in extended spells off duty, his love of beautiful girls, fast cars and gambling for high stakes drove him to seek the company of the hard-living Berlin movie crowd. Yet Galland was no man to pull rank; arriving unheralded on the primitive strip, wearing only flying kit, the unit's new commander asked some mechanics, grouped round an old-fashioned well, to draw him some water. The reply was terse: the well was full, he'd only to wind up the bucket.

Tactfully, sparing them the shock that their new G.O. was among them, Galland did as he was bidden.

To his pilots, Galland was a man who'd pull no punches putting their point of view to the top brass – and this afternoon, as the Horch purred through Karinhall's high gateway, surmounted by marble lions, this was what Galland intended. Why Goring had summoned him he didn't know – but as always he felt out of place here, away from fighting men, jostled by natty staff officers with their white-and-raspberry-striped trousers. On the Ebro River in Spain, Galland had flown in bathing trunks, returning from each sortie dripping with sweat and oil, his bare chest black with cordite – and this was the world he knew and trusted.

As Goring stomped across the entrance hall to pump his hand, Galland knew the Reichsmarschall didn't really like him. He spoke out too forcibly for that. At the Channel coast, only recently, General Bruno Lorzer, of No. 2 Flying Corps, chewing over the campaign, had remarked complacently: "It's just like the last war, Herr Reichsmarschall – a little faster and a little higher, that's all." At once Galland had jumped in: "It couldn't be more different."

Now as the Reichsmarschall proffered a box of fine Havana cigars, Galland guessed he was expected to play "the cigar game". All Goring's favourites covertly tucked a few extra up their sleeves, and the Reichsmarschall, thwacking their forearms in farewell, would break the cylinders, hooting with laughter, before making good the loss. Somehow it was a game Galland couldn't bring himself to play.

But today, Goring, as bland as could be, overlooked the slight: Galland was a guest of honour. Today, he and Werner Molders, who had received a similar summons, were to be formally invested with the Gold Pilot Medal with Jewels as a token of their prowess.

Major Adolf Galland half suspected more was to follow – and too soon events proved him right. The ceremony over, Goring led him and Molders to his vast library, crammed with books on venery, biographies of Genghis Khan – and the mood changed as abruptly as the setting. Both pilots had earned their decorations, Goring granted that – but as a whole the fighter effort just wasn't good enough. There wasn't enough effort, enough aggression – and their co-ordination with the bomber units was shameful.

And Goring went further: this farce of rendezvous going awry had got to stop. From now on, a single aircraft from the bomber formation would circle the fighter escort's airfield, to signal they were ready to go. Then the fighters must get airborne, follow the bomber to its main formation, and stay with that formation all the way. Clearing the sky ahead of the raiders would be the task of special fighter units – but the bulk of the fighters would cling to the bombers, no matter how the R.A.F. tried to deflect them.

Before Galland could lose his temper, Goring forestalled him: the true solution to the problem had eluded him, but he had it now. Much of the faulty leadership was due to the present group commanders – they were all too old.

Take Major Martin Mettig, commanding the 54th Bomber Group – no wonder the man complained about working an eighteen-hour day. He was thirty-seven years old, virtually an old man in this game, and the Luftwaffe's Inspector General reported him "the wrong temperament for a fighter pilot". From now on, this was Goring's personal decree: no group commander would be older than thirty-two, no wing leader older than thirty, no squadron commander older than twenty-seven. In this way they'd mount a really vigorous offensive against the British.

Beaming, Goring now offered his piece-de-resistance: in four days' time Molders would take over the 51st Fighter Group at Wissant. Galland would relinquish his 3rd Wing at Caffiers and succeed Major Gotthard Handrick, 1936 Olympics champion, as group leader at Audembert.

Now, to the surprise of the ambitious Molders, Galland protested hotly. His wing was all he asked for – already they were responsibility enough, and the last thing he wanted was to be tied to the ground. Surely it wasn't the fighter leaders who were lacking in aggression – the whole concept of the battle was against them. And he instanced: with the ME 109's operational range pinned to 125 miles at most, every fighter battle was confined to southern England. Perhaps one-tenth of the British Isles – and in the other nine-tenths, the R.A.F. could build and repair aircraft, train their pilots, well out of fighter range.

He wound up: "All I ask is combat, combat with my wing" – but Goring reassured him. He'd see all the combat he wanted, and more: this was the whole beauty of the scheme. The eight group commanders and seventeen wing leaders then operational would all be young thrusting pilots, men like himself, Molders and Mettig's successor, Major Hannes Trautloft, who'd personally lead their units in action.

Angry and suspicious, Galland still smouldered as Goring hashed over final points, then as Goring wound up the meeting – "Any last requests?" – he stubbornly resumed his old stand. "Yes, Herr Reichsmarschall – to remain a wing leader." Goring went purple: "Request refused."

The meeting broke up then. Outside in the main banqueting hall, knots of staff officers stood gossiping: servants were carrying round trays of champagne. The rich aroma of cigars filled the air. Galland wandered out onto the terrace. He felt suddenly useless and alone. He wondered how his 3rd Wing back at the Channel were doing.

–

South of Canterbury, Oberleutnant Gerhard Schopfel, leading the unit in Galland's absence, knew his luck was in. Not one but nine Hurricanes were flying unsuspectingly 1,000 metres below him, in the strange tight formation the British flew – "the bunch of bananas", the Luftwaffe dubbed it. They were climbing in tight circles on this soft, hazy Sunday morning, seeking to gain height, apparently quite oblivious of the Germans above them. At that moment, Schopfel glimpsed the squadron's two weavers, quite alone, to the rear of the formation. As they veered north-west, away from Canterbury, he dived.

His two cannons, each loaded with sixty rounds, blasted out, and two rear Hurricanes of No. 501 Squadron, airborne from Gravesend at 8.30 a.m., fell flaming. Now Schopfel was hard on the tail of a third, and he watched, almost incredulous, as this, too, spiralled burning from the sky. Still the squadron flew serenely on, and Schopfel's confidence grew. Too close for safety, he jerked the firing button again and the Hurricane blew up almost across the nose of his 109. Debris jarred his airscrew; a viscous Niagara of oil swamped his windshield. Hastily, unable to see any longer, Schopfel broke upwards.

The battle had lasted just four minutes – and still he'd fifteen bullets left, enough for another victory.

Now, on the return flight, Schopfel had just one headache: wouldn't claiming four in four minutes sound like the tallest of tales? But back at Caffiers airfield his wing reassured him: they'd seen the whole incredible venture and his claim would be sustained. Schopfel's first thought: Galland would be proud. His second: if that's the way things are going today, we must be winning.

This morning, August 18, the same confident feeling gripped all the pilots of Air Fleet Two. For twenty-four hours their morale had been at lowest ebb: low-lying cloud had closed in on England and four bomber units between them couldn't locate the priority fighter airfields at Debden, Duxford and Hornchurch. Now, with the ceiling lifting, their spirits soared, too; even if the first sorties had gone less well than they'd hoped, the top brass could be expected to iron out the wrinkles.

It was the same on every airfield. At Calais-Marck, Pilot Officer Ralph Roberts, No. 64 Spitfire Squadron, a newly arrived prisoner-of-war, was astonished when his German hosts, chatting over drinks, assured him: "We shall be home by Christmas all right – and so will you." At St. Inglevert, near Boulogne, Hans-Otto Lessing, a twenty-three-year-old ober-leutnant, tried to convey in a letter to his parents the champagne exhilaration of a fighter pilot's life. He apologised: "This is a short report – but I'd have to write a book to give you the whole picture."

But he had to confess it: "For me this is the most exciting time of my life – I wouldn't wish to change places with a king. Peacetime will seem very dull after this."

The confidence wasn't misplaced – yet every Luftwaffe success this day was achieved at a fearful toll of human lives. At 1 p.m. (2 p.m., to the Germans in northern France) soon after the people of southern England had filed from morning service, thirty-one Dorniers of Oberstleutnant Frohlich's 76th Bomber Group were churning inexorably from Cormeilles-en-Vexin airfield in Normandy towards the English Channel, along with twelve Junkers 88 dive-bombers. Their targets, though the crews didn't fully appreciate it, were two of Fighter Command's most vital sector stations, covering the southern approaches to London – Kenley, which the unlucky Hauptmann Rubens-dorffer hadn't located, and Biggin Hill. Contrary to the R.A.F.'s belief, the Luftwaffe never once suspected these for what they were – the nerve-centres of Dowding's command. From first to last they assumed that priority command posts would be sited underground away from the centre of operations – not in unprotected building plumb in the airfield's centre, lacking sandbags or blast walls, locations that had served well enough until the Luftwaffe had reached the Channel. Like every other sortie, these raids were aimed solely at putting Kenley and Biggin airfields out of action – though with a novel difference.

To fox the radar stations, a spearhead of nine Dorniers would fly at wavetop height, creating maximum confusion by homing in on Kenley and Biggin Hill at nought feet, in concert with the high-level raids. It all sounded so intriguing that one war reporter, Otto Sommer, decided to hitch a ride on a Kenley-bound plane.

Farther west, on the Cherbourg peninsula, Sperrle's Air Fleet Three planned no surprises – merely the mixture as before. Twenty-eight planes of Stuka Group 77, escorted, under Goring's new decree, by no fewer than three fighter wings, would fly in decoy attacks on a broad thirty-mile front against the airfields at Thorney Island, Gosport and Ford – all of them Coastal Command or Fleet Air Arm stations.

It would be a dovetailed raid from first to last, involving mammoth staffwork – yet again, contrary to all the lessons of the past ten days, Goring was stubbornly placing the onus on Stukas, protected by ME 110s, with ME 109s allotted the taxing role of protecting both formations at once.

At Uxbridge, Middlesex, headquarters of No. 11 Group, Fighter Command, the duty controller, Lord Willoughby de Broke, didn't know where to turn. On him lay the responsibility of planning the first steps of the battle like a gigantic game of chess, before relinquishing on-the-spot control to the sector stations – but already more then 600 plots swamped the situation map. Now Lord Willoughby begged Fighter Command's Filter Room, which sifted incoming details from the radar stations: "Is there a lot of mush building up behind?"

To the Filter Room, the request made sense – how many formations might be mustering just outside radar range? But at

1 p.m., no man could be certain – and suddenly it was every Sector Controller for himself.

In Kenley's Ops Room, Squadron Leader Anthony Norman, the duty controller, was on the horns of a dilemma: the Observer Corps had spotted those low-level Dorniers before any warning from No. 11 Group. Norman's hunch was instant-aneous: *They're coming for me.* For a second he hesitated: Croydon was only four miles north, and six miles due east lay Biggin Hill Sector Station. By rights, 11 Group should make the final decision – but though the Dorniers were only ten minutes flying time away, no word came.

So, Norman acted fast. Across the airfield Spitfire pilots of Squadron Leader Aeneas MacDonell's 64 Squadron got the call: "Freema Squadron, scramble. Patrol base, angels twenty." At the same time Squadron Leader John Thompson's 111 Squadron at Croydon had wind of their role: their Hurricanes were to make for Kenley and circle the airfield at 100 feet, poised for a head-on intercept of the low-level raiders. Another Hurricane squadron, No. 615, was patrolling, too, leaving one flight, under Pilot Officer Keith Lofts, at stand-by – strapped in their cock-pits, engines turning over.

At Biggin Hill, Group Captain Richard Grice, the station commander, came to the same decision: still he had heard nothing from 11 Group, and if the raiders were flying with fighter escort, his planes needed fully twenty minutes to reach a 109's operational height. On his own initiative he ordered the controller to scramble the two squadrons available – No. 32 and No. 610.

Now in both Ops Rooms, the tension mounted by the minute; at Kenley, Squadron Leader Norman told the floor supervisor quietly: "Get them into their battle bowlers… tin hats everybody." Nearing Biggin Hill, Oberleutnant Rudolf Lamberty, among the first nine Dornier pilots, peered anxiously for the twisting spiral of smoke and flame that should mark the airfield – unaware that the high-level strike, encountering rendezvous difficulties, still hadn't arrived. In the Kenley spearhead, the war reporter, Otto Sommer, made a hasty note: the nerve of these Dornier pilots was astonishing. They were flying at nought feet now, heading for the white chalk quarry that singled out Kenley – so low they were clipping the tops from fruit trees. Next instant the concussion of the Dornier's bombs was crashing and ricocheting from the bellies of the planes.

On the dais of Biggin Hill Ops Room, the petite, red-headed Corporal Elspeth Henderson heard the phone ring stridently; it was Lord Willoughby de Broke, ordering Biggin's squadrons to get airborne without delay. Replying, Group Captain Grice was withering: "You're too bloody late; they're already scrambled."

Over Kenley, the pilots of No. 64 Squadron were completely in the dark, even when Squadron Leader MacDonell's voice came high-pitched with urgency: "Freema Squadron, going down." Sergeant-Pilot Peter Hawke was one of several who thought, Why down? We need all the height we can get. Then he knew: a black pillar of smoke shot skywards like a gusher from Kenley's hangars. As the Spitfires fell like avenging furies for the earth at 490 miles an hour, fleeting irrelevant thoughts raced through the pilots' minds. Pilot Officer Richard Jones thought: Surely they won't hit the mess? My best tunic's there. Sergeant Peter Hawke saw a mighty flash like exploding helium from a Dornier and thought appalled: My God, did I do that? Then he checked himself: Peter, this is what you were trained to do.

Fifty feet above the airfield, Squadron Leader Thompson's Hurricanes, racing for their head-on attack, got the shock of their lives: ack-ack fire burst above them and the air seemed full of whirling wires. No one had warned them that the station defences were firing P.A.C. (parachute and cable) rockets at the raiders – electrically fired rockets whooshing upwards at forty feet a second, mounting to 700 feet to grapple their wings with four hundredweight of steel wire. Anguished, Thompson thought: My God, if one of those hits us we're finished.

It was a day of surprises – for the grounded as well as the airborne. At 615 Squadron's dispersal, Flight Mechanic George Budd was busy whipping away the stand-by flight's chocks when the low-level Dorniers swept like monstrous eagles above; with only fifty feet to spare, Pilot Officer Keith Lofts took off through a curtain of bombs. Sergeant Jackie Mann, of 64 Squadron, grounded through a leg injury, was musing restfully in the sergeants' mess toilet as the first bombs came whistling; caught literally with his pants down, Mann blushed to see that the blast had stripped away all four walls of the flimsy hutment.

Things were as bad up above. Pilot Officer David Looker, 615 Squadron, racing to take off, found his own machine out of action; undaunted he took off in an obsolete 1937 Hurricane with fabric-covered wings, innocent of armour-plating or bullet-proof windscreen. Tangling with German fighters, Looker spun out of control for 7,000 feet, the tattered fabric streaming like bunting from his wings. Force-landing at Croydon airfield, he again escaped death by inches; convinced he was a German, the ack-ack gunners greeted him with a solid sheet of fire.

Now almost sixty bombers were aloft over Kenley, moving back and forth like tractors ploughing a field – and suddenly everyone was eager to join the battle. Flight Lieutenant Robert Stanford Tuck was lunching twenty miles away in the officers' mess at Northolt, with the station administration officer, Wing Commander "Tiny" Vasse, when word came of the alarm: at once Vasse, a mountain of a man, propelled the protesting Tuck into a dug-out: "Down the bloody bunker for you."

For preposterous moments they wrangled over protocol: Tuck's squadron was based at Pembrey, South Wales; he couldn't operate under Northolt's control. Clawing from the bunker, a tin hat tilted over his eyes, Tuck barely heard; only Vasse's giant hand, clamped firmly on his ankle, held him from pelting for his Spitfire, the only one still parked at dispersal.

Finally in despair, Vasse gave in; racing for his machine Tuck was airborne in two minutes, streaking to join the battle over Kent.

A few were more phlegmatic. Corporal Albert Jessop, a Kenley air-frame fitter, was five miles away at Carshalton, off-duty with his family, preparing for the hallowed British ritual of Sunday lunch. Today it was roast beef with all the trimmings – and his wife had barely placed the joint on the table when Jessop saw the first bombs spilling, minute black specks against the sun. Calmly, still plying knife and fork, Jessop remarked: "That's Kenley, but I'm going to finish this first."

It was a sage decision; the Dorniers had done their work too well. At Biggin Hill, the damage was minimal; in the confusion caused by the high-level raid's late arrival, the bulk of 500 bombs landed wide, on the airfield's eastern periphery. Still Group Captain Grice paraded the station personnel to utter a well-timed warning: "What's happened at Kenley today can well happen here, so don't think you've escaped." In the W.A.A.F. ranks, Corporal Elspeth Henderson unconsciously stood taller; she'd opted to be in the front line, so she could scarcely complain. For weeks now, Grice had never failed to ram this message home – though Elspeth and her friends, after long compulsory practice hours on the range with Lee-Enfield rifles, felt life could offer no more pain than their bruised and aching right shoulders.

But at Kenley, the bombers had scored and with deadly accuracy… destroying six Hurricanes on the ground… shattering ten hangars and damaging six more… putting the vital Ops Room out of action… reducing buildings to trembling shells. Only one factor saved the station from total destruction: many bombs were released so low they landed horizontally and didn't explode.

Yet the 76th Bomber Group had paid a heavy price: four Junkers 88 dive-bombers, six Dorniers, and all their crews. When the news reached Karinhall, Goring's reaction was decisive: no further low-level raids would be launched from this day forward.

Sixty miles west, the losses were appalling; of the twenty-eight Stukas that attacked the coastal targets around Portsmouth, in one more endeavour to draw up the British fighters, eighteen were lost or severely damaged. Again, the bombers made their mark – pounding hangars and workshops at Gosport, Thorney Island, and the Fleet Air Arm station at Ford – but at a cost no air force in the world could have counted.

To the R.A.F., the aircraft of Stuka Wing 77 seemed the surest targets they'd ever held in their sights. From Warmwell, the Spitfires of No. 152 Squadron alone claimed nine, battling at any height from 100 feet to sea-level, seeing bomber after bomber vanish in a depth charge of white water. From West-hampnett, near Tangmere, No. 602 Squadron were airborne, too, in a no-holds-barred battle, diving undeterred through ack-ack so lethal that one pilot plunged blindly into a high-tension cable.

As the Channel water boiled over the last of six Stukas, Flight Lieutenant Finlay Boyd, a man with a cold and deadly flair for killing, chuckled without pity: "Good, no survivors."

Those Stuka pilots who did get back made it by a hair's-breadth. Oberleutnant Karl Hentze saw the powdery black spirals of smoke as his bombs struck Ford airfield, but somehow, try as he might, he couldn't retract his diving-brakes: the first onslaught by British fighters had shot away most of his hydraulic system. The Stuka seemed top-heavy and jolting violently – "like riding over cobbles" – and he knew that whoever had him in their sights could hardly fail to score.

Nor did they. Suddenly two Spitfires were on his tail, circling and feinting like vicious birds; a bullet struck his radio telephone then ricocheted back, furrowing through the skin at the base of his skull. Momentarily, he blacked out, then a roar from the gunner awoke him to life; the plane was skimming the water like an albatross and in one second of stark terror he felt the wheels dip beneath the waves.

North-west of Bayeux in Normandy, he landed almost blind in a meadow, his wheels skidding and scarring the soft turf, then blacked out again; somehow his gunner hauled him out and when Hentze came to he found a party of French peasants pressing perfumed handkerchiefs to his nose to revive him. One, not realising he was concussed, pressed a flask of brandy on him and within minutes Hentze was doubled up, vomiting painfully. Then a jolting, horse-drawn cart took him to a field hospital where a case-hardened doctor, probing the bullet from his skull, chaffed him: "You'll pay duty for importing English metal."

Oberleutnant Kurt Scheffel, striking for Thorney Island, knew moments as bad; even as he prepared for the attack, his Stuka was colandered by fifty-two cannon shells, killing his gunner, peppering Scheffel from head to foot with glass fragments that stung like darts. Now he doubted whether he could even press the bomb-button; a splinter had lodged in his right thumb, a pain so agonising he couldn't pluck other splinters from his face, and even his left hand lacked power to doctor his injured thumb and end that throbbing nightmare.

Then, to starboard, he saw the unit's commander, Hauptmann-Freiherr von Dalwick, waggling the wings of his Stuka, the signal to attack, and he fought with all he knew against the pain and nausea, mechanically running through the nine automatic checks that preceded every dive-bombing attack… diving brakes out… bombs fused… reflector sights on… tail trimmed for altitude… propeller blades in to increase the streamlining… water and oil coolers off. Then he pressed forward on the stick. At 2,000 feet the bombs were hurtling, and even as they went, Scheffel saw planes rising unscathed from Thorney Island and wondered how long the end would be.

Now he, too, found he couldn't retract his diving-brakes – not like Hentze's, because of enemy action, but through sheer lack of muscle power. He came back across the Channel fewer than five feet above the water, "crawling like a street car", Blenheim fighters from Thorney Island blasting at him, knowing his gunner was dead long minutes back and could do nothing to shield him. Once he laughed weakly because a British submarine surfaced briefly and a head peeped from the conning tower, then, seemingly appalled by the flying lead, dived back out of sight. Tyres riddled, Scheffel came down near Caen, not far from where Hentze had landed, but he could only beckon feebly to the ground crews until they realised the import – he was so weak from loss of blood they must lift him bodily from the plane.

At his Cherbourg headquarters, even the iron-willed Baron von Richthofen was appalled at the losses; to his chief of staff, Oberst Hans Seidemann, he announced bluntly: "This price is too high." And in his leather-bound diary he wrote more dramatically: "A Stuka wing has had its feathers well and truly plucked."

From this moment on, the Stukas – 280 planes – were virtually out of the battle; the first casualty in Goring's thrust.

At "The Holy Mountain", Air Fleet Two's advance headquarters, the losses totalled up were in no way comparable, yet Oberst Theo Osterkamp, regional fighter commander, whose office was at Le Touquet close by, was at his wits' end. Since the afternoon's sortie began, Generalfeldmarschall Albert Kesselring had barely given him a moment's peace... hastening from the fetid underground dug-out to his private look-out post – feverishly enumerating every returning plane he could see... then back to the dug-out to telephone Osterkamp afresh. "What has happened? Where are the planes? At least thirty flew out awhile back, but I've only counted seven returned."

Osterkamp groaned. Only recently he'd urged his chief: "You're driving yourself mad sitting down in the dug-out all day – no fresh air, no relaxation. How can you help the war effort by sitting underground and worrying?" And he'd extracted a firm promise from the over-conscientious Kesselring: in one month's time he'd return to his main headquarters in Brussels. Prudently, Osterkamp had noted that date in his diary. But there were still weeks to go, so, bridling his temper, Osterkamp assured him: "I'm dealing with the problem now. They haven't been signalled in yet."

Unappeased, Kesselring roared: "Well, they're long overdue. And you should know where they are already. It's your job."

Patiently Osterkamp explained: if Kesselring tied him up on the phone all day, he couldn't check with the airfields what planes they'd logged in. Then he hung up. It would be hours before the final figure was known to him – but among them was numbered young Hans-Otto Lessing, who "wouldn't have changed places with a king". He had posted the letter to his parents only that morning.

One man was given up for lost – but he wasn't going to die if he could help it. Now, ten days after the battle began, Hauptmann Herbert Kaminski's "throat-ache" – his ambition to win the Knight's Cross – was keener than ever, but that afternoon, twelve miles east of Foulness Point, he fleetingly bade this ambition farewell. Spitfires had shattered his port and starboard engines; there was nothing for it now but to ditch the ME 110 in the choppy sea. To his long-suffering gunner, Unteroffizier Strauch, he cried "We're landing – so pay attention and get the dinghy ready. And remember – don't ditch your hood until I've ditched mine." As he released the canopy, it spiralled away into the wind, and in that instant Kaminski saw with horror that the 110's nose was head-on to the waves.

Still flying without harness straps, because of the unhealed wound in his right shoulder, "The Last of the Prussians" knew the impact would be hard indeed. The engulfing sea swept up to meet them, and though Kaminski vainly threw his arm before his face, he was hurled forward with such force against the instrument panel that he broke his nose. Then he swooned downwards in pain and oblivion; the world grew cold and dark and wet and Kaminski came to. His first thought was one of unrelieved joy: It's wet. Hell is not wet. I'm alive.

He struggled upwards to the water's surface, his nose pouring blood, calling, "Strauch, Strauch, where are you?" Then he saw Strauch, too, come thrashing to the surface, spitting water, bleeding from a head wound. Severely, Kaminski taxed him: "A head wound? That came of disobeying my orders. You ditched your hood before I told you and my hood knocked you out." Strauch said miserably: "It's not so important now, Herr Hauptmann."

At this moment, the ME 110 tilted forward, vanishing in a flurry of bubbles. Both men saluted it solemnly; it seemed the thing to do.

Now, swimming steadily, they sought to inflate the dinghy, and Kaminski grew rapidly furious: Strauch hadn't even connected up the oxygen flask in advance, and there was the angry hiss of escaping air. Still swimming, Kaminski roared: "I sentence you to ten days' close arrest. Do you realise we are going to die because of your foolishness?"

Still spitting water, Strauch thought this over, then said stolidly: "Herr Hauptmann, I ask you to withdraw that punishment, because if we're going to die, I want to die without a stain on my service record."

"Well," said Kaminski grudgingly, "I'll think it over. But I don't haggle over things. Punishments are fixed."

Strauch was still fiddling vainly with the flask and now he announced triumphantly, "Herr Hauptmann, the punishment has no foundation. Even if the flask *had* been connected, there are twenty bullet holes in its bottom." Kaminski only grunted: "We'll see about that later. Orders are orders."

Nonetheless they still propelled the dinghy ahead of them, for there was no other way to ferry the two water-tight canisters with provisions for downed airmen – Very pistols and ammo, chocolate, brandy, grape-sugar and Pervitin tablets.

Then, to their joy, a plane was circling them, and both men ripped off the yellow scarves all Luftwaffe pilots wore for recognition purposes and waved them wildly. But Kaminski noticed that it was flying on one engine, perhaps crippled from the same sortie, and whether it would even make the French coast to alert the rescue services was doubtful.

Now the enormous weight of their water-soaked clothing seemed to tug them deeper into the sea, and soon they had recklessly stripped off their flying overalls and boots and helmets and swam on in their underwear. As the cold numbed his powerful hands and attacked his strong legs, the stocky, fair-haired Kaminski noticed their boots still kept pace with them, gliding like periscopes. They ripped their fluorescine packets open, and the yellow-green patch of marker dye swirled outwards from them.

It was twilight before the rescue plane zoomed low over the water, but after three despairing circuits the pilot gave up all hope of a landing; the rising waves had come close to swamping his struts. Urgently, both men fired their Very pistols and the pilot circled again, making imperative signs: Don't shoot, don't shoot. The implication was plain – a long night lay ahead and they must conserve their ammo for the morning that seemed so far away. Impotently, Kaminski shook his fist at the pilot and yelled "God damn you!"

Then, to their undying relief, the navigator came perilously down the collapsible ladder, inflating a yellow rubber dinghy, and launched it onto the waves. But it fell fifty yards away from them, and the waves were head high. Nonchalantly, Kaminski asked, "How long did it take a youngster like you to swim fifty yards in peacetime? Sixty seconds?" Prudently, Strauch said: "No."

Magnanimously, Kaminski decided: "Well, I suppose I'd better try it myself." On an impulse he shook Strauch's hand, adding: "If I don't make it, goodbye, and the punishment will be rescinded."

Mercifully the rescue plane still hovered – for it was ten icy minutes before Kaminski reached the second dinghy and now, in the gathering darkness, he'd quite lost sight of Strauch. It was the navigator, craning from the escape hatch who guided him back again – but it was a good half-hour before Kaminski, puffing and cursing, had paddled the dinghy back. Clumsily the gunner tried to clamber in, swamping his chief with icy water.

Exasperated, Kaminski roared: "How many times have I told you to practise boarding a dinghy? This is the third order disobeyed – climb aboard, for the love of God." But each time Strauch manoeuvred afresh, the dinghy bobbed like a balloon, tipping Kaminski back into the water. Splashing and floundering like men sporting with a porpoise, they made it finally – but now the bulky Kaminski was lodged in such a way that every fresh wave swamped his rear, while the lightweight Strauch sat snugly in the dry.

Past all patience, forgetting it couldn't hear, Kaminski shook his fist again after the retreating rescue plane: "And don't forget to come back in the morning!"

–

In southern England it was like a resurgence of hope. As news of this day's fighting spread, the people, for the first time since Dunkirk, showed more than passing interest in the news; the battle seemed almost won. Only twenty-four hours earlier, the Minister of Information, Alfred Duff Cooper, had assured the nation: "If the air raids are the prelude of invasion, we can only say that the prelude has proved... a melancholy failure... we are quite ready to receive [Hitler] now and we shall really be very disappointed if he doesn't turn up."

On all sides, there seemed cause for jubilation, even complacency; the R.A.F.'s mounting losses, the shortage of trained pilots, were still a closely guarded secret. Travelling the south coast, *P.M.*'s Ben Robertson noted that newspaper sellers already chalked up the day's result in terms of a cricket match: "R.A.F. V Germans, 61 for 26 – Close of Play To Day, 12 for 0." A cocky farmer put a novel proposition to Kent County Council: he'd rope off a meadow, charge sixpence admission for the Spitfire Fund, and bill it as "The Only Field in East Kent in which No German Aircraft Has Yet Fallen."

The vainglory was premature. Thousands had yet to come of age and realise that new burdens must be shouldered – and that, however heavy those burdens, this was their war, too. To many, the air battle raging on the edge of the stratosphere was still a vast aerial circus staged for their diversion – and before the last grand parade they craved a souvenir.

At Bembridge, Isle of Wight, youngsters whooped through the streets, clips of live 303 ammunition festooning their belts – but on many battlefields, the adults were as avid. At Kenley airfield, smoke still plumed from gutted hangars as airmen toiled to haul away every unexploded bomb in sight, pursued by burly sergeants bawling, "Put them down, you fools – they may be delayed-action!" Outside Tangmere airfield, one man, inside a shattered Stuka, calmly toiled with a work-bench and tools until he'd dismantled its electric wiring. Near Poling in Sussex, R.A.F. salvage crews, arriving to fly a German aircraft away, found they couldn't; souvenir hunters had removed the entire tailplane. At Portisham, Dorset, hearing a Stuka had force-landed, garage proprietor William Duck set off at a trot; its tail-wheel would be just right for his old wheelbarrow.

Shuttling from site to site, examining every shot-down German aircraft to collate up-to-the-minute modification details, Flight Lieutenant Michael Golovine and his crash invest-igation team were at their wits' end: how could they determine if the armament was standard when souvenir hunters had stripped the guns? Sometimes a placard, "Bombs On Board – Keep Away" did the trick – but most often relic-hunters stole the placard.

Some wanted grimmer keepsakes. Two schoolboys from Smallfield, Surrey, chancing on a German flying helmet, weren't one whit perturbed to find a chunk of the pilot's skull adhering to it; threading it on a length of string, they hung it in their father's cowshed. At Braishfield in Hampshire, pub regulars spent all that evening passing round a crony's memento of the day: a bloody flying boot with the foot still in it.

Few had as yet grasped that the future they cherished was at stake, and that all civilisation depended on the outcome of this battle.

But many were learning: one brief dog-fight could impose indelible sights on the memory. At Five Ashes in Sussex, a direct hit on his cowshed from a bomb jettisoned in flight cost one farmer, James Berry, thirteen cows and his two sons James and Alfred. Boat-builder Herbert Merrett, returning to his bungalow workshop, near Bosham, Sussex, after a peaceful Sunday afternoon outing, was riveted to the ground: a Stuka had crashed in his willow-bed, the gunner, baling out 100 feet above the marshy ground had dashed his brains out on Merrett's old car, and now an R.A.F. salvage team had commandeered the boat-builder's gate to carry the body away. Sightseers swarmed everywhere, oblivious to two fifty-kilo bombs still attached to the Stuka's smouldering wings.

At "Highleigh", a house fringing Kenley airfield, Mrs Kathleen Marshall ducked from her garden shelter to see the broken body of a Dornier, caught by the parachute cable's soaring wire, strewn within yards of her fence. Then she recoiled in horror: the long white fingers of Otto Sommer, the dead war reporter, were stretched towards her as if in supplication.

For some the horrors were not fleeting: the war struck mercilessly at all they cherished most. At 2 p.m., though the air-raid warning had sounded, there was nothing to warn Mrs Doris Addison, a coalman's wife and mother of two, that the tiny cottage called "The Warren", close by the millstream at Hurst Green in Surrey, stood in imminent danger. She was glad the children were safe indoors; when the siren sounded, Delma, aged six, ten-year-old Frank, and Jimmie Murrell, their young evacuee, had dashed back from paddling in the stream – so fleetly that Delma, clad in her swimsuit, left her navy-blue knickers behind on the bridge.

Doris Addison was just dishing up the Sunday joint – roast lamb, with blancmange and fruit to follow – when all of them heard the droning of an engine, louder and louder, until the drone gave place to a high-pitched scream. Even Bob, their two-year-old liver-and-white springer spaniel, huddled uneasily beneath the table. Though the Addisons didn't know it, one of Kenley's retreating Dorniers, hotly pursued by the pilots of III Squadron, was in dire distress.

Just south of "The Warren", the Dornier struck the ground, with the inhuman screech of tortured metal, already disintegrating in a sweeping sheet of flame... ripping through a hedge... shedding its bomb-load everywhere, bouncing partly over "The Warren"... spraying everything in its path with blazing fuel. From the Fire Service post up the lane, from where he'd seen everything, Auxiliary Fireman Dick Addison was racing furiously to protect his family.

Inside the cottage, Doris Addison and the children were taken unawares: one appalling explosion and then the open kitchen door was a shaking yellow curtain of flame. Resourceful Mrs Addison bustled the children into the downstairs bathroom and out through the window, then turned back once more for Bob. For a second her heart failed her; the spaniel had bolted panic-stricken through the open door, into the leaping heart of the flames.

Tumbling through his garden gate, Dick Addison was numb with outrage; his little cottage and garden seemed somehow desecrated. An unexploded bomb, one of eighteen thrown clear, lay beneath the kitchen table, a man's severed arm beside it... Delma's new doll's pram had been gutted to its frame... the ravaging fury of the flames had stewed the fruit on his plum trees, roasted his chickens in their run.

Hastily collecting two bucketsful of human remains from his own kitchen, Addison carried them out of sight of the children, though at this moment he needn't have worried. All three were crouching petrified in the laurel bushes as infantrymen who'd arrived on the scene frenziedly opened up on the blazing plane with a light machine-gun.

Somehow, though they never forgot this day, the Addisons managed to come through. At first, the children were inconsolable, lamenting the loss of Bob; it had been Delma's whim to dress him up in a bonnet and shawl and wheel him round in her new doll's pram. But when the dog was found, a few fields away, badly burned but alive, McConnachie Ingram, the local vet, took Bob into his care and six weeks later delivered him alive and well – his black nose scorched pink, four bootees protecting his damaged paws.

And the Addisons, after only one night spent with neighbours, moved back into "The Warren"; the damage had been superficial, after all. Opening the larder door, the first thing Doris Addison saw was the blancmange, still untouched, and she told Dick triumphantly: "I think if I dust it off we can eat it after all."

And others were as philosophic. To C.B.S.'s Ed Murrow, their calm unflinching demeanour was what impressed him most: the question he and other U.S. newsmen had asked themselves – Could the British people take it? – seemed answered now. Only two days back, in a Sussex village street, he had marvelled; a police loudspeaker had suddenly announced, "Clear the streets for His Majesty the King. Hold that horse's head," and King George VI's big maroon car purred sedately past. Though the country was on the brink of invasion, Murrow noted the King's sole escort was a lone patrolman on a motor cycle.

Today, outside Kenley airfield, Murrow marvelled again: a company of uniformed W.A.A.F.S had marched with drill-ground precision through the airfield's main gates, ranks steady, every girl smiling. Eight men had died and eight – among them a W.A.A.F. – had been wounded in that lunch-time raid, but the clerks, cooks and waitresses were going on duty just the same.

Not all were heroes. At Manston, on the Kent coast, the morale of many was at lowest ebb, their officers' example notwithstanding; for six days many airmen had not ventured forth from the deep chalk shelters. To the pilots of 266 Spitfire Squadron, operational flights from Charlie Three spelt frustration from start to finish – the first devastating Eastchurch raid had cost them their Mae Wests and parachutes, and at Manston no storeman came on duty to replace them.

Only today Flight Lieutenant Dennis Armitage had spent a dusty half-hour groping through the labyrinth of caves, vainly seeking a station electrician he'd entrusted to complete a job. Finally, blinking in the strong sun-light, he emerged to check on the squadron's Spitfires – and cursed forcefully. Though no German aircraft had been sighted in two hours, the man hadn't even started. Patiently, holding himself in check, Armitage bent to the task himself.

Across the airfield's 500 acres, every officer could tell the same story. At 600 Squadron's dispersal, Pilot Officer Henry Jacobs just had to chuckle: though it was Sunday, the station accountant officer had wandered disconsolately by yet again, weighed down by two bags of chinking silver, vainly seeking enough airmen above ground to organise a pay parade.

By now, after four all-out raids, few buildings were even tenable. With all water cut off, men shaved at the pre-war swimming pool – if they shaved at all. Many were close to breaking-point; in the nick of time Squadron Leader James Leathart, 54 Squadron, stopped an overwrought technical officer firing blind down the shelters to flush the scrimshankers out. Manston's chaplain, the Reverend Cecil King, acted as promptly. Near-berserk, another officer had burst wild-eyed into the mess, a revolver trembling in his hand, threatening to finish off himself and every man present. Gently, King led him from the room, talking of God's infinite mercy, until the man broke down and surrendered his gun.

In Manston's smoke-filled horror and confusion, the thirty-four-year-old chaplain was an inspiration to all who saw him. Armed for safety's sake with his uncle's Webley revolver – which he later found would have blown up after one round – King had helped to organise every detail of the shattered station's routine. Often, he'd noticed the Germans zoomed in from Cap Gris Nez at mealtimes, when many airmen were queuing outside their dining halls; his suggestion that all mealtimes were put back an hour kept casualties low. Even burial services needed careful planning; for German airmen he had thoughtfully procured a German flag, captured at Narvik, to drape the coffins. And few would forget King's dispersal-hut services, his text from Psalm 63 hand-picked for pilots: "In the shadow of Thy wings will I rejoice."

But King and all of them divined the bleak truth; for Manston, now, the end was very near. Pilot Officer Henry Jacobs still recalls bitterly: "Manston was literally taken from us piece by piece." It had needed more than the brave primitive armament of 600 Squadron to stop the Luftwaffe.

At 3.30 p.m., on August 18, Manston was again, without warning, under fire. The Spitfires of 266 Squadron were still on the ground, being serviced by the flight crews, when sixteen ME 109s burst from the sun, machine-guns hammering. Planes took fire with a white incandescent flame, and everywhere men fell wounded.

There was no time for anything but evasive action. Spitfire pilot Dick Trousdale, a canny New Zealander, too weighed down by flying kit to run for it, presented his rear-end to the raiders; obligingly, his low-slung parachute stopped three bullets. Sergeant Don Kingaby, hitting the deck, saw the earth spout ahead of him and marked the line of fire; rolling rhythmically back and forth for five minutes, gauging the spouts, he escaped with a nicked thumb.

Others sought shelter as and where they could. Pilot Officer Henry Jacobs, at the base of an apple tree while Squadron Leader Graham Deverley tossed down fruit to him, dived without hesitation for a bed of stinging-nettles; when Deverley fell clean on top of him he judged himself amply screened. Flying Officer David Clackson and six others lay prone beneath the mess billiard table – while raking shots sheared the baize from the slate as cleanly as a knife might have done.

Crawling from beneath the table they stared, unbelieving: it was as if the Germans had meant to do that. They felt a sudden unutterable sense of helplessness.

–

At Headquarters, Fighter Command, the hour was late. Behind stifling black-out shutters, under naked electric light bulbs, the night staff worked on. As Pilot Officer Robert Wright entered Dowding's room with the day's figures, he thought his chief had never looked so old. There was the usual abrupt "Yes?" as Dowding's craggy eyebrows shot up – then total stillness as he bent to the reports.

Though the R.A.F. had claimed 140 German planes – swiftly amended to seventy-one, including thirty ill-fated Stukas – it was his own command's casualties that held Dowding spellbound now. Twenty-seven planes had been written off altogether, as many were badly damaged. Ten fighter pilots were dead; eighteen others severely enough wounded to need hospital treatment.

It was small wonder Dowding looked grave. On the previous day, the Air Ministry had at last acceded to his long-standing request: the thinning ranks of Fighter Command would be stiffened now by many Fairey Battle pilots, Army Co-operation Command pilots, by Allied pilots such as Squadron Leader Ernest McNab's No. 1 R.C.A.F. Squadron. But again the training period had been slashed – from one month to two short weeks. Many of these pilots, like those now serving, would never have fired the guns on a fighter, were unable to use a reflector sight, and would have done exactly twenty hours on Spitfires and Hurricanes.

These were the pilots who would bear the brunt of the battle that lay ahead.

To Robert Wright, it seemed a long time before Dowding, with a superhuman effort, aroused himself. Almost it seemed as if he found difficulty in arising from his chair. Then, shrugging slowly into his greatcoat, the Air Officer Commanding-in-Chief contrived to put a brave face on things: "Must be on parade in the morning, Wright, must be on parade in the morning."

Wright watched him, miserable, wanting to help. He wished he could think of something to say.

Chapter Six

"...and for So Little"

August 18–28

At Kirton-in-Lindsey, 100 miles from the battle-line, on the Lincolnshire fens, the pilots of No. 264 Defiant Squadron were agog with excitement. For weeks now, their sole link with the war had been the B.B.C.'s nightly news bulletins; never had the shepherding of convoys along England's peaceful East Coast seemed more irksome. But soon after breakfast on August 20, Squadron Leader Philip Hunter, the dark, dapper C.O., had warned that tomorrow they'd be moving out.

Though secrecy precluded him from naming their destination, the twinkle in Hunter's eyes told the assembled crews it lay in the right direction. "Just stuff a toothbrush in a parachute bag," was all Hunter would say. "Don't worry about kit."

And by noon on August 21, his pilots were past all worry; airborne from Kirton, Hunter set a southerly course from the first, and soon the grey ribbon of the Thames curved beneath their wings as they touched down at Hornchurch airfield, Essex. Now in the thick of the battle once more, the crews held their heads higher – those thirty-eight Stukas the squadron had claimed in one May day over Dunkirk hadn't been a fluke after all.

The fate of the nine-strong 141 Defiant Squadron – so lethally mauled on their first mid-July sortie, six weeks after Dunkirk, that the Defiants were at once withdrawn – only fleetingly occurred to them. As Pilot Officer Desmond Hughes put it, "It's up to us to regild the image."

At Hornchurch, hardened veterans shook their heads. If 264 Squadron was part of the battle, it showed the desperate straits Dowding had reached. A two-seater fighter with an unwieldy power-operated gun-turret, the Defiant's Dunkirk success had been the merest fluke: no Luftwaffe pilot had then met a "Hurricane" boasting a rear-gunner. But the surprise had been minimal. Within weeks the Germans knew the Defiant for what it was; a hump-backed non-starter, lacking all forward armament, with a maximum speed of 304 miles an hour.

Since the pilots relied solely on their gunners' verbal instructions to manoeuvre into a firing position, they were almost powerless against frontal attack.

Yet Dowding saw no other choice. By August's end, 181 fighter pilots had been killed in combat or on training flights, another 145 wounded. Some 426 aircraft had been written off, with fully 222 undergoing repairs. Already, by August 20, six squadrons had been pulled from the battle-line, but no commander could risk withdrawing the still unblooded outfits affording fighter cover to the north and midlands. Those who fought in the south must find strength to fight on.

The flimsy green combat reports flooding in to Fighter Command's headquarters showed what a beating pilots and planes had taken in the days just past. Pilot Officer "Scruffy" Joubert, blown clean through the side of his Hurricane when his radiator exploded, mercifully pulled his ripcord just in time. Sergeant Kim Whitehead, force-landing on Whitstable Beach, fell clear of his blazing plane with seconds to spare. Pilot Officer Tony Woods-Scawen, crash-landing on the Isle of Wight, smashed his front teeth to pieces; angrily he first repaired to Southampton's Polygon Hotel, threw a mammoth champagne party for all his girl friends, then 'phoned the Adjutant to come and pay the bill. Flight Sergeant "Taffy" Higginson, skid-landing at 100 miles an hour, vacated his burning Hurricane so fast he fell face down in a cowpat and broke his nose.

On every airfield, flight mechanics and maintenance men had hourly proof of how tough things were. At Hornchurch, Flying Officer Robert Lucy, 54 Squadron's engineer officer, wrenched the armour plating from the back seat of one write-off, coaxed the village garage to fashion it into two stout fish-plates, used them to patch up another fighter's badly holed starboard wing root. Lacking spare wings or replacement parts, it was the best Lucy could do – but each night he religiously removed the fairing to make sure it was standing the strain.

If tools and spares were lacking to keep planes airborne, maintenance men improvised. Faced with an eighteen-inch gash in a Spitfire wing at Biggin Hill, Aircraftman Harold Mead cut a slice from a petrol can and tacked it into place with four rivets. Always time was of the essence. At Duxford, Leading Aircraftman William Eslick and his mates saved precious minutes by switching the access point to the compressed-air bottles powering the guns – from an inaccessible trap in the cockpit floor to a point behind the pilot's seat, with ingress through the sliding hood.

In peacetime, these planes, like the men who flew them, would have got prolonged observation and rest – but now most, if the damage couldn't prove mortal, were in there fighting again. As veterans they couldn't be spared.

To the squadron commanders it made no sense at all. Why go on sending up units twelve strong when the bulk of that strength was made up by novices who were downed on their first flight? A small cadre of veterans who knew the ropes would be twice as effective. At Biggin Hill, where he often spent an hour each night wrestling with letters to next-of-kin, Squadron Leader John Ellis, commanding 610 Spitfire Squadron, bravely broached this very point with Air Chief Marshal Dowding. As Ellis saw it, it was a futile waste of planes and personnel.

Replying, Dowding was stony: if twelve planes were service-able, twelve planes would at all times be airborne.

Sadly, Ellis retired to a corner of the mess to nurse his pint. Beyond a point, you couldn't wrangle with the Air Officer

Commanding-in-Chief – but to him the whole policy seemed a needless sacrifice of lives.

And other commanders were as baffled. At Tangmere, 601 Squadron's commander, Flight Lieutenant Sir Archibald Hope, put a personal request to Air Vice-Marshal Keith Park, commander of No. 11 Group. If 601 withdrew to Scotland for one week's rest and training they'd return like giants refreshed.

For answer, Park switched the squadron to the sector station of Debden in Essex, covering the hotly contested Thames Estuary approach to London, then back to Tangmere. In one sortie, the weary Hurricane unit lost four men; by early September, below strength, they'd been pulled out altogether.

At Kenley, this same problem faced Flight Lieutenant Denys Gillam, moving spirit of the newly arrived 616 Auxiliary Squadron. Forcefully he put his case to Air Vice-Marshal Park: he'd no time to train the green replacements sent him, the older hands were too weary to give of their best. He, too, sought brief respite – one short week to teach the new boys the tricks of survival.

To Gillam, Park's reaction was as violent as if he'd preached sedition. He couldn't under any circumstances agree to front-line squadrons being released to study tactics.

Still Gillam couldn't see it; this thin-red-line outlook, geared to foolhardy sorties from forward strips, such as Manston and Hawkinge, made no sense. If the R.A.F. withdrew to the airfields north of London, they'd be out of the 109s' range – and the pilots would have time to gain operational height before speeding south. True, airfields would be within bomber range – but shorn of fighter protection, the bombers were easy meat. At Hawkinge and Manston, the R.A.F. invariably climbed beneath hovering fighters, knowing they'd be jumped at 18,000 feet before they'd ever had time to gain height.

It was hard for any pilot to grasp – yet Dowding and Park saw a show of front-line strength as paramount. As yet, with large-scale daylight raids on British cities an unknown bogey, the morale of the people was in doubt – and even retaining advance bases such as Manston, tactically wrong, was as politically expedient as the Navy's attempts to force the Channel passage. To keep morale at peak, every plane available must be up there in the sky – fighting against any odds Goring chose to decree.

Yet Dowding and Park spared no efforts to save life. On August 19, Dowding had stressed that Britain just couldn't afford to lose pilots through forced-landings in the sea. From now on, Sector Controllers must eschew sending fighters beyond the coastline to tackle small German formations. Three days later, after one year of war, the Air Ministry stepped up its meagre air-sea rescue effort: Coastal Command spotter planes and naval patrol launches would play their part, along with twelve Lysanders borrowed from Army Co-operation Command.

But if losses on the sea were lessening, losses over the land weren't: the steady induction of novices into front-line units precluded that. Down to nine pilots, 111's Squadron Leader John Thompson greeted two unfledged sergeants wearily: "I'm sorry, but I'm afraid you'll have to go in today – you see, we're so terribly short." Outside the mess, he saw their old jalopy, jam-packed with luggage. By the afternoon's tea-break, one was dead, the other in hospital – their gear still unpacked.

The man in hospital was Sergeant Raymond Sellers, who had proudly noted twenty minutes actual dog-fighting practice in his log-book. Now the young pilot was so deeply in shock that, though medical orderlies pressed him, he couldn't even remember his name.

It wasn't surprising few saw themselves as heroes: press eulogies and parliamentary oratory alike left them unmoved. At Kenley, the pilots of No. 64 Squadron, ranged beside their planes, could scarcely contain their laughter as Under Secretary of State for Air Archibald Sinclair paid warm tribute to these Hurricane pilots of No. 12 Group; until then, to the best of their belief, they'd been Spitfire pilots of No. 11 Group. On August 20, when Churchill, before a packed House of Commons, paid his immortal homage to "The Few", the reactions of most aviators were affectionately ribald. At North Weald, Pilot Officer Michael Constable-Maxwell chuckled: "He must be thinking of our liquor bills." Flying Officer Michael Appleby thought instead of the meagre fourteen shillings and sixpence a day at which the country valued his services. Irreverently he capped the speech: "...and for so little."

Most saw themselves as expendable and Red Tobin's wise-crack, as he tapped the wings on his tunic, summed it up for all of them: "I reckon these are a one-way ticket, pal."

Both Red and Andy Mamedoff had good reason to know. Until their first August 16 combat they, too, had had a bare twenty hours on Spitfires – and now, within five days of Churchill's speech, both had looked death squarely in the face.

At 6 p.m., on August 24, there was nothing to alert Red and the others that the Germans were planning a daring 100-plus divebombing attack – Junkers 88s escorted by *Zerstorers* and ME 109s – on this Dorset forward base. One moment the pilots were sprawled on the dusty grass at dispersal, swapping stories – the next they were staring unbelieving at scores of German planes flying in perfect stepped-up box formation. It was all so orderly that Aircraftman Laurence James, peeping from a slit trench, applauded aloud: "Have you ever seen anything so damned cool?"

Until this moment, Red Tobin had scarcely known a care in the world. Outwardly he was as light-hearted as could be – secretly Squadron Leader Horace Darley wondered whether he took the battle as seriously as he should. To date, the Americans had faced no greater problem than that of protocol: two days back, Group Captain the Duke of Kent had arrived to meet the pilots, and Andy, anxious to do the right thing, had asked, "Do we call him 'Duke'?"

Hastily, the Britons put him wise – the more usual style was "sir" – though few, as it turned out, had much chance to address the Duke. Absorbed in a heart-to-heart with Shorty Keough, the Duke listened enthralled to the narrative of those 480 parachute jumps – and of how often Shorty had delayed pulling the ripcord for 8,000 feet to give the crowds more kicks.

Now the Americans faced problems more urgent: the choice between life and death. Airborne so swiftly the raiders had no time to scatter more than a score of bombs, 609 Squadron were soon blazing across the four-mile channel of the Solent, between Portsmouth and the Isle of Wight. Now at 15,000 feet, Red made to turn on his oxygen, then knew a sudden disquiet. Somehow the feed had jammed – and already Darley, at the tip of the arrowhead formation, was climbing higher. The altimeter showed Red how steeply – as high as 25,000 feet.

Red Tobin worried: as yet he didn't feel sick, but as he sucked in the thin air a strange sensation was overtaking him. To fly at 25,000 feet without oxygen was courting disaster, and his mind flew back to the narrow squeak Andy had had only yesterday, August 24.

Though it had been Andy's twenty-eighth birthday, both Red and Shorty had ribbed him that it would go unobserved – "by all means don't give him a thing," Red had noted in his diary. But when Andy, intent on upholding the honour of all the White Russians, had tangled with a 110 so savagely that cannon shells smashed his tail wheel, his radio, and his trimming tab, blowing a foot of fabric from his elevator, piercing his armour plating and parachute harness, Red had swiftly shown his true concern. "They must have thrown the whole Krupp factory at you," he'd consoled Andy, standing treat.

If he flew on without oxygen, Red knew, a worse fate could befall him. They'd dropped to 19,000 feet now, but he'd better ask Darley's permission to break. Then, flying level, ahead of them, he saw the 110s.

In this frozen moment, as he later recalled, he had just one thought: There we are and there we go.

This was typical of Red Tobin: no man to push himself forward, he was more often than not, if a challenge arose, there to meet it. Once in school amateur dramatics when the leading player fell suddenly ill, the popular Red, president of his student body, had been jockeyed into taking over; though he'd hated the idea, he couldn't let his classmates down. Improvising his dialogue for most of the way, he'd won thunderous applause. It had been the same years later when friends talked him into entering a crooning contest in a night club. Though Red admired Crosby too much to fancy his own chances, he wouldn't chicken out – and won first prize.

Now he showed the same determination; oxygen or no, he couldn't let down 609 Squadron. An ME 110 was drifting in a gentle bank ahead of him, enormous, seemingly impregnable with its fifty-foot wing span. Before the rear-gunner could swing his long barrel round, Tobin thumbed the firing button, holding the gunsight steady just to starboard of the gunner's goggled face. Tracer sparkled along the whole length of the fuselage, and then the ME 110 was climbing, almost vertically, as if the pilot was trying to loop.

For a moment it seemed to hang like that, motionless, a giant silver projectile aimed at the evening sun. Then it caromed steeply to starboard, vanishing from sight.

A veteran within seconds, Red remembered in time the caveats of those who knew: Don't follow him down – if you do you're wide open to an attack on your own tail. Why worry whether you scored a bullseye? There are plenty more where the first came from.

It was true. Barely had he broken, jinking through a lethal latticework of curving, glowing tracer, then another Messerschmitt swam into his sights. As if by reflex, Red jerked the firing button; the 110 see-sawed and a thin straight ribbon of black trailed from its engine. Then the German was losing height in a giddy succession of spins and turns, and Red, on fire with the chase, followed after him, banking steeply at more than 370 miles an hour. In that instant, 18,000 feet above the water, he blacked out.

Now, for the first time, the thrust of G was pushing him deep against the bucket aluminium seat, bending his backbone like a bow, pushing his chin downwards onto his chest. The inexorable centrifugal force was driving the blood from his head towards his feet, turning it to the weight of molten iron, and for a second his brain was no longer working; his jaw sagged like an idiot's and a yellow-grey curtain swam before his eyes. And at this moment he had a dream so terrifying that no man could ever persuade him to reveal it, until suddenly a gentle insistent voice was urging him: "You are in an airplane and you are fighting. You'd better come to."

Then, drowsily, Red found his brain clearing, and he was flying absolutely level, only 1,000 feet above the water. Back at Warmwell airfield, he excused himself shakily to Darley: "I blacked out colder than a clam," but the squadron were all solicitude. Sick at heart, they'd watched him spin all the way, fearing the worst.

From this moment on, Red felt less light-hearted – and even the veterans were the same. Flight Lieutenant James MacArthur, Andy's Canadian flight commander, was mordant: "If the clouds sock in, they might keep the Grim Reaper off a while." Red's flight commander, the imperturbable Frank Howell, felt the same: "Our luck can't really last at this pace."

Yet in most ways, Red and Andy Mamedoff were lucky: their mistakes hadn't been irretrievable. For scores of pilots now entering the battle, there would be no second chance.

At Northolt airfield, outside London, Squadron Leader Ernest McNab, leading No. 1 Squadron, Royal Canadian Air Force, had reached "the lowest point in my life" – though the pilot shortage decreed that McNab's Canadians should be operational from August 17, he knew his men weren't ready for combat. Like most outfits, they'd fired at a moving target in the air only once. Their sole aircraft recognition training had been an instructor hastily shuffling through a pile of silhouettes like a gambler riffling a deck of cards.

Ninety minutes before Andy Mamedoff's near-fatal sortie, McNab's Canadians, twelve strong, were bulling west towards Chichester Harbour, eyes squinting against the blinding white orb of the afternoon sun. Word had come that German bombers were heading north across the Isle of Wight and at H.Q. 11 Group, Park's controller feared the worst: the raiders must be once more bound for Tangmere Sector Station. The Canadians' orders were explicit: intercept the Germans over Selsey Bill, the southernmost part of the West Sussex coastline.

Nine miles north-west, at R.A.F. Station, Thorney Island, three slow-paced Blenheim patrol planes of No. 235 Squadron, Coastal Command, were ordered up on the same mission.

It wasn't until the bombers pressed steadily on that the controllers spotted their intention: a mass strike against Portsmouth Harbour. Over Selsey, Squadron Leader McNab's Canadians realised, too; black oily puffs of smoke hung motionless in the sky to the west. At 4.40 p.m., flying at 10,000 feet, the Canadians swung towards Portsmouth.

Briefly, for the first time, they were aware what fear could do to a man's mouth – McNab's own palate was suddenly "as dry as cotton wool". Flying Officer Dal Russel of Montreal, rhythmically chewing gum, felt the wad cleave to the roof of his mouth; later he had literally to prise it clear.

Then McNab's fears were past, because ahead of him, at 6,000 feet, north and east of Thorney Island, three aircraft were flying in line astern, heading away from Portsmouth. Through the dark sifting curtain of ack-ack puffs, he saw them as Junkers 88s, though sifting smoke and sunlight didn't make for easy identification. Flight Lieutenant Gordon McGregor still recalls with fascinated dread: "Those planes were black – black against the sun."

And now, in the fearful instant before the attack, McNab, leading his section of three, called, "Echelon, starboard – go!" and for every pilot the scene tilted sharply as they put the Hurricanes' noses down and their right thumbs took the first light pressure on the gun buttons. Then they were diving at 300 miles an hour, faster and faster, too fast for all to hear McNab's electrifying scream in their earphones: "Break, break, break! Don't attack!"

For at 3,000 feet above the dark silhouettes, McNab had seen the gun turrets that Junkers 88s conspicuously lacked and the white flash on the aircrafts' fins, marking them as British; he and his section broke violently to port and didn't attack. But the following planes saw what they took to be long yellow spears of tracer curving towards them, and opened fire – not realising the Blenheims' gunners were firing yellow and red Very pistol flares, the colours of the day, which were the recognition signal.

Tyres holed, undercarriage wrecked, Blenheim pilot Sergeant Naish was within an ace of disaster; he escaped the Hurricanes' point-blank fire only by crashlanding on Thorney Island airfield. Starboard engine holed, his windscreen starred with thick opaque blotches, the second pilot, Flight Lieutenant Flood, was lucky to follow suit. It was the purest tragedy that the third Blenheim, Pilot Officer David Woodger's, never made it. Smoke was streaming from its tailplane, its starboard engine was already on fire, as it spiralled towards the sea, then another two-second burst came as the coup-de-grace.

East of Thorney Island, over Bracklesham Bay, it fell apart, blazing like a petrol-soaked brand, in the second before it struck the water. Pilot Officer Woodger had never stood a chance.

Even now the Canadians didn't appreciate the full enormity of what had happened. Back at Northolt, their home base, it was the station commander, Group Captain Stanley Vincent, who broke the news as gently as might be, to the shaken Squadron Leader McNab. When McNab, appalled, cried: "My God, what have we done? What can I do?" Vincent was compassionate. "There's nothing you can do, these things happen in war – the one thing you must do is to fly down and see them and explain."

It was war indeed – for now the Luftwaffe's revised tactics were working triumphantly. From August 19, Sperrle's Air Fleet

Three, on the Cherbourg peninsula, had been stripped of every single-engined fighter; by August 24, all were transferred to the Pas de Calais, operating under Oberst Theo Osterkamp, regional fighter commander for Air Fleet Two. Now the main onus of the battle lay with Generalfeldmarschall Kesselring: the main concentration of effort was in the east, and the bombers that droned in over Kent would be escorted by almost every single-engined fighter the Luftwaffe had.

To the German pilots it seemed that the pressure was stepping up almost hourly. At Audembert, whence he'd transferred as the 26th Fighter Group's new commander, Major Adolf Galland told his younger brother Wilhelm, a junior officer in an ack-ack training camp: "Things can't go on much longer like this. You can count on your fingers when your turn will come." Oberst Carl Viek, Osterkamp's chief of staff, knew the truth of it: despite all protests, Goring would permit no rest days, no rotation of frontline units. Even decimated units must fight on; the ruthless watchword was "The last man shall go again."

At Manston, No. 264 Defiant Squadron felt the full impact of this new tempo. Not long after 5 a.m., on August 24, they'd been ordered by their home base, Hornchurch, to furnish Manston's fighter cover – a near-insuperable task for an aircraft whose rate of climb barely exceeded 2,000 feet a minute. Yet in the first shattering attack, only one section, under Flight Lieutenant John Banham, even had time to climb. As Banham's section circled on sentry-go, three other sections were on the ground refuelling.

Then, as seven Defiants prepared to take off anew, came the emergency Fighter Command dreaded most: twenty JU 88 dive bombers, with a powerful fighter escort, hurtled from the early morning mist, their bombs falling in black ugly salvoes among the taxi-ing planes. Above the howling confusion of the attack, one clamour rose, more deadly than the rest – the clanging of machine-gun bullets raining on the fighters' wings and noses.

Aloft the confusion was as great. Flying Officer Peter Bowen, in the nick of time, realised the 109s were on a reciprocal course;

he was due to meet them head-on. Miraculously, there were no collisions; at a converging speed of 600 miles an hour, the fighters flew clean through the Defiant formation, neither side firing a shot. To his eternal surprise, Flight Lieutenant Banham found himself diving with the bombers, hauling both feet onto the control column to keep level. Pilot Officer Eric Barwell, trying for a nose-shot, turned so steeply he blacked out his gunner. Caught up in his first sortie, Pilot Officer Desmond Hughes saw the looming black crosses and thought: This is it. They really *do* come over here.

One Defiant pilot, Flight Lieutenant E. W. Campbell-Colquhoun, was as confused as any; promoted to command a flight after one trip in a Defiant, he couldn't even identify the buttons and switches on his instrument panel. Within minutes, thus preoccupied, he'd joined formation with three ME 109s, whose cannon shells exploded his Very cartridges. Choking with smoke, his Defiant alive with bouncing coloured balls, Colquhoun touched the plane down somehow, pelting for a slit trench.

Within the hour, he heard the worst news yet; his C.O., Squadron Leader Philip Hunter was dead, shot down pursuing the raiders across the Channel, and two other Defiants were missing. The five-minute skirmish had cost 264 Squadron six men, three machines – and soon they must face the Germans yet again.

Manston airfield was suffering as cruelly. In 600 Squadron's Ops Room, Pilot Officer Henry Jacobs was relaying a blow-by-blow commentary to Headquarters 11 Group when a hollow note like a gong echoed up the wire, then the line went silent. Jacobs didn't know that a bomb had struck the telephone and teleprinter lines, severing 248 circuits at one blow; he only knew the bombs seemed too close for comfort. Dashing from the Ops Room, he saw the East Camp guardhouse next door had vanished – nothing but chalk dust mushrooming above a crater forty feet deep.

Now in a savage frenzy of impotence, 600 Squadron were hitting back with everything they had... firing rifles... Very pistols... the pole-mounted Vickers called "The Armadillo"... Corporal Francis De Vroome hurling stones and clods of chalk skywards. Close by, dashing from a slit trench, the Reverend Cecil King stooped among the ruins of the guardhouse, beside himself with grief as he uncovered fragments of human flesh, passionately shaking his fist at the raiders. Later, told by eye-witnesses he'd cursed like a trooper, he couldn't remember a word of it.

From Dover's Shakespeare Cliff, C.B.S.'s Ed Murrow watched the raid with a weird sense of unreality: against the sun the dive-bombers looked like ducks with broken wings, yet even as the hollow grunt of bombs went home, it was hard to believe that men were killing and being killed. As Dover's ack-ack pounded, an American newsman told the *Daily Herald*'s Reg Foster: "It used to be a five-dollar box of fireworks. Now you are bringing out the ten-dollar box."

Close to, it seemed worse. Defiant gunner Freddie Sutton couldn't believe his eyes; as the bombs tore up the airstrip, men ducked beneath petrol bowsers, seemingly too dazed with shock to realise the danger. Leading Fireman Herbert Evans, Margate Fire Brigade, tut-tutting through the airfield's main gates on a motor cycle, as spearhead of the main fire force, felt he'd hit a ghost airfield. Hangars... the armoury... aircraft at dispersal... all were burning with a yellow lambent flame – yet the grass acres were as deserted as a prairie.

Only a lone R.A.F. officer, pipe in mouth, hands in pockets, stood gazing at the devastation, tears streaming down his face. Then, seeing Evans, he turned ashamedly away; the firemen never saw him again.

Now Margate's Chief Officer Albert Twyman arrived on the scene; though unexploded bomb craters pitted the ground all round them, there was work for his firemen to do. Dashing into the blazing armoury, Twyman's men time and again stumbled forth with armfuls of precious Browning machine-guns, while a blazing Very light store next door spangled the afternoon sky with whooshing red and white lights.

Only when the roof-timbers sagged ominously inwards did Twyman lead his smoke-grimed shock-troops to safety – a feat that was to earn him the George Medal for bravery.

Hastily, Flight Sergeant John Wright, a maintenance N.C.O. of 600 Squadron, piled a truck to overflowing with vital spares. In the prevailing chaos, civilians from nearby Ramsgate were moving in to loot tools marked "Air Ministry", even live ammunition, from the main stores.

On the same day, the bulk of the station personnel were moved out. After twelve bitter days of attrition, all attempts to hold Manson had proved in vain.

It was almost as if despair was contagious. At Hawkinge, nineteen miles down the coast, Aircraftman Thomas MacKay saw armed N.C.O.s flushing the perimeter hedges like beaters at a shooting party, driving unwilling ground crews back to work. At North Weald, Essex, the first bombs of August 24 saw a flood of men surge like frightened sheep from the main gates, bound for the leafy glades of Epping Forest close by… officers and civilians first… followed closely by N.C.O.s… lastly by ground crews themselves.

Arriving back from a sortie to find his station badly strafed, Wing Commander Victor Beamish, the C.O., reached for the tannoy loudspeaker, and his powerful Irish brogue boomed out over the airfield: "Any officer, N.C.O. or airman who leaves his post while on duty is a coward and a rat – and I shoot rats on sight." At North Weald, no man panicked again.

Now, sixteen days after the battle began, the pressure was stepping up; under such mounting strain, men were bound to crack. Day after day the vast formations swept across the Channel to clash with the spearheads of 11 Group, so many now the Controllers rarely knew when the next attack would come or from where. So many German planes were in the battle-line that even a fleet of 100-plus might be a feint to draw up the fighters – the main attack sweeping in unopposed once they'd landed to refuel.

And though many squadrons were due to withdraw, making way for new blood, the irony was that the veterans, even dog-tired, were still scoring. All too often men fresh to the battle could contribute little more than bravery, the ability to face death with disdain.

Consider the case of Sergeant Ronnie Hamlyn, a dashing twenty-three-year-old of 610 Squadron, veteran of Dunkirk. Soon after 8 a.m., on August 24, Hamlyn's Spitfire, off Rams-gate, was diving from 12,000 feet onto a Junkers 88, hosing it with fire, watching it rip like a hydrofoil along the water's surface. Banking, he fastened on the tail of an ME 109, firing until this, too, fell, trailing a red garland of flame. By 9 a.m., Hamlyn was back at his home-base, Biggin Hill – preparing to face a different kind of ordeal.

A few days back, the young sergeant had made a care-less wheels-up landing at Gravesend – and now he must face his station commander, Group Captain Richard Grice, on a charge of negligence. But at 10.35 a.m., as he lined up outside Grice's office door, the tannoy loudspeaker blared into life: 610 Squadron was to scramble. Politely, Hamlyn excused himself to Warrant Officer George Merron, his escort: trouble threatened, but he'd be back.

As things turned out, Hamlyn very nearly wasn't. Vectored first to Gravesend, then over Dover, 610 Squadron had patrolled for a full hour before they swept into six ME 110s – all of which swung abruptly for France. Now the Messerschmitts had a head-start; even flying at full throttle, Hamlyn couldn't open fire until he'd crossed the French coast. Then, closing to 150 yards, he sent six three-second bursts blasting into the centre of the fuselage, aiming from beneath and astern. Black smoke vomited from the stricken port engine as the ME nose-dived beyond control into a field. Hamlyn saw no one walk away.

About 4 p.m., bare-headed, braced to attention, Hamlyn was in Group Captain Grice's office, as the group captain pondered his offence. Again the loudspeaker rasped, calling 610 Squadron, and Hamlyn, blushing to the roots of his hair, apologised profusely: there was man's work to be done. Then he was away, hareing for his plane, and the swift flight towards the intercept at Gravesend.

North of the Isle of Sheppey, the Spitfires roared into battle with twenty 109s, and Hamlyn, holding his machine in the tightest turn ever, hauling with both hands on the control column, flayed fire at two more 109s until both fell flaming for the water. Homing for Biggin Hill, he pondered: it had been a busy day, but somehow no busier than most. Hamlyn couldn't know, as yet, that an unprecedented toll of five victims would earn him the D.F.M.; he thought only that today, as never before, everything had seemed to click.

As he touched down at Biggin Hill, Group Captain Grice, poker-faced, came forward to meet his aircraft: "As it seems impossible to meet you in my office, Hamlyn, I hereby officially admonish you."

–

Hauptmann Herbert Kaminski breathed a silent prayer of relief. To the east, pale, primrose-yellow light streaked the sky, and he knew that dawn was near. Now he could look back with something like detachment over one of the most wretched nights he had ever spent.

For more than six hours of total darkness, the dinghy had bobbed awkwardly on the choppy Channel waters – and every rising wave soaked Kaminski's rear-end anew, while Unteroffizier Strauch sat comfortably in the dry. Early on, Kaminski had decided, "We'll change positions," but Strauch said truthfully: "It's impossible, Herr Hauptmann. We'll capsize her."

Then Kaminski remembered what a downed comrade, Hauptmann Kogler, had cautioned only recently: "If you spend a night in 'the brook', don't fall asleep. Because then you may fall off the dinghy and lose the paddle." He told Strauch: "We'll sing by turns. You sing a song, and then I sing a song. Whatever happens, we do not fall asleep."

But after a long hour the singing had drawn to a melancholy close, and Kaminski, racking his brain for new diversions, had ordered: "Now we'll recite poems for a change – you first." Though Strauch shook a regretful head – "Herr Hauptmann, I don't know any poems" – Kaminski didn't think he sounded sorry at all.

A man driven beyond endurance, Kaminski growled: "You have not memorised one single poem and I know almost all of *Faust* by heart? Have I got to recite *Faust* all night?" Strauch saw it as the ideal solution. "Go on, Herr Hauptmann," he said smugly.

As Kaminski embarked on the floodtide of Goethe's master-piece, he lost all count of time. Both men's watches had stopped soon after entering the water; he knew only from his compass that the wind was driving them to the east. High above the clouds, bombers throbbed and searchlights were weaving far away. German bombers bound for England or English bombers en route to France? They didn't know.

At intervals, suspicious of the silence, Kaminski stopped reciting and yelled: "Are you still awake?" Each time Strauch said eagerly, "Go on, Herr Hauptmann. It's really very nice." Groaning, Kaminski continued.

But now, as dawn broke, Kaminski shelved all thoughts of Goethe and there was only one thing on his mind: rescue. Already the first German planes were soaring across the Channel, and again both men waved their vivid yellow scarves. Though the last fighter in the formation got a signal flare almost across his nose, the pilot took no notice at all. Almost paralysed with cold, Kaminski said: "We will now have breakfast. Open the first canister, and we will divide it equally." Generously, he offered Strauch first swig at the small stone bottle of *steinhager* gin, but Strauch, wry-faced, passed it back after one sip. "It's too strong."

But Kaminski's throat, after a long night of *Faust*, salt water and sing-songs, was so rasped he couldn't taste it. The *steinhager* gurgled down like water, and before he knew it he'd emptied the bottle. He was aware of nothing, not even the fact that he was now as drunk as any man could be. Masterfully he ordered Strauch: "We will now take the paddle and row to the French coast."

Strauch protested forcibly – it just wasn't feasible, they must conserve their strength – but Kaminski was in no mood to be reasoned with. He enquired with steely disdain: "Who has three times been placed in close arrest and who is the commandant? Lower that kedge anchor!"

At this moment, three icy waves hit him in the face in sharp succession, and all at once Kaminski was sober again. He ordered judicially: "End of manoeuvre."

At Lille North airfield, the pilots of *Zerstorer* Group 26 were settling to breakfast when their commander, the wooden-legged Oberstleutnant Joachim Huth, who'd vainly tried to check Oberst Fink's attack on Eastchurch, stumped into the mess. Worriedly, he asked: 'Where is "The Last of the Prussians'?"

Nobody knew for certain, so Huth 'phoned the German Navy. The Navy were apologetic: the rescue plane had reported two fliers in the water, but the Channel was still too turbulent for a naval launch to set out. Furious, Huth roared: "You leave my pilots in the water and tell me nothing? Send a minesweeper, not a launch – and *my* unit will guide you to 'The Last Prussian'."

In the dinghy, still light-headed, Kaminski had temporarily forgotten rescue: he was out to save Strauch from himself. All night he'd noticed the gunner fiddling at intervals with an unidentified object, but now daylight revealed it for what it was – a small pearl-handled revolver. Convinced Strauch was about to do away with himself, he ordered: "Throw that pistol overboard. We will have no suicides here."

Strauch protested: he had no such intentions. It was a present from his fiancée and he was trying to keep it dry. Incensed, Kaminski roared, "Throw the God damn thing overboard," but the gunner shook a mutinous head. Kaminski sighed. There was nothing for it: Strauch would have to stay in close arrest another ten days.

Just then, far to the east, they saw four ME 110s sweeping over the water, until one pilot spotted the eddying green marker dye. Now the *Zerstorers* roared above them in ever-decreasing circles; gleefully Kaminski and Strauch brandished their yellow scarves. But when the minesweeper at last hove to, Kaminski hadn't even strength to take the line they cast him; he fell top-heavily into the water.

The Navy had to rig a bowline and haul him on board, and as he sprawled on the minesweeper's deck he was palsied alternately with cold and laughter. For as Strauch, in turn, was hauled aboard, the gunner's pistol plopped into the water after all.

Oberstleutnant Huth and his pilots were so elated to see Kaminski alive they prevailed on Dunkirk's hospital authorities to let them spirit him back to Lille. They soon regretted it. Above all, Kaminski needed heat to thaw the ice from his stocky frame, and the fire they had to build in the billet was a roasting torment in mid-August. Sweat-soaked and swooning, the pilots fed the blaze with logs, but Kaminski, sipping iced champagne in bed, felt life was just fine.

Then Kaminski, his "throat-ache" still unappeased, flew to Dusseldorf; he and Strauch would be shot down and wounded five times more before he won his coveted Knight's Cross, but first a plastic surgeon must fix his broken nose. To celebrate, he rang up Grete Sima, the famous film-star, and invited her to supper at the Rauchpass, Dusseldorf's toniest restaurant. The headwaiter was at his haughtiest but "The Last of the Prussians" quelled him with a glance: "Give us the best damn table in the place and bring champagne. I've come from the English Channel."

One squadron that wasn't giving up without a fight was 264 Defiant Squadron – though by late afternoon on August 26, two days after entering the battle, it seemed more akin to gallantry than common sense. Only that morning, orbiting between Deal and Herne Bay, the Defiants had slammed resolutely into a dozen incoming Domiers.

Pilot Officer Desmond Hughes, jockeying for position as his gunner, Sergeant Fred Gash, chanted instructions, was one of the lucky ones; as Gash's fire jolted home on the Dornier's cockpit, splinters of metal flew like chips from an axe. Then it was gone, dragging a black scar of smoke across the sky.

At this moment more than fifty 109s came hauling up beneath them, a vicious welter of cannon shells spurting from an angle the Defiant gunners couldn't reach.

Hard as they fought back, the squadron was outnumbered and outgunned. Flight Lieutenant John Banham had just seen a Dornier leap like a landed salmon under his gunner's fire when an explosive shell struck his plane amidships. Now his greatest fear was for his gunner, Sergeant Baker: cramped in their turrets, their heads within inches of the gunsights, Defiant gunners, of necessity, wore their parachutes high on their shoulders. Until the pilot turned the plane on its back, his gunner had no freedom to bale out – and even then the chute harness almost always snagged on a projecting lever.

Now, with seconds to spare, Banham swung the blazing plane clean upside down, yelling urgently over the intercom: "For God's sake get out." They were over the Channel, ten miles off Margate, and as he jumped he wasn't even sure whether Baker had heard. After a chilly ninety minutes, Banham was picked up by an air-sea rescue launch, but Baker was never found.

Three more Defiants had fallen to the German cannons – and two gunners were missing.

And still the losses were rising. On August 24, twenty-two fighters had been written off, and two days later the toll was steeper – thirty-one aircraft lost, four pilots killed, twelve wounded. At H.Q. 11 Group, Air Vice-Marshal Keith Park was in despair: compared with the sorties flown, the R.A.F.'s interceptions were negligible, and thanks to low-lying cloud, the height and strength of many German formations were being imperfectly assessed.

Despite the hazards, the Defiants were living up to their name – and at Hornchurch, the station staff, under the terrier-tempered Wing Commander Bouchier, worked like beavers to aid them. But though new Defiants came from the assembly line as fast as they were lost, many had vital modifications left undone. Some had no self-sealing tanks... others had the wrong plugs... none of the guns were harmonised. Working all night in blacked-out hangars, under dim blue pilot lights, the mechanics were dropping on their feet.

But the crewmen weren't defeated. Defiant gunner Freddie Sutton put a bold front on it: "There are plenty of us left yet" – and whatever their status, men were weighing in to help. Pushing aside paper work, Squadron Adjutant John Kimber and his clerks learned to handle bowsers and re-arm turrets; putting a match to the wordy Air Ministry memos that might have detained him, Kimber solemnly announced them "destroyed by enemy action". When the squadron jammed into pilot Hugh Percy's Bentley to speed from mess to dispersal, Wing Commander Bouchier was always on tap to help give a push start.

It was cruel fate that at 8.30 a.m., on August 28, under their new C.O., Squadron Leader Desmond Garvin, the Defiants should have clashed with a mixed bomber formation, heading for Rochford and Eastchurch airfields – a task force escorted by the ace some feared more than death itself, Major Adolf Galland.

Ten days commander of the 26th Fighter Wing, despite all his protests, Galland was growing daily more withdrawing. The small framed plaque, bearing a quotation from Nietzsche, that hung above his desk in the red-brick farmhouse at Audembert embodied his most urgent prayer: "Praised be all things that harden us." Only this pitiless front could keep at bay the doubts that tortured him with every loss: Did I lead in the best way? It was his life, but did I lose it for him? Was it his fault – or my fault?

And the paper-war fought after each day's battle taxed Galland, too; no chance to relax in the mess over a drink and get to know his pilots better. Instead, lonely hours grappling with reports… airfield modifications… billeting… food supplies… long abstruse discussions with Prufmeister Sander, the technical officer, and Waffeninspektor Breitmeier, the armaments chief.

Worse, Galland knew his men were under heavy stress. Often they couldn't touch a bite before 10 p.m.; one jangle of the alarm bell set them vomiting. If Galland himself kept going, warm milk mixed with a little red wine was all he could choke down at breakfast. The strain of adjusting their cruising speed – 298 miles an hour – to a Dornier's snail-paced 265, was an endless frustration. So great a howl for protection had the bomber men set up that the fighters were all the time throttling back to screen them.

Now, most humiliating of all, Goring had forbidden fighters to do the very job they were designed for – to range free and fight. Hugging the bombers – "furniture vans" to the embittered fighter pilots – they must wait tamely until the R.A.F. came and blasted at them.

There was no time for further introspection at 7.30 a.m., on Wednesday, August 28. Already a lone Heinkel of Oberstleutnant Exss's 1st Bomber Group had circled Audembert airfield, ready to guide the fighters to the main formation, and the alarm was blurting. As Galland pelted for his ME 109, his mechanic, Unteroffizier Egon Meyer, was already standing by. The sunlit grass was suddenly alive with running men in pale-blue overalls, and on all sides mechanics were doubling like scene-shifters to remove the grass and matting camouflage.

Clambering into his plane, Galland observed a brief second of ritual: a black Brazilian cigar clenched in his jaws, he puffed contentedly as the Daimler Benz engine roared into life. Then, still puffing, he was skimming at 130 miles an hour across the flattening grass, soaring after the retreating Dorniers, climbing at more than 3,000 feet a minute. Three minutes, then regretfully he stubbed out his cigar in the ashtray, wafted the fumes from the cockpit, clapped on his oxygen mask.

Droning across the Channel, astern of the glinting bombers, Galland knew the kind of combat he sought today – if combat was joined. Always he prayed for what he called a "You or Me" fight – a relentless kill-or-be-killed duel, which only the best man could win. Easy victories were always a strange burden on his conscience – and if Kesselring or Osterkamp congratulated him, that made it worse.

It was now 8.30 a.m. At heights ranging from 16,000 to 21,000 feet, 159 German planes slid unopposed across the coastline of North Kent: 120 of Galland's fighters escorting thirty-nine bombers. Now the two formations parted: the Dorniers of the 3rd Bomber Group swung north-west for Rochford airfield, the Heinkels turned west for Eastchurch. Beneath the Heinkels, Galland bored on. Abruptly, over Ashford, Kent, his eyes narrowed behind his goggles. Nobody had warned him that Stukas would be part of this formation.

It was a second before he spotted them for what they were: eleven British two-seater fighters, flying in close formation just below the Heinkels, closing in to attack from astern. At any moment the four Browning machine-guns in their power-operated turrets would be raking the Heinkels' bellies.

It was now or never. Slamming his throttle forward, Galland hauled back on the control column. Momentarily G clamped him to his seat, then he was blazing upwards, followed by his staff flight of three, and the too-tight Defiant formation, at the Messerschmitts' mercy, scattered and broke.

Scrambled so hastily most were still wearing pyjamas, few of the Defiant crews even stood a chance. At the rear of the formation, Pilot Officer Freddie Sutton, left elbow over the high-speed button, threw his turret from side to side, blazing away at the hurtling 109s – then, as one fell like a torch, the world spun before his eyes.

Suddenly, his pilot, Peter Bowen, had turned the plane upside down, and now centrifugal force was crushing Sutton's neck and spine against the turret's roof. Very pistol, cartridges, the axe for cutting trapped gunners loose, floated crazily past his eyes. Dimly Bowen's voice came: "Hit – fire – jump."

But Sutton hadn't even power to raise his hands to the release catches on the turret doors; the whistling roar in his ears threatened to burst his head apart. Icy sweat bathed his body and he screamed hoarsely, in pain and fear.

Miraculously, after an inverted spin of 10,000 feet, Bowen brought the fighter under control, to find the fire in the engine nacelle had blown out. The Defiant was flying straight and level, and Bowen was heading hard for Rochford airfield.

Not all were so lucky. At first the combat flared so fiercely that Adolf Galland couldn't even hold a Defiant in his sights: the first jinked away between other 109s, and he couldn't fire for fear of hitting them. Flying alongside a second, he was about to open fire when Oberleutnant Horten got in first. At Hinxhill in Kent, the machine, with the pilot, Peter Kenner, and the gunner, Johnny Johnson, still aboard, hit the ground in a wailing all-out dive – ripping so far beneath the earth that though men dug for a day they couldn't reach it.

Again, Galland dived – but this third machine he over-shot completely; the Defiant was gliding slowly downwards on a dead engine. He saw a fourth pressing downwards, and dived again, opening fire at 100 yards, closing to twenty. His cannon ammunition was expended now – but his machine-guns were still working.

Now Galland was caught up in a duel to the death with Flight Lieutenant Clifford Ash, the Defiant's gunner; though the plane, piloted by Squadron Leader Garvin was already on fire, Ash wasn't giving up. Four times his bullets holed Galland's 109, but Galland, even as he fired, thought: What right have they to put such tragically outmoded planes into the firing line? Chunks rained from the Defiant's fuselage; white flames blossomed from the wing tanks. As Galland broke away, he didn't see Ash, baling out, swing mortally against the Defiant's tailplane. Garvin, too, baled out, badly shaken, his eyebrows singed clean away.

Five crewmen were dead, and now only three planes remained serviceable: the massacre of the Defiants was complete. Four days in action had cost them eleven aircraft, fourteen lives.

On August 29, withdrawn from the battle, 264 Squadron flew back to Kirton-in-Lindsey – led now by Pilot Officer "Tommie" Thomas, a twenty-year-old Dunkirk veteran, the one experienced man left. Some couldn't even get airborne; Flight Lieutenant E. W. Campbell-Colquhoun sent for his wife to motor him to Kirton. His hands shook so, he couldn't even light a cigarette, let alone grip a steering wheel.

Bitterly, Major Adolf Galland set course for Audembert; it had been no "You or Me" combat that, merely slaughter. But within seconds Galland was in trouble: the circuitous route the bombers had taken, the combat itself, had taken up precious minutes. Now Galland wondered: could he get himself and his group home? Already his earphones exploded with anxious voices: "Red light showing! Red light up!"

That meant pilot after pilot after pilot had seen a red warning bulb glow on his instrument panel: very few litres of petrol left from the initial 400. Fifteen minutes' more flying time – twenty at most.

Below loomed Manston, strangely deserted, dotted with the charred shells of hangars, and the realisation struck Galland: in the last resort he might have to force-land and surrender on the airfield he'd so often strafed. Then responsibility drove all thoughts of self from his mind: for better, for worse, the 26th Fighter Wing was his and he must survive to lead them. Sweating minutes of tension – but somehow he nursed his 109 across the Channel, roaring along the hard packed sand of the beach below Gap Gris Nez at 130 miles an hour. He was lucky: at least seven of his pilots, ditching in mid-Channel, were narrowly fished from the sea.

Had Galland hit Manston he would in all probability have been brought face-to-face with Winston Churchill who was just then, as part of a two-day coastal visit, trudging its cratered acres. Not surprisingly Churchill was both angry and perplexed. For thousands of civilians and servicemen now, the war was coming home with a violence they'd never experienced – and even the bravest could wonder what lay ahead. Six days back, on August 22, Dover had come under fire from the giant guns of Cap Gris Nez; for eighty minutes shells had fallen like cabers among the grey winding streets. On August 24, during the heavy attack on Manston, 500 bombs had hit nearby Ramsgate, damaging 1,000 houses in three minutes.

So Churchill worried: how would his people stand up to it?

None knew better than Churchill the faith they needed. With Lieutenant-General Alan Brooke, he'd toured almost every mile of Britain's threatened coastline... striding briskly out wherever crowds gathered, despite his weariness, to boost morale... creating chaos each time he flung away a cigar butt as onlookers scuffled for a souvenir. And on all sides, the moral was plain: if "Operation Sea-Lion" wasn't to become a grim reality, everything depended on the R.A.F.

The ground defences were pitiful. All over southern England only one Home Guardsman in three had a rifle – and the Army were in poor shape, too. From Dover to Southampton, there was just one machine-gun to defend each 1,500 yards of beach. At Deal, Private Alfred Neill and his mates of the 5th Battalion, Shropshire Light Infantry, had one Bren gun among 750 men. Private Ben Angell, one of twenty trainee signallers defending a concrete pill-box outside Dover, had only a rifle he barely knew how to fire.

All along the coast, the weird barricades showed the shape of the war to come, a guerilla war with the people caught up in its midst... at Chilham in Kent, tree trunks from the sawmill... at Tonbridge, tar barrels from the distillery... at Goring in Sussex, a flimsy latticework of old iron bedsteads. Inland, at Sidcup crossroads, the police had dumped 100 tons of glass, as for a medieval siege. At Deal, an agricultural contractor, Reginald Blunt, each night waited until 11 p.m., when the last bus had gone, then dutifully blocked the road with his three traction engines and a steamroller.

Yet strangely, Churchill had no cause for alarm: with blind faith that the R.A.F. would win through, his people were preparing to stick it out. At Ramsgate, 60,000 of them had settled in for a long war – in caves seventy feet below the chalk cliffs, known locally as "The Persian Market". Together with beds, tables and chairs made from barrels, most had brought their own alarm clocks, ears attuned to sleep through every clangour save their own. Even groceries were no problem; at week-ends, local tradesmen lowered provisions down the bluff with a rope and pulley.

Those who didn't fancy shelter life clung doggedly on in their houses – scrubbing their doorsteps as white as a bleached bone after each air raid. Outside Ramsgate's blitzed Assembly Hall, a notice loomed: "Cheer up – the best part of history is still to be written."

It was the same in every coastal port. At Dover, those young-sters who remained had new standards of barter: one Messer-schmitt cannon shell changed hands for three large lumps of shrapnel, Even the errand boys carried on, wearing tin hats to deliver their goods. Under shellfire on the broad cliffs that rimmed St. Margaret's Bay, Reginald Blunt and his minder Bill Harris were at work threshing several thousand quarters of corn, labouring from dawn to dusk. Some, cannily, used danger to their own advantage. At a Chilham poultry auction, one man stood resolutely fast as bombers zoomed low and the bidders scattered, got his lot dirt cheap.

Though Churchill only half suspected it, the German's day-by-day attacks were stiffening British resolution: a slow inoculation of danger in the blood. Each day that the battle raged further inland brought the people closer to war.

All over southern England, people prepared to meet the Germans with all the sang-froid they could muster. At Hadlow Down in Kent, Alan Henderson, a sharp-eyed ten-year-old, noted men kept their pitchforks at the ready, the girls their lipsticks: Luftwaffe aces could be very devastating. In Mercery Lane, Canterbury, a puzzled Home Guard hastened into George Woods' high-class cigar store: was there a brand of cigarettes called State Express 555? When Woods obliged, the man explained: "We've bagged a German pilot and he's sent me to get them." At Buckhurst, Earl De La Warr's Sussex estate, the butler with flawless composure announced: "An officer of the German armed forces is waiting to see you in the drawing-room, my lord."

Often the Germans proved equal to the occasion. At Duxford, a captured bomber crew begged the guardhouse for the loan of some boot polish: they were booked for inter-rogation and their flying boots were a disgrace. Farmer John Hacking, racing to the capture of a German pilot on Cadbor-ough Farm, near Rye, saw the man had lodged half-way through the tiled roof of a farm worker's backhouse. In faultless English he hailed Hacking: "I seem to have come from the shit into the shit."

Whether formal or frivolous, their morale measured up. Assistant Mechanic Alfred Lacey of Margate lifeboat, still recalls: "If they could stand at all, they stood at attention."

At Biggin Hill, the pilots of 32 Squadron liberated an ME 110 pilot from the guardhouse, bore him off to the mess for a drink, then took him for a tour of their dispersal. It wasn't until Pilot Officer Pniak, one of the squadron's Poles, chalked "Made in Germany, finished in England" over the squadron's trophies – a JU 88 machine-gun, the fin of a Heinkel – that the atmosphere grew noticeably starchy. Hastily his British hosts led the German away. And in Biggin Hill sick bay, Flight Lieutenant Robert Stanford Tuck, chatted so warmly with a shot-down Junkers 88 pilot that the lad, on an impulse, unslung the Iron Gross he still wore above his hospital-issue nightshirt.

He explained: "For me, the war is finished, but it would be nice for me to know that my cross is still flying – still free."

Flying or free, tactics were the topic when combatants met. Feldwebel Alfred Fraas, a Heinkel pilot of the 53rd Bomber Group, had barely crash-landed near Hornchurch, when his aggressor, Pilot Officer Pat McLintock, touched down and hurried up to him: would the German offer his candid opinion of McLintock's deflection shooting? And Pilot Officer Pyers Worrall, 85 Squadron, suspecting that Spitfire pilots of 65 Squadron were likely to claim *his* Dornier, landed beside it to seek the Germans' support.

To his glee, the pilot backed him to the hilt: Worrall had put out his compass and his starboard engine before the Spitfires ever started on him.

It was harder for the civilians – often each day was a twenty-four-hour vigil, as they awaited their own personal crisis. At 5 p.m., on August 28, the war, as never before, at last found Farmer Robert Bailey.

Until recently, Bailey hadn't for a second regretted his decision to stay on at Ladwood Farm. That deep shelter he'd dug behind the house had been finished days back – but to date not one of the family had needed to set foot in it. Yet now he worried – the lads from the searchlight crew at Blandred Farm were often at the back door, begging milk and home-made buns from Vera, his wife, and they brought strange rumours. They said that Hawkinge airfield might soon be evacuated – already the clerks and the main stores had been moved to quarters a mile away.

So Bailey had wondered: were the R.A.F. pulling out to leave civilians to their fate? Each day the B.B.C. news bulletins announced victories to cheer the heart – but from where Bailey stood at Ladwood, each German formation seemed to sweep through unopposed.

At 5 p.m., on this day, his thoughts were far from the war: weighed down by buckets of swill he was in the farmyard, with ninety plump grunting pigs clamouring for their feed. Five hundred yards away, on the crest of the hill by Ladwood Copse, old Rodney, the horse, was grazing peaceably, along with the cows and heifers. Bailey loved Rodney because the old horse belonged to the leisured past – though at twenty-three he still did his daily bit, hauling the cold sweet water from the 200-foot deep well in forty-gallon buckets.

Then, high above him in the sky, too far away to hear the roar of their engines, Bailey saw a formation of three Hurricanes flying from the direction of Canterbury. Suddenly, though he'd seen no German plane, one of the pilots baled out.

All unknown to Bailey, Sergeant George Smythe, of 56 Squadron, duelling with a 109, had no sooner got his man than his own petrol tank blew up. Drenched with petrol, benumbed by fumes, he somehow got clear at 20,000 feet.

As far as Bailey could judge the pilot would land some three miles from Hawkinge airfield – but though his eyes scanned the hazy blue, he couldn't see the abandoned Hurricane. Next instant he glimpsed it and his blood ran cold. It was spiralling to earth at 450 miles an hour, coming straight for Ladwood Farmhouse.

So petrified he couldn't even run or shout, Bailey watched, arms bowed like hoops under the weight of the swill buckets. He could hear the Hurricane now, the harsh, shrill screech of engines out of control, the plane coming straight for the farmhouse as if it planned a perfect three-point landing. Now a breeze teased gently at one wing, now the other, swerving it this way, then that – a swerve that could mean life or death to the people at Ladwood Farm.

Old Rodney and the cows were listening now, ears pricked as the shrieking tore, like a factory siren, at the warm almost windless air.

At that moment, Bailey's heart clenched. He saw now that the plane wouldn't hit the farmhouse, the direction was wrong – either it would hit the copse or it would rip a path across Barn Field, massacring the huddled animals. Why did they stay huddled like that? Why didn't they run?

Now, 500 yards from where he stood, the Hurricane struck the wood's topmost branches with idiot violence: the tall trees ripped white like matchwood, and it shattered on, cutting a swathe like a sickle for 100 yards, ploughing against the great stock of an ash tree. Then it blew up.

For Bailey this was the moment of truth. Suddenly "the whole wood seemed to take on leaves of fire" – a blaze so fearful that Folkestone fishermen, trolling for mackerel eighteen miles away off Dungeness, saw that red shifting skyline. Then, with a high-pitched scream of terror, old Rodney broke from the pasture. Followed by twenty thundering cows and heifers, he stampeded direct for the yard where Bailey stood rooted to the ground.

Abruptly, within yards of the farmer, the whole horde wheeled, screaming and blundering back towards the fire, and suddenly Bailey was running, too, pounding, he didn't know why, towards the fire. The air was thick with charred green leaves floating gently from the sky over Barn Field, and as he ran he saw a Spitfire corkscrewing out of control over Alkham, three miles away.

Above the crackling roar of the flames, running feet were audible: it was Bailey's neighbour, Mr Tobit of Standard Hill Farm. Dazedly, the two men exchanged news: three planes had crashed within seconds of one another, the ME 109 coming down in Garden Wood.

Now, though other locals were collecting, Bailey couldn't bring himself to stay and gossip. Irrationally, though there was nothing any man could do to protect the things he cherished against total war, he felt the need to be near Vera and the farmhouse. As he hurried back for Ladwood, a car packed with R.A.F. officers tore through the farmyard gate; a tall officer, cursing like a trooper, leapt out and hastened up to him. What had happened to the pilot? Had Bailey seen anything?

When Bailey reassured him, "He's safe enough. I saw him bale out, but there wasn't anything we could do for the plane," the officer seemed content. "We can get another plane," he said. "We can't get another pilot."

Robert Bailey said nothing. It hadn't occurred to him until then that pilots were hard to come by, and he wondered just how this battle would end. Moments earlier, the war had reached out to destroy everything that was most dear to him, then, unpredictably, had stayed its hand. He needed time to think, to readjust.

–

About this time, eight miles to the east, Winston Churchill's Humber staff car was squealing and skidding round the lanes north of Dover, hot on the trail of another falling plane. At intervals Churchill urged chauffeur Joseph Bullock, "Faster, man, faster." Deeply stirred by every aspect of the battle, Churchill had seen the plane hit and losing height 18,000 feet above the ramparts of Dover Castle; at once he commanded Bullock: "Follow that plane!" Beside him, secretary Mary Shearburn shut her eyes, unable to look: she was so afraid it would be a Spitfire.

In fact, it was an ME 109, which crashed on fire at Holly Lodge, Whitfield, three miles north of Dover; minutes earlier, the pilot, Leutnant Hans-Herbert Landry, had baled out. Surveying the molten wreckage, lost in thought, the old warrior grunted. "Well, that's *one* less."

It was true – yet in northern France, Air Fleet Two still had fighters and to spare. And at the same hour on August 28, Fighter Command approached their gravest pilot shortage yet.

More and more squadrons were so tired they must be plucked from the battle-line – and others, decimated by grass-green combat tactics, were withdrawing, too. The Defiants of 264 had already gone: a week earlier, after just eight days of battle, 266 Squadron had been pulled out. At Gravesend, 501 Squadron had a nominal strength of twelve officers – including the doctor, the intelligence officer and three men in hospital. Next day, after 470 hours operational flying, 615 Squadron must withdraw to Prestwick, Scotland.

Their C.O., Squadron Leader Joseph Kayll, summed up what many felt: "They're sending raids we're quite incapable of dealing with. It's just a matter of weeks before attrition."

And others were destined to go. By September, the pilots of 56 Squadron who'd flown with Geoffrey Page had left North Weald; at Hornchurch, 54 Squadron had five more days to go. As old Dunkirk hands they'd lost only nine aircraft, one pilot, in ten days, but survival was different from scoring.

It was hardly for want of trying, as none knew better than Flight Lieutenant Al Deere. Only that day, the young New Zealander and the pilots of 54 Squadron, up on one of five patrols, had joined in a low-level combat so frenzied Pilot Officer George Gribble shot a cow – while Sergeant Jock Norwell got back with a tree adorning his tailplane. Deere himself had kept up his amazing nine-lives record by baling out yet again.

What irked Deere most, on this third sortie over the North Foreland, was that his cine-guns had just recorded one of the strangest sights ever – an ME 109, caught by Deere's tracer, steadily inflating like a squat silver balloon until, balloon-like, it burst into a thousand shining pieces. Relieved that the film would confirm his marksmanship, Deere was delighted to see a Spitfire moving in to support, fully banked in a steep turn behind him. Abruptly the Spitfire opened up, and Deere's pleasure changed to fury – the trigger-happy pilot had severed his rudder control cables and smashed his port elevator.

Throttling back, Deere knew there was nothing for it: he'd have to abandon both plane and film. Whether he could maintain elevator control at lower, more turbulent altitudes was anybody's guess—and if he misjudged his approach, the Spitfire would be uncontrollable. He was at 10,000 feet now, and the engine was smoking ominously. Time to go.

Wary after that last near squeak that had almost pinned him to his plane, Deere made no attempt to turn the aircraft on its back; with the Spitfire almost stalled he went headlong over its side like a swimmer from a springboard. Near Detling airfield, sideslipping to dodge the roof of a farmhouse, Deere's 175 pounds landed comfortably in the farmer's plum tree, sending bushels of ripe fruit cascading to the earth.

Quivering with anger, covering him with a double-barrelled shotgun, the farmer roared: "Did you have to choose a prize tree to land in? I was saving that crop."

Back at Hornchurch, Deere reported to the squadron intelligence officer, Tony Allen: the cine-gun would have confirmed a 109 destroyed, but lacking witnesses he couldn't claim it as more than probable. He'd taken bursts at fully six others, but somehow they hadn't seemed to connect.

Shrugging, Deere spoke for every hard-pressed unit in the south: "We're so bloody tired we're just not getting them."

Chapter Seven

"Don't You Know There's a War On?"

August 28 – September 3

Pilot Officer Geoffrey Page lay in the Royal Masonic Hospital, Hammersmith, West London, sobbing helplessly. Minutes earlier, three old friends from 56 Squadron – "Jumbo" Gracie, Michael Constable-Maxwell, and Barry Sutton – had roistered from the room – and now, despite the hectic gaiety of their visit, Page felt an overwhelming sorrow.

For all their nonchalance, the charcoal circles under their eyes told him the strain 56 Squadron were facing, and no matter how great the personal disaster they must needs make a joke of it. "Jumbo" Gracie, his neck now in plaster, had joked, days back, that he could no longer crane round in the cockpit when fighting; his neck must be broken. Then Adjutant Basil Hudson prevailed on him to see the M.O. for X-rays and Gracie returned white and shaken: "My God, it *is* broken." Constable-Maxwell had escaped death as narrowly, wrecking his plane in a crash-landing that had left him with the radio in his lap, only the cockpit intact.

Others were dead, and the three had passed it off as light-heartedly as if they'd been discussing cricket scores.

Now, though he wept, Page couldn't have said why – was it self-pity, the knowledge that friends had died, or regret that he was no longer part of squadron life? He didn't know – and within hours he was to suffer the worse setback yet.

For the first time the staff nurse looking after him, who'd fed him and tended him ever since his transfer, days back, from Margate General Hospital, brought a Red Cross trainee to help with the dressings. To Page, she was one of the loveliest girls he'd ever seen – but what went through him like a knife was the uncontrolled horror in her eyes.

Hypnotised, Page saw, as if for the first time, the solid slough of boils covering his forearms from elbow to wrist. From wrist to finger tips his hands were blacker than ebony, smaller than he'd ever remembered them. Then the staff nurse's voice came drily, "That black stuff's tannic acid. It's not the colour of your skin."

As Page felt relief flow through him, the trainee, her face working, ran headlong from the room.

The silence seemed to stretch for ever, and now the fear that had obsessed Page ever since Margate was surging uncontrollably: What had the fire done to his face? Why wouldn't they tell him? His voice icy, he commanded: "Get me a mirror, please, nurse."

Still working carefully at the dressings, the nurse soothed him: "That girl is a brilliant pianist, but an inexperienced nurse. The sight of your wounds was a great shock to her." Coldly, Page ignored her. "I should like a mirror, please, nurse."

Evenly, selecting sterile wool with forceps, the nurse answered, "You'll see yourself in a mirror all in good time." But now Geoffrey Page's blood was up: hectoringly, he repeated the request. For the first time the nurse's voice was as cold as his own. "You'll be allowed to look in a mirror, Pilot Officer Page, when I see fit to permit it and not before."

For ten silent minutes Page lay there hating her, until at last dropping the tweezers with a clank into a kidney dish, she propelled the trolley from the room, without one parting word. Now, with a twenty-year-old's stubbornness, Page vowed: "Right – I'll look in the bloody mirror if it kills me." In fact, the mirror hung over the washbasin, only two steps distant from his bed – but how to dislodge the bedclothes, which were tucked with hospital efficiency beneath the mattress? Five minutes painful heaving with his elbows, sobbing for breath, had moved them as far as the cradle that kept the sheets from his injured leg. Now he'd only to sit up and swing his legs over the edge of the bed – no easy task when he couldn't even use his hands for support. A wave of dizziness swept over him, teetering high on the edge of the bed, above the polished floor.

Gingerly, straightening his back, Page slid feet first to the ground. But the movement jolted his elbow painfully; his leg muscles were growing weaker by the second. As he took the first trepidant step forward, icy sweat bathed him; he felt his knees buckle. One lurching pace further, squeezing the moisture from his eyes, he reached the mirror.

Then two things happened as one: the door swung suddenly open behind him and he saw the staff nurse's face, shocked and drawn, loom beyond his left shoulder. For one hideous second the black swollen mass that had been his face swam and bobbed in the mirror glass. Then mercifully, the room reeled and he smashed unconscious against the washbasin.

The battle to be a fighter pilot was over; for Page another, greater, battle was just beginning.

But for scores of Dowding's pilots, the shooting war had only now begun – and with little concept of what lay ahead, they greeted the news with gold-rush fervour. At Prestwick, Scotland, the officers of 253 Hurricane Squadron had word towards midnight that they were heading south. At once, trussing up a cushion to simulate a football, they invited the N.C.O. pilots over for a massive free-for-all that smashed all the mess furniture and left Squadron Leader Tom Gleave, the G.O., with a black eye.

And as 603 Squadron flew south from Turnhouse, Scotland, one pilot, Richard Hillary, recalled a moving moment: the children of the Tarfside valley, hands raised in silent farewell as the squadron dived in salute, immobile on the sunlit grass beside the white boulders they'd arranged to spell: "Good Luck". On August 27, 603 landed at Hornchurch airfield, Essex – and 222 Squadron landed soon after, parking their Spitfires wing-tip to wing-tip as neatly as in peacetime.

Promptly the fiery Wing Commander Bouchier hailed Squadron Leader Johnnie Hill: "What the hell do you think you're doing lining up planes like that? Get them staggered and dispersed – don't you know there's a war on?"

Within hours, both squadrons knew. In Hornchurch mess, an Old Etonian pilot had just said flippantly to Pilot Officer Bill Read, a newcomer to 603, "Half of the Germans we're fighting haven't had a decent education – not what *we'd* call a decent education," when the first scramble came; from this first sortie, Flight Lieutenant Don MacDonald didn't return. Of the twenty-four who'd flown south on this August day, just eight would fly back.

That night, a New Zealander, Donald Carbury, voiced the sober truth to Pilot Officer Richard Hillary: "You don't have to look for them – you have to look for a way out."

It was as bad for 222 Squadron. Scrambled within thirty-five minutes of reaching Hornchurch, they lost seven planes on their first day – with one pilot killed, two injured. Few had seen any action until now; one man trustingly landed at Rochford, Hornchurch's satellite, through the lane of yellow flags marking unexploded bombs, assuming it was a flight-path. The survivors retired to make their wills on toilet paper.

It was a wise precaution. Despite their two weeks' crash-course, pilot losses were fast outstripping the training units' yield; in all August they'd turned out only 260 pilots, and casualties had totalled 300. Now the pilot wastage was approaching 120 men a week; from May right through August, losses had averaged 476 pilots a month – 346 killed or missing, 130 wounded. And aircraft production was falling, too – in the thirteen days following August 24, 466 fighters had been destroyed or damaged as against a total of 269 new or repaired. From July onwards, aircraft production had fallen by 19 per cent; aero-engines by 26 per cent.

As the losses mounted, the men close to Dowding knew that only a miracle could save the R.A.F. now.

But some men were in the mood for miracles. At Northolt airfield, Squadron Leader Zdzislaw Krasnodebski had seen his pilots' spirits sink daily lower – and their hatred for Group Captain Stanley Vincent grow daily more intense. Though more than 100 Poles serving with British squadrons had played their part in the Battle's first three weeks, the all-Polish squadron was still grounded – for Vincent felt their grasp of English was still too rudimentary to risk their lives in the air.

Conscious that it was he who'd led these men on their 2,000-mile crusade, the dark intense Krasnodebski felt deeply responsible. Each small link that forged a fraternity between Pole and Briton had become a landmark in his life... the night Squadron Leader Ronald Kellett, the joint-commander, first drove them all to dinner at the glossy "Orchard" restaurant in his Rolls-Royce... the way the pilots had so taken to Winnipeg-born Johnnie Kent, the flight commander, that they'd christened him "Kentowski"... the riotous night when an English pilot wouldn't stand for the Polish officers' anthem, *Jeszeze Polska nie Zgineta* (Poland Is Not Yet Lost) and "Kentowski" bloodied his nose, hauling him to attention.

From the first, Krasnodebski and Kellett had been of one mind on tactics; those tight V-shaped formations were out from the start. Weaving and straggling, Polish-style, like a small independent air force, they flew fully four yards apart, line abreast with each clutch of four planes fifteen yards apart, each man keeping a sharp eye peeled for the safety of his neighbour.

Relaxed in a deck chair at the Polish dispersal, Krasnodebski surveyed affectionately the men who'd come so far with him – blonde, blue-eyed Flying Officer Ludwig Paszkiewicz; a shy, unassuming boy, Jan Zumbach, with his deep rumbling voice; the handsome clean-cut Witor Urbanowicz. All of them had shared warm moments together since Warsaw burned – like the time when they first arrived in England, and learned the phrase, "Four whiskies". It was a drink they'd come to like better than vodka – but till they'd learned the meaning of "four" it had always been four whiskies, no matter how many or how few Poles were in the party.

Now Krasnodebski would have welcomed action, to stifle the memories of Wanda, his wife – it had been weeks now since he'd heard from her. But he still had patience to contain himself – unlike some others who'd militantly asked Johnnie Kent: "If we've got to train, why can't we go and train over the French coast?"

Then, at 4.35 p.m., on August 30, at the hour of Air Chief Marshal Dowding's deepest despair, No. 303 Squadron, by blindest chance, became operational. As they took off from Northolt at 4.15 p.m., gaining height to 10,000 feet, their training flight was as routine as could be: north of St. Albans in Hertfordshire, they were to rendezvous with six Blenheims and execute dummy attacks on them. Twenty minutes later, at 4.35 p.m., young Ludwig Paszkiewicz, glancing down, stared, perplexed. Below, the tiny cathedral town slept in the August sun, but smoke furled steadily from a cluster of roofs like the prelude to an Indian attack.

At that moment Paszkiewicz saw another smoke trail, plunging downwards to meet the first: a Hurricane much like his own. A thousand feet above them, to port, sixty German bombers, as many 109s and a handful of British fighters were caught up in a running battle. At once he alerted Squadron Leader Kellett: "Hullo, Apany Leader, bandits ten o'clock." But if Kellet had heard he made no rejoinder. Pressing the emergency control, which sent his supercharger to a maximum twelve boosts, Paszkiewicz broke for the battle.

In fact, the phlegmatic Kellett had heard the warning clearly, grunting, "If you want to be a hero, be one" – but though it was too late to restrain Paszkiewicz, he wouldn't allow others to follow. There was still an exercise in progress – and with 109s on the warpath they must now scrap the dummy attacks and escort the Blenheims safely to Northolt.

But Krasnodebski saw it differently: this was his beloved squadron's turning point. For now, as Paszkiewicz winged towards the formation, the young Pole saw a strange plane turning towards him, then banking into a steep dive; following in a half-roll he saw the black cross marking its wing – a Dornier. From 100 yards dead astern, Paszkiewicz fired 303 Squadron's first symbolic burst, firing until the starboard engine gouted flame. He was still firing when a crewman baled out, then the bomber dived, more steeply still, lurching for the ground.

Watching, Krasnodebski felt a glow of love and pride. He knew how hard Paszkiewicz had fought to become a pilot; resisting all contentions that his temperament was wrong – and now this boy's sheer dogged determination had given the squadron its first victory.

Back over Northolt, when Paszkiewicz threw his Hurricane into a victory roll, the Polish maintenance men, under tough old Flight Sergeant Starzynski, grinned but kept on working; the only wonder was that Kellett had kept his unruly pack on the leash so long. But Paszkiewicz, as he touched down, knew a sudden qualm: had the squadron been engaged in a really worthwhile battle somewhere while he'd wasted all that time on a lone bomber?

In fact, though they hadn't, it was the forerunner of many to come. Air Staff officers might explode that the Poles were incapable of observing discipline, but Kellett, seeing their morale at fever-pitch, knew it was time to act. Phoning Fighter Command, he urged: "Under the circumstances, I do think we might call them operational."

Without hesitation, Dowding had agreed. The Poles were needed now, as never before.

Worse, for the first time since the battle began, the German raiders were getting through for steadily diminishing losses:

small compact bomber units, no more than twenty strong, shielded by three times as many fighters, probing for – and finding – their targets.

And time and again, the newcomer squadrons ignored Air Vice-Marshal Park's edict: Strike for the bombers that will do the damage; whenever possible, leave the fighters alone. On August 28 their disregard of this order had cost the R.A.F. twenty Hurricanes and Spitfires for thirty-one German planes – and twelve of those had been bombers. Next day, with 564 ME 109s and 159 ME 110s in a massive fighter sweep over Kent, Park kept his squadrons on a tight rein – but it was plain now that, unhampered by the Stukas, the Germans could get through.

To Reichsmarschall Hermann Goring, it was vital that they should. Plans for "Operation Sea-Lion" had reached a crisis point now: on August 23, the German Army and Navy had clashed decisively. Gross-Admiral Erich Raeder, the Navy's Commander-in-Chief, had urged that landings must be confined to the narrow Straits of Dover; naval strength just wasn't adequate to win command of any larger area. To the Army, a landing on so cramped a front was plain suicide. As Generaloberst Franz Haider, Chief of the Army General Staff, had put it: "I might as well put the troops that have landed straight through a sausage machine."

Then, on August 27, Hitler stepped in with a compromise. Why not confine the landings to four main areas – between Folkestone and Dungeness, Dungeness and Cliff's End, Bexhill and Beachy Head and Brighton to Selsey Bill? Still the Navy were dubious. To land eleven divisions between the North Foreland and the Isle of Wight might call for two million tons of shipping.

In the last resort, it was plain, everything must depend on the Luftwaffe's vanquishing the R.A.F.

The trouble was that few Luftwaffe pilots had much belief in the invasion as such. Though by no means beaten, the invasion preparations they'd seen to date seemed as amateurish as could be. Off Le Touquet, Oberleutnant Victor Bauer's 3rd Wing, Fighter Group Three, saw only a weatherworn fleet of apple barges; near Calais, Hauptmann Hans-Heinrich Brustellin of the 51st Fighter Group, choked with mirth to see a fussy flotilla of old Rhine steamers assembling. Incredulously, he said: "But it's like a travelling circus."

Major Max Ibel's 27th Fighter Group felt the same: in their one combined operation with the Army, thirty pontoons had broken from their moorings and been carried away by the tide. Before the exercise could proceed, the Luftwaffe had to lay on rescue launches to tow the drifting pioneers back to safety.

At Audembert, Major Adolf Galland impatiently took time off to hear a commission of staff officers praise his 26th Fighter Group to the skies: following a successful invasion, they would have the honour of being the first unit to land in England. When a long memo followed, minutely detailing how to prepare trucks for sea transport, Galland, shrugging, tossed it in his out-tray. The top brass were always on about something.

It wasn't that Galland and his men were disheartened: by now the Cap Gris Nez-Dover route was so familiar, pilots christened it "The Reichs Autobahn" – and sometimes "*Flak-strasse*". But neither Galland nor Werner Molders believed that the R.A.F. could be destroyed on the ground – though at Kesselring's underground H.Q., despite Galland's protests, bombers no sooner strafed an airfield than Kesselring personally struck from the map every unit stationed there.

As a result, Baron Speck von Sternberg's 3rd Wing, 27th Bomber Group, told that the British fighter arm no longer existed, sent twenty unescorted Heinkels along the English Channel to wipe out a whole chain of targets. To the bomber crews' chagrin, six didn't return, fourteen were severely damaged. The top-brass insistence on "the last fifty Spitfires" seemed perilously close to whistling in the dark.

Yet the Luftwaffe were faring better than they knew. All that week they'd punched home their attacks... the successful

Eastchurch–Rochford raid that Major Galland had escorted… a punishing strike against the 300-acre sector station at Debden in Essex… a strategic fifty-bomb sortie on Detling airfield, which cut the mains cable and fired the oil tanks.

Then by sheer mischance, a mains supply failure along the eighty miles of coastline between Whitstable and Beachy Head put the radar stations out of action. At 6 p.m., on August 30, when young Ludwig Paszkiewicz was just touching down at Northolt, there was nothing to warn Squadron Leader Roger Frankland, the duty controller at Biggin Hill Sector Station, that nine Junkers 88 dive-bombers, loaded with 1,000-pounders, feinting towards the Thames Estuary, had now turned south, driving for Biggin Hill.

Already Major Max Ibel's 27th Fighter Group, stepped up at any height between 15,500 and 25,000 feet, had free-hunted ahead of the bombers – and now, to make doubly sure, Major Hannes Trautloft's 54th Group flew with them as strong fighter escort. But today, with the cloud layer at 7,000 feet, the Observer Corps knew nothing of this – they were plotting by ear alone.

At Biggin Hill, there were only minutes of warning before the bombers were upon them. Biggin's Spitfire Squadron, No. 610, was too high and too far away from base to tackle the raiders: only one unit, No. 79 Hurricane Squadron, remained as defence. As they banked in their first circuit after take-off, the 1,000-pounders were already scattering from the bomb-bays. Distractedly, Squadron Leader Frankland tried to raise 501 Squadron, then patrolling from Hawkinge, but the first bombs severed the radio telephone link-up; though a few of Squadron Leader Harry Hogan's 501 pilots heard Frankland's cry, "Mandrel Leader, they're bombing Rastus," Hogan himself heard nothing. Now Frankland called the look-out on the officers' mess roof: "Identify aircraft making low-level attack."

Back came the look-out's anguished cry, "Hello, Control, have no time to identify – am being attacked by a swarm of bees."

In the shelter at the far end of the WA.A.F. quarters, Corporal Elspeth Henderson, at this moment off-duty from the Ops Room, felt the walls transmit every salvo like a depth charge through water, yet strangely she knew no fear. Ever since Group Captain Grice's stirring words following the bombing of Kenley, she'd steeled herself for this. Hadn't she, of her own free will, forsaken the parties and dances of her unthreatened Edinburgh to come south and see it through in the front line? A steel helmet on her trim red hair, Elspeth sat determinedly on.

It was a quaking nightmare to come. Flat on his face near the main guardhouse, Leading Fireman Patrick Duffy saw an old hydrant-plate leap like a jack-in-the-box from the solid earth. In a slit trench close by, Section Officer Pamela Beecroft noticed that few were talking: the sharp crack of lightweight bombs followed by the deep vibrant roar of the 1,000-pounders ruled out speech. Beside her, Flight Lieutenant Michael Crossley, a Hurricane ace who yearned to be airborne, hummed "It's Only a Paper Moon", and mimed the strumming of a ukelele. Soundlessly, in the thick darkness, a W.A.A.F. repeated the Lord's Prayer. There was no panic, no hysteria.

In another trench, a W.A.A.F. who still had her voice had just remarked, "I think we're being dive-bombed," when the concrete walls caved in like a medieval torture chamber, smothering more than forty girls with tons of chalky earth and stones. Suddenly, from the choking darkness, they heard the W.A.A.F. Flight Sergeant Gartside exclaim, "My God, they've broken my neck" – then, incongruously: "And they've broken my false teeth, too!" Pinned there in the darkness, waiting to be dug out, there wasn't a girl who could help laughing.

Some saved their lives by sheer chance. Corporal John Tapp and his mate Amos Collins had just emerged from the airmen's mess when the first bombs came tumbling; at once they joined the throng of running men, carrying their mess tins, streaming across the tennis courts for the nearest shelter. On an impulse, both men decided to stay in the open, ducking round the side of the building. Behind them, machine-gun bullets ripped through a line of dustbins as if they'd been tinplate.

When next they looked the shelter was gone – nothing but a monstrous jagged crater, strewn with blue shreds of uniform cloth and the butchered bodies of airmen.

Aircraftman Harold Mead hadn't fancied the shelter either. Tagging onto the end of the queue, he'd just passed in when the thought struck him – they wouldn't allow him to smoke. Among the last to enter, Mead was now the first out, pelting through falling bombs, hitching a ride on a truck to 610 Squadron's dispersal. Fitter Bertie Alkins made for dispersal, too – diving from the mess window, with a man-sized bread and jam sandwich, grabbing a handy bicycle, bent double and pedalling furiously. As a low-flying Dornier swooped, a bullet hit his front wheel, sending Alkins flying.

Furious, oblivious to bombs and bullets, he dashed his jam sandwich to the ground, shaking his fist at the Germans.

Others survived as narrowly. W.A.A.F. driver Jackie Day was piloting two officers in her Humber station waggon when the raid began; ten seconds after they piled out into Elspeth Henderson's shelter, a bomb fell twenty-five feet away. Airborne above the drome, Pilot Officer George Nelson-Edwards, saw the Humber whoosh skywards to meet him, landing sixty feet up on a hangar roof before plunging through to the concrete floor. In the sergeants' mess, the N.C.O.s, ignoring the bombing, were clustered round the radio, tuned in to Sergeant Ronnie Hamlyn's broadcast on his bag of five German planes. As Hamlyn finished speaking, their appointed slit trench close by was wiped out.

On all sides, the devastation was appalling. Ninety per cent of the station's transport had been damaged or destroyed... one hangar had taken a direct hit... two aircraft had been burned out... the workshop and many barracks made uninhabitable... all electricity, water and gas mains cut... a staggering death-roll of thirty-nine dead, twenty-six injured.

Now, as the fury of the bombing passed, an eerie silence fell: slowly, dazedly, people began to emerge from their shelters. In the distance, Elspeth Henderson heard a faint far droning: with empty magazines, the Hurricanes of No. 79 Squadron were returning. A panting messenger, thrusting into Section Officer Pamela Beecroft's trench, begged the chaplain, the Reverend A. J. Gillespie: "Could you come at once, sir? A trench has been hit."

Scrambling in their wake, the W.A.A.F. C.O., Section Officer Felicity Hanbury, felt in urgent need of a cigarette; it wasn't until she'd lit it and was nearing the ruins of the W.A.A.F. guardhouse that she noticed the poisonous tang of coal gas. With unwitting irony, a stentorian voice hailed her: "Put that cigarette out, or you'll blow the place to pieces."

It was an unforgettable sight... grey-white mounds of chalk and concrete looming everywhere... the pungent reek of gas and plaster-dust ... hangars burning as brightly as birthday candles... the blue shadows of evening gathering over the hayricks and apple orchards in the peaceful valley below.

But the blind fury of the raid had one result: every man and woman on the station was seized by the urge to help. Already airmen, helped by an old countryman who tended the officers' mess garden, were digging in tight-lipped silence to reach all those entombed inside their shelters. Pilots came running from their cockpits to lend a hand; ambulance and stretcher parties stood by, along with a Salvation Army canteen, the first on the spot. Clawing with bare hands at the rubble, Corporal John Tapp winced: the black, congested face of one of his own airmen was staring vacantly up at him.

For eighteen-year-old Harold Mead it was suddenly too much; he'd quit the airmen's shelter for a smoke and now lads he knew were being hauled "like rag dolls" from the debris. Trembling with shock, he was led by a W.A.A.F. to the officers' mess for a strangely unpalatable snack: kippers and hot sweet tea. As he choked it down, a, man circled on a bicycle, blowing a bugle, as dusk fell on the dead.

Mead wasn't surprised to find himself in such surroundings; tonight everyone was weighing in as and where they could. Leading Fireman Patrick Duffy joined Sergeant Joan Mortimer from the Armoury in marking every unexploded bomb on the airfield with a red flag; the hangars were too well ablaze now to need a fireman's attentions, but when the fighters took off at first light, they'd need a flight path charted for them. Elspeth Henderson's place was normally in the Ops Room, but it wasn't her shift and there was work to be done freeing the W.A.A.F.s still trapped in their shelter. One by one the bodies were brought out, their faces barely recognisable under a sticky paste of chalk and blood, but all save one, Corporal Lena Button, a Tasmanian nursing orderly, was alive.

Briskly, doing as an officer had bidden her, Elspeth and other W.A.A.F.s began to propel the shaken survivors up and down to restore their circulation – until a medical officer, with a cry of protest, stopped them short. Others besides the W.A.A.F. Flight Sergeant Gartside had broken their backs.

In the small village school at Hermalinghen, now the officers' club of the 54th Fighter Group, Major Hannes Trautloft and his pilots were having a party; two officers had this day been awarded the Iron Cross and Hauptmann Dietrich Hrabak had been newly promoted leader of the 2nd Wing. From upwards of 10,000 feet, the fighters' lowest level, they'd seen nothing of the Biggin Hill raid; they were celebrating for purely personal reasons.

Though the Germans couldn't know it, there was more than promotions to celebrate. At the height of the raid, the main London-Westerham cable connecting Biggin Hill with the outside world had been severed north of the airfield. Now the hard-pressed Hornchurch Sector Station, covering the Thames Estuary, must assume control of Biggin's squadrons and satellites, Gravesend and Redhill, as well as its own, Rochford – six squadrons to manoeuvre in combat over 5,000 square miles of sky.

The key to Dowding's whole system was constantly open telephone lines – but now, with Biggin Hill's lines out, how would the R.A.F. intercept the bombers if they chose the direct southern route to London lying within Biggin's orbit? As the hours crawled, Headquarters Fighter Command didn't know.

In Biggin Hill village, it seemed they didn't care. As Section Officer Felicity Hanbury with Pamela Beecroft trudged from house to house, seeking billets for all whose barracks had been blitzed, they met up with bitter opposition. Door after door was slammed in their faces – if the R.A.F. hadn't settled in, the German raiders would never have come. It was nine hours before they'd found the billets they needed, and time was running short. With water at a premium, Biggin's airmen got just half a cup of tea that morning – to drink or shave in, as they chose.

But the Post Office had taken Biggin Hill's troubles to heart. Inspector Abraham Thomson, a brawny Scottish maintenance engineer, was at home in Tonbridge, sixteen miles away, when word came through of the severed cable: though the airfield's Post Office maintenance officer had been blown clean out of a shelter trench, he'd still stumbled to the nearest Post Office Exchange to report the damage. The operators had evacuated – but with the aid of a lone workman the engineer manned the switchboard to alert Maintenance Control at Tunbridge Wells.

About 9 p.m. – three hours after the bombing – Thomson, his foreman, Mossy Adams, and their six-strong working party set out for Biggin Hill, Thomson and Adams in the Inspector's Ford Prefect, the working party following by truck. Now the true urgency of their mission struck home to them; the night was inky-black; somewhere above the clouds a German bomber droned; beyond Westerham the Home Guard refused them even parking lights to steer by. Towards 10 p.m., after hitting a bank with bone-jarring impact, Thomson and Adams had scaled the long gradient that led to Biggin Hill.

By now the airfield was as quiet as a plague city; only a man from the Metropolitan Water Board, looming from the darkness, warned that it was prudent to walk warily. Opposite the officers' mess, a crater split the earth; near the Met Office, north of the airfield, was one larger still – twenty-six yards wide, thirty feet deep. In the silence, Thomson heard the hiss of gas, a broken water main gurgling like a brook. Until first light, at least, there was nothing the engineers could do. Cramped in a rat-infested shelter, they settled to a game of cribbage.

At dawn, on Saturday, August 31, Thomson and his crew set to work... slithering down the shingly sides of the six-feet-deep fissure by the officers' mess, where the main cable was severed... Jointer Sid Sharvill and his mates armed with blow-lamp, lead cutters, wire brushes, crowbars, lead sleeves to seal the repaired wires. The cable, made up of seventy-four pairs of wires, with a gauge of forty pounds to the mile, was ruptured in three places; it would be a three-hour job, at best, before they could hope to effect repairs.

But this morning, luck wasn't with the engineers. After half an hour below ground, Thomson's limbs were heavy as lead, he gulped thickly for air – carbon monoxide from a leaking gas main was making them all sick and dizzy. As they clawed from the crater, the siren, for the first time that day, whined up over the Kentish valleys. It was 8.30 a.m.

Sixty miles south-east, over Dover, Oberleutnant Hans von Hahn, 3rd Fighter Group, his sights set at 600 yards range, fired a long burst, banking sharply away to avoid collision as one of Dover's barrage balloons, sixty-five feet wide by twenty-five deep, burst into vivid scarlet flames. As it sank towards the seaport, bannering pitch-black clouds of smoke, other pilots of the 3rd Group opened up as one: wave after wave of fighters blasted at the balloons like boys at a shooting gallery. Soon fifty of them, spaced 450 yards apart, had fallen, trailing fire and smoke towards the sea.

Often in the past, returning from a mission, fighter pilots had shot up the balloons for the sheer fun of seeing them burn – until Goring grumpily vetoed it as a waste of ammunition.

But this morning the attacks had the Reichsmarschall's entire approval. Clearly visible from the French coast, the burning balloons signalled that the skies were clear for the day's all-out onslaught.

At Biggin Hill, Abraham Thomson's working party had scant warning of the raider's return. Group Captain Grice had briefed them: pay no heed to air-raid warnings from north or south, wait for the camp's bugler to signal imminent danger. Before noon, the bugle had blared three times – and three times the airfield had come under spasmodic attack. Scrambling from their crater, Thomson's men each time took to their truck, careering off the aerodrome into the trees – then toiled back to their repair work yet again.

But each half-hour, raiders or not, they crawled out beaten, greedy for oxygen, their heads throbbing and weak from coal gas. No food came their way, and there was no water to quench their thirst.

But miraculously, the morning's main raids had been well to the east – at Detling, Eastchurch and again at Debden. By midday, groggy from the foul air, Thomson could report to Flight Lieutenant Osmond, Biggin Hill's signals officer, that the main cable was restored. The telephone links with H.Q. 11 Group, the Observer Corps, the radio telephone transmitting and receiving links with the squadrons were intact again – and Biggin Hill was back on the air.

But the local cables, connecting the Ops Room with the Met Office and the pilot's dispersals, were still out. Soon after noon Thomson's crew set to work.

For everyone at Biggin Hill it had been a memorably unhappy Saturday. For Elspeth Henderson, life as a shift worker was never easy; though her quarters were a bare 150 yards from the Ops Room, outside the main airfield on the Westerham-London road, there was no running water, so that even taking hot baths was a complex rigmarole of firing an old-fashioned boiler beneath the tub. Then, too, the W.A.A.F. plotters' mess was in a converted cafe three miles away at Keston village. No man to ring the changes, the cook doled out corned beef three times a day – but to eat at all Elspeth had to hitch transport there as and when she could.

On August 31, Elspeth had done her best to help spruce up the billet – the quarters were still habitable, though bombing had shaken tiles and some of the brickwork loose. Often, before a late afternoon shift, she and other plotters enjoyed a game of tennis, but today even tennis was out. Incendiary bombs had cratered the courts; broken shards of concrete, scattered all over the camp, cut the shoes to ribbons.

Just before 4 p.m., showing her pass to the armed sentry, Elspeth entered the main Ops Room – sited directly opposite the airfield's main gates, across the London Road. A few moments earlier, a passing housewife had pressed a bag of apples on her – they'd help to stave off hunger pangs on the six-hour shift that lay ahead.

Already, as the outgoing crew, thirty strong, handed over, the small oblong room, facing north towards the officer's mess, was alive with murmuring figures, shuffling papers, consulting scribbling pads. Swiftly Elspeth took up her station on the long wooden dais, raised five feet above the main room, where plotters, connected by head-and-breast sets to the Observer Corps centres and Fighter Command's Filter Room, were huddled round a huge glass wall-map of the sector. Fitting on her own headset, Elspeth now checked her own permanent line to H.Q. 11 Group, who'd control the first moves of the battle. This afternoon, two duty controllers had slipped into the seats on her left – Senior Controller Roger Frankland and 32 Squadron's former C.O., John Worrall. To her right, Pilot Officer Arthur Bennett manned the keyboard linking him with 11 Group and with Biggin's squadron dispersals.

Now Elspeth felt a subdued stir of excitement. Of all the controllers she found the quiet, nonchalant Worrall easiest to work with – but two controllers on duty was a sign that something might break. Since no controller could handle above two squadrons at a time, two men on duty spelt trouble.

It was a shrewd intuition. For more than an hour, there was only subdued activity... checks on unidentified aircraft entering the sector... Elspeth carefully entering up the Ops Room log... noting that as yet none of Biggin's machines were airborne. The wall-display panel showed the newly-arrived 72 Spitfire Squadron now at readiness; at dispersal the pilots were still pondering why 610 Squadron, whom they'd relieved, had seemed so anxious to depart. Across the airfield, 79 Squadron also stood by.

At 5.37 p.m., the Observer Corps were on the line: twenty miles east in the Maidstone area, the air-raid warning had sounded. The crew around the Ops Room wall-map were plotting furiously now: an unknown number of raiders was approaching from the south-west making for the line of the Ashford-Redhill railway. Eight minutes later, Elspeth was scribbling frantically: in her earphones, 11 Group Control were ordering Biggin's squadrons airborne. The message passed to Pilot Officer Bennett then swiftly to Frankland and Worrall.

Worrall seized the microphone; all over Biggin Hill's 500 acres his voice echoed, metallic, weirdly impersonal: "Tenis Squadron, scramble. Tenis Squadron scramble. Patrol base." Twenty-plus Spitfires of 72 Squadron were airborne within minutes, heading *for* Maidstone.

A pause, then the unemotional voice again: "Pansy Squadron, scramble. Pansy Squadron, scramble. Protect base." With only six machines serviceable, it was doubtful whether 79 Squadron could put up more than token resistance – but they were more vulnerable still on the ground. Simultaneously Frankland ordered the flight supervisor: "Sergeant Greave. Steel helmets!" And he added a rider: the old Ops Block had no reinforced concrete roof; everybody not urgently required on duty should take shelter.

Gingerly fitting on her steel helmet, Elspeth Henderson ignored the suggestion: even now it was hard to master the art of

195

balancing a helmet on top of headphones. As for taking shelter, it never once occurred to her: someone had to keep the line to 11 Group manned until the squadrons had intercepted – and it was her job, too, to check how long they'd been airborne, warning the controller if fuel was running short. And who knew where danger would strike? Time and again raids had feinted towards them, then struck for Croydon or Kenley – it was a philosophy she'd carefully cultivated as the weeks went by.

In the tiny telephone exchange outside the main Ops Room, Sergeant Helen Turner, a World War One veteran, reached the same decision. Often in leisure moments, she'd made Elspeth chuckle over stories of a telephone operator's life at the Savoy Hotel and the strange quirks of the rich: here, with equal composure, she sat on at the switchboard linking the Ops Room to the rest of Biggin Hill.

Aching silence now; the ticking of the synchronised wall clock fretted the nerves like water on stone. On this sultry evening, the temperature was in the eighties; like everyone else in the room, Elspeth had thrown off her tunic, was working in blouse and skirt. As if mesmerised, she watched the plotters coloured counters, bringing the raid closer second by second.

Worrall again, his voice measured: "This is an air-raid warning. This is an air-raid warning. All personnel except those employed on essential services are to take cover immediately. Switching off." Now Frankland to the squadrons: "Hello, Tenis leader, this is Rastus. Enemy approaching base, angels ten. Attack imminent. Attack on Rastus imminent. Do what you can."

Split seconds later, Pilot Officer Bennett and all of them heard the voice of the look-out, breathy with excitement, from the officers' mess roof: "Twenty Dorniers, sir, coming from the sun – they're coming straight at us." At once Group Captain Grice, who'd just then entered, ordered: "Now, all you girls, under the table."

Elspeth Henderson was never too certain what happened then. She'd kept the line open for Group's instructions as long as she could, but no plotting or controlling was possible now; along with Frankland, Worrall and the rest, she piled beneath the table. What struck her most was the uncanny silence: the guns had all ceased fire to leave the few fighters aloft unimpeded. Suddenly, as Pilot Officer Arthur Bennett will always recall, a telephone rang stridently, and Grice asked: "Who is going to be brave enough to answer that?"

As fast as a falling curtain, chaos descended. With a thin, high whistling, a 500-pounder loosed by one of Oberst Johannes Fink's Dorniers tore through the Ops Room roof, bouncing violently from a steel safe, exploding in the Defence Teleprinter Network room next door. Simultaneously, as the lights went out, the glass plotting screen burst from its frame, shattering on the steel helmets of the crouching W.A.A.F.s, spraying slivers of glass everywhere. Peering from the table where she'd hastily taken shelter, Sergeant Helen Turner saw knife-edged steel fragments slice her switchboard in two.

Strangely, nobody seemed unnerved; despite the whirling blizzard of plaster dust, they acted as if danger was their heritage. One of the first men on his feet, Aircraftman Townsend, the Ops Room runner, had already hit on a way out – through the window and along a narrow crevice between the Ops Room and the outer blast wall. He exhorted Elspeth Henderson: "Come along, Miss, you can get through here, show them how to squeeze through." Peppered in the face and elbows by flying glass, Group Captain Grice was groping on hands and knees for his pipe, cursing strenuously: not until he'd located it, undamaged, would he follow on. Pilot Officer Bennett, checking a girl who moved back to the wreckage, was told: "If you please, sir, I forgot my knitting."

Courage or not, it seemed as if the end was near. By 6.30 p.m., the Observer Corps at Bromley had warned Fighter Command: "Biggin Hill Operations Room on fire. They cannot take any more." Nine minutes later, Kenley Sector Station pressed Bromley: in this emergency they'd have to handle Biggin's squadrons, but they had no note of either call signs or radio frequencies. One hour later, with still no word from Biggin, Kenley's C.O., Wing Commander Tom Prickman, sent a motor cycle despatch rider speeding for Biggin. Sickened, the cornier reported back: "The place is like a slaughterhouse."

In fact, there'd been few deaths – only devastation. Inspector Abraham Thomson's temporary lash-up of lines and power cables had been severed yet again – within six hours of completion. Grimly, Thomson and his men resigned themselves to the worst; there was still two hours' work to be done on the local cables, and by then it would be too dark to see. Tomorrow, they'd start work on the main cable all over again.

Still Elspeth Henderson found it hard to take in; the plaster dust had lodged deep in her lungs and she couldn't stop coughing. At intervals she explained, almost fiercely, that the blood on her shirt-front had been spilt by someone else, and she didn't need first aid at all. On the airfield two Spitfires burned with a white incandescent flame, and a truck circled the perimeter, its driver shouting: "Any airwomen want somewhere to sleep tonight?"

At this moment Elspeth didn't know whether she lacked a billet or not; the road was so cratered she couldn't even get back to see if her quarters were still intact. Then the question was decided for her, because word came through that the Emergency Ops Room would be functioning within the hour in a commandeered butcher's shop in Biggin Hill village, and the duty watch, bloody, dusty, and still in their shirtsleeves, would repair there to carry on.

It was better that way, Elspeth decided; there was less time to think of what had happened. She could not then know that this day's endeavour was to win her the Military Medal, one of only six awarded to W.A.A.F.s through the entire war. To herself, she said, with no sense of drama or occasion: "All right, then, let's get, on with it."

At Fighter Command the news of Biggin Hill's ordeal was heard with consternation – did the Germans plan to concentrate the might of their bombers against the sector stations? Just five hours earlier, at 1.15 p.m., the Dorniers of Oberst Fink's *Kampfgeschwader* 2 had broken through to Hornchurch, just then holding the torch for Biggin, with alarming ease. In the Ops Room, Wing Commander Cecil Bouchier, the airfield's C.O., was standing on the dais as the look-out, on top of a hangar, signalled the first of sixty bombers; in the gloom the white faces of the W.A.A.Fs seemed upturned as if in supplication. At that instant, Squadron Leader Ronald Adam, Duty Controller, was scrambling No. 54 Squadron.

Eight planes, led by Squadron Leader James Leathart, made it narrowly, but now as the raid swept like a cyclone across the aerodrome, a stick of bombs followed the last three Spitfires up the runway. Again, the look-out's voice came, all dispassion gone: "Three aircraft Rabbit Squadron being bombed as they take off – three aircraft Rabbit Squadron crashed."

From their slit trenches, scores now saw a sight they'd never forget. Pilot Officer Richard Hillary, strolling for 603's dispersal, saw with alarm the bombers' bellies slide from the August heat haze, glinting like slugs in the sunlight, seconds before three Spitfires took off with a roar down-wind. One moment they were twenty feet up, in close formation; the next they catapulted apart "as though on elastic" – one screaming down the runway on its back, the second plunging on its airscrew, the third spinning wingless into a field. Dazed, Hillary thought: That's the shortest flight *he's* ever taken. From 603's dispersal, Pilot Officer Bill Read saw it, too: a puff of smoke, a blinding flash, then the Spitfire poised on the peak of the bomb blast "like a bee on a flower petal".

Within seconds, Squadron Leader Adam had word through his look-out: "The chap on the runway – it's Al Deere."

At this moment the young New Zealander needed every one of his nine lives. Clamped in his cockpit like an astronaut in a capsule, he was skidding at 100 miles an hour, upside down along the tarmac for more than 100 yards, in a spark-whirling screech of metal, the thundering friction of the earth bludgeoning through his leather flying helmet, scoring an awful wound in his scalp. Then the plane came to a grinding halt, and Deere, trapped and helpless, heard the bombs still reverberating across the airfield and smelt with fear the rich sweet reek of petrol.

The second man to crash, Pilot Officer Eric Edsall, was luckier; his Spitfire had landed right way up. Now, despite a dislocated hip, he crawled painfully across the tarmac to Deere's plane, wrenching at the cockpit door while Deere pushed from inside. Concussed and shaken, Deere tumbled to the earth – only to find that Edsall, who couldn't even walk, was bent on carrying him. Cursing, Deere rejected any such indignity; along with Flying Officer Robert Lucy, 54's engineer officer, they helped Edsall hobble to station sick quarters.

The third pilot, Sergeant Davies, blown clean off the airfield into marshy ground, scrambled out unharmed and made for the nearest garage. To his fury, the accountant officer wouldn't refund his taxi-fare: Air Ministry regulations offered no provision for downed pilots to charge up hire-cars.

Almost the only man who didn't rush to greet the survivors was Pilot Officer Derek Smythe, who'd thoughtfully unharnessed an abandoned shirehorse from a grass roller and led it to an air-raid shelter.

An early arrival on the scene was Wing Commander Cecil Bouchier – as irate at the 100 craters pitting his airfield as a groundsman plagued by moles. Promptly all leave passes were cancelled, and Bouchier himself led the working parties... filling in the holes with pick and shovel, placing yellow cardboard cones to mark the sites of unexploded bombs. Pilot Officer Henry Jacobs, whose squadron, No. 600, had been transferred from Manston, recorded: "Whatever your rank you were in there pitching." By 8 p.m., Hornchurch was operational

– and Al Deere, head bandaged, wrist in plaster, begged a stiff brandy from the doctor. To be bombed on the ground after all his vicissitudes was too humiliating to stomach.

At Fighter Command, Pilot Officer Bob Wright, decorum forgotten, hastened into Dowding's room with the report of Deere's escape: "*This* you must read, sir."

It was hard to believe that anyone but Deere could have lived through it – yet as the battle gathered force, man after man was surviving by the skin of his teeth. On this day, August 31, Fighter Command had suffered the heaviest losses yet – thirty-nine fighters shot down, fourteen dead – and as the hours raced, it was amazing they hadn't lost more.

Even those who got back unscathed needed all the valour they could muster. Sergeant Geoffrey Goodman, breaking from two ME 109s that had blasted six feet from his starboard wing, put his Hurricane into a dive so steep he screamed for the earth like a meteor; pulling out, he hauled so hard on the stick his feet were braced on the instrument panel. Above Sittingbourne, Sergeant George Booth, on the tail of an ME 110, abruptly levelled off; as his air-speed indicator showed 400 miles an hour, the fabric on his Hurricane's wings was literally ripping at the seams. Flying Officer Eric Beardmore, of McNab's Canadians, wasn't even so lucky; shots had carried away his air-speed indicator, his elevator controls, the whole inner framework of his tailplane.

Gauging his speed by instinct, his tailplane "like a piece of Swiss cheese", he gingerly nursed his Hurricane down on Northolt airfield.

Sheer ingenuity saved some. Airborne from Fowlmere airfield in Cambridgeshire, on his first sortie of the battle, Flying Officer Jimmie Coward was at the controls of one of the few cannon-equipped Spitfires in the R.A.F. when disaster struck. As he took his section shearing in on a flight of Dorniers, his cannons jammed – and simultaneously, the Spitfire shuddered all over. Briefly Coward felt a dull pain "like a kick on the shin in a rugby football scrum", then saw his bare left foot lying on the cockpit floor, severed from the leg by all save a few ligaments.

As the Spitfire tilted uncontrollably forward, Coward baled out with ease – then the agony of his foot spinning crazily by its ligaments drove him to desperate action. Pulling the ripcord, he was floating for earth from 20,000 feet, but already blood was jetting from his tibial artery, vanishing in thin swirls far away below. Worse, the slipstream had sucked away his gloves – and now, his hands blue with cold, he couldn't budge the clamping parachute harness to reach the first-aid kit in his breast pocket. Yet if he was to survive at all, he must improvise a tourniquet, and fast.

Frantically, fumbling with numbed fingers, he picked open the strap and buckle of his flying helmet – to which his radio telephone lead was still attached. Then, raising his left leg almost to his chin, he bound the lead tightly round his thigh, choking the flow of blood, drifting slowly across Duxford airfield where the rest of his squadron were now landing. Within the hour, Coward was in a Cambridge hospital where a doctor amputated his leg below the knee.

Others survived less through ingenuity than luck. Canada's Vernon Corbett jumped from his blazing plane to find his parachute harness had failed; at a heart-stopping 300 feet a second, he fell for a mile head-first until his parachute opened – wafting him gently into a hospital garden. Pilot Officer George Nelson-Edwards, from Biggin Hill, made a split-second, wheels-up landing in a walled Elizabethan garden, at Oxted, Surrey, checking his Hurricane within inches of a brick wall. To his astonishment, a country gentleman of the old school stepped courteously forward to greet him – cut-glass tumbler of brandy for his guest, parrot perched on a leather-patched shoulder sprinkled liberally with bird lime.

He wasn't the only one to fall in good hands. Near Lympne airfield, Pilot Officer Richard Hillary force-landed alongside a brigadier's cocktail party, relaxed while the Army plied him with double whiskies "for shock". Flight Lieutenant Robert Stanford Tuck, covered in hot black oil from his Spitfire's ruptured tanks, baled out at Plovers, the old-world estate of Lord Cornwallis, Kent's future Lord Lieutenant. As he soaked in a scalding tub, His Lordship encouraged him: "Drop in for a bath any time, my boy."

When British ack-ack holed his plane over Dunstable, Sergeant Stanislaw Plzak, a cheerful Czech whom his comrades called "Big Nose", force-landed to meet up with a friendly policeman. Since the bobby suggested a drink, the Czech wasn't averse – not realising that it was Dunstable's market day and the pubs didn't close. Nine hours later, as smug as a man who'd been making do on milk-shakes, "Big Nose" delivered the euphoric policeman back to his wife.

But many men, unable to master their machines, lived sweating moments of terror. Spitfire pilot Desmond Sheen, swooning over his control column from a painful leg wound, awoke to find the fighter wailing for the ground at 500 miles an hour – a speed so sheer he couldn't level out. Sucked from the cockpit through the open hood, he fell straddled along the fuselage, his feet trapped by the top of the windscreen. He kicked free with only seconds to spare. Montreal's Bill Sprenger, his Hurricane's controls shot away, dropped a mile before he could slip from the emergency hatch; it took him barely seven minutes to drift to earth.

Pilot Officer David Bell-Salter, springing from a Hurricane he couldn't control, hadn't even pulled his ripcord before losing consciousness; he revived to find himself upside down, hanging by one leg, suspended by a single rigging line snagged behind his knee. Above him, a long rent across its canopy, the parachute was flapping wildly – yet the speed of his fall had ripped the harness clean from his body. Hitting the ground so violently he crushed several vertebrae and smashed his right heel, Bell-Salter thought that either aerial mast or tailplane, catching his parachute pack as he jumped, had ripped it to pieces. Only the miracle of hooking his leg in a rigging line had saved his life.

Some held on to the last, fearful of the danger to others. Pilot Officer Jeff Millington, a lively, fair-haired youngster, made to abandon his blazing Hurricane, then risked it for three more minutes; it might easily have hit Tenterden in Kent, one of the prettiest places he'd ever seen. Hurricane pilot, William "Ace" Hodgson, had the same motives; ablaze over the Shell Oil Company's tanks at Thameshaven, on the estuary, he foresaw the havoc a blazing Hurricane could cause below. Switching off his engine and side-slipping violently, he kept the flames in check until he'd made a rocky wheels-up landing in an Essex field.

For others the luck was running out like sand from an hourglass. All along Pilot Officer Tony Woods-Scawen, 43 Squadron, had sworn by his lucky parachute; four times he'd baled out and four times it hadn't let him down. The fifth time he left it too late; he was within 1,000 feet of the ground when he left his Hurricane. Before the parachute could snap open, the plane exploded above him. His elder brother Patrick, of 85 Squadron, had been shot down and killed a day earlier; the only two brothers to serve all through the battle had died within hours of one another.

Lucky or not, the wounded put a brave face on it – as if courtesy was as great a requisite as courage. Swaying towards the earth, his left toe smashed by a cannon shell, Squadron Leader Peter Townsend saw two housemaids standing in a garden, staring open-mouthed. With the urbanity that was later to serve him as equerry to King George VI, Townsend called: "I say! Do you mind giving me a hand when I come down?" Pilot Officer Robert Rutter, wounded in the right foot, baled out in a ploughed field and hobbled into a lane, bathed in blood and oil, to accost a passing civilian, "Do you know anything about pressure points?" and 253's Squadron Leader Tom Gleave took the palm for understatement: baling out from a blazing

Hurricane "like the centre of a blow lamp nozzle", the skin drooping in folds from his body, he was already on the dangerously ill list when his wife arrived at Orpington Hospital, Kent.

When Beryl Gleave asked, "What on earth have you been doing with yourself, darling?" her husband shrugged it off. "Had a row with a German."

Some had landings as bizarre as could be. Sergeant Mike Bush, putting down his Hurricane in a Kentish field to check his bearings, was wheedled indoors by a wild-eyed woman who dabbled in astrology: if Bush supplied the time, date and place of his birth, she could fix on the date of his death. Hastily the sergeant took his leave. And as Flight Lieutenant Gordon Sinclair struck a wood near Caterham in Surrey, he recognised the first man to reach him as Lieutenant Derek Cooper, Irish Guards. With a Guards' officer's traditional imperturbability, Cooper drawled: "What are you doing here, Gordon, old boy? Haven't seen you since we were at school."

A few came back to earth to meet with a mixed reception. One sergeant baled out in the grounds of a girls' school, roosting uncomfortably in a tree above a horde of giggling pupils until firemen arrived to cut him down. Near Canterbury, a pilot officer ran the length of a village street pursued by housewives armed with rolling pins, convinced he was a German. An ambulance picked him up in the nick of time. 603's George Gilroy, pounded almost insensible by Local Defence Volunteers, received a £10 whip-round in his hospital bed when the shamefaced locals realised their mistake.

If a few men were roughly handled on landing, it wasn't surprising. Despite the Air Ministry's endeavour to play down losses, the feeling of loss was in the air; baling out over a Kentish hopfield, Pilot Officer Robert Deacon-Elliott was told: "We'd hoped you were a German – we're picking up too many R.A.F." And as the battle continued, not every man on English soil was in the mood for mercy.

At Tandridge in Surrey, blood-crazed troops did a tribal dance round a hayrick, parading a German's head on a pitchfork. On the beach at East Wittering in Sussex, a local gardener, Ernest Collier, saw a Heinkel belly-land at the high watermark; as the first crewman, unhurt, clambered out on the wing, a soldier raised his rifle and shot him dead. Local Defence Volunteer Richard May, hastening towards Coulsdon Golf Course in Surrey, where a German had baled out, met two soldiers who'd get there first. One of them, carrying a pilot's gauntlet glove, announced tersely: "We've fixed him." In the field, May found a tall man wearing the Iron Cross, his head smashed to pulp.

There were flashes of the same ugly mood all over. At Chatham in Kent, Chief Fire Officer E. G. Maynard was outraged to learn one of his foam tenders was saving a German airman from a blazing plane; seizing the phone he roared: "Stoke it up and let the bastard burn." At Rochester, a few miles away, aircraft-factory workers saw an ME 109 pilot, parachute in flames, hurtle for the ground like a shooting star. Aloud they applauded: "Terrific — let's have more of it."

Above Crowhurst, Sussex, as Oberleutnant Hasse von Perthes, 52nd Fighter Group, swung like a tiny black pendulum on the end of his parachute, R.A.F. fighters filed past, opening fire at point-blank range. Miraculously von Perthes lived through it, landing with bullet-riddled legs in a tangle of telephone wires at Hurst Green in Surrey. And Pilot Officer James Caister, airborne on one of his first sorties from Hornchurch, wondered what kind of battle he'd come into: as a German pilot baled out, a Spitfire was circling him watchfully, flying lower and lower until the German reached the ground. From the air, Caister watched in fascination: as an ever-narrowing circle of troops converged on the German, it was like a slow-motion film.

Suddenly, as the Spitfire swooped for the last time, its pilot opened fire. For an instant the wings were barbed with blue and orange flame, then the German crumpled, dead.

For some men on both sides it was abruptly a war of no quarter. Pilot Officer Janos Maccinski had been with Squadron

Leader John Thompson's III Squadron just four days when he baled out east of Folkestone; as he drifted towards the sea, despite all Pilot Officer Ben Bowring's efforts to protect him, German bullets scythed him to pieces. Near Woldingham in Surrey, War Reserve Constable Tom Dadswell saw a Spitfire fall flaming over the green acres of Marden Park; as the pilot baled out, a German fighter swooped, machine-guns chattering. An ambulance worker, John Lunt, one of the first to reach the airman, found scarcely a bone intact in his body.

It wasn't only with their adversaries that men grew callous. Hating their intimacy with death, they strove to immunise themselves against caring as young Geoffrey Page had done. As Pilot Officer "Rafty" Rafter's Spitfire spun for the earth over Maidstone, Pilot Officer Bill Read heard an angry 603 pilot break radio silence: "Bugger – he owed me a fiver!" In fact, Rafter, after hospital treatment, survived to repay it – but nobody knew that then. And 253 Squadron, witnessing David Bell-Salter's terrifying one-foot bale out, had written him off prematurely, too. A girl friend phoning the mess to speak with him heard curtly from a fellow pilot: "You can't – he's dead." With that, he hung up.

But as often the imminence of death brought out the best in men; there was compassion on both sides, too. As a former naval chaplain, the Reverend Edward Bredin, Vicar of Ulcombe in Sussex, had lost an arm in the Battle of Jutland, but when the badly burned Leutnant Werner Kluge landed in a nearby field it was the one-armed vicar who carried him to safety. At Stourmouth, in Kent, the Reverend Harry Whitehouse's parishioners were up in arms: the vicar had not only taken a captured German to the vicarage but entertained him to tea.

Unrepentant, the vicar, as the text for the next day's sermon, chose the parable of the Good Samaritan.

Even in the heat of battle chivalry won the day. Squadron Leader Michael Lister Robinson, running out of ammunition, chased an ME 109 for forty miles, carrying out such realistic dummy attacks that the German force-landed in a field.

Then, leaning from the cockpit, Robinson threw him a packet of cigarettes, waving cheerfully as the German waved back. Hauptmann "Assi" Hahn, tumbling his 109 about the sky in a fierce duel with a Spitfire, realised he and his adversary had run out of ammunition at the same moment. As the R.A.F. pilot spread his hands, ruefully, Hahn did the same – and suddenly both men were flying, side by side, laughing uproariously. It was a moment before Hahn realised his friendly flight was carrying him towards England. Hastily he broke for home.

For most it was the sudden knowledge of a life in the balance that turned the scale: abruptly a machine became a man. Hauptmann Erich Dobe was heading back over the Channel, escorting a returning Dornier formation, when Spitfires bounced the ME 110s beneath him. Vainly, the *Zerstorers* milled to form a circle of death; but before the manoeuvres were complete, two were plummeting from the circle, engines smoking. In his earphones, Dobe heard one of the *Zerstorer*'s gunners cry, "I'm hit, I'm wounded"; not even knowing who it was, he yelled urgently, "Bale out, bale out." Then, with a bull-roar of "*Scheisse*", Dobe's adjutant, furious, broke from the formation, blazing into battle with the Spitfires.

Now Dobe's earphones came alive with the wounded gunner's screams and he put his 109's nose down, flying close to the *Zerstorer*, shouting: "Keep calm, stay close to the bombers, we'll see you home." It was too late; the plane had broken from the circle and at that moment a Spitfire dived for the kill. Somewhere beyond Margate, the 110 went down in wrapping flame.

The shock of it made Dobe reel in his safety harness. He wanted nothing now but to kill, to empty his magazines into a British plane until the Perspex canopy was a seething mass of yellow flame. Six thousand feet below, he saw a Spitfire break from the battle, trailing a thin white stream of glycol like blood from a wounded animal, and he set off in pursuit, closing slowly as he stalked it... 800 yards... 700... 650. His body was rigid with hatred against the harness, and at 200 yards he would open fire.

Then his eyes had dropped from the shining graticule of the gunsight, swiftly checking his turn-and-bank indicator, but the black needle quivered at dead-centre – his reading was true and he couldn't miss. The 109 was hovering like a hawk, and still the Spitfire suspected nothing. Abruptly, Dobe cursed; in his blind hate, he'd forgotten to turn the safety ring surrounding the gunsight from safe to fire.

But at this moment, looking down, Dobe saw the British pilot's face craning up at him – the eyes dilated behind the goggles, in mindless imploring terror, like an animal at bay. Suddenly the hatred drained from him and he felt shabby and ashamed; you couldn't kill a man when you'd looked in his eyes. You couldn't even fire. Abruptly he swung his 109 away, heading east for Marquise airfield, but the battle seemed cleaner now.

–

At Fighter Command, Air Chief Marshal Dowding paced his room slowly, back and forth, like an automaton. His calls on Pilot Officer Bob Wright were increasing now, yet as often as not, Wright had no sooner entered than he found himself dismissed: The Old Man had momentarily forgotten why he'd issued the summons. And Wright knew there were reasons. On August 31, Fighter Command was 166 pilots below strength – and seven days later the figure had soared to 209. If the losses for September 1 were lighter – fifteen aircraft, six pilots – the next day they had risen alarmingly: thirty-one aircraft lost, eight pilots killed, seven wounded.

And still the Germans pounded the airfields – raid after raid with the deadly precision of a hammer driving home nails. Eastchurch… Hawkinge… Detling… Lympne… Biggin Hill again – all were priority targets on September 1. Next day Eastchurch was raided again, an eighteen-bomber attack that destroyed an ammunition dump and five planes. Now, like Manston, the main camp was evacuated. Then Detling again... Debden... Biggin Hill... North Weald... Rochford... it seemed as if the bombers would never stop.

At Warmwell airfield, Flight Lieutenant David Crook recalled to Red Tobin the Duke of Wellington's words at Waterloo: "Hard pounding, gentlemen – let us see who pounds the longest."

And even seasoned pilots looked askance at the lengthening odds. Flight Lieutenant Johnnie Kent, losing sight of 303 Squadron's main formation, was leading his flight of six Poles when Northolt's controller hailed him: "Garter calling Apany Red Leader, vector one-four-zero, Angels one-five, one hundred and fifty-plus twenty miles ahead of you." When Kent, aghast, pointed out his force was just six strong, Northolt replied: "Understand you are only six – be very careful."

On the same day, September 3, Dowding cut official squadron strength from twenty-two aircraft to eighteen – though, as things stood, it was little more than a gesture. At Croydon, 111 Squadron were down to seven pilots; at North Weald two Hurricane squadrons between them often mustered only two serviceable aircraft. From 1,438 men available, pilot strength had slumped to 840 – a casualty rate that assured the Germans victory in just three weeks.

Few conceded this more readily than Dowding. Already, in the long hours of pacing, he had made a bold decision: "I'll lose no more fighters until the Germans cross the Channel." His relations with the Chief of the Air Staff, Air Chief Marshal Sir Cyril Newall were worse than they'd ever been; only ten days back, at the height of the battle, the Air Staff had told him he must relinquish his command on August 25. Abruptly, within hours, came an as-you-were; they'd once more changed their minds.

To withdraw his fighting line beyond the range of the 109s was now the one trump left to Dowding – though fearing Air Staff intervention, he told no man what was in his mind.

Many pilots were nearing the end of their tether. At Hornchurch, even the cheerful Al Deere found his nerves at snapping point; an expected shout over the radio-telephone set his heart pounding like a trip-hammer. His fellow-countryman, Colin Gray, was biting his nails to the quick. At mess supper the lively George Gribble slumped fast asleep, face first, into a plate of bacon and eggs.

It was the same with every squadron. At Croydon, Squadron Leader Thompson's pilots averaged four hours unrefreshing sleep a night — then crawled from their beds to fight again. Sergeant James Lacey, a young Hurricane ace from Hawkinge, had to fly with his right foot tucked in the loop of the rudder bar; in combat his left foot twitched so uncontrollably he just couldn't check it. At Stapleford, Essex, the pilots of the incoming 46 Hurricane Squadron were staggered to find the seven surviving pilots of the departing 151 Squadron taking lunch at 11 a.m.

When a breathless telephone orderly reported, "Controller says one fifty-one scramble," the jaded flight commander threw back: "Tell him we're finishing our bloody lunch first."

At Duxford, No. 19 Squadron heard the worst; their eighteen cannon-equipped Spitfires jammed so often that they were being pulled north to Lincolnshire, out of the battle for good and all. Following a swelling chorus of protest, the command fitted them out with the only planes available — old eight-gun Spitfires, rushed from a training unit, streaked with oil leaks, adorned with brightly painted airscrews, reeking of vomit.

At this crucial moment, about 2 p.m., on September 4, Dowding returned from lunch at "Montrose" to hear the worst news yet. Not only had Eastchurch and Lympne been attacked yet again, but from a whirling confusion of 300 German planes, fourteen Junkers 88s had broken through to the vital Vickers Armstrong aircraft factory at Weybridge, Surrey, bringing all production to a standstill... killing eighty-eight... injuring 600.

Now every fighter squadron Dowding could spare must be diverted to give cover to four top-priority Hurricane and Spitfire factories – while all reports stressed that the invasion of England was only days away.

Chapter Eight

"You'll See All the Black Crosses in the World"

September 4–14

Reichsmarschall Hermann Goring had no such confidence in "Operation Sea-Lion" at breakfast on Tuesday, September 3. This morning, his valet Robert Kropp knew there was just one gramophone record to slip on the turntable – "The March of the Heroes" from *Gotterdammerung*, which always helped restore Goring's humour. The battle that should have been over in four days was becoming a deadly war of attrition, with each side fighting itself to a standstill.

Oh September 1, the Luftwaffe had lost only fourteen planes, but twenty-four hours later there were few crumbs of comfort – a loss of thirty-five as against the R.A.F.'s thirty-one. Worst of all, it seemed that Hitler had gone cold on the invasion plans.

General Kurt Student, commanding all airborne troops for "Operation Sea-Lion" never forgot taking tea with Goring at Karinhall on the afternoon of September 2; rarely had he seen *Der Dicke* so depressed. Without ceremony, he cut into Student's monologue: "The Fuhrer doesn't want to invade Britain."

Shocked, unbelieving, Student pressed him: "Why not?" For answer, Goring gave a massive shrug: "I don't know. There'll be nothing doing this year, at any rate."

Despite Hitler's reluctance, the Armed Forces High Command were going through the motions. On September

3, the day following Goring's tea party, Feldmarschall Wilhelm Keitel, Deputy Supreme Commander, ordered the embarkation of invasion material – but not troops – to begin in eight days' time, on September 11. The Navy had its orders, too – to lay mine-barriers on the flanks of the invasion.

Later, Student nourished the intriguing theory that, from now on, Goring was engaged in an all-out bid to force Hitler's hand – for on September 3, the Reichsmarschall, along with Kesselring, Sperrle, Oberstleutnant Josef Schmid, Luftwaffe intelligence chief, and the heads of each Flying Corps, was involved in an angry no-holds-barred conference at The Hague. Now Goring was putting the pressure on his Air Fleet Commanders; the time had come to alter tactics and switch their forces to an all-out, piledriving attack on London.

Just one problem remained: had Fighter Command been sufficiently depleted, or would the bombers be running too great a risk?

Now words flew hotly. Kesselring, who saw it as his duty to infuse every man in his command with optimism, jumped in at once; of course the R.A.F. was finished; a study of combat reports made that plain. All along he'd urged this mass attack on one key objective, rather than against so many diversified targets – now ports, next airfields, then factories. In fact, Kesselring, who'd sounded out No. 2 Flying Corps' Oberst Paul Deich-mann on this topic, had received only qualified assurance, but this didn't bother him now.

Next Generalfeldmarschall Hugo Sperrle took the floor. A sceptic who loved disagreeing with Kesselring whenever possible, he found it all too easy now. So the R.A.F. were finished, were they? This was just playing up the need for optimism; he didn't believe a word of it. He'd wager a good dinner that the R.A.F. had every one of 1,000 fighters left. (The truth: they had only 746 serviceable.)

Now tempers rose dangerously; fists pounded the long, polished table. Hotly, Kesselring reiterated his credo: the R.A.F.

were done for, figures proved it. Coldly, Sperrle sneered his disbelief – and his regional fighter commander, Oberst Werner Junck, lent strong support. A finished force couldn't inflict such losses. Junck wound up: "This is a Verdun of the air."

Goaded, Kesselring rounded on Oberstleutnant Schmid, the intelligence chief: "Well, are they finished, or aren't they?"

Caught between the crossfire of two Air Fleet commanders in fighting mood, the unhappy Schmid temporised. Perhaps the R.A.F. had between 100 and 350 planes left – no man could be sure.

At once Sperrle cut in: a London attack would have his support, provided target selection had top priority. As he saw it, the whole object of the battle was the destruction of British ports and shipping – not the loss of German bombers. The priority target should be the London docks, handling the greatest bulk of Britain's sea-borne traffic, and to cut down bomber losses they should be raided by night. He summed up: "Raid their docks by night, their airfields by day."

Kesselring would have none of it. The object of the battle was to defeat the R.A.F., but airfield attacks weren't the answer. Shrewdly he anticipated Dowding's secret resolve: the R.A.F. didn't need airfields like Manston when they could withdraw to fields north of London, out of fighter range. Why they hadn't done so weeks ago, God alone knew.

He urged: "We haven't a chance of destroying the British fighters on the ground – they're always in the sky. We must force them to fight with their last reserves of Spitfires and Hurricanes."

The 2nd Flying Corps' General Bruno Lorzer saw this as sound sense. A heavy London raid might produce useful results, political as well as military – either forcing the R.A.F. to come up and fight, or the Government to sue for peace.

Right from the start of the battle, Kesselring and Lorzer had urged this all-out London attack – yet stubbornly, all through August, Hitler, still hopeful of peace, had refused. Nothing in the battle had made him so angry as Rubensdorffer's Croydon attack: only narrowly had Oberst Paul Deichmann, as the officer who'd triggered off the raid, escaped a court-martial. Then, on the night of August 24, the navigational error of a few bomber crews started a chain reaction. Probing for the oil tanks at Thameshaven on the estuary, they drifted over central London – and for the first time in twenty-two years bombs were scattered across the City and the East End.

Angrily, Winston Churchill ordered immediate reprisals – and eighty-one twin-engined Wellington, Whitley and Hampden bombers set out for Berlin. In fact, fewer than ten found the target – but four times in the next ten days the British tried again.

As early as September 2, the Luftwaffe's Command Staff drafted its tentative reprisal plan. At Wissant, near Calais, Major Adolf Galland and seven other group commanders heard from Oberst Theo Osterkamp: "There may be a massed attack on London on September 7." But until September 3, no one had been too certain: Hitler's reluctance to carry the war into the empire's capital was well known.

Then, on September 4, at Berlin's Sportpalast, came Hitler's angry decision: "If they attack our cities, then we will raze *theirs* to the ground. We will stop the handiwork of these air pirates, so help us God."

Now, as The Hague conference broke up, Kesselring, jubilant, noted that his optimism had carried the day: in four days' time, soon after 4 p.m., 625 bombers and 648 fighters would cross the coast, striving to embroil the last of the few in a battle to the death over London.

And Goring, with a penchant for high-sounding names, thought up the code-word for the operation: Loge. The old German god who had forged Siegfried's sword sounded just right; he might well forge a new chapter in the history of the Luftwaffe.

On the Channel coast, Goring's pilots as yet had no knowledge of the Reichsmarschall's plans. They were waging their own private battle with fatigue.

The business of escorting the bombers back and forth to Kent was taking its toll – up to five sorties a day, and each time the fear: Will I get back? If combat wasn't joined now, few worried as they would have done a month back: that anxious eye on the fuel gauge made it all too fraught. Oberleutnant Hans-Ekkehard Bob, 54th Fighter Group, put it this way: "Blessed are they who leave space behind them, for they will see the Fatherland again." Leutnant Erich Hohagen saw it more starkly: "The Channel's a blood-pump – all the time draining away our strength."

To Major Hannes Trautloft, newly appointed 54th Fighter Group commander, it was all strangely unreal. In his diary, he noted: "Today, a year ago, the war started in Poland. Who would have thought a year later we'd be fighting against England?"

And every pilot felt the stress. In Leutnant Eduard Neumann's unit the red warning bulb glowed so often now, they'd evolved a code-cry: "*Trubsal*" (Distress). From Colembert, Oberleutnant Hans von Hahn, leading the 1st Wing, 3rd Fighter Group, reported home: "There aren't many of us who haven't made a forced landing in the Channel in a badly shot-up plane, or without a propeller." Leutnant Hellmuth Ostermann noted the same at Guines – a tension so marked pilots, for the first time, talked of a posting to a quieter base.

It wasn't surprising; daily their tasks were stepped up. With Sperrle's Air Fleet Three given over to night bombing, his single-engined fighters were detached to Air Fleet Two – and Kesselring found work for them to do. The August 31 raids against Hornchurch and Biggin Hill had seen 1,301 fighters escorting 150 bombers; in twenty-three days, the Luftwaffe had lost 467 fighters, none of them replaceable.

To some at least, it was a wonder they hadn't lost more. On the eve of posting from the battle-line, Leutnant Johannes Steinhoff had puzzled, "The R.A.F. seem so hesitant – perhaps they never realise how scared to death we really are."

It was Goring's cherished *Zerstorers* that suffered most. At Arques, near St. Omer, Hauptmann Schalk's 3rd Wing, Z.G. 26, could sometimes muster only three planes. Within weeks, Oberstleutnant Friedrich Vollbracht's Z.G. 2 would be disbanded entirely: hardly a man was left alive. Only twice in the battle did Oberleutnant Hans-Joachim Jabs get his 110 back undamaged; on September 3, shepherding the bombers back from Debden, he ditched in the Channel within sight of the French coast. Five of his unit ended up in the bathroom, scrubbing away blood and oil, while the station commander, Oberst Schellenberg, dosed all of them with cointreau.

In truth the five were lucky; it was a black week for the 110s. On September 4, seven were shot down in sixty-five minutes around Worthing alone. August 30 was a bad day, too – with *Zerstorers* crashing all over Essex, in used car dumps, on railway lines, even in a man's greenhouse, hurling the pilot clean through an open bedroom window and imbedding him in the wall.

But Goring's infatuation with the *Zerstorers* was short lived. Again, like a capricious child, he now wouldn't hear a word in their favour: "Don't even speak of them – they haven't delivered the goods." And he added a rider: he'd heard they called their tactical manoeuvre "the circle of defence", and he expressly forbade it. The Luftwaffe was never on the defensive: it would be "the offensive circle" from now on. One *Zerstorer* commander sighed: "Well, it's still the same old circle."

The truth was that Goring and his commanders were less and less in touch with the realities of air war, and the pilots sensed it and were angry. At Samer, near Boulogne, Hauptmann Erich von Selle was beside himself... today his fighter wing was only eighteen machines strong... the weathermen's forecast was so far out they'd lost the bombers they were escorting in cloud... by the time they'd sighted the French coast they were fewer than 250 feet above the earth, and every man's red bulb was glowing... there wasn't even time for a circuit. Eighteen machines somehow touched down, eight of them without one drop of fuel left.

Two hours later, with the cloud ceiling worsening, von Selle had Kesselring's advanced headquarters on the line: the 2nd Wing, Fighter Group Three, would take off on another protection flight. Bluntly, von Selle refused; his wing was twenty-two aircraft below strength; only blind chance had preserved those planes he had brought back.

When Kesselring's office grew steely – "This is an order, not a request" – von Selle dug in his toes. "If it's an order, we'll fly it – but if I see no land again at a thousand feet, I'll take the wing up to thirty-five hundred feet and order every man to bale out." No more orders were forthcoming.

Other commanders beside Adolf Galland noted how tired men were – and the errors that fatigue engendered. One *Zerstorer* pilot, Oberleutnant Schafer, circled so long before touching down that the three 110s on his tail narrowly escaped a crash landing. Profusely, he apologised: forgetting he wore sunglasses, he thought night had fallen and was searching for a flare path.

Hauptmann Eduard Neumann, ordered to free-hunt over Portland, was too weary to spot that his magnetic compass was faulty; he led forty planes to Brighton, 126 miles east. Unteroffizier Delfs, not even realising he was duelling with another ME 109, baled out over a railway siding near Calais, snagging his parachute harness in the points. Only the swift thinking of Oberleutnant Josef "Pips" Priller saved him from death beneath an oncoming train; firing Very lights that the train driver ignored, Priller had to swoop again, a head-on attack with cannon, until it shushed to a halt.

Often two hours' readiness in the cockpit before take-off robbed a man of all appetite: Hauptmann Helmut Wick nearing fifty-six confirmed victories, refused all solid food, kept going on black coffee and English cigarettes. Though alcohol was tabu until evening, Oberleutnant Ludwig Franzisket found a small flask of rum before a battle gave him renewed strength. In the 53rd Fighter Group, Oberleutnant Werner Ursinus noted more readiness "to do a Cap Gris Nez" – turn homewards with suspected engine trouble.

No man lacked resolution – but where would the slaughter end? Leutnant Hans Ebeling, one of Galland's pilots, shot down in the Channel after his thirteenth victory, spent ninety minutes in the water before noon on August 31. When the German Navy fished him out, he set about reviving himself with a tumbler of brandy and hot pea-soup: a man who'd been thrown from a horse must remount to gain confidence. Six hours later, he was flying as escort to the Biggin Hill bombers.

Often heavy losses only strengthened a unit's determination; at Mardyck near Dunkirk, Major Hennig Strumpell and his men solemnly toasted their dead each evening before dinner. Yet, inevitably, superstition was on the increase... Oberstleutnant Freidrich Vollbracht's men rarely shaved before a sortie, avoided Friday flying when possible... Feldwebel Karl-Heinz Bendert was one of many who wouldn't have his photo taken before a flight... it had done for Manfred "Red Devil" von Richthofen in World War One... Oberleutnant Josef Fozo, who claimed Hungarian parentage, forced to fly a plane with a white 13, was shattered to find himself alongside another 109 that bore a black 13. Hastily, both planes turned home.

Few looked as far ahead as Feldwebel Johannes Lutter: determined not to fly on his birthday, December 17, he hoped he wouldn't have to disobey an order.

As the tension mounted and men made it back only by a hair's-breadth, a few went to pieces. South of Gravesend, en route to London, the pilots of No. 1 Wing, 27th Fighter Group, saw their red bulbs already aglow; despite all Goring's caveats, the bombers had arrived half an hour late, then picked the most circuitous route ever. As the shouts of "Red lamp! Red lamp!" crackled in his earphones, Oberleutnant Gert Framm was one of several squadron commanders who ordered: "It's hopeless – forget the bombers, we turn back." Now machine after machine banked steeply; the pilots flew for their lives towards Guines airfield, Calais.

Even before it loomed in sight, Framm ordered, "Down at once when you see the field, no circling" – but to his horror, one pilot, a callow eighteen-year-old, dived for the airfield like a bullet, without even throttling back. As Framm breathed, "My God, this can only end in disaster," the boy's fuel gave out forty feet above the ground. The Messerschmitt "fell like a piano", strewing wings and engine parts across the field, and already Framm could see the fire·tender rocketing towards the wreckage.

Then, as the planes touched down, the pilots were unbuckling their harness, vaulting onto the wings of their planes, racing to free the boy still trapped with his cockpit crushed about him. To Framm's relief he saw him move, and suddenly the youngster had freed himself and jumped to the ground, blood pouring from his face, his eyes as vacant as an imbecile's. When he saw Framm, his head jerked furiously like an epileptic's and he began to shout hysterically: "I'm a bloody fool, I did the one thing I was told not to. I did the one thing my squadron leader told me not to."

Stricken, Framm tried to calm him, but it was useless; the boy raved on in shock. Fatherly Major Max Ibel, their Bavarian C.O., was as gentle as could be: "My dear, dear boy, calm down". The lad didn't even hear him. Again he screamed, "I'm a bloody fool – the one thing I was told not to," and now Framm saw the tears streaming down his face and recognised that hysteria was taking hold of him.

Muttering, "Leave it to me," he stepped forward, and suddenly, at the pitch of his lungs, he shouted: "Be quiet, you swine, in the presence of a senior officer – and stand to attention."

Abruptly, the boy snapped to attention like a marionette and the raving stopped. Instead, he began to whimper like a child, and very gently they led him, shivering and shuddering, away from the battle, away from the airfield called Guines.

–

Pilot Officer Robert Oxspring had the shock of his life. Two days back he'd been enjoying a blissful leave in the Lake District; now, urgently recalled to No. 66 Spitfire Squadron, he arrived at Kenley airfield, Surrey, to find his comrades in a sorry plight. As Oxspring lugged his suitcase up the drive, he saw them ranged on the mess steps like hospital inmates – some with bandaged heads, others with their arms in slings, one man picking glass from an open wound. On all sides groans assailed him: "Oh, you don't know what you've come into."

Appalled, Oxspring heard what two days of fighting in the south had cost his squadron, fresh to the battle-line from Colt-ishall in Norfolk – two men were dead, six others had been badly shot up, too. He thought only: Why 66 Squadron? What's the matter with us? He had no way of knowing that it was the same on airfield after airfield – and that in this first week of September, with the massed German onslaught on London only days away, Headquarters Fighter Command faced a grave crisis in leadership.

As Air Chief Marshal Dowding saw it, the truth was hideously simple. Of the fifty-plus men who had commanded squadrons since Eagle Day, ten were dead, nine were in hospital, almost twenty more had been withdrawn from the battle. And many now taking command, accomplished enough as aviators, hadn't so much as one hour's combat flying.

At Hornchurch, Flight Lieutenant Norman Ryder heaved a sigh of relief as his new C.O., the slightly built Squadron Leader Lister, strolled into the bar; days earlier, he'd seen Lister's predecessor, Squadron Leader "Robin" Hood collide head-on with another pilot in his very first sortie, his Spitfire "spiralling like a sycamore leaf" for the ground. Now, puzzled by Ryder's warm greeting, Lister saw his flight commander's eyes fastened on the purple-and-white ribbon of his Distinguished Flying Cross and gently broke the news: "I'm afraid I got this for dropping leaflets on tribesmen in the Khyber Pass."

Patiently, Ryder steeled himself to inform yet another commanding officer: "This is quite definite – for the time being you'll fly as my Number Two. When you know you're O.K. and I know you're O.K., *then* you take command."

Close by, at 54 Squadron's dispersal, Flight Lieutenant Al Deere and his friends felt the same; after handing over to Squadron Leader Donald Finlay, their former C.O., James Leathart, had returned within twenty-four hours. A backroom boy who'd been eager to play his part, Finlay had flown a Spitfire for exactly two-and-a-half hours before baling out badly wounded.

It was no lone example. Flight Lieutenant John Banham, a survivor of the savagely mauled 264 Defiant Squadron, was just now taking over No. 229 Squadron; three circuits in a Hurricane, and Banham was ready to lead his unit in battle. And Squadron Leader A. R. Collins, a photographic expert, twice wounded in two days of leading 72 Squadron from Croydon, just had to hand over to Wing Commander Ronnie Lees. On his first sortie, lacerated in the thigh, Lees, too, retired for a spell in hospital.

Time and again it was only the flight commanders who saw the neophytes through – though not all gave advice as salutary as Oxspring's own, Ken Gillies: "When you go up tomorrow morning, you'll see all the black crosses in the world – but don't get too excited about shooting them down. There'll be someone a lot more experienced waiting to play the same dirty trick on you."

It was advice worth heeding. Dowding's decision on August 19, not lightly taken, to cut training time to two weeks, decreed most newcomers had just ten hours' experience on Spitfires or

Hurricanes – many could barely land a Spitfire, let alone fly it. Some, after one night's cockpit drill by torchlight, did their first training flight at dawn. And the reserve squadrons still held in the north were often as unpolished. At Usworth in Northumberland, 607 Hurricane Squadron, though veterans of France, had little enough gunnery practice; told to conserve engine-hours because spares were short, they'd had to use engine tests as an excuse to get airborne at all.

To the veterans just quitting the fray, the newcomers often seemed as cocky as could be. Squadron Leader Joseph Kayll's 615 Squadron had moved north to Prestwick, but Kayll himself lingered on at Kenley, anxious to save the relieving 253 Squadron from their own folly. Flying in tight air-parade formation, lacking even weavers, the squadron seemed unable to grasp that German fighters hovered in the sun – swooping once the R.A.F. tackled their bombers.

In vain Kayll stressed: "You must keep your eyes peeled for fighters – only take on the bombers if there's a good chance." To his chagrin, the pilots of 253 found him the funniest man alive: "Nuts to caution – we've come south to see some action." When Kayll next heard, they'd lost thirteen planes, nine pilots, in seven days.

The losses weren't surprising: few of the newcomers had ever flown in any save the tight, vulnerable V-shaped formations. At Debden, 73 Squadron had two pilots wounded, six planes destroyed or damaged in their very first sortie; 46 Squadron at Stapleford had four wounded, lost six planes. Incredibly, though some squadron commanders – Robert Stanford Tuck, Adolph "Sailor" Malan – were known to have evolved looser fluid formations, with pilots grouped in pairs, nobody found time to pass on this news to the novices.

At Northolt, Squadron Leader Ronald Kellett put it harshly to Squadron Leader Zdzislaw Krasnodebski: "The squadrons they're bringing in now are as near valueless as makes no odds."

To Krasnodebski, it was undeniable truth; so eager were his Poles for action, they already seemed to be doing the work of two squadrons. At the moment that Elspeth Henderson and the duty watch were groping from Biggin Hill's shattered Ops Room, 303's Poles, now fully operational, were east of the airfield, diving from the sun on three 109s – an attack so audacious that at seventy-yards range they couldn't miss. But Biggin Hill was too close to home for Krasnodebski's men; two days later, after a running battle over Dover, Flying Officer Zdzislaw Henneberg was eight miles inside France, down to 3,000 feet, and still attacking before he broke for base.

Alarmed, Air Vice-Marshal Keith Park cautioned from 11 Group: "There *is* good shooting… within sight of London."

But the Poles, after their ignominy on the ground, were past checking – and Krasnodebski, looking back to his long months of stewardship, daily saw signs that it hadn't been in vain. There was the sortie when every returning pilot signalled his score by victory rolls over Northolt, one even flying clean through an open hangar, until faces grew grave: the devil-may-care Jan Daszewski hadn't returned. When the tiny black speck of his plane loomed at last on the horizon, Krasnodebski wasn't surprised to see many Poles weep openly. What warmed his heart was to see the gruff, no-nonsense Kellett, finding no words, fervently pump each man's hand.

Most Poles, after initial reservations, he knew, gave their allegiance to this brawny Englishman, who could lift a man to shoulder height with one arm – and Johnnie Kent hadn't become Kentowski without proving himself a fighting leader. Following one recent sortie, Flight Lieutenant Zyborski, the adjutant, had awarded him the highest praise possible: "Kent, you very good boy. Finish off Germany, then come to Poland – help us fight Russia."

Though Krasnodebski didn't then suspect it, the Poles' action on September 5 had set the seal on things. At Northolt, Group Captain Stanley Vincent, noting 303's spiralling victories, told his intelligence officer: "Treat these claims with a lot of reserve – go through them with a toothcomb." When the officer, despairing, complained that each man corroborated the other, Vincent was resolved. Northolt's Station Flight would be airborne: he'd go up and see for himself.

What Vincent saw, at 21,000 feet over Thameshaven, astern of the Poles and 1,000 feet below, was a sight he'd remember till he died... tier upon tier of glinting, well-drilled Dorniers... two Hurricanes, poised 1,000 feet above, suddenly crash diving into space with near-suicidal impetus... a sudden ripple of agitation running through the mighty horde as the leading Dorniers, foreseeing head-on collision, turned and broke.

This was the spearhead. As the bombers scattered, Pole after Pole was diving – holding their fire until twenty yards distant, accepting the awful risk that the last great explosion would destroy them, too. Amazed, Vincent saw planes and parachutes fluttering like charred paper through the sky... Kellett, an ME 109 and Sergeant Kazimierz Wunsche duelling only 100 yards apart... the sergeant closing to sixty yards to save Kellett's life... Flying Officer Waclaw Lapkowski baling out with a broken arm... Polish fighters angrily nosing Vincent's Hurricane aside, grudging him so much as one chance shot at a crippled bomber.

Back at Northolt, fevered with excitement, Vincent sent for the intelligence officer: "My God, they *are* doing it; it isn't just imagination." Now, hearing of the group captain's doubts, it was Krasnodebski's turn to be flabbergasted: hadn't all his pilots fought for forty-three non-stop days in Poland, so that most had two years' training, 500 flying hours, before ever arriving in Britain? How could Vincent ever have doubted that the Poles were a force to be reckoned with?

At dawn on September 6, Krasnodebski had little doubt that 303 Squadron would figure as one of the most successful units Dowding ever had.

Then, soon after 9 a.m., trouble broke. West of Biggin Hill, Krasnodebski and all of them sighted the mightiest German formation they'd ever seen: a solid air-bridge of fighters and bombers blackening the sky for twenty miles. Worse, every course they'd been given to steer was the wrong one. The sun dazzled from a milky haze, blinding their eyes; above them, the vapour trails seemed as if a sinister invisible spider was weaving a gigantic web across the sky. They'd have to attack on the climb, Krasnodebski knew – and at a sluggish 140 miles an hour.

Few got so far. From the spider's web above, Messerschmitts came spinning; with height, speed, sun and numbers, they overwhelmed the climbing Poles. Flying Officer Miroslaw Feric, a 109 in his sights, saw the black crosses actually take fire under his bullets; his luck was rare. Sergeant Stanislaw Karubin, hit by a Heinkel's cannon shell, force-landed near Pembury in Kent, his thigh laid wide open. Kellett, the ammunition boxes in his wings exploding under cannon, saw fabric drifting in strands from his tailplane; his starboard aileron was shot away; holes a man could have leapt through were torn in his wing surface. At 160 miles an hour, he landed on Biggin Hill's cratered airfield, narrowly dodging a German bomber, its port engine ablaze, yawing helplessly above the aerodrome in a left-hand circuit.

Kellett didn't know it, but from this moment on the Poles were all his. One burst of fire, and flying glass had sprayed from Zdzislaw Krasnodebski's instrument panel, peppering his face and hands. Petrol slopped from the bullet-holed tank into his Hurricane's cockpit, and fire was lapping greedily. Somewhere over Farnborough in Kent, Krasnodebski baled out.

He fell free for 10,000 feet before pulling his ripcord; above him 100 planes were milling tightly in the sky, and it was politic not to drift gently while there was a chance of stopping a bullet. With 10,000 feet still to go, Krasnodebski pulled his ripcord – and once more saved his life. His trouser legs were smouldering ominously; trembling yellow flames licked at the tough overall cloth. As he hit the earth, barely conscious, the fire had already reached his knees – for all the world it seemed as if he was wearing ragged shorts.

Had he pulled the ripcord at 20,000 feet, the fire would have clawed up his body to the rigging lines of the chute, and nothing could have saved him.

At Northolt, Group Captain Stanley Vincent heard with dismay of Krasnodebski's injuries; barely conscious, under morphia, it would be a full year before he flew again. But as the survivors touched down, one by one, they were crowding eagerly round Kellett; watching from his office window, Vincent chuckled: "Look at them rubbing their hands – all boys together." The English squadron leader had knocked down a 109 in a head-on attack without once looking behind to assess the danger – an attack in true Polish Cavalry tradition if ever there was one. Krasnodebski's trusteeship was complete.

–

Squadron Leader Zdzislaw Krasnodebski had done better than he knew. Towards 6 p.m., on September 7, as the last Hurricanes of 303 Squadron were touching down at Northolt, they knew they *were* the one squadron to have scored triumphantly. To the east, the livid, shifting skyline of London showed how staggeringly successful the Germans had been; at a score of dispersals in southern England, the fires of dockland glittered ruddily on aluminium wings.

From Bermondsey to West Ham, mile after mile of London was ablaze – and by 8 p.m. 247 bombers of Sperrle's Air Fleet Three, operating under cover of darkness, would stoke up those fires until 4.50 a.m., on Sunday, September 8.

But the long testing-time of Krasnodebski's Poles was over. Before three weeks was out, their score had mounted to 11 Group's highest total – forty-four German planes in five days' fighting over London alone. And today, the height, the luck and the skill had been all theirs.

Scrambled late from Northolt, as the first bombs fell, they'd first climbed steadily to 24,000 feet, away from the combat zone; never again would German fighters surprise them from above. Then, as Northolt's No. 1 Hurricane Squadron took on the bulk of the fighter escort, they fell without mercy on a Dornier formation forty strong – from left flank, from right flank, a broadside at point blank range.

His blood on fire with the fury of combat, Flying Officer Witor Urbanowicz reported back to Intelligence: "It was like twelve hounds tearing a boar's body to pieces."

It was a rare example. On this calm, sultry Saturday, Fighter Command's controllers had nothing so urgent on their minds as the safety of the sector stations: above Northolt, Biggin Hill, Kenley, Hornchurch, circled weaving networks of planes, alerted to stave off the attacks that might soon put the command's control system out for good and all. No man realised, until too late, that the Germans had switched from the sector stations – or that the way to London lay clear.

It was a cruel necessity – yet Dowding and his commanders knew it was a godsend. Twisting above the inky pall of smoke swathing London River in his Hurricane, O.K.1, Air Vice-Marshal Keith Park saw 75,000 tons of food supplies burning, and breathed: "Thank God for that." As Park saw it, the Germans' focus on London meant precious breathing time for his sector stations – now so devastated that London might soon lack any fighter defence.

Outnumbered, scrambled too late and too low, few squadrons had the chance to operate, like 303, at full strength: it was a day for lone wolves. Pilot Officer John Bisdee, 609, swam as stealthily as a shark beneath a 110, pumping lead into its belly for seven furious seconds. Eighteen-year-old Sergeant John McAdam, who'd never flown at high altitude before, found himself 19,000 feet above the grey mushroom dome of St. Paul's Cathedral, hosing tracer at a line of Dorniers. Six thousand feet above the blazing boundary line of the Thames Estuary, Flying Officer Dennis Parnall played a grim game of hide-and-seek with an escaping Heinkel 111, hammering at its starboard engine each time it broke smoke-cover, never letting up until it belly-flopped on the mudflats at Sheerness.

To the German bomber crews the run-up to the target had been child's play; each time shrapnel rat-tatted against

Oberleutnant Karl Kessel's Dornier, his gunner, Oberfeldwebel Felix Hipp, cheerily called: "Come in!" Only on the return journey, with the defenders alerted, did the going become tougher. In Oberst Johannes Fink's plane every man save Fink was wounded: a buzzing bullet even tore the flight chart from Fink's hand. Ahead of him an excitable rear-gunner, convinced he was under heavy attack, was heedlessly riddling his own tailplane with bullets.

Back in northern France, the Germans now had urgent reports to render. At Guines, near Calais, Major Hannes Trautloft spoke for most: "Only single British fighters which could do nothing… there were thick black clouds drifting with the wind all the way across the Channel." Major Max Ibel added a rider: the fighters had stuck with the bombers but it had been a close thing – every warning bulb was glowing red as they reached the Channel. Oberst Johannes Fink took time out to disillusion the trigger-happy gunner, now the centre of an admiring throng: "You yourself were your own worst enemy, my dear boy – you have shot away your entire tailplane."

For the R.A.F. it had been a bitter, frustrating day: the sky so crowded you could scarcely single out friend from foe. Sergeant Cyril Babbage, seeing his friend Andy McDowall with six 109s on his tail, had yelled, "Hang on, I'm coming," and Andy still hadn't quite forgiven him: the quixotry had brought another dozen Messerchmitts down on top of them. Canada's Keith Ogilvie found the 109s, "zooming and diving… like masses of ping-pong balls," disconcertingly swift; aiming at the first he was mortified to find he'd hit the second. His friend Flight Lieutenant James MacArthur felt worse; back at Middle Wallop airfield, Mess Steward Joseph Lauderdale couldn't even tempt him to the pink, flaky Scotch salmon on the cold buffet.

Bitterly, MacArthur told him: "I couldn't face a bite of it, Mr Lauderdale. We've been up there all afternoon and done nothing – there wasn't a British plane in the sky."

Though MacArthur wasn't strictly accurate, he had come uncomfortably close. For forty-one German planes, the bulk of them bombers, the R.A.F. had lost twenty-eight fighters. Nineteen of their pilots were dead – and only one German plane in thirty had been harmed at all.

–

Across the Channel, Reichsmarschall Herman Goring had already arrived at Cap Blanc Nez in his private train, code-named "Asia", with its ornate mahogany-panelled-saloons. To Goring, at this eleventh hour, all the magic formulas of the past weeks – Stukas, *Zerstorers*, radar attacks, closer fighter escort – boiled down to this: *he* must infuse the Luftwaffe's fighter arm with the belly-fire they so sorely lacked.

To a wireless reporter with a recording van, he announced: "I personally have taken over the leadership of the attacks against England... for the first time we have struck at England's heart... this is a historic hour." Watching him, Hauptmann Hans-Heinrich Brustellin wondered why he was wearing pink patent-leather boots.

But today what Goring saw at the Channel coast didn't entirely please him. Despite the mighty air armada of 1,200 shining war planes, the attitude here, in the front-line, seemed all too light-hearted. Only recently Goring had ordered his regional fighter commanders to shift their quarters to overlook the Channel itself – and how, standing, binoculars levelled on the cliffs at Cap Blanc Nez, he heard the irrepressible Oberst Werner Junck, Sperrle's fighter chief, announce: "I'm going to build a new headquarters right in the Channel. When the tide's in I'll be up to my neck, when it's out I'll be up to my waist – but I shall be looking the enemy squarely in the face."

Grunting, Goring pretended not to hear. He hadn't seen the irreverent notice outside Junck's dug-out headquarters, "Tell Me About Your Leadership, And I'll Tell You Where To Put It," but the placard he'd already espied outside Oberst Theo Osterkamp's had riled him enough: "What Sort of Leaders will the English need if they want to lose the War?" Sucking his diamond-studded baton, Goring ordered peremptorily: "Osterkamp, that's a slight against me. It comes down."

Goring was too far gone in fantasy to see that this light-hearted cynicism was prompted by his own on-again, off-again policies: he wanted to hear of nothing now but plain unadulterated victories. What cheered his heart most was to meet four of Adolf Galland's pilots – Gerhard Schopfel, Joachim Muncheberg, "Micky" Sprick and Hans Ebeling – with seventeen victories apiece. Beaming, Goring shook hands with every one – if only every pilot showed this spirit!

Less gratifying was the sight of Hauptmann Heinz Bar, a dour Saxonian, shot down by a Spitfire under Goring's very eyes, within sight of France. No sooner had a patrol boat fished him from the water than Bar, still dripping and chilled to the bone, was hauled before the Reichsmarschall. When Goring, like a jovial uncle, asked him what he'd thought about in the water, the Saxonian replied grouchily: "Your speech, Herr Reichsmarschall – that England isn't an island anymore."

But as a teleprinter clacked out the day's results at Kesselring's advanced H.Q., Goring's gloom deepened: fighter losses had been few enough, but a loss of forty bombers was insupportable. It bore out what Golring had all along felt – even given brand-new commanders, the fighters had no stomach for the battle. On impulse, he barked orders: each fighter group and wing commander was to report to his private train.

It was poor psychology – and even worse timing. Already the fighters had flown on a relentless mission; most pilots hadn't even touched solid food that day. Now their leaders found themselves marshalled, like errant schoolboys before a headmaster, in a windy field near the Pas de Calais, while Goring harshly rebuked their lack of courage.

He upbraided them: "The bombers are more important than a fighter pilot's record of kills. Your job is to protect them and each time you fall down on it." When someone raised the question of British fighters, Goring swung on him: "Don't tell *me* the sky's full of enemies – I know they haven't more than seventy fighters left."

Standing in line between his friends Helmut Wick and Werner Molders, Adolf Galland just had to speak up: he thought of brave fliers he'd known, their wings for ever folded, and to see Goring shrug aside their tenacity was like a sickness welling in his throat.

Replying, Galland strove to stick to facts: the ME 109 was a plane built for attack, not for protection. The Spitfire, though a slower plane, was yet more manoeuvrable. On escort flights the 109s were for ever throttling back – it was like chaining a yard-dog and then asking it to fight. Impatiently, Goring brushed him aside: this was defeatist talk.

Galland stood silent. In this moment he saw quite clearly the beginning of the end: the bitter clashes with Goring that would one day see him slam down his Knight's Cross on the table in front of his commander, the enmity between the two that would end in Galland's total disgrace and flight.

Now Goring was addressing himself to group commanders only: what were their immediate needs? Werner Molders was prompt: more powerful engines for his 109s. Curtly, Goring swung on Galland: "And you?" Poker-faced, his voice modulated, knowing full well the sensation he'd cause, Galland replied: "A squadron of Spitfires."

In truth, though the Spitfire was more agile for escort duties, Galland preferred the 109, but the stubborn incomprehension of the High Command drove out all thoughts of caution.

Goring went purple, flashed him one long look of hate, then stamped off, growling. Galland wasn't sure, but it looked as if he'd reached the point of no return.

–

As the bombers forged above southern England, en route for London, 10,000 eyes followed their progress – some frankly curious, some in silent awe: were the R.A.F. powerless to stop the Germans getting through?

In some districts, raiders were commonplace now; as Fink's Dorniers swept heedlessly over Canterbury's Cattle Market, a newsboy by the traffic signals hailed them cheerily: "Hey, wait for the lights to turn green!" Others just didn't comprehend the danger. At Shepperton, on the Thames, writer Basil Woon, sprawled on the grass at a Saturday afternoon cricket match, heard a crackle of applause from the pavilion as a batsman's stumps flew: "Well bowled, sir – a beauty!"

Looking upwards, he saw Heinkels at 15,000 feet, sliding into the blue haze that marked the city's boundary, and thought comfortably: But they'll never get to London.

The assurance was short-lived. By 6 p.m., the throb of the bombers was unceasing – to Probationer Nurse Jacqueline Smith, at a Haywards Heath, Sussex, hospital, it was "like a wind tunnel all the time getting nearer". At Dover, seventy miles south of the capital, the people faced with the most chilling sight they had ever seen – a crimson sun setting in the east – ironically feared the worst.

Nobody saw it as a raid to preface peace terms or to draw the R.A.F. up into combat; the non-stop air armada convinced them of just one thing. The invasion fleet was coming.

None knew it more certainly than Robert Bailey. Why else would the Luftwaffe drop bombs on *him*? At this hour on the Saturday evening, Bailey had some of his 100 sheep in a pen beside the garden, shears poised for clipping, when the bombers roared overhead. Now, as he stood transfixed, a sheep in his arms, he heard Vera call from the house: "Are they Germans, Robert? If they are, you'd better come in."

Bailey could see no good reason. "It's not likely they'll drop anything on us – they're heading for Hawkinge." He was still holding the sheep, craning upwards to count the planes, when the first bombs came whistling.

Suddenly the sloping canyon of the valley, flanked by the tall groves of beech trees, was like a battle-field; the ground shook as if an earthquake threatened, and then chalk and earth were founting. Inside Ladwood Farmhouse, the kitchen ceiling rained plaster dust and wooden beams, and Vera Bailey staggered out, groping towards her husband. For a moment both she and Robert stumbled as if in a fog; the whole valley was filled with choking smoke.

Alarmed, Bailey shouted, "They're branching off – they're coming back," and with that he and Vera were running to collect the Swaffer family from the farmhouse annexe, all of them bent double and racing for the high, fern-covered banks of nearby Elham Lane. As they ran, a bomb, with a monstrous snapping crack, struck the giant beech tree in Nine Acre Wood, cleaving it clean in two.

At this moment, it didn't strike Bailey or any of them that German bombers, faced with trouble, were jettisoning their loads. To them, it seemed the end of Ladwood, the prelude to invasion.

From the High Command down, the belief was common: this was H-Hour. At 8.7 p.m. Brigadier John Swayne, unable to locate his chief, Lieutenant-General Alan Brooke, had issued the codeword "Cromwell", signifying Alert No. One to Eastern and Southern Commands: "Invasion imminent and probable within twelve hours." At Gosport Army Co-operation Station, on Portsmouth Harbour, Pilot Officer "Nobby" Clarke, in a Skua target-towing plane, had word: "Get cracking – light all the points, working from east to west." From Weymouth 150 miles east to Beachy Head, Clarke knew that on every available landing-beach petrol pipelines jutted almost level with the water's surface. Now his task was to dive-bomb each with incendiaries, to transform the inshore waters into a raging cauldron of fire.

On the main roads leading inland to Canterbury, Maidstone and Horsham, troops stood grimly by 600-gallon tanks sited ten feet above road level, ready to spray a petrol and gas-oil mixture on the advancing Germans – a jetting thirty gallons a minute, to burn at a heat of 500 degrees Fahrenheit. Professor Lindemann, Winston Churchill's scientific adviser, had grimly assured the Premier: "Nothing could live in it for two minutes."

But why had the Germans delayed? Flying east towards Littlehampton, Pilot Officer Clarke could see no invasion barges: only the grey wash of the sea at sundown, white surf creaming on the sand. Then abruptly his radio-telephone crackled. Without explanation he was recalled to Gosport.

Along the coast confusion multiplied. At Folkestone's Hotel Mecca, panicky officials whipped out Mrs Lillian Ivory's telephone, then remembered her boarding house was Intelligence Corps Headquarters; hastily they brought it back again. On a night drive from Brighton to Worthing, Miss Vera Arlett kept her pass at the ready; bayonets glinted eerily at every checkpoint. At Dover, bugles sounded along the white cliffs; in a score of villages from Portsmouth to Swansea, Home Guardsmen, unbidden, rang the church bells to warn against invasion, a lonely tolling over dark fields. In Reg Cooke's little coastguard cottage at Pett, Sussex, the telephone shrilled, and the Home Guard was on the line. "They've landed at Lydd."

Peering east through the darkness, Cooke could see nothing – and in any case he had only a duck-gun. He and his wife Lydia went to bed.

All that night, the Home Guard stood by, alerted for the first invasion for nine centuries, gripping a weird armoury of weapons – from assegais to four-dozen rusty Lee-Enfield rifles, relics of a spectacle, supplied by London's Drury Lane Theatre. Around Southampton, troops of the 4th Division dozed in motor coaches, fully clothed, rifles by their sides. At Stubbington, Hampshire, Colonel Barrow told his Home Guard company: "They may be landing paratroops behind you, but there will be no turning back." Doggedly his farm-workers and shepherds agreed – though only one among them had a .22 rifle; the rest had stout sticks.

Some units had word early. At Gosport, Pilot Officer Clarke and his fellow pilots stood by all night with four bombed up Roc target-towing planes, only one of them fully armed or equipped with wireless. Others knew nothing until dawn; although Fighter Command's signal A 443, was issued at 9.50 p.m., it was, ironically, one of the night's few cipher messages to be allotted no priority. Some units didn't even decode their copy until 10.30 a.m., on Sunday, September 8.

Then, as the full impact struck home, station commanders jumped to it. At Middle Wallop, Red Tobin and the pilots of 609 sat strapped in their cockpits, engines turning over, facing downwind. At Hornchurch, airmen at 603's dispersal heard Wing Commander Cecil Bouchier rasp over the tannoy loud-speaker: "Stand by – be ready to draw rifles and ammunition from the armoury." Bouchier was now at his wits' end: his instructions were to wreck all electrical transformers, gut the hangars, blow up the water supply and defend the airfield to the death – but whether before or after demolition, Bouchier didn't know. In the end, feeling faintly ridiculous, he did nothing.

At Hawkinge, Aircraftman Jock Mackay and his mates, given much the same instructions, could hardly begin to comply. Issued with five rounds of ammunition per man, they had never learned to fire a rifle.

A few decided to be safe, rather than sorry. Lifeboatman Ernie Barrs set off for Margate's boathouse with his dinner parcelled in a red handkerchief, knife and fork lodged in the knot; if things got busy, he wasn't going to miss his dinner the fourth Sunday running. Private Ben Angell set out for morning service at Dover's Baptist Chapel. Though this was a National Day of Prayer, some in his unit were bent on getting drunk – but Angell thought a prisoner-of-war would need all the faith he could get.

All that day, strange rumours multiplied. Station Officer Thomas Goodman, a London fireman on relief at Dover, heard of an attempted landing at Sandwich Bay, fourteen miles north: the inshore waters were black with German dead. Taking a staff car, Goodman set off – to find only baking sands and blue sea, not a soul in sight.

In Folkestone, the people numbered Dover's fate in hours: the Germans had completed a cross-Channel tunnel and were preparing to launch bombs against Dover torpedo-fashion. Dover knew the worst about Folkestone: because their ground defences had caved in, German planes had launched that London raid from Hawkinge. Worthing's citizens knew well enough why no bombs had come their way – Goebbels's mother lived there. (She didn't.) Croydon had the buzz that Goring was striking at food supplies: thirty milkmen had been machine-gunned in the streets. (They hadn't.)

Only two days earlier, Winston Churchill had warned the House of Commons: "We must prepare for heavier fighting in the month of September. The need of the enemy to obtain a decision is very great."

Ironically, it seemed to the Germans that with every sortie the British got stronger: the unopposed flights of September's first days were past now. Days before, Major Hannes Trautloft's outfit had been cheered to see German convoys steaming blithely along the coast, transport horses at the water's edge growing accustomed to the splash of waves: now at 21,000 feet over the Thames Estuary, endless flights of Spitfires and Hurricanes were diving at the 54th Fighter Group head-on. To keep their bomber formation intact, Trautloft's pilots fought as they'd never fought before.

Back at Guines, Trautloft reported gravely on what seemed like a turning point: "The sky was full of roundels. For the first time we had the definite feeling we were outnumbered."

Other pilots agreed: to battle over England was to battle for life itself. One Trautloft pilot, Unteroffizier Fritz Hesselmann, was still being harassed when he baled out at 400 feet; smashing against a housetop in Hope Street, Maidstone, he escaped with broken legs. Gefreiter Heinrich Werner, pursued as hotly over Kent, was glad enough to bale out and surrender to the police; when record crowds gathered to gape outside Sittingbourne Police Station, the resourceful bobbies took round the Spitfire Fund collection box.

For some there seemed no peace even when battle was done. At North Weald guardhouse, Leutnant Ernst Fischbach, a captured Heinkel III pilot of the 53rd Bomber Group, was astonished to see an excitable Irishman, wearing a boiler suit and airmen's boots, storm into his cell brandishing a flying log-book. The unconventional Wing Commander Victor Beamish wanted confirmation that *his* Hurricane had delivered the coup-de-grace – though Fischbach, deep in shock, could only gawk at him.

It was as well the fighting spirit was there; daily the pilot shortage worsened. Faced with a steady drain of 120 men a week, Dowding saw nothing for it: from now on his squadrons must be split into three categories – Category A squadrons, to bear the brunt of the southern fighting, a small operational reserve of B squadrons, C squadrons stripped of every pilot still capable, virtually reduced to training units. Useless against German fighters, these squadrons were no longer fit to tackle anything save unescorted bombers.

If pilots were lacking, so, too, were the planes. At North Weald, on September 8, John Grandy's 249 Squadron had just seven Hurricanes available; at Westhampnett, 602 Squadron were down to eight Spitfires. Two days before the great dock-land blitz, Professor Lindemann had warned Churchill: all through August, fighter losses had totalled a steady fourteen per day. Now cannon production had slumped, too – so alarmingly, the output barely equalled one gun per fighter.

In fact, as Churchill was fast discovering, the position was worse: all told, twenty-six eight-gun fighters – roughly 800 per month – were being written off each day. When Churchill called for explanations, Lord Beaverbrook clarified: in fact, these figures included aircraft sent for repair. Ultimately, they'd be back in the fighting line – though it might be a matter of weeks.

Now, for the first time, Churchill realised the gravity of the situation: the Air Ministry wastage figures he'd been studying all the time took no account of damaged planes, only of total losses. The Under Secretary of State for Air, Archibald Sinclair, was forced to admit it: there were only 288 fighters, eleven days' supply, still in reserve. The losses had eaten into Britain's reserves to the tune of 45 per cent.

If Britain's aircraft factories and storage units came under concentrated pinpoint attacks by lone bombers, as Generaloberst Hans Jeschonnek, Luftwaffe Chief of Staff, had advocated as recently as September 2, the position would be desperate.

Now Churchill was at his wits' end: was Britain producing steadily more fighter aircraft, as he'd been led to believe, or not? Patiently Lindemann explained: it was indeed, but since more squadrons and training units were being created to absorb them, output remained virtually stationary. And Lindemann, a passionate statistician, added his own acid rider: between May 10 and September 12, the Air Ministry's gains and losses calculations involved a cumulative error of 500 aircraft.

It was small wonder that Churchill grumbled: "It is always very difficult to deal with the Air Ministry because of the variety of the figures they give."

The Air Ministry had statistical problems of its own. To Dowding's anger, their crash investigators raised sceptical eyebrows over Fighter Command's claims; checking wrecks over a sample area of Kent, they just couldn't find planes enough to support the figures. At once Archibald Sinclair sent for Dowding, urging: "Look here, you must give us accurate figures – the neutral countries aren't being convinced which side is telling the truth."

Replying, Dowding was glacial: "All I can say, sir, is that this war isn't being fought for the benefit of the neutral countries – it's being fought for the survival of civilisation."

It was a characteristically loyal defence of his hard-pressed pilots – yet Air Ministry saw the facts as clear. The raw two-week pilots, their leaders scarcely more experienced, were still, with no intention to defraud, overclaiming. Flight Lieutenant Michael Golovine, the leading crash investigator, summed up: "To get any true picture we shall have to divide by three."

It was a daunting realisation. Already Wing Commander Geoffrey Tuttle's Photographic Reconnaissance Unit, operating with eleven high-flying Spitfires from Heston, Middlesex, had spotted hundreds of invasion barges moving towards the Scheldt and the Straits of Dover: on the night of the 6th, 200 were massed at Ostend alone. On September 11, Winston Churchill warned the nation: "If this invasion is to be tried at all, it does not seem it can be long delayed." From Berlin, with grim humour, Hitler announced: "In England they're filled with curiosity and keep asking: 'Why doesn't he come?' Be calm, be calm. He's coming!"

But Hitler wasn't coming just then. Already, the alert for "Operation Sea-Lion", scheduled for September 11, had been postponed for three more days: only then would the Navy move out to sow the boundary minefields for D-Day, September 24. And though the commander-in-chief of the invasion forces, Generaloberst Gerd von Rundstedt, thought it likely he could reach Reigate in Surrey, by September 30, Gross-Admiral Erich Raeder didn't. On September 10, he reported: "There is no sign of the defeat of the enemy's Air Force over southern England or the Channel area."

Hour by hour, Dowding's pilots were living for the day, and their nerves were at full stretch. At Tangmere, Pilot Officer Frank Carey recalls, the morale of No. 43 Squadron "was really slipping" – and to 607 Squadron, moving in as their relief, it seemed that 43's pilots "couldn't leave Tangmere fast enough".

Soon enough they knew why. Since July, 43, at whiplash speed, had lost three squadron commanders; their last, Squadron Leader Caesar Hull, hadn't even survived long enough for his batman to sew on his third rank stripe. Now, settling into Tangmere, 607's pilots gazed with awe at tiny Tiger Moth biplanes, lashed up with racks of twenty-pound bombs. If training planes were in the battle against the invasion fleet, they knew how bad things were.

It wasn't something men often shaped in words. At Stapleford in Essex, the hard-pressed Flight Lieutenant Alexander Rabagleati, a South African, listened with mounting impatience to a Czech pilot's tale of woe; he'd be happier with a posting to another squadron. Angered, Rabagleati tossed back: "We don't care whether you're *happy*! Don't you realise we're fighting for your bloody existence?"

Pilot Officer Charles Ambrose, standing nearby, nodded thoughtfully. It was the first serious statement of war aims he'd heard since the battle started.

Some men had a frightening sense of disintegration. On leave in rural Buckinghamshire, Sergeant Ronnie Hamlyn tried vainly to check himself; one tinkle of a bicycle bell, so akin to the dispersal telephone, set him running like a hare. Pilot Officer Bill Read knew the same primal fear; let an ambulance bell jangle and he wildly took to his heels. At Croydon, Pilot Officer Christopher Currant, 605 Squadron, cursed unrestrainedly at any airman who hastened by; there was that awful jungle compulsion to run, too.

Fearing for his men at Digby in Lincolnshire, was Squadron Leader James McComb. Word had arrived that the pilots of 611 Squadron must, for the first time, patrol south, over London – yet now, as they stood by at dispersal, there came the solemn, disquieting notes of Chopin's Funeral March. By cruel mischance, a hard-drinking pilot of No. 29 night-fighter Squadron had crashed fatally two nights earlier; the funeral cortege, complete with band, was passing within feet of where McCombs pilots stood bow-taut at attention.

Covertly, McComb stole a glance at Pilot Officer Colin MacFie beside him: for this gentle nineteen-year-old, such an ordeal prefacing his first sortie could prove too much. Momentarily he saw MacFie's face crumple, then knew a blessed relief; the boy was battle-hardened before even a shot was fired. As the gun-carriage passed, MacFie, lips barely moving, muttered, "First time he's been on the wagon in weeks."

Few men found the strain as beneficial as Flying Officer Bryan Considine, 238 Squadron: a man who kept a hawk-eye on the bathroom scales, he was cheered to find that the stress had lost him a stone in weight.

The tension wasn't surprising. On all sides men saw their comrades die tragically and sensed the precious fragility of life. Near Westerham, Sergeant Stefan Wojtowicz, one of the first Poles to die, crashed in the deep abyss of a chalk-pit; the heat beat up the cliff-face like flames up a chimney flue, and the firemen couldn't reach him. Over Weybridge in Surrey, on their second patrol, every 611 pilot saw Sergeant Frederick Shepherd's Spitfire, hit by ack-ack, plunge flaming into the youngster's parachute, catapulting him to the ground.

This was September 11, when Fighter Command lost twenty-nine aircraft and seventeen pilots, with another six men wounded. As Red Tobin put it to Andy Mamedoff: "The death of one experienced guy is worth ten Spitfires."

Off-duty, each fought against the pressures as best he could. At Hornchurch, Flight Lieutenant Norman Ryder nightly steered the youngsters of 41 Squadron to the bar for a round of beers, counselling: "Drink up, now – you can't sleep on cold ham and celery." Ryder's own ration was three pints of beer and six gins, but he had a flight commander's worries. At Croydon 605 Squadron, packed into an open truck, ran the gauntlet of ack-ack to The Greyhound Hotel for a party to end them all – heedless of an unexploded parachute mine in a tree across the way.

No man was gayer than Pilot Officer Christopher Currant, striving to blot out the most awful sight he had then seen – an airman drifting slowly on a parachute, whom he'd circled during that afternoon's combat, watching the smoke curl slowly from his boots, up towards his back, until flames spurted for the harness, and the pilot, still beating frantically at his overalls, hurtled downwards, his speed fearsomely increasing.

Until closing-time at The Greyhound, Currant could forget it; until the time came to sob himself to sleep.

It was the same in every squadron. All night Pilot Officer Bill Assheton, 222 Squadron, screamed from a pit of nightmare, but when the squadron took over the bandstand at Southend's Palace Hotel, he was always first to seize the mike, ad-libbing combat chatter as Squadron Leader Johnnie Hill pounded the drums: "Achtung, Spitfire – 109s to starboard." For most, sleep was time ill-spent; when Air Chief Marshal Dowding warned 249 Squadron at North Weald, "The need for you to rest is paramount – soon we may have to fight for thirty-six hours non-stop," Squadron Leader John Grandy and his pilots were of one mind: "Christ, let's get to London for a party."

Not all carried it to the extremes of No. 92 Spitfire Squadron, just then moving into the relief of Biggin Hill. Thumbing their noses equally at danger and discipline, they rigged up their billet, Southwood Manor House, two miles from the blitzed drome, as a non-stop night club, with a combo of batmen posted for their skill on sax or trumpet... imported London fashion models to keep the party spirit alive... snipped off the ties of any VIPs reckless enough to impede them.

It wasn't all living it up; with the cornered courage of men whose backs were to the wall, the R.A.F. were growing wary. From September 5 on, Air Vice-Marshal Park was operating every squadron in pairs – the agile Spitfires to deal with the fighter screen, the sturdier less manoeuvrable Hurricanes to tackle the bombers. And most, now conscious that the Germans' morning raids came from the south-east with the sun behind them, from the west in the afternoon, took care to place themselves up-sun before they dived.

At Duxford, a No. 12 Group station west of Cambridge, the legless Squadron Leader Douglas Bader had carried Park's idea a stage further: why not meet strength with strength? A formation of three squadrons, flying as a wing, was a better match for 100-plus Germans than a scant twelve planes. For 11

Group squadrons, covering the approaches south of London, such formations just weren't practicable: one squadron, quickly airborne, could hinder deliberate precision bombing while a wing was still gaining height. Then, too, to employ a wing meant committing all one's machines against a possible German feint.

But Air Vice-Marshal Trafford Leigh-Mallory, Air Officer Commanding No. 12 Group, had nothing to lose: his airfields lay north of London and in East Anglia, which allowed precious time for a wing to manoeuvre. And though there were teething troubles – thirty-nine fighters could scramble in three minutes flat but it took ten minutes, climbing hard, to get them as high as 2,000 feet – Bader was persevering. On September 14, he planned to lead an armed pack of sixty fighters into the air for the first time.

Bader wasn't the only man to have second thoughts on tactics. Those head-on attacks the Poles so relished took all the nerve a man had – the aggregate rate of closing was 550 miles an hour, and the quick pull-out to avoid collision could turn you sick and dizzy. Though the Air Staff discouraged them as "unorthodox", some squadrons, such as John Thompson's 111 Squadron, had all along used them to good effect; now other outfits, such as the headstrong 92 Squadron, were trying them, too. As Thompson enthused: "The bombers scatter like a flock of starlings."

Often, to Keith Park's fury, squadrons just ignored the controllers' orders now, gaining height and climbing steadily. Airborne from Croydon, Flight Lieutenant Archie McKellar and the pilots of 605 heard the Kenley sector controller's voice in mounting irritation: "Confirm that you are indeed on vector oh-nine-zero." In fact, the squadron, as always, was flying not southwards but on the reciprocal course, due north, steering 270 degrees magnetic, all the time gaining height. From Hornchurch, Flight Lieutenant Norman Ryder used the same tactics, determined his pilots wouldn't even cross the Thames until they'd reached 18,000 feet.

Often it meant tangling with high-level fighters while the bombers got through, but pilots who'd been bounced too often saw survival as paramount. Somehow, they must live to fight another day.

And though Fighter Command had issued no contrary orders, many pilots hotly questioned the wisdom of those tight-packed V-shaped formations. At 66 Squadron's Kenley dispersal, young Robert Oxspring, learning fast, was the centre of nightly heated arguments: surely the losses were a pointer towards scrapping the whole formation?

When some argued that the height of a battle was no time to switch tactics, Oxspring countered: "The Guards don't go into battle as if they're Trooping the Colour – they fight from trenches. We're trying to fight a battle like an air display." Confronted with the standard Fighter Command attacks, Oxspring was withering: "That book's a criminal document – the whole formation sticks out like a dog's balls."

All through this week, in the warm smoky twilight of the pubs they used, the pilots thrashed out the tactics that could wrest victory from defeat... Biggin Hill men in The White Hart at Brasted, Kent... Gravesend pilots in Charles Dickens's beloved Leather Bottle at Cobham... North Weald pilots in The Thatched House, Ingatestone, on the leafy fringe of Epping Forest... Red Tobin and other Middle Wallop pilots in the still room of The Black Swan, Monxton, irreverently christened The Mucky Duck.

Expertise was the currency. At 28,000 feet, nearing the height of Mount Everest, where the 109s lurked, the grease in your guns might freeze solid and you couldn't fire a shot. If you took off in wet boots, your feet, even 3,000 feet below that height, could freeze to the rudder pedal. At Westhampnett, 602's pilots found that a sliced potato rubbed over the bullet-proof windscreen was the sure way to stop it icing up. At Croydon, 605's pilots teased one flight commander unmercifully: forced on the edge of the stratosphere to relieve the needs of nature, he hit his compass in error, watched in horror as it promptly froze up, leaving him completely lost.

Those who had tips to survival passed them on – to others who listened because their lives depended on them. One pressure of the thumb on the gun button might push the control column slightly forward, depressing the plane's nose – so to aim true, first lock the stick with your left hand, then fire with your right. See that those last fifty rounds in your guns were glinting tracer – then you'd know you were running short. Use your mirror to watch your rear like a canny motorist – the top brass hadn't incorporated them in fighter planes, but wise men fitted their own.

Prudent men nursed their eyesight, too: the man who saw farthest shot first. At Middle Wallop, 609's Poles, Novierski and Ostazewski sat for hours, inert as zombies – staring at flies on a faraway wall to strengthen the six muscles of the eyeball. 605's Archie McKellar was most often relaxed on his bunk, pads of lotion-soaked cotton wool restoring his vision.

And at Hornchurch, tyros listened open-mouthed to Pilot Officer George Bennions, 41 Squadron's Yorkshire-born deadshot: "You want to be slightly above them or just under their bellies, lad – dead astern, at two hundred yards range, and you just can't miss…"

—

About 9 a.m., on Thursday, September 12, Winston Churchill was hoping that the R.A.F. couldn't miss. As things stood now, only 1,381 pilots of Dowding's force stood between England and annihilation.

On the face of it the old warrior was as buoyant as ever – as if challenge was meat and drink to him. Fearing the worst, his bodyguard, Inspector Walter Thompson, had begged him to consider his own safety; now the London raids had begun, anything could happen. For answer, Churchill, quivering with indignation, had poked his stick towards the worn grey facade of 10 Downing Street: "Thompson, the Prime Minister of the country lives and works in that house – and until Hitler puts it on the ground, *I* work there."

Then, despite all Thompson's admonitions concerning security, he posed patiently on the front steps for a group of press photographers. Gently he chided his bodyguard: "They have to get some copy, Thompson – they're all God's children, you know."

And this morning, at London's Holborn Viaduct Station, awaiting the Prime Minister's special train that would carry them to Shorncliffe in Kent, Thompson witnessed one of the war's most moving sights. As Churchill, deep in conversation with Lieutenant-General Sir John Dill, Chief of the Imperial General Staff, Lieutenant-General Alan Brooke and Admiral Sir Dudley Pound, the First Sea Lord, paced the station platform, a horde of office workers, streaming from suburban trains, suddenly espied Churchill across the tracks.

In that moment, it was as if a skilled stage director had pulled the strings; the concourse halted, and a great impromptu cry rang out over the whole station: "Thank God for the guns." Deeply stirred, Churchill raised his right hand in his famous victory gesture, to rally them: "And for every bomb they drop we will give them back ten."

To Sir John Dill, his aside was caustic: on the night of September 11 the ack-ack had put up its first-night barrage of 13,500 rounds, excellent for morale, no doubt, though they hadn't scored one hit.

And Churchill had a busy day ahead of him. There'd been alarming reports of the vulnerability of the Dover guns and the Premier had to see for himself… on the way down, he talked long and earnestly with General Brooke on the defence of the Narrows… a searching inspection of the coastal guns at Dungeness… then on to Dover to lunch at The Castle with Admiral Sir Bertram Ramsay, Flag Officer Commanding.

Yet hectic as the day had been, Brooke noted the Prime Minister had been as piqued as a youngster who'd missed a birthday treat: the front had stayed quiet and there hadn't been a single air battle for him to see.

Neither Churchill nor his party knew it, but Fate would recompense them. The greatest air battle of all time was just seventy-two hours away.

Chapter Nine

"There'll Be Someone There to Meet Them"

September 15

As Air Vice-Marshal Keith Park settled to his morning conference at H.Q. 11 Group, at 10.30 a.m., on Sunday, September 15, he and his staff officers were startled to see the beaming face of Winston Churchill framed suddenly in the open window. Courteously, Churchill reassured them: he'd no wish to disturb anyone, but as he was passing with his wife, Clementine, he'd looked in to see if anything was afoot.

He ended up: "But if there's nothing on hand, I'll just sit in the car and do my homework."

At once, Park rang Wing Commander Eric Douglas-Jones, the Duty Controller, in 11 Group's underground Ops Room: "Anything doing, D-J?" The controller wasn't certain, though he conceded, "Well, sir, there could be something up." Now, as one officer present, Wing Commander Thomas Lang, would always remember, Park's staff exchanged covert glances. Had the old warrior, in some uncanny way, scented a raid even before the radar stations?

In fact, Churchill often dropped into "The Hole" at Uxbridge – a bomb-proof nerve-centre fifty feet below ground, camouflaged from above by gaily-striped deck chairs, and green lawns merging unobtrusively into the nine-hole Hillingdon Golf Course beyond. This was the first focal point of every battle, where the duty controller, sifting information from radar stations and observer posts already processed by Dowding's Filter Room, allotted incoming raids by sectors – planning the opening gambits like a gigantic game of chess until the squadrons were airborne.

Park didn't realise that Churchill's sense of history had drawn him hence – recalling that Waterloo had been fought on a Sunday, too. But now it struck him that over breakfast he'd apologised to his wife, Dorothy, a member of his cipher staff; though today was her birthday, he'd been too pressed to buy her a present. Smiling, Dorothy Park had assured him: "The best present you can give me is a good bag of planes."

Now, as Churchill's party trooped down sixty-three blackened stone steps to the Ops Room, Park wondered: Had Churchill sensed there would be a good bag? It seemed prudent to warn the Prime Minister: "I don't know whether anything will happen today, sir. At present all is quiet."

All over the airfields of southern England, from Hornchurch in the east to Warmwell in the west, the pilots shared Park's feelings: if trouble was afoot, there was no sign of it as yet. It had still been cold and dark when Pilot Officer Red Tobin, sleeping off a late night at The Black Swan with Shorty Keough, awoke to find Pilot Officer John Dundas shaking his shoulder: "I say, better wake up."

When Red, irate, demanded why, Dundas, yawning, replied: "I'm not quite sure, old boy – they say there's an invasion on or something."

Hastily, Red had scrambled from bed – just how calm could an Englishman get? – but outside there wasn't a hint of trouble. Nothing but goblin wraiths of mist above the chestnut trees, the measured thud of the bowsers refuelling the planes, the Spitfires' silhouettes, dark against the dawn, like some weird immobile flight of prehistoric birds.

There was that same relaxed air at every squadron dispersal – as if each pilot sought relief from tension in calm workaday routine. At 229's dispersal, Northolt, Squadron Leader John

Banham sat as stiff as a statue while the famous war artist Cuthbert Orde limned a swift portrait in charcoal, then relaxed thankfully as Orde first sprayed the sketch with fixative, then dated it – September 15, 1940. For neither man then could this date hold significance.

At Debden, the pilots of 73 Squadron were agog over a current sweepstake: the sex of Flight Lieutenant Mike Beytagh's forthcoming baby. (It was a girl, Molly, born on September 26.) At Croydon, 605's pilots, sprawled in deck chairs in the gardens of commandeered villas along the airfield perimeter, were absorbed in calculations of their own: how many rose-bushes and cigarette butts would their voracious billy goat, brought south as a mascot, eat before breakfast this morning?

Covertly, their squadron commander, Flight Lieutenant Archie McKellar, studied every one of them, checking that each man had taken time to shave. If a 605 pilot died this morning, the fastidious McKellar, as always, was determined he'd die barbered and clean.

Despite the outward gaiety, a few squadron commanders sensed an aching tension beneath. At Biggin Hill, Flight Lieutenant Brian Kingcome rallied the incorrigibles of 92 Squadron: "Any of you chaps war-weary, want a posting? If so, speak now, or for ever hold your water." At Duxford, the legless Squadron Leader Douglas Bader, making the rounds of his sixty-strong fighter wing, quietly assured the Poles of 302 Squadron: "You'll soon be back in Warsaw."

Some felt weary beyond all belief. At No. 1 R.C.A.F.'s Northolt dispersal, Flight Lieutenant Gordon McGregor stared glazedly at the brimming cup of tea his batman had just then placed in his right hand. Nowadays it was a safety precaution McGregor forced himself to take: if he fell asleep, the tea would spill and scald him, but at least he'd be alert and ready to go. No such problems faced 504 Hurricane Squadron at Hendon. This morning General Declos Emmons, U.S. Army Air Corps, and Rear-Admiral Gormley, U.S. Navy, were booked in on an important visit – stop-watches poised to check just how long a British fighter squadron took to get airborne.

For others it was a time of dedication. Many men, in later years, would recall this morning's services, and how the chaplains, with uncanny prescience, had picked their text from the 139th Psalm: "If I take the wings of the morning, and dwell in the uttermost parts of the sea, even there shall Thy hand lead me." At Northolt, Zdzislaw Krasnodebski's Poles voiced a poignant prayer of their own: "It does not matter that so many must perish on the way, that our hearts are eaten up by longing… we believe that You have not forsaken Poland."

Squadron after squadron sought distraction in music – nostalgic, ragtime, any music so long as the tune was familiar, something each man had heard a hundred times before. At Hornchurch, Pilot Officer "Razz" Berry's gramophone was forever grinding out "Sweet Violetta" or "She Had to Go and Lose It at the Astor"… Squadron Leader Rupert Leigh, at Gravesend, spun Dorothy Lamour's "These Foolish Things" so often, his pilots begged for mercy… at Duxford, a doggerel pop of the day, "Three Little Fishes", grating interminably over the loudspeaker, was a blaring diapason above the sound of Merlin engines roaring into life:

Down in the meadow in the iddy biddy poo
Thwam three little fishies and a mama fishie too.

In the Ops Room at H.Q. 11 Group, Winston Churchill felt this tension, too. To Churchill, the compact, two-storeyed underground room, sixty feet across, was for all the world like a small private theatre, the controller's dais on which he sat sited roughly where the dress circle would have been. Beside him, on a green, leather-covered swivel chair, Wing Commander Eric Douglas-Jones kept a sharp eye on the battery of six telephones linking him with the fighter sectors – and on the six bulb-lit panels covering the opposite wall, charting the state of every sector's squadrons.

The thought crossed his mind: at least the lacquer-red telephone that marked the "hot line" to 10 Downing Street would stay silent this morning. Whatever danger threatened, the Prime Minister was here to see for himself.

And to Churchill and every man on watch it was plain trouble was imminent. Already the W.A.A.F. plotters at the map below, earphones adjusted, were expertly piloting the coloured discs with their long croupier's rods: forty-plus coming in from Dieppe, corrected swiftly to sixty-plus. Seconds later, eighty-plus, this time direction Calais. Even Douglas-Jones, a seasoned controller, now felt a brooding sense of crisis.

A dead cigar gripped in his teeth – though he yearned to smoke, Keith Park had tactfully explained that the air conditioning just wasn't equipped to cope – Churchill now broke silence. "There appear to be many aircraft coming in." As calmly, Park reassured him: "There'll be someone there to meet them."

All along the coastline of southern England, 50,000 silent men and women – the watchers of the Observer Corps – binoculars levelled, peered intently towards the mist-shrouded sky, striving to interpret the danger signs – then, as the faint, far specks grew in number, their officers, prone among yellow gorse on the chalky clifftops, lifted their field-telephones. Now their warnings, speeding inland, lent weight to the reports from the radar stations, along the low-lying marshes. At Pevensey, Rye, Swinggate and Poling, the German formations had swum into focus: wide, deep, steadily beating echoes, arising from the mists of the morning.

From Rye Radar Station, Corporal Daphne Griffiths reported urgently to Fighter Command: "Hello, Stanmore, Hostile Six is now at fifteen miles, height fifteen thousand." At once Stanmore queried, "How many, Rye?" and as swiftly the answer flashed back: "Fifty-plus. Plot coming up. Read."

Still, in 11 Group's Ops Room, Wing Commander Douglas-Jones made no move. Behind him, Keith Park stood immobile:

no man to interfere with his controllers, Park's sole hint of his presence was never more than a firm hand placed quietly on the shoulder, token of encouragement. For one long second, Douglas-Jones hesitated. The squadrons needed height and sun – but supposing, as so often happened, this was a German feint?

But at 11.30 a.m., he could wait no longer. Already the lighted bulbs showed every squadron standing by, some men already in their cockpits, and Fighter Command had warned both 10 and 12 Fighter Groups to be alerted, too. He reached for the first of six telephones and, automatically, thirty-five miles away, a lighted bulb glowed on the desk of Squadron Leader Roger Frankland, controlling at Biggin Hill.

As Douglas-Jones, using the direct secret line, ordered, "Seventy-two and Ninety-two Squadrons to patrol Canterbury, angels twenty," Frankland seized his microphone; simultaneously identical instructions, further coded to fox German fighters, volleyed across Biggin Hill airfield: "Gannic squadron, scramble – Gannic squadron, scramble…"

Now every man sensed the shape of the battle that lay ahead.

To the first pilots airborne, it seemed that this morning the Luftwaffe, as never before, held the sky. Twenty thousand feet over Canterbury Cathedral, craning over his Spitfire's starboard wing, Pilot Officer Anthony Bartley, 92 Squadron, noted small, black, cotton-wool puffs of flak staining the sky and at once saw why: a vast gaggle of bombers was winging inland, evading the guns with ease, closely escorted by ME 109s, 3,000 feet below and astern. Awed, he muttered: "Jeepers, where the hell do we start on this lot?"

Then, to port, he saw ten Spitfires, soaring to join them, and felt suddenly less lonely: 72 Squadron were in the battle now, and with no more hesitation both units, guns blazing, closed in combat.

And more were destined to do so. At 11.50 a.m. Wing Commander Douglas-Jones had alerted Debden's controller: Hurricane Squadrons 17 and 73, this minute airborne, were to patrol over Chelmsford, Essex. Fifteen minutes later two more Hurricane squadrons, Krasnodebski's Poles and John Banham's 229 Squadron, got wind at Northolt: scramble and orbit Biggin Hill. Simultaneously Hurricane Squadrons 253 and 501 were climbing steeply from Kenley, heading for Maidstone at 18,000 feet.

Five minutes later, at 11.25 a.m., learning that every 11 Group squadron was now in action, Duxford's station commander, Wing Commander Woodhall, sent Douglas Bader's sixty-strong 12 Group wing speeding to lend support over London.

At H.Q. 11 Group, Winston Churchill watched with growing dismay: twenty-one squadrons were airborne now, and on every squadron panel a red bulb glowed ominously beside the legend "Enemy intercepted". Now he asked Douglas-Jones, "Good Lord, man, all your forces are in the air – what do we do now?"

Replying, Douglas-Jones strove to sound more confident than he felt: "Well, sir, we can just hope that the squadrons will refuel as quickly as possible and get up again. The fighter stations will report immediately when any aircraft are available."

In fact, the position, in many squadrons, was worse than even Churchill could know: the hard-pressed 501 Squadron, at Kenley, could this morning muster only two planes serviceable. It was worse for 73 Squadron at Debden: twenty-four hours earlier, their thirteen Hurricanes had been savagely trounced by a squadron of trigger-happy Spitfire pilots. One life – and six aircraft – had been lost before this last great battle was ever joined.

And still the Luftwaffe streamed across the Channel... slim logger-headed Dorniers... glinting shark-nosed 109s... slow, scantily-armed Heinkel 111s... many of them decorated with insignia as colourful as any air force had ever boasted... the green dragon signifying Hauptman Hans von Hahn's 1st Wing, 3rd Fighter Group, picked out by a high and watery sun... Major Adolf Galland's Mickey Mouse, armed with gun and hatchet, puffing a cigar strangely like Galland's own... the eagle's head of Werner Molders... Major von Cramon-Taubadel's jet-black ace of spades.

Outside the Receiver Block at Rye Radar Station, Corporal Daphne Griffiths, shielding her eyes against the glare, watched now in silent awe the very planes that she herself had plotted roaring overhead – as if a dense black swarm of insects was advancing upon her, each one trailing ever-lengthening miles of white ribbon. Minute by minute the swarm grew denser, the morning sun gilding yet more legends and emblems... the green heart of Major Hannes Trautloft's 54th Fighter Group... the white-and-red lightning flashes of *Kampfgeschwader* 3... the poised black sledgehammer that marked Oberst Johannes Fink's Dorniers... the bared shark's teeth of No. 2 Wing, *Zerstorer* Group 76.

Some, as the Spitfires of 72 and 92 Squadrons, dived over Canterbury, veered back towards the coast – but many more, among them the Dorniers of Oberst Chamier-Glisczinski's K.G. 3, bored on towards London.

High above the city's grey huddled rooftops, Pilot Officer Red Tobin, watching them come, perversely knew relief: almost since dawn 609 Squadron had patrolled over London, first at 25,000 feet, then at 20,000... up to 25,000 feet once more, the Controller heartlessly juggling the heights like a puppeteer, until half an hour had passed. Then suddenly they saw them – 100-plus German planes – and mercifully the suspense was broken.

Simultaneously in Red's earphones sounded Squadron Leader Darley's measured Oxford drawl: "Many, many bandits at seven o'clock," and the young American winced. The Germans were right behind them – and again Red was "Arse End Charlie", weaving back and forth to protect his section's rear.

Then it was Andy Mamedoff's turn to wince, because his own section leader, John Dundas, had yelled as suddenly:

"Many, many bandits at four o'clock!" The meaning was crystal clear: the Germans were surrounding them.

Now, peering skywards, Red Tobin saw, 4,000 feet above them, fifty hovering 109s, but to the right and 1,000 feet below were twenty-five Dornier bombers: and these Flight Commander Frank Howell was readying to attack. He called to Red, "O.K., Charlie, come on in."

Then, in this last moment, feral instinct once more saved Red Tobin's life. In the second of closing in, something prompted him to make one last check, swinging the Spitfire violently to port, and as he swung back on the last weave of all he saw, almost dead astern, three yellow-nosed Messerschmitt 109s.

Like most R.A.F. pilots, Red assumed yellow noses symbolised ace pilots, though in fact these were mere identification symbols, in no way implying a crack unit. But aces or no, the planes spelt trouble, and now Red's voice, "loud enough to be heard in Kansas", blasted in Howell's eardrum: "Danger, Red Section, danger, danger, danger!"

In that instant, he saw Howell break frenziedly to starboard, down towards the bombers, while the No. 2 man did a tight climbing turn to port, and Red himself, reefing his Spitfire into a steep 360-degree turn, threw on the emergency boost, slamming his propeller into high pitch as he spun round. Again instinct was a screaming voice: Keep chasing your own tail and they can't touch you. They're too fast to pull out of that dive.

And Red was right. Engines snarling at full throttle the 109s hurtled past at upwards of 400 miles an hour, and now Tobin was in turn the pursuer, sending long bursts of tracer hammering in their wake. Smoke bellied from the last plane's motor, then all three were gone, streaking for the anonymity of cloud-cover.

Climbing again, weaving violently at 275 miles an hour, Red felt the blood pounding in his temples, and just then, 200 yards to port, he saw a Spitfire spin away in an uncontrollable dive, its whole cockpit made invisible by fire. Whether it was Howell or Geoff Gaunt he could not know, but whoever the pilot was, there was no hope for him, so to himself, Tobin said quietly: "Whoever it was, he's flying in clearer sky."

Suddenly, dead ahead of him, Tobin saw a slim, cigar-shaped Dornier nose into a shallow dive, heading for cloud-cover, and now he dived again, thinking: If he makes the cloud, he's lost, so get him now. And with this thought he thumbed the firing button. Tracer broke in a chain of sparks against the bomber's port motor, and abruptly white smoke was bannering. So the radiator was hit – or maybe the glycol tank.

Gingerly, Tobin eased the Spitfire round, waiting until the port wing was steady in the gunsights, firing again until the aileron collapsed and fragments of wing fluttered emptily through space. As it gained cloud-sanctuary, he momentarily lost sight of it, then plunging through, he was in time to see it crash-land shakily, grinding to a halt, across a wide meadow. As Tobin circled, three of the crew clambered out, sprawling dazedly across the still-intact starboard wing.

And now Red Tobin stopped short: was this really *his* Dornier – or another that had crashed in a field a quarter of a mile away, alongside a wrecked ME 110? A mile distant, both a Spitfire and a Hurricane were down, too; as far as a man could see, there was nothing but crumpled aluminium grasshopper-shapes, and the white billowing shrouds of parachutes.

It wasn't surprising: out of twenty-one squadrons airborne since 11 a.m., fully twenty-one had intercepted, though not all of them had met with marked success. At 18,000 feet over Biggin Hill, Squadron Leader McNab's Canadians never saw the group of 109s that slashed at them from the sun: only two of the Hurricanes even closed with the raiders. It was the same with 41 Squadron over Gravesend; baulked equally by 109s, they watched yet more bombers slide through to London.

Few were yielding to the odds without a struggle. Twenty thousand feet over Maidstone, Belgian pilot Georges Doutre-pont sheared single-handed into twenty-five ME 109s in a vain attempt to divert the bombers' escort, then, fatally wounded, plunged with a sickening downwards twist into the railway station at Staplehurst, Kent, strewing fire and devastation.

A few miles away, at Cranbrook Police Station, even war-hardened bobbies such as Police-Constable Jack Hood heard the news with consuming grief. Only a few days back the little Belgian had been sitting with them, chatting in broken English over a cup of tea, after being downed over the same district.

Now, as Big Ben boomed noon, 148 German bombers broke through undeterred to central London, showering bombs to southwest and south-east, landing one bomb, unexploded, in King George VI's back-garden at Buckingham Palace. Yet from the ground, few civilians witnessed this historic combat: thick white clouds hung low above the city's spires. Fifteen-year-old Roy Owen Barnes wrote it down as the most disappointing day on record: this morning, as always, he'd thrilled to the sound of the siren, yet now, peering at the clouds above Catford, South London, his aircraft recognition booklets were no help at all. At Chislehurst, Kent, schoolteacher Ernest Mann was as piqued: machine-gun clips clattered on the suburban pavement and engines droned and wailed, but he never saw a plane all day.

It was easier for Squadron Leader Douglas Bader and the fifty-nine pilots of the Duxford wing. Arriving late over London from the north, they swiftly spotted the bombers five miles distant, "like drilled black flies sliding towards the naked city". As they gave chase to the west, they little by little gained height and sun – and suddenly, miraculously, the bombers had turned, sweeping into their sights.

And now, the radio-telephone was an urgent pandemonium; at the spearhead of No. 302 (Polish) Squadron, Squadron Leader Jack Satchell heard Bader shout: "Weigh-in, everyone for himself." Ten thousand feet above, where 12 Group's Spit-fires waited to tackle the fighters, Flight Lieutenant Jack Leather chuckled to hear Bader explode: "There are the buggers –

come on, let's get at the bastards." Promptly, the soothing voice of Wing Commander Woodhall sounded from Duxford's Ops Room: "Douglas, remember there are ladies in the Ops Room this morning."

At H.Q. 11 Group, one lady didn't mind at all: while Winston Churchill remained tensely on the controller's dais, his wife, tuned in to a radio-telephone link-up in a nearby annexe, heard a sudden flood of medieval oaths as Krasnodebski's Poles sighted the bombers. When a shocked staff officer made to switch off, Clementine Churchill restrained him: "It's lovely, I wouldn't have missed it."

Twenty-seven thousand feet over London, Squadron Leader James McComb, of Bader's Spitfire force, throttled back his machine with mounting impatience. At this height the intense cobalt blue of the sky, the sun's fiery radiance, his breath condensing like frosted glass on the cockpit canopy, were among the most exhilarating sights he'd ever seen – but though his Spitfires had waited for seven long minutes to engage the hovering 109s, the German fighters had made no move.

Most, with growing apprehension, were watching their fuel gauges, knowing that the moment to break for the Channel must come within seconds now – but though McComb didn't divine this, he saw Bader's Hurricanes below had the monopoly of the action. At fever-pitch, McComb broke radio-silence: "To hell with this – we're coming down! Squadron echelon port – St. George for Merrie England, rah-rah-rah."

And down they went.

Now the sky became a wheeling, snarling saraband of warplanes – as Bader later recalled it, "the finest shambles I'd ever been in." Flame and black smoke spewed from a Dornier's bursting engines; aircraft spun everywhere in blurred and fleeting confusion. On his first sortie with 302 Squadron, Flying Officer Julian Kowalski watched two of his comrades fall like stones; though his Hurricane was riddled with seventy-six bullets, he alone survived from his section.

Close at hand, two of the crew leaped from a burning Dornier 17; as the bomber dived for the earth, another Pole, savagely slicing the tail from the burning aircraft, wrenched his own, port wing away at the root. To port, the sky rained rudders and sheet metal; to starboard, a Spitfire carved clean through the fuselage of an abandoned Messerschmitt, then spun away fearsomely, beyond control. High above, more crewmen baled out – from a Dornier that broke evenly and terribly in half, level with the black crosses.

In a combat so frenzied, few men could know with certainty who fired at whom – or with what results. Sergeant Ray Holmes, a Hurricane pilot of 504 Squadron, hot on the trail of a bomb-shedding Dornier, was convinced it was the very plane that had bombed Buckingham Palace; no sooner had it blown up than Holmes himself, his Hurricane hit, baled out. Landing in a dustbin in Ebury Bridge Road, South London, he phoned his home-base, Hendon, with an interim bulletin: his victim had crashed with spectacular force in the forecourt of Victoria Station.

Unknown to Holmes, Pilot Officer Keith Ogilvie, of Red Tobin's outfit, was just then making this same report to 609's intelligence officer – a feat that earned him a personal commendation from Queen Wilhelmina of the Netherlands. A Buckingham Palace guest who had witnessed the furore, she was anxious to thank Ogilvie for guarding her so zealously.

To the Germans, both fighters and bombers, this morning run-up to the target seemed a veritable ambuscade. Oberleutnant Ernst Dullberg, a young 109 pilot, never forgot the eerie sensation of crossing the coast escorted by a silent phalanx of Spitfires – the contrails streaking the sky far above his unit, keeping pace all the way to London. Worse by far was the gauntlet run by Oberst Johannes Fink's scantily armed Dorniers, a sortie culminating in unmanned guns, with the dead and wounded sprawled out on the floor. Horrified, Fink saw one Dornier fall from the sky before a shot was even fired, knowing its pilot had reached the peak where the strain could be borne no longer.

As Fink recalls September 15: "No man could be asked to bear more tension – mental or physical."

And many men, gripped by the heat of battle, became, on a sudden, primal. Swooping above the black shape of a slowly descending German pilot, Squadron Leader Bryan Lane, one of Bader's wingmen, watched gleefully as his Spitfire's slipstream rocked the parachute violently towards the topmost branches of a wood, screaming: "I hope that breaks your neck, you bloody swine!" Above Rotherfield, Sussex, dozens, homeward bound from morning service, watched horror stricken to see a Dornier trailing fire towards their village – the gunner's parachute snagged hopelessly on the tailplane, a flight of Hurricanes in pursuit raking him relentlessly with bullets.

Chastened, Major Hannes Trautloft confided in his diary: "Who'd know that it was Sunday if it hadn't been announced on the radio?"

By 12.29 p.m., the Observer Corps' 19 Group H.Q. at Bromley, Kent, could report no further raids coming in, only a slow ebb of Channel-bound planes high above the oast-houses and apple orchards. Though the sky was scarred with contrails, and burning metal pulsed and flickered amid the stubble, the last great wave had receded.

The lull would not last long. Even now, on the airfields of northern France, the Germans, determined that the morning's score should somehow be reversed, were refuelling and bombing-up for the biggest sortie of all.

–

Beneath the sultry heat of early afternoon, Middle Wallop airfield lay silent – a silence that Pilot Officer Red Tobin could equate only with despair. For Red, the morning's brief, heady triumph – a Dornier officially confirmed – had ended in bitter anti-climax: homing in on Wallop, his landing gear down, just seven gallons left in his fuel tanks, he'd never espied the crash waggon that shot from behind a hangar into his line of flight until too late.

Next instant, one of his wheels had grazed the top of the truck, the impact jarring it back into the fuselage. Effecting a tricky landing on one wheel, Red knew the plane was a write-off – and now, though the rest of the squadron, including Andy and Shorty, had scrambled hastily once more, Red himself was grounded. There simply wasn't one spare machine left at Middle Wallop.

It was hours before Red Tobin could fully appreciate why, but by 2 p.m. on September 15, this was the measure of things all over. In this last effort to force the R.A.F. into a fight to extinction, the Luftwaffe had committed every plane they could muster – and to meet the challenge, any R.A.F. plane still serviceable was airborne to join the fray. At H.Q. 11 Group, Winston Churchill himself, noting that every red bulb now glowed ominously, had asked Air Vice-Marshal Park: "What other reserves have we?"

Park had to admit it: "There are none."

His face a graven mask, Churchill said nothing, but his thoughts were anguished. If refuelling planes were caught on the ground by other raids of forty- or fifty-plus, the chances for the R.A.F. were minimal.

Even the decimated 264 Defiant Squadron were just now up over Kirton-in-Lindsey, Lincolnshire, orbiting base at 15,000 feet, with six planes – all that could be mustered.

At Rye Radar Station, Corporal Daphne Griffiths had seen the shape of things to come as early as 1 p.m.; already the screen showed a steady build-up of returning formations. At 2 p.m., with a new watch manned under blonde Betty Graham, Daphne and her friends adjourned to the canteen, hadn't even finished their jam tart and custard before the sirens whined over the marshes. At once, determined not to be penned in camp, the W.A.A.F.s bolted for their bicycles, pedalling up Rye's Leasam Hill, intent on a grandstand view.

Now, in the breathless moments of early afternoon, Sector Controllers all over southern England were marshalling their squadrons as 11 Group so instructed them, and the radio-telephones crackled with call-signs that held a strange ring of Alice-in-Wonderland: "Hello, Garter, this is Caribou, your message received and understood"… "Hello, Turkey Leader, hello, Turkey Leader, this is Runic, patrol Maidstone, angels twenty"… "Laycock Red Leader, this is Dory… about forty bandits heading for Lumba… will you patrol?" "Laycock Red Leader to Calla Leader… watch it, Calla Leader, here the bastards come!"

It was 2.25 p.m. All along the south coast, hundreds craning upwards saw now the last classic interception of the Luftwaffe by Dowding's fighters: tiny black specks, flashing silver as the sun's rays caught them, machine-guns rattling, as if a boy ran a stick along a line of palings, the white drifting motes of parachutists pulling on their guide lines, like the first faint flakes of a snowfall.

To Major Adolf Galland, the spearhead of this mighty force, whose task was to clear the skies over Maidstone, it seemed that fresh, larger-than-life squadrons had suddenly been conjured from the ground. For ten hectic minutes – one of the longest combats he could ever remember – Galland wheeled in battle with Hurricanes and Spitfires – to achieve precisely nothing. Then, sighting a squadron of Hurricanes, 2,500 feet below, he swooped to test his skill anew, launching a lightning attack from the rear at the last plane on the port flank, closing to within ramming distance. Chunks of molten metal beat a fierce tattoo on his windscreen and now, as Galland tore past and above, he was, for one fearful instant, penned in on all sides by the Hurricanes. Again he attacked, an onslaught so stunning that not one Hurricane opened fire, and then the whole formation had burst apart, plane after plane peeling skywards and down-wards, and 1,500 feet below, Galland saw two pilots bale out.

Fully 3,000 feet below a third Hurricane loomed, and again Galland dived, firing without cease until flames burst from the

265

cowling, yet still the R.A.F. pilot seemed undaunted; in a series of gentle curves the machine glided serenely on. Three times more Galland banked, opening fire – then stopped abruptly. The Hurricane was still spiralling towards the ground, as if piloted by a phantom hand – while the pilot, relaxed in the open cockpit, sat stone dead.

For most German fighters this whole afternoon proved to be a vicious circle of frustration. Leutnant Hellmuth Ostermann, of the 54th Fighter Group, knew he'd never felt more impotent; tugging like a man berserk at the controls of his ME 109, he could feel the very fuselage shaking, yet still the bright blue bellies of the R.A.F. fighters stayed tantalisingly out of range, diving and firing each time the bombers turned, while the 109s, forbidden to pursue, looked helplessly on.

The same outfit's Oberleutnant Hans-Ekkehard Bob had troubles all his own; 12,000 feet above Canterbury, a cannon shell struck his radiator, and Bob knew that if he immobilised his airscrew, letting the machine glide on its own power, the wounded Messerschmitt couldn't carry him more than twenty-five miles – perhaps to mid-Channel, no more.

But Bob, determined to make it somehow, tried a bold experiment. Cutting his motors, he let his machine glide gently, while the airflow from the still-turning propellers served to cool his engine as the radiator fluid would have done. Then, priming the motors, he swiftly gained height – taking the Messerschmitt as far as he could until the engine was near to boiling. Hastily, Bob again cut the motor, reverting to a gentle glide, until the airflow had done its work – then once again started up. As he skidded in a hair's-breadth forced-landing along the sandy beach near Calais, he whooped joyfully: "Cape Horn in sight."

To the Luftwaffe, ever after, this last-ditch mode of navigation was known as "bobbing across the Channel".

To a few bombers, shorn of fighter-escort, it seemed fruitless even to attempt the journey. Airborne from Juvaincourt in a Junkers 88 of the 77th Bomber Group, Oberleutnant

Dietrich Peltz found the whole sky empty of 109s; without hesitation he sent the whole 4,000-pound bomb load tumbling towards the Channel. And other bomber pilots saw the gesture as eminently practical; the piled clouds ruled out all hope of precision bombing, and everywhere the R.A.F. were waiting. With his pilot slumped bloodily on the cockpit floor, Oberleutnant Heinz Laube, a Dornier observer, took over the shattered bomber's controls for the return journey, somehow achieving a jolting, juddering emergency landing on Antwerp-Deurne airport.

Equipped only with a B-2 civil licence, Laube had never, until this day, flown a bomber in his life.

With aces like Galland bemused by the whirl of fighters, it was small wonder the bombers of the afternoon wave paid a bitter price: almost a quarter of all those engaged, with many more seriously damaged. The crucial two hours' delay had given the R.A.F. time to re-fuel and re-arm, and, even more, to stir men to epic endeavour. Those who had known success that morning knew they just couldn't miss – and those who had failed hitherto were out for blood.

Ever since that tragic August 24 encounter with the Blenheims, Squadron Leader Ernest McNab's Canadians had ached to acquit themselves in battle – and now over Biggin Hill, at 2.30 p.m., on September 15, their chance had come. Diving like angry eagles on a formation of twenty Heinkel bombers, eleven Hurricanes cut them to ribbons – to McNab, the white plumed exhausts of the wheeling aircraft were suddenly "like sky-writing gone mad". From the carnage, one Canadian, Flying Officer Phil Lochnan of Ottawa, emerged to fulfil ambitions of his own. Belly-landing his Hurricane beside a crashed bomber in the mud-flats of the Thames Estuary, he personally escorted the crew from the aircraft – one of the few fighter pilots ever to take a prisoner.

It was a notable exception. The battle was suddenly a clawing, stalling mass of fighters bent on destruction, battling within a cube eighty miles long by thirty broad, more than five miles high: a battle that within thirty minutes would number above 200 individual combats. So crowded was the sky that Sergeant James "Ginger" Lacey, a twenty-two-year-old Hurricane pilot, happily tagging on to a flight of 109s, painstakingly shot down two before they'd ever spotted him. As a Dornier's port wing flashed over his cockpit, veteran Squadron Leader Bryan Lane, ducked involuntarily, breathed: "Why, it's the whole Luftwaffe." Pilot Officer Patrick Barthropp, operational for the first time that day, felt as awed. After the morning's sortie, he'd noted in his log-book: "Thousands of them." This afternoon, he returned to note again: "*Still* thousands of them."

But even the novices were well to the fore – among them, young Robert Oxspring, who'd so taken his flight commander's caveats to heart that on his first seven sorties he'd never once fired his guns. Now, still finding himself no match for a 109, Oxspring was cruising his Spitfire home at 2,000 feet, when he suddenly saw a Dornier climbing for the cloud. Scarcely able to believe his luck, he turned in pursuit, firing for the first time to see four crewmen bale out – then, to his horror, saw the stricken Dornier crash like a thunderbolt onto a rooftop near Rochester, Kent. In that moment the whole house fell in, a yellow-white cone of plaster dust trembling above the ruins.

It was no wonder newcomers such as Oxspring were awed by their own prowess: even the veterans achieved feats that surprised themselves. At the very moment Oxspring was closing on his Dornier, 611's Squadron Leader James McComb, diving on another Dornier from the sun, put out its port engine, pulled up into a loop, then dived again – upside down. To his astonishment, his guns worked perfectly; as he came to from a momentary blackout, he saw the Dornier dissolve in flames.

For now, with sun and height and numbers at last in their favour, few R.A.F. pilots any longer took thought of the risks. To Krasnodebski's Poles, under Squadron Leader Ronald Kellett, the whole afternoon battle recalled the Charge of the

Polish Light Horse at Somosierra, when Polish cavalry, annihilating the Spanish gunners at the mouth of a canyon pass, paved the way for Napoleon's advance on Madrid. Pilot Officer Miroslaw Feric, sending an ME 110 flaring towards the sea, felt a savage exultation; on the third day of war a German fighter had shot away his control column at the base, leaving him petrified with fear, but accounts had been squared now. Flying Officer Witor Urbanowicz, seeing a Dornier on the point of force-landing, saw no good reason why the crew should survive; one lethal blast across the cockpit sealed the bomber's fate.

And Sergeant Stanislaw Karubin, his ammunition exhausted, was still determined to finish off the Messerschmitt that had assailed him; carolling an old cavalry song, "Oh, it's fine when the uhlan rides to war," he flew head-on at the plane like a suddenly loosed torpedo, breaking to reef his Hurricane a yard above the cockpit hood. For a second, he glimpsed the German's face distorted in mortal terror – and the man's hand on the controls gave one fatal tremor.

A mighty muffled crash sounded from far below, as the Messerschmitt hit a meadow in a rending all-out dive, tearing the body of the plane apart, scattering the wings 100 yards across the pasture.

The battle was only fifteen minutes old, yet already so many parachutes blossomed across the sky that one cheerful Pole, floating down, yelled a warning: "They'll take us for a bloody parachute division."

Chapter Ten

"Here Come Those Last Fifty Spitfires"

September 15 and after

High above the Dorniers of the 76th Bomber Group, London-bound, hovered the escort fighters of Major Max Ibel's JG 27 – and as the glinting cohorts of Spitfires hove into view, Ober-leutnant Ludwig Franzisket sardonically broke radio silence: "Here come those last fifty Spitfires!"

Franzisket felt no fear as such, but with him, as with many Luftwaffe pilots, the promises of the top brass now held a hollow ring. For six long weeks they'd been assured the R.A.F. were a write-off – and now at 2.30 p.m., on this mellow September Sunday, the British fighters were more numerous and fresh-seeming than ever.

The truth was that Air Chief Marshal Sir Hugh Dowding was still 170 pilots under strength – but at this eleventh hour a fierce elation had seized every man airborne. Squadron Leader James McComb still recalls seeing his second-in-command, Jack Leather, airborne on the second September 15 sortie, "grinning hugely, his hood open, German bullets ripping past his flying helmet". As McComb flew alongside, Leather, switching his radiotelephone to send, remarked happily, "Kee-rist, this is dangerous."

Many took risks that later turned them cold to think about. Above Maidstone, Pilot Officer Mike Cooper-Slipper, 605 Squadron, felt something jar his Hurricanes undercarriage, knowing the plane had taken fire, then saw dead ahead three Dorniers closing in. Accepting that his machine was finished, Cooper-Slipper now made a sudden snap decision: "I'll ram them."

As he later recalled, his main preoccupation was to ram the middle plane; all thoughts of death or pain passed him by. The impact came, and again, recalling an early automobile accident, Cooper-Slipper thought clinically, "It's quite different – not a big bump at all. It's just a swishing and a swooshing." Dimly, he was conscious of his Hurricane's port wing catapulting away into space, smoke enveloped the shattered Dornier, then that too had fallen steeply away. At 20,000 feet, ripping three finger-nails from his right hand, Cooper-Slipper baled out.

–

Over Appledore, Kent, Pilot Officer Paddy Stephenson, 607 Squadron, came to the same decision. Two Dorniers were approaching so fast he just hadn't time to take aim. The sole recourse was charge them with a right and left blow from both wings. Baling out above the blazing bombers, to land outside the local lunatic asylum, Stephenson was probably the only Battle of Britain pilot to bring down two German aircraft without firing a shot.

And others had experiences as bizarre. Toronto-born Stanley Turner, one of Bader's aces, his Hurricane's tailplane afire over the Thames, was about to bale out when he realised there was no necessity – the heavy rain cloud he'd just flown through had as promptly extinguished the flames. And, in Squadron Leader Jack Satchell's outfit, one Polish pilot – intent on finishing off a Dornier – flew so close a crewman baled out clean into his airscrew, smashing it to pieces, stoving in the radiator. Somehow, the Pole contrived to force-land his scarred and bloody Hurricane near North Weald.

Most were so afire with the chase that all thoughts of time and place were suspended. Implacable Sergeant Janos Jeka, a

Polish Hurricane pilot, pursued a 110 so close to the earth his bullets were literally scything up yards of turf. Sergeant David Cox, a Spitfire pilot, chasing a 109 all the way to France, only turned back when his oil temperature went right off the clock. Sub-Lieutenant George Blake, Fleet Air Arm, took his Spitfire so close to a Dornier "it was like Nelson firing a broadside at Trafalgar".

Curiously, few pilots this afternoon were notching up top scores; it was teamwork from first to last – and so numerous were the crippled bombers few men could miss. Over the English Channel, leading 609 Squadron in pursuit of two limping Dorniers, Flying Officer Michael Appleby, deciding the time was propitious to launch one of Fighter Command's classic attacks, rapped out: "Number One attack, Number One attack, go."

To Appleby's mortification, nobody had even heeded him. Without waiting for instructions, Andy Mamedoff, Shorty and the rest had all dived blindly to attack, blasting the bombers to pieces in mid-air, each man duly claiming "one-sixth of a Dornier". Intent on leading a superb charge, Appleby found he had arrived last of all.

Just a few men were on their own all through. At Northolt, forty-three-year-old Group Captain Stanley Vincent, World War One adversary of the famous Richthofen Circus, saw no good reason why his squadrons should monopolise the combat. Mobilising the Station Defence Flight – his own Hurricane – Vincent set off in search of action.

Abruptly, at 19,000 feet over Biggin Hill, Vincent found it; a flight of eighteen Dornier 215s escorted by twenty 109s, droning inexorably for London. Without hesitation, Vincent flew steadily towards them, opening fire at 600 yards, closing to 200 yards, seeing his bullets strike home. Minutes later, the Heinkels had turned, breaking for the Channel, and Vincent, streaking in pursuit, sent a fusillade of tracer after them, before pulling sharply up to engage the fighters.

To his astonishment, the nearest 109 burst into flames before he'd even fired a shot, its pilot baling out – and now Vincent realised that in the shrieking confusion, a second 109 had been stampeded into shooting down his own leader. Before his ammunition ran out on this memorable day, Vincent had just time to attack and destroy the second.

To some, it seemed the most routine day ever. Pilot Officer Vernon Simmonds, 238 Squadron, sailed through a barrage of ack-ack over London, blew up the starboard engine of a Heinkel 111, realised that cannon had riddled his own tailplane, was back at Middle Wallop in fifteen minutes flat. To Sergeant Cyril Babbage, the day spelt tedium all the way. Abandoning his Spitfire over Shoreham, Sussex, shortly before noon, he found the battle so disrupting rail traffic that it took five hours to cover the twenty-five miles from Shoreham to 602 Squadron's dispersal at Westhampnett airfield.

It was a day of stark tragedy for some. Far below the swirl of the battle, at Hanns Farm, Bilsington, a village above the Romney Marshes, thirty-one-year-old Alice Daw was getting her small daughter, Vera, ready for an outing. Her husband, William, who farmed the smallholding, had promised them both a run in the car, and already four-year-old Vera was on tiptoe with excitement.

Neither Daw nor his wife saw the jaunt as a calculated risk. Aerial dog-fights in this part of Kent were now so commonplace few villagers even bothered to take shelter. At this moment, tinkering with his old rattletrap inside the barn, Daw wasn't even conscious that there was a plane overhead – or that Oberstleutnant Hassel von Wedel, the Luftwaffe's official historian and World War One comrade of Goring, was in dire trouble.

Ever since his arrival on the Channel coast, attached to the 3rd Fighter Group, he had put in creditable flying hours for a man of forty-seven. Determined to record every facet of the battle, he'd flown twenty-three dangerous missions – and today was no exception. When the unit's commander, Major Gunther Lutzow, and ten others were briefed to "free-hunt" across the Channel, von Wedel determined to join in.

It was a hazardous decision – hazardous because the myopia that had grounded von Wedel from operational flying was a grievous handicap on such a no-holds-barred mission. At 6,000 feet over Maidstone, von Wedel never even saw the Hurricane that riddled his yellow-nosed Messerschmitt 109 with bullets. Circling frantically, losing height by the minute, it was cruel misfortune that his engine seized up as he glided over Hanns Farm.

In the barn below, Farmer Daw heard nothing; he was still servicing the car when the Messerschmitt ploughed through the roof of the barn above his head… knocking Daw unconscious and reducing the car to scrap metal… strewing its severed wings across a field near by… fatally fracturing Alice Daw's skull as she ran from the cottage… killing four-year-old Vera outright.

The first men on the scene, the local Fire Brigade, found von Wedel unhurt, his fall from the plane broken by a pile of manure, yet plainly the bald, eagle-faced man was on the verge of crack-up. Near to tears, he could only repeat, "I've killed a woman, I've killed a woman," over and over again. As one of the Fire Brigade hastened to the farmhouse to brew the stricken pilot a cup of tea, somehow no one had the heart to break the news concerning the child. Repatriated in 1943, to die outside Berlin in 1945, von Wedel until the end believed that this tragic day had offered one compensation; a child's life had been spared.

A few would always see the day as one of total failure. At Duxford, Squadron Leader Douglas Bader was cursing like a trooper; the scramble had come too late, the Germans had had the height on the 12 Group wing all the way, the controlling had been inept from start to finish. Given expert guidance, his pilots could have shot down every raider that crossed the coast – and from now on this was Bader's insatiable ambition.

To the newsmen, by contrast, it seemed a day for tributes. *The New York Times's* Robert Post reported: "The German loss of air crews is tremendous." The London *Daily Express* was sardonic: "Goring may reflect that this is no way to run an invasion." The London *Times* was cautiously confident: "The figures... give grounds for sober satisfaction."

Ordinary civilians felt the same. At Folkestone, Grocer Fred Turner, working peacefully on his allotment as the fighters duelled above, saw an old man with a wheelbarrow capturing the mood of the moment. Following behind Folkestone's only horse-drawn vehicle; a milk-cart, he was carolling, "There'll always be an England", as he shovelled up the dung. Inland, at Marden, Kent's Civil Defence boss, Alderman E. S. Oak-Rhind, saw a sight to touch the heart; a gang of, field labourers, rising as one man to doff their caps, as a lone squadron of Spitfires roared overhead.

At Maidstone, a downed German fighter pilot added a tribute of his own to Home Guardsman A. H. Terry: "Well done, Spitfire."

Yet, at top level, many felt concern. At 3.50 p.m., as the all-clear sounded at H.Q. 11 Group, Air Vice-Marshal Park confessed to Winston Churchill: in the last twenty minutes of the raid, Control had been so swamped with information they hadn't been able to handle it. Nor had the interception been by any means fool-proof; everywhere the German bombers had broken through. Still, Churchill felt moved to praise Wing Commander Douglas-Jones, clapping him on the shoulder with an unexpected "Good show, old boy".

It was hours before Fighter Command knew the extent of their losses – twenty-six planes, thirteen pilots – but it was known that many planes had taken a cruel beating. If the Germans came again in such force, could the R.A.F. still contrive to stem the tide?

At many airfields, they were wondering, too. At Northolt, the plight of Zdzislaw Krasnodebski's 303 Squadron was typical of many. By the day's end, only four aircraft remained service-able. Ten others had cables cut, control surfaces shot away, radiators smashed, wings and engines riddled, one with its main wing spar nearly broken at the junction with the fuselage. Without more ado, the servicing flight, under Flying Officer Wiorkiewicz, a Warsaw factory engineer, settled to a gruelling all-night vigil, nourished only by cups of tea, to present twelve planes serviceable by first light. It was the same on airfield after airfield.

And nobody among Dowding's pilots thought in terms of a final victory. If many messes held parties that night, it was because the nerves demanded one to relax the aching tension, for no man knew now which party might be his last. 73 Squadron's pilots packed out the Fox and Hounds at Steeple Bumpstead, Essex, for just one reason; they'd found a cunning way of sabotaging the clock to allow an hour's extra drinking. At Northolt, Group Captain Stanley Vincent threw an oyster-and-stout party for a few close friends – but it wasn't every day a Royal Flying Corps veteran got back into action.

At Middle Wallop, Mess Steward Joseph Lauderdale sought out Flight Lieutenant James MacArthur, recalling his deep depression on September 7, when the R.A.F. had fared so badly over dockland. Wasn't he ready for a plate of the cold Scotch salmon now? Again, MacArthur shook his head: "I've no stomach for it, Mr Lauderdale. There were so many British planes up today I never got one squirt at a German."

Only at 8 p.m., did there seem some cause for jubilation. At Chequers, Winston Churchill, peeling away the black satin eye-band he always wore for sleeping, was just waking from a nap; it had been 4.30 when he'd arrived back from 11 Group and the drama had tired him out. He rang the bell, and Principal Private Secretary John Martin brought a dismal budget of news... the Italians were advancing on Alexandria... fifty British tankers had been destroyed. Then Martin wound up: "However, all is redeemed by the air. We have shot down one hundred and eighty-three for a loss of under forty."

Within days, Flight Lieutenant Michael Golovine's crash investigators had arrived at the truth; the German losses totalled no more than fifty-six. In addition to twenty-four ill-fated Dorniers and ten Heinkel 111s, the R.A.F. had accounted for eighteen Messerschmitt 109s, three ME 110s and one Junkers 88. Yet within days, too, further truths were emerging; the German attempts were slackening as the Luftwaffe tried to thrash out some feasible way of continuing the assault.

From August, through September, their losses had totalled some 1,140 planes of all types – and at such a rate of bomber losses the force would surely bleed to death. Even isolated fighter units, such as 54th Group's 1st Wing, after losing fourteen pilots in two months, were being pulled from the line.

Crimson with rage, Goring summoned his commanders for a stormy September 16 conference, charging furiously: "The fighters have failed." In vain, Oberst Theo Osterkamp defended them; if they were restricted to escorting bombers, how *could* they fulfil their original function? Then, too, the British were employing new tactics, gathering large numbers of fighters with express orders to concentrate on the bombers.

For answer, Goring could only roar: "If they come in large numbers, we should be pleased – they can be shot down in large numbers."

Osterkamp was silent. In the face of Goring's irrational outbursts, there was no more that any man could usefully say. Attacks by single fighters, rendered clumsy by 500-kilo bomb-loads, would drag on until December – their losses spiralling as the surprise element that Hauptmann Walter Rubensdorffer had pioneered were lost altogether. The Battle of Britain might be over – but the battle between Goring in Berlin and the Luftwaffe commanders in the west could only intensify from now on.

In any case, air supremacy was no longer geared to the logistics of "Operation Sea-Lion". One day earlier, in Berlin, Hitler had stressed that "Four to five days good weather are required to achieve decisive results". But, by September 17, Gross-Admiral Raeder had dictated for the War Diary: "The enemy air force is by no means defeated. On the contrary, it shows increasing activity. The Fuhrer therefore decides to postpone 'Sea-Lion' indefinitely." Within two months, Hitler's resolve was crystallised – the onslaught on Russia, "Operation Barbarossa," assumed full priority.

When Generalfeldmarschall Wilhelm Keitel queried the wisdom of this, Hitler was icy: "I have come to this decision and no more discussion will follow." To Oberst Martin Harling-hausen, 10th Flying Corps' chief of staff, he elaborated; "I want colonies I can walk to without getting my feet wet." A few still felt the decision rankled. To Sperrle's chief of staff, Oberst Karl Roller, Hitler burst out angrily: "The world would have been very much better off if the aircraft had never been invented."

Reichsmarschall Hermann Goring veered from the frus-trated to the philosophical. On September 14, at his hunting lodge in the Rominterheide, East Prussia, he assured Haupt-mann "Assi" Hahn at the height of a stag hunt: "Two weeks more and Britain will be forced to her knees." Within days he confessed ruefully to General Kurt Student: "We'd forgotten that the English fought best with their backs to the wall."

It wasn't an admission he'd make at all levels. When Gener-alfeldmarschall Albert Kesselring suggested that it was high time to concentrate solely on night bombing, Goring exploded: "Night raids? What insanity! I can finish the air war without that." But, within days, he saw the solution as the one factor that must break down British morale, reasoning: "After all, man isn't a nocturnal animal." He rallied the disillusioned Oberst Johannes Fink: "You must give the German people air superi-ority as a Christmas present to hang on their trees."

All this lay in the future. For most people, as September 15 drew to a close, it was a matter of overwhelming relief that after six fateful weeks they were still alive and free.

Pilot Officer Geoffrey Page lay in a clean white hospital bed, not moving, not speaking. By now he knew well enough what the battle had done to his face and hands. Fifteen major surgical operations were to be endured before Page, through bitter determination, fought his way back to operational flying, vowing to take one German life for every operation he had undergone. Only once this was achieved did the bitterness drain from him, leaving him void and spent, but this was not yet. There was nothing in his heart now but hate.

Zdzislaw Krasnodebski, at thirty-seven, could summon more philosophy. Barely conscious at the Queen Victoria Hospital, East Grinstead, he blessed the opiates that dulled his pain. The noise of the last great air battle seemed very far away, but he knew that until he flew again his stewardship had not been in vain. Each time Jan Zumbach and young Ludwig Paszkiewicz came to visit him, the squadron had eclipsed its past endeavours. He wondered how soon the Polish Underground would assure Wanda he was alive and well.

For most pilots, the evening of September 15 was as uneventful as any other. Young Barrie Heath, a 611 Spitfire pilot, got back late to his rented flat near Digby airfield to make his peace with his wife. It wasn't only combat that kept him so long; they'd had a few drinks in the mess. When Joy Heath chided him, "I *do* wish you'd let me know if you're going to be late for dinner," the young pilot apologised meekly. The cast-iron excuse – that he'd been fighting for his country – never occurred to him until later.

Others had to come to terms with things. At Gravesend, Pilot Officer Robert Oxspring couldn't face a drink until he'd first rung the Rochester police. Had the house wrecked by his very first German victim been tenanted or empty? But the police were reassuring and he felt better. Only twenty-five years later did he learn they'd spared his feelings, that a woman and child had died.

Mike Cooper-Slipper, who'd rammed the Dornier head-on, wondered if his own experiences in some way crystallised the whole upside-down day. First, drunken hop-pickers had tried to lynch him, convinced he was a German... then, assured of his nationality, they'd been ready to fight the police for the honour of his custody... Though a doctor gave him a cup of tea, his hand shook so with shock he couldn't drink it ... then, having lost both doctor and police, he'd found himself in a stranger's house at a children's party, young hero-worshipping faces upturned to his.

Then the children faded as in a dream, and suddenly he was in an unidentified Army mess, intent on being driven back to Croydon airfield. But his escort, with mistaken charity, halted at many pubs along the way, and when Cooper-Slipper at length reached Croydon he'd collected two German Mae West lifejackets and a rubber dinghy, and was more dead to the world than he had ever thought possible.

For Red Tobin and the pilots of 609, it was a routine evening at The Black Swan, Monxton. Red knew now that it was Geoff Gaunt who had gone down in flames, and he drank that much harder to forget. He was missing Ann Haring tonight, too; then, snapping out of it he told himself: "Hell, Tobin, why don't you quit your beefing? You'll live through it."

Three days from now, he, Andy and Shorty would go north as pilots of the first Eagle Squadron, forming at Church Fenton, Yorkshire. He would miss the British right enough, but maybe action with the new outfit would be rougher yet. As Andy always said: "Time will tell."

In northern France, the Germans, as yet, had no inkling that the invasion was off. Only gradually would that realisation sink in, and some would know relief, others regret. Major Hannes Trautloft, a diarist to the end, noted: "It seems very unlikely we shall end the war against Britain this year – and who knows what will happen next spring?" At Sempy, in the Pas de Calais, Major the Baron Gunther von Maltzahn voiced what some perhaps already felt: "We're never going to win this war; we can't."

At Guines, Major Martin Mettig, hearing of the cancellation, asked the officers assembled in the Casino, "What were all the deaths for then, eh?" and nobody could answer him.

Oberst Theo Osterkamp carefully checked the date in his diary – September 15 – then, lifting the phone, ordered Generalfeldmarschall Albert Kesselring's car to stand by, along with a Storch airplane. The local anti-aircraft band, too, were placed on the alert before Osterkamp, poked-faced, reported to Kesselring: "We're truly sorry to see you go." When Kesselring gaped, Osterkamp produced the diary as a witness: on this day Kesselring had given his solemn promise he'd return to Brussels and leave them in peace.

Blinking, Kesselring emerged at last from the "Holy Mountain" into the strong sunlight, grumbling: "A fine thing, a colonel throwing out his own field-marshal." Then Osterkamp gave the signal, and at once the military band struck up lustily, "*Muss i denn, muss i denn, zum Stadtele hinaus?*" (Oh, must I leave my hometown?) Chuckling hugely then, Kesselring flung up his arms in surrender.

Adolf Galland was in Lille, playing ragtime on a cafe piano, a score of others clustered round. The pilots had hijacked every military road-sign for blocks around, and carted them to the cafe: one of the officers was swinging rhythmically from the central chandelier. It was long past midnight, but when the provost's men strode disapprovingly in to check on his papers, Galland just played faster than ever, black cigar still clenched in his teeth. He said: "Just look in the *Berliner Illustrierte* – front page." It featured his latest decoration, as large as life. At this moment, he hated provosts as much as staff-officers, anybody who wasn't a pilot, the whole stinking war.

Across the Channel, in southern England, the night seemed mercifully quiet. Outside Ladwood Farmhouse, Robert Bailey was lost in thought, hearing the gentle pulsing of the bombers en route to London. It had been the usual quiet evening at Swingfield Baptist Chapel, and he and Vera had been back well in time to hear the B.B.C.'s 9 p.m. bulletin, when announcer Alvar Liddell read the news: "Wave after wave of raiders tried to approach the capital... some planes got through, but the rest were harassed and shot to pieces by our Spitfires and Hurricanes."

Now, Bailey had dimmed the oil-lamp and stood quietly in the darkness, wondering: the news seemed more cheering, but who knew how much the public were told? Some of the Swaffers' children, clustered behind him in the porch, heard the bombers, and one asked timidly, "Is that a German?" "*No*," Bailey said quickly, "they're ours. Don't worry. They're ours."

It was quiet on the airfields too – save at Hornchurch, where the four-gun ack-ack battery on the officers' mess lawn made sleep almost impossible. Wing Commander Cecil Bouchier was still in the Ops Room, writing citations and sifting combat reports: in days like these it seemed the only time a station commander had to catch up... Soon the trucks would race past like fire-engines, bearing the pilots to dispersal, but that would be the dawn of another day.

Through the darkened corridors of Fighter Command, Air Chief Marshal Sir Hugh Dowding threaded his way like a ghost. Current Air Ministry propaganda was suggesting that his command was stronger now, towards the end of the battle, than at the beginning, and the false emphasis made Dowding angry: it hardly took into account the victories that had been achieved at the cost of pilots killed or wounded – or that many fighter squadrons were now little more than training units. It had been a long and awful struggle, and so much lay ahead.

A W.A.A.F. plotter passed ahead of him, and, exhausted as he was, the Air Officer Commanding-in-Chief didn't omit to open the door for her or to raise his hat as he said, "Goodnight." Now his car would bear him back to "Montrose". With luck, there might be two hours' sleep before the Prime Minister was again on the line, to ask how the night had gone.

It was late at Chequers, too, when Winston Churchill at last left his study. Outside the door, Inspector Walter Thompson was almost dropping on his feet, and Churchill, concerned, peered through the gloom: "You're tired out, Thompson." Thompson admitted it: "Yes, I am, sir." He remembered that day because it was the first time Churchill had ever put an arm round his shoulder. Then Churchill said: "It will be worth it in the end. We're going to win, you know."

They walked along the corridor like that, the Prime Minister's arm still round the shoulder of his faithful shadow.

At Biggin Hill, Corporal Elspeth Henderson was going off-duty. Northwards, the sky glowed with driven fires as 180 bombers pounded London, and the ack-ack barrage studded the night with golden sparks. Pausing for a word with the sentry, Elspeth wondered just how crowded the public air-raid shelter would prove at this hour; it was too stifling to sleep in the little room above the butcher's shop that was now Biggin's Emergency Ops Room, and meanwhile, their old billets were still unrepaired. To the problems of feeding and keeping clean was added now the problem of sleeping.

Ahead lay the long nights of bombing, and the day battles were all but over, but Elspeth Henderson did not know that then: tomorrow would be just another working day. Slowly, her trim resolute figure passed from the sentry's view; the darkness swallowed up the sound of her footfalls.

Facts About the Battle of Britain

This is not, and was never intended to be, the full story of the Battle of Britain: few campaigns in recent history have been subjected to such a working over by the military and air strategists. It is the story of a handful of people who lived out their lives against the battle's six most fateful weeks – their hopes and fears, what the battle sounded like to them, how it felt. And, since most of them were too involved emotionally to be aware of the neat phrases charted by the historians, even basic statistics must be accepted with caution.

Nonetheless, given these reservations, here is an attempt to answer some fundamental queries:

What was the span of the battle? Even today, twenty-five years later, leading authorities are at loggerheads here. Basil Collier's *Defence of the United Kingdom* voices the official Ministry of Defence viewpoint – a five-phase campaign starting on July 10. In direct variance, the Royal Air Force Association's *Battle of Britain Souvenir Book* gives the start as August 8 – along with *Newne's Directory of Dates and Anniversaries*. *Whitaker's Almanack*, though, favours August 11 – while the battle's close is varyingly given as September 15 (official British celebration day), October 5 and October 31 (the Ministry of Defence's official date). And many German historians place the battle's climax as late as May, 1941.

For the purposes of this book, my choice has been arbitrary: August 6 to September 15, the six crucial weeks when the battle for air supremacy was most closely linked with the preparations for "Operation Sea-Lion".

What types of British planes were involved? British legend obstinately gives pride of place to the Vickers–Supermarine Spitfire, Mark I and II – most of them armed with eight Browning .303-guns, capable of climbing 2,530 feet a minute, a maximum speed (at 19,000 feet) of 355 miles an hour. But, in fact, only nineteen Spitfire squadrons took part in the Battle: at peak, on August 30, exactly 372 Spitfires were ready for operations. By contrast, Hawker-Hurricane squadrons totalled thirty-three – with 709 planes available for front-line operations on August 30. Reliable up to 20,000 feet, with a sturdy gun platform, the Hurricane was essentially a slower performer – with a climbing rate of 2,380 feet a minute, a maximum speed of 342 miles an hour.

Other fighters marginally involved were the Bristol-Blenheim two-seater, used primarily by eleven pioneer night-fighter squadrons; the short-lived Boulton-Paul Defiant; the twelve wooden Gloster Gladiator biplanes of 247 Squadron, defending Plymouth's Royal Naval dockyard; the Fairey Fulmar fighter-bombers operating with No. 808 Squadron, Fleet Air Arm, from Wick, Scotland.

What planes could the Germans call on? Star performer in the German camp was the Messerschmitt 109, whose worth was proven in the Spanish Civil War; most of Fighter Command's spiralling losses could be laid at the door of the eight single-engine fighter groups – accounting for 805 of Goring's August 10 front-line strength – that took part in the battle. As fast as the Spitfire (maximum speed 354 miles an hour), faster than the Hurricane, it could out-dive and out-climb both; its sole drawback was that a Spitfire could out-turn it. Less certain were the 224 ME 110 *Zerstorers* (destroyers) that took part; initially successful as a long-range fighter, its speed (340 miles an hour maximum), its weakened tail unit, made it no match for the agile Spitfires. Among German bombers: the short-lived JU 87 Stuka dive-bomber, withdrawn after ten days' fighting; the Heinkel 111, inadequately armed with its hand-operated gun; the slim-nosed Dornier 17, "The Flying Pencil," originally a high-speed Lufthansa commercial plane; the Junkers 88 medium dive-bomber, best suited to the pinpoint bombing of industrial targets.

What were the total strengths? On August 13, "Eagle Day," the German Quartermaster General's returns show 4,632 aircraft in all countries – with an average of 3,306 serviceable at any one time. Total front-line strength, though, whittled down to 3,358 aircraft – with 2,550 planes immediately serviceable. The breakdown: 80 close and 71 long-range reconnaissance planes, 998 bombers (in *Kampfgeschwaders*, or bomber-groups, of 74 planes), 261 Stukas, 31 ground-attack planes, 1,029 single- and twin-engined fighters (each *Jagdgeschwader*, or fighter group, totalled 120 planes), 80 coastal reconnaissance planes. By contrast, Fighter Command had only 708 fighters, 1,434 fighter pilots, immediately available on August 3 to bear the brunt of the battle – though the trained pilot strengths of other commands were 1,147 (Bomber), 889 (Coastal), 206 (Army Co-operation), 702 (Overseas Commands).

Who flew the most sorties – and when? Here again, historians differ violently – according to the time-span they allot to the battle. In the six-week period under survey here, the Luftwaffe, on August 15 alone, set the record for the battle – 2,119 planes of all types, according to the most recent German figures. Other Luftwaffe peaks were achieved on Eagle Day, August 13 (1,485 sorties), August 16 (1,715), and August 31 (1,450). By contrast; only on one day, August 30, did Fighter Command's sorties pass the thousand mark – 1,054 sorties flown. Main R.A.F. efforts wore concentrated on September 6 (987 sorties), August 31 (978) and August 15 (974). Ironically, on September 15, "Battle of Britain Sunday", Fighter Command launched only 700 sorties.

Who lost what – and when? Undeniably, the most vexed of all questions concerning the battle. Beyond a point, neither Air Force had any way of checking whether a plane was a total write-off – and few pilots, in the heat of combat, could know with certainty whether a hit had proved mortal, or whether plane and pilot survived to fight again. Highest German losses came on September 15 (56 planes) and August 15 (55 planes); British losses were equally at peak on August 15 (34 planes destroyed) and August 31 (39 planes). But German Quartermaster General records for August and September, taken in conjunction with Ministry of Aircraft Production figures, show, significantly, that the German fighters gave rather better than they got: 558 single- and twin-engined fighters totally destroyed cost the R.A.F. 715 Spitfires and Hurricanes reduced to scrap. Total bomber losses, though, show Goring's cause for concern – 348 bombers, 47 dive-bombers.

What were the casualties? Again, figures tell only part of the story – because of varying time-spans and incomplete documentation. Of 2,949 British fighter pilots, 515 were killed between July 10 and October 31: apart from Britons, highest casualties were suffered by the Poles (29), Canadians (20), New Zealanders (15), Australians (13). Hardest hit units were both Hurricane squadrons – No. 238 and No. 501, with 17 casualties apiece. Casualties among German fighter pilots were smallscale compared with the home-defence losses of 1943/5: for example, Adolf Galland's JG 26 lost 293 pilots in 1944, only 82 during the whole of 1940. Bomber crew casualties were never totalled up, but Hans Ring (*The German Fighter Forces in World War Two*) shows 261 fighter pilots killed, missing or died in accidents between July and December, 1940, another 79 known to have been taken prisoner. Units that suffered most were Major von Cramon-Taubadel's JG 53 – 68 killed, missing or taken prisoner – and Werner Molders' JG 51 – at least 63 suffering the same fate.

Who were the top scorers? Here, too, statistics are but a pointer – according to which span of the battle the experts are surveying. In one respect, though, the two Air Forces differ markedly: the R.A.F. aces who later became legends – Bader, Malan,

Tuck – were all eclipsed, until December, 1940, by dead-shots the public barely knew. Among them: Pilot Officer Eric "Sawn Off" Lock, 41 Squadron (22 at least), Sergeant Herbert Hallowes, 43 Squadron (21), 605's Squadron Leader Archie McKellar (20), Sergeant James "Ginger" Lacey, 501 Squadron (19 at least), Pilot Officer Harbourne Stephen (19). But Hans Ring's German tally, taken up to the end of December, 1940, shows that the top aces were already men in the public eye: JG 26's Adolf Galland (57), Helmut Wick, JG 2 (56, up to 28/11/40), JG 51's Werner Molders (55), the same unit's Walter Oesau (39), JG 53's Hans Mayer (30, up to 17/10/40).

How did production measure up? Ministry of Aircraft Production figures, contrasted with German statistics held by the United States Strategic Bombing Survey, show that Goring's experts, in urging a switch in priorities, were wiser than their master. July, 1940, saw British fighter production given topmost priority – 536 fighters out of a total 1,757 planes from the assembly line. (The remainder: 451 bombers, 88 general reconnaissance planes, 517 training aircraft, 47 Fleet Air Arm planes, 117 miscellaneous.) As a result, the month's total fighter gain was 215 aircraft; even allowing for heavy losses, Lord Beaverbrook, on August 30, could signal that 1,081 fighters were at once available, with 136 Hurricanes, 116 Spitfires, ready for use within 4 days. (Another 191 Hurricanes, 81 Spitfires, were undergoing long-term repair.) By contrast, Germany's ME 109 production had been 164 planes in June, 220 in July, 173 in August, 218 in September. According to Professor Willy Messerschmitt, total aircraft production, at this time, never exceeded 460 aircraft a month, with bombers – on Goring's orders – taking top priority.

What did people say? There are no imaginary conversations in this book. Apart from contemporary documents and intelligence reports, such dialogue as is quoted represents a genuine attempt by one or more individuals to remember what he or she said at the time.

When did various events occur? Official papers *do* confirm that Squadron Leader John Peel's 145 Squadron fired what may have been the Battle's first shots at 9 a.m. on August 8 – and that the "All Clear" following September 15's second raid sounded at 3.50 p.m. In between, though, there are wide discrepancies; every time given in the text follows an existing log or report, but in the maelstrom of the battle, weeks could elapse before squadron diaries were made up. For example, Flight Lieutenant David Crook, 609 Squadron, writing at the time, placed the August 14 Middle Wallop raid as "soon after lunch"... Red Tobin's diary fixed it more accurately as 4.45 p.m.... the Middle Wallop Station Diary as 4.30 p.m., before the bombers had even crossed the coast.

Every care was taken to check that the incidents described pertain to the right day or time-span, but the time phases at the head of each chapter are a rough guide only. Inevitably, some incidents began earlier and finished later than the compass of that chapter.

Acknowledgements

Over pre-lunch drinks in the pillared hush of the R.A.F. Club, London, an oberstleutnant of the new Luftwaffe dropped his bombshell. A Battle of Britain veteran, like his host, Group Captain Peter Brothers, R.A.F., he looked back wryly to that summer of 1940 – when many Luftwaffe aces like himself vowed that their first drink on British soil would be taken here in this bar. Now, though contrary to all known club etiquette, he sought a favour: for auld lang syne, he'd like to buy a drink for every man in the house.

An unprecedented request – but then hadn't it been an unprecedented campaign? So promptly the group captain went into a huddle with the club's secretary, who in turn cajoled a quorum of committee members into reaching a drumhead decision. For a former adversary and a Battle of Britain survivor, anything was possible – and shortly the oberstleutnant, in the chair, was standing treat to an imposing cross-section of that year's Air Force List.

The story – and the sentiment – are typical. Air chief marshals, generals, pilots of every grade, flight mechanics, farmers, fishermen – 505 people in all, throughout Britain, the Commonwealth, Germany and the United States – showed similar generosity during the compilation of this book. All of them unselfishly gave up countless hours of time, to ensure that this human record of the battle might be as complete as could be.

The chivalrous jousting of the skies seems to have engendered this universal mood: nothing is ever too much trouble. It is symbolised, in many ways, by three unique associations, the Battle of Britain Association, the *Gemeinschaft der Jagdflieger*, and the *Gemeinschaft der Kampfflieger*, and to the officials of all three go my undying thanks – most especially to Air Commodore Aeneas MacDonell and Group Captain Tom Gleave, in London; to Herr Hans Ring, Herr Werner Andres and Herr Hans-Joachim Jabs, representing the German fighter pilots and to Oberst Robert Kowalewski, who fixed up many bomber interviews. They made possible contacts that I and my research team would never otherwise have made, and to Hans Ring I am forever indebted for permission to draw freely from his work in progress, *The German Fighter Forces in World War Two*. And many others, rifling through old diaries and address books, furnished valuable introductions: Generalleutnant Adolf Galland, Group Captain Peter Brothers, Oberst Freiherr Fritz von Schroetter, Wing Commander Robert Wright, Wing Commander John Cherry, Oberst Erik Hartmann, and Wing Commander Robert Stanford Tuck, in whose house some of the first crucial problems were thrashed out.

To the secretaries of many squadron associations, too, goes my deepest gratitude for their help in tracing literally scores of survivors. In particular, the help furnished by G. J. Rothwell (17 Squadron), Dennis Fox-Male (152), Ken Battrick (600), W. J. Cornish (601), G. Greenwood (605), Wing Commander Francis Blackadder (607) and Wing Commander Kenneth Stoddart (611) saved endless time and trouble. Lieutenant Earl Boebert, U.S.A.A.F., and Bill Matthews, both of the American Aviation Historical Society, cut many corners in tracing the first United States fliers. On the W.A.A.F. side I had help beyond price from Wing Officer Margaret Green, Mrs Violet Hime and Mrs Daphne Carne (then Griffiths) who initiated me into the mysteries of those 1940 radar stations.

Many survivors went far beyond the scope of the book to help get a better feeling of what it was all like. You sense how infinitely precious life was then, when Group

Captain Zdzislaw Krasnodebski, now reunited with Wanda in a quiet Toronto apartment, recalls the electric excitement of young Ludwig Paszkiewicz's first combat, and the comradeship of those long-ago nights at The Orchard restaurant… when Wing Commander Geoffrey Page, now a top aircraft company executive, shows the livid scars that the fires of battle imprinted on his hands… when Mrs McWatt Green (then Elspeth Henderson) beside her pin-neat rock-garden in Craiglockhart, Edinburgh, recalls the simple problem of getting a good night's rest at Biggin Hill. For a moment her eyes glow as she re-lives the danger, the sense of purpose, the fun of being a pretty young W.A.A.F. in England's front-line.

Superficially, most of these people can look back to that far-off summer with detachment – it's almost as if somebody else's snapshot had been pasted in their album. Yet all of them, having come close to death, seem to have achieved a greater maturity, a deeper understanding of their fellow men, than falls to many – most often in their readiness to laugh. Leaning on his five-barred gate, Robert Bailey chuckles and confesses ruefully: "I'd give anything to see a dog-fight up there again – provided nobody got hurt." From the streamlined ease of an executive suite in Bonn, Germany, Adolf Galland stresses that life with JG 26 wasn't all combat – sometimes there were parties where you could always sober the fuddled ones with a roar of "Achtung, Spitfire!" Oberstleutnant Herbert Kaminski, of the new Luftwaffe, recalls those days, too. "There was more discipline then," muses "The Last of the Prussians", "you didn't have to ask a general's permission to put a private on kitchen fatigue."

To these and many other survivors I am truly grateful, for without their help this book could not have been written. To record even part of the story has been a task equalling nine years' research: a 30,000-mile journey by a team thirteen-strong throughout 230 cities, towns and villages in Great Britain, Germany, Canada and the United States. The testimony of 434 eye-witnesses was the raw material from which this book was fashioned.

I must stress that none of the people here acknowledged necessarily agree with all – or in some cases with any – of my conclusions. For the views expressed or implicit in the course of the narrative, for any errors that may have crept in, I alone am responsible.

Despite personal testimony, this book is founded essentially on the hard core of records: on war diaries, flying log-books, police blotters, private diaries and contemporary letters. In this respect I am lucky enough to have been the first Battle of Britain writer to have had access to the invaluable studies of the United States Strategic Bombing Survey, and to the private papers of Lord Cherwell (then Professor Frederick Lindemann), Winston Churchill's scientific adviser. My deepest thanks thus go to the many archivists who made records available or suggested contacts: to Victor Gondos, Jr., Elmer O. Parker and John E. Taylor, of the National Archives and Records Services, Washington; to Sir Donald MacDougall and Miss Christine Kennedy of Nuffield College, Oxford; to Mr L. A. Jackets, Chief of the Air Ministry Historical Branch, London, and to Mr W. J. Taunton, Mr E. H. Turner, Mr S. H. Bostock, and Mrs G. A. Fowles, of that department; to Chris Coles, of the Ministry of Defence's Air Information Department; above all, to Generalleutnant Panitzki, Brigadegeneral Rudolph Jennett, Oberstleutnant Technau and Dr Lupke, for their generous long-term loan of many records from the Fuhrungsakademie, Hamburg.

How the Battle reacted on the people of southern England has remained, for the most part, a closed book; a special word of thanks, therefore, to Dennis Knight and Peter Foote who generously made available the private archive they have amassed over seven years. Their painstaking transcription of police registers, Civil Defence occurrence books, borough and rural district council records amounts to a veritable repository of unplumbed local lore. Time and again Messrs Knight and Foote emerge as the men who can pinpoint to the second when a plane crashed, where, what happened thereafter.

Others, too, worked like beavers to fill in blank passages in the narrative. Wing Commander R. V. Manning, Director of Air Force History, R.C.A.F., Ottawa, proved the final authority on all things Canadian; Mr. W. R. Wybraniec of the Polish Air Force Association in Great Britain, and most especially Major L. W. Bienkowski, lent essential colour to the Polish narrative; Mr I. Quimby Tobin and Mrs Phyllis Harrington went to untold trouble in furnishing the private diary of the late Pilot Officer Eugene Tobin as well as answering a host of supplementary questions. Generous help came, also, from Mr James Lucas, Mr Vernon Rigby and Mr John Sutters, of the Imperial War Museum; from Leonard England and Mary Taylor, of Mass Observation Ltd., from Herr Ziggel and Dr Schmalz, untiring in their help at the Bundesarchiv, Koblenz; from Mr. L. G. Hart and E. J. Grove of General Post Office Headquarters, London, and Malcolm Miles and C. A. Allen of the Royal Air Force Association.

At the British Broadcasting Corporation, G. A. Hollingworth and P. G. Curtis miraculously unearthed the text of the original B.B.C. news bulletin broadcast at 9 a.m., on September 15, 1940; Jackie Robertson, of Scottish Television, most kindly lent a set of shooting scripts covering the war story of 602 Squadron; Bill Herbert and Norman McBain, respectively of the Canadian Broadcasting Corporation's Vancouver and Montreal offices, dug out useful tapes. Vexed questions on Battle of Britain weather were the province of the Meteorological Office's John Grindley at Bracknell. At the outset Mrs Ilse R. Wolff, of the Wiener Library, London, provided useful leads.

On the R.A.F. side I was lucky enough to have valuable consultations at Fighter Command level with Air Chief Marshal Lord Dowding and his former deputy Air Chief

Marshal Sir Douglas Evill. At Bomber Command, Air Chief Marshal Sir John Grandy proved a gracious host; Air Chief Marshal Sir Keith Park sent a cogent narrative all the way from New Zealand; Air Vice-Marshal Sir Cecil Bouchier spent hours recalling the triumphs and tribulations of life at Hornchurch. Air Vice-Marshal George Chamberlain and Air Vice-Marshal Laurence Fuller-Good provided useful written accounts. Others who afforded sterling help were Air Vice-Marshal Harry Hogan, Air Vice-Marshal Frank Hopps, Air Vice-Marshal Stanley Vincent, Air Vice-Marshal John Worrall; Air Commodore Harold Bird-Wilson, Air Commodore James Coward, Air Commodore Robert Deacon-Elliott, Air Commodore Alan Deere and Air Commodore Desmond Hughes. And Air Commodore John Thompson not only took the time to talk about 111 Squadron, he arranged an intriguing, on-the-spot tour of the now disused 11 Group Ops Room, from where Winston Churchill watched the last great battle.

In Germany, I had valuable advice and encouragement from first to last – notably from General Alfred Bulowius, General Paul Deichmann, an ever-present help, General Johannes Fink, General Martin Harlinghausen, General Max Ibel, General Werner Kreipe, General Hans Seidemann, and General Hannes Trautloft, an indefatigable diarist even in the heat of combat. The exemplary patience of Brigadegeneral Walter Enneccerus, Brigadegeneral Paul Hozzel, Brigadegeneral Karl Kessel and Brigadegeneral Johannes Steinhoff deserves special mention, too.

Many others spent far more time and trouble than I had a right to expect – in suggesting untapped sources, in authenticating dates, in helping locate survivors. On the lifeboats, K. F. Speakman and H. B. Fleet gave indispensable guidance in Ramsgate and Margate. H. R. Pratt Boorman, *The Kent Messenger's* director, and Tony Arnold, of the Dover bureau, helped enormously by making public my appeal for survivors.

Peter Williams, of Southern Television, and Arthur Streatfield were equally towers of strength... Peter Corbell and Christopher Elliott freely lent long-out-of-print books and papers... Derek Wood selflessly devoted a hard-won Saturday to sorting through nuggets omitted from his mammoth study, *The Narrow Margin*... David Irving not only gave sterling leads but lent generously from his unique private collection of German and American microfilms.

Finally, the uncomplaining hours put in by my own research team deserve a chapter all their own. Joan St. George Saunders and her researchers provided enough solid fact to nourish a hungry computer; Marguerita Adey's contribution, though brief, was telling; Lila Duckworth's pioneer translations saw the German side of things proceeding smoothly from the start. Marise Dutton's coverage of the Vancouver scene was as exceptional as Jean Farrer's work across 6,000 miles of Great Britain – of inestimable value in assembling the jigsaw.

Pamela Hoskins proved all over again that the fact – or the eye-witness – that can elude her is rare indeed. Dennis Knight and Peter Foote worked back and forth like beavers across southern England... Elisabeth Leslie filed invaluable transcripts with the habitual serenity that took her undaunted through a blizzard in the Pass of Glencoe. Robin McKown weighed in from New York. In Los Angeles and throughout 5,000 miles of Germany, Nadia Radowitz made an untold contribution, standing in as interpreter at upwards of seventy interviews before devoting the next six months to translating bales of German documents. The finished work would have been poorer without her.

Above all, my deepest debt is to my wife, who handled almost all of the Canadian and United States research, beside card-indexing, conducting many other interviews, typing the final draft and offering the moral support that saw it through. Hers was the hardest task of all – for she had to live through the writing.

Eagle Day: The R.A.F.

Fighter Command

Order of battle: August 13, 1940

HEADQUARTERS, FIGHTER COMMAND. Bentley Priory, Stanmore, Middlesex
  Air Officer Commanding-in-Chief:
  Air Chief Marshal Sir Hugh Dowding

HEADQUARTERS, No. 10 GROUP. Rudloe Manor, Box, Wiltshire
  Air Officer Commanding:
  Air Vice-Marshal Sir Christopher Brand

PEMBREY SECTOR STATION
Wing Commander J. H. Hutchinson

No. 92 Spitfire Squadron – Squadron Leader P. J. Sanders (to Biggin Hill, 9/8/40)

FILTON SECTOR STATION
Group Captain Robert Hanmer

No. 87 Hurricane Squadron – Squadron Leader T. G. Lovell-Gregg; Squadron Leader R. S. Mills (from 8/18/40) (based at Exeter Satellite Station, then to Bibury)

No. 213 Hurricane Squadron – Squadron Leader H. D. McGregor (based at Exeter Satellite Station; to Tangmere on 7/9/40)

ST. EVAL SECTOR STATION (Coastal Command)
Fighter Section H.Q.: Group Captain L. G. le B. Croke

No. 234 Spitfire Squadron – Squadron Leader J. S. O'Brien; Flight Lieutenant C. L. Page (to Middle Wallop on 14/8/40, returning to St. Eval 11/9/40)

No. 247 Gladiator Squadron – Flight Lieutenant H. A. Chater (One flight only, operating from Roborough Fleet Air Arm Station)

MIDDLE WALLOP SECTOR STATION
Wing Commander David Roberts

No. 238 Hurricane Squadron – Squadron Leader Harold Fenton; Flight Lieutenant Minden Blake (acting C.O. until 15/9/40) (to St. Eval on 14/8/40, returning Middle Wallop 9/9/40)

No. 609 Spitfire Squadron – Squadron Leader Horace Darley (also operating from Warmwell Satellite Station: Wing Commander George Howard)

No. 604 Blenheim Squadron – Squadron Leader Michael Anderson

No. 152 Spitfire Squadron – Squadron Leader Peter Devitt (also operating from Warmwell)

HEADQUARTERS No. 11 GROUP. Hillingdon House, Uxbridge, Middlesex
Air Officer Commanding:
Air Vice-Marshal Keith Park

DEBDEN SECTOR STATION
Wing Commander Laurence Fuller-Good

No. 17 Hurricane Squadron – Squadron Leader C. W. Williams; Squadron Leader A. G. Miller (from 29/8/40) (detached Tangmere 19/8/40, returning Debden 2/9/40)

No. 85 Hurricane Squadron – Squadron Leader Peter Townsend (to Croydon from 19/8/40, returning Castle Camps, Debden Satellite, 3/9/40, thence to Church Fenton)

NORTH WEALD SECTOR STATION
Wing Commander Victor Beamish

No. 56 Hurricane Squadron – Squadron Leader G. A. Manton (also operating from Rochford Satellite Station; transferred Boscombe Down 1/9/40)

No. 151 Hurricane Squadron – Squadron Leader J. A. Gordon; Squadron Leader Eric King (from 21/8/40); Squadron Leader H. West (from 4/9/40) (to Stapleford Satellite Station on 29/8/40; thence to Digby 1/9/40)

HORNCHURCH SECTOR STATION
Wing Commander Cecil Bouchier

No. 54 Spitfire Squadron – Squadron Leader James Leathart; Squadron Leader Donald Finlay (from 26/8/40) to 28/8/40 only); Squadron Leader Pat Dunworth (from 6/9/40) (also operated from Manston; transferred Catterick 3/9/40)

No. 65 Spitfire Squadron – Squadron Leader A. L. Holland (also operated from Manston; transferred Turnhouse 27/8/40)

No. 74 Spitfire Squadron – Squadron Leader Francis White; Flight Lieutenant Adolph Malan (from 28/8/40) (to Wittering on 14/8/40, thence to Kirton-in-Lindsey, from 21/8/40, and Cottishall, from 10/9/40)

No. 266 Spitfire Squadron – Squadron Leader R. L. Wilkinson (detached to Eastchurch Coastal Command Station during 13/8/40; operated from Hornchurch and Manston until 21/8/40; then to Wittering)

No. 600 Blenheim Squadron – Squadron Leader David Clark (based at Manston, for night-readiness only; trans-

ferred Hornchurch 24/8/40; thence to Redhill, forward
airfield for Kenley, from 15/9/40)

BIGGIN HILL SECTOR STATION
Group Captain Richard Grice

No. 32 Hurricane Squadron – Squadron Leader John
Worrall; Squadron Leader Michael Crossley (from
16/8/40) (to Acklington 28/8/40)

No. 610 Spitfire Squadron – Squadron Leader John Ellis (to
Acklington 31/8/40)

No. 501 Hurricane Squadron – Squadron Leader Harry
Hogan (operating at Gravesend Satellite Station, then to
Kenley from 10/9/40)

Other forward bases in the Biggin Hill Sector were:
Hawkinge – Squadron Leader E. E. Arnold
Lympne (the emergency landing field) – Squadron Leader
D. H. Montgomery

KENLEY SECTOR STATION
Wing Commander Tom Prickman

No. 615 Hurricane Squadron – Squadron Leader Joseph
Kayll (to Prestwick 29/8/40)

No. 64 Spitfire Squadron – Squadron Leader Aeneas
MacDonell (to Leconfield and Ringway, 19/8/40)

No. 111 Hurricane Squadron – Squadron Leader John
Thompson (operating from Croydon Satellite Station until
19/8/40; transferred to Debden until 3/9/40; returning to
Croydon 7/9/40; thence to Drem)

No. 1 (R.C.A.F.) Hurricane Squadron – Squadron Leader
Ernest McNab (based at Croydon, non-operational until
16/8/40; transferred to Northolt Sector, fully operational
17/8/40)

NORTHOLT SECTOR STATION
Group Captain Stanley Vincent

No. 1 (R.A.F.) Hurricane Squadron – Squadron Leader D. A. Pemberton (to Wittering 9/9/40)

No. 303 (Polish) Hurricane Squadron – Squadron Leader Zdzislaw Krasnodebski (until 6/9/40); Squadron Leader Ronald Kellett (non-operational until 31/8/40)

No. 257 Hurricane Squadron – Squadron Leader H. Harkness (until 12/9/40); Flight Lieutenant Robert Stanford Tuck (to Debden 15/8/40; from 5/9/40 operating from Martlesham Heath Satellite Station)

TANGMERE SECTOR STATION
Wing Commander Jack Boret

No. 43 Hurricane Squadron – Squadron Leader John "Tubby" Badger; Squadron Leader Caesar Hull (from 1/9/40); Squadron Leader Tom Dalton-Morgan (from 16/9/40) (to Usworth 8/9/40)

No. 145 Hurricane Squadron – Squadron Leader John Peel (operating from Westhampnett Satellite Station; to Montrose Flying Training Command Station and Dyce Coastal Command Station on 14/8/40)

No. 601 Hurricane Squadron – Squadron Leader the Hon. Edward Ward; Flight Lieutenant Sir Archibald Hope, Bt. (from 16/8/40) (to Debden 19/8/40, returning Tangmere 2/9/40; thence to Exeter, 7/9/40)

HEADQUARTERS No. 12 GROUP. Watnall, near Nottingham, Nottinghamshire
Air Officer Commanding:
Air Vice-Marshall Trafford Leigh-Mallory

CHURCH FENTON SECTOR
Group Captain C. F. Horsley

No. 73 Hurricane Squadron – Squadron Leader M. W. Robinson (to Debden 5/9/40)

No. 249 Hurricane Squadron – Squadron Leader Eric King; Squadron Leader John Grandy (from 21/8/40) (to Boscombe Down 14/8/40; transferred to North Weald 1/9/40)

No. 616 Spitfire Squadron – Squadron Leader Marcus Robinson; Squadron Leader H. E. Burton (from 3/9/40) (operating from Leconfield Satellite Station; to Kenley 20/8/40; to Cottishall, then Kirton-in-Lindsey from 3/9/40)

No. 302 (Polish) Hurricane Squadron – Squadron Leader Jack Satchell and Squadron Leader Mumler (non-operational until 20/8/40; attached Duxford 13/9/40)

KIRTON-IN-LINDSEY SECTOR
Wing Commander S. H. Hardy

No. 222 Spitfire Squadron – Squadron Leader Johnnie Hill (to Hornchurch 30/8/40)

No. 264 Defiant Squadron – Squadron Leader Philip Hunter; Squadron Leader Desmond Garvin (from 24/8/40) (to Hornchurch 22/8/40; withdrawn to Kirton-in-Lindsey 28/8/40)

DIGBY SECTOR STATION
Wing Commander Ian Parker

No. 46 Hurricane Squadron – Squadron Leader J. R. MacLachlan (to Stapleford Satellite Station, North Weald Sector, 1/9/40)

No. 611 Spitfire Squadron – Squadron Leader James McComb (operating from Fowlmere Satellite Station, Duxford Sector, from 11/9/40)

No. 29 Blenheim Squadron – Squadron Leader S. C. Widdows

COLTISHALL SECTOR STATION
Wing Commander W. K. Beisiegel

No. 242 Hurricane Squadron – Squadron Leader Douglas Bader (to Duxford 2/9/40)

No. 66 Spitfire Squadron – Squadron Leader Rupert Leigh (to Kenley 3/9/40, then to Gravesend from 11/9/40)

WITTERING SECTOR STATION
Wing Commander Harry Broadhurst

No. 229 Hurricane Squadron – Squadron Leader H. J. Maguire; Squadron Leader John Banham (from 7/9/40) (to Northolt 9/9/40)

No. 23 Blenheim Squadron – Squadron Leader C. Heycock (from Colly Weston Satellite 16/8/40; to Middle Wallop and Ford (Fleet Air Arm Station) 13/9/40)

DUXFORD SECTOR STATION
Wing Commander A. B. Woodhall

No. 19 Spitfire Squadron – Squadron Leader P. C. Pinkham; Squadron Leader Bryan Lane (from 5/9/40) (operating also from Fowlmere Satellite Station)

No. 310 (Czech) Hurricane Squadron – Squadron Leader Douglas Blackwood; Squadron Leader Sasha Hess (non-operational until 18/8/40)

HEADQUARTERS, No. 13 GROUP. Blakelaw Estate, Ponteland Road, Newcastle-on-Tyne, Northumberland
Air Officer Commanding:
Air Vice-Marshal Richard Saul

CATTERICK SECTOR STATION
Wing Commander G. L. Carter

No. 219 Blenheim Squadron – Squadron Leader J. H. Little

No. 41 Spitfire Squadron – Squadron Leader H. R. L. Hood; Squadron Leader Lister (from 8/9/40) (to Hornchurch 3/9/40)

USWORTH SECTOR STATION
Wing Commander Brian Thynne

No. 607 Hurricane Squadron – Squadron Leader James Vick
(to Tangmere 9/9/40)

No. 72 Spitfire Squadron – Squadron Leader A. R. Collins;
Wing Commander Ronald Lees (for 2/9/40 only); Flight
Lieutenant Edward Graham (operating from Acklington
Satellite Station; to Biggin Hill on 31/8/40; operational
from Croydon after 1/9/40)

No. 79 Spitfire Squadron – Squadron Leader Hervey
Hayworth (operating from Acklington; to Biggin Hill
27/8/40; transferred to Pembrey 8/9/40)

WICK SECTOR STATION (Coastal Command)
Fighter Section H.Q.: Wing Commander Geoffrey Ambler

No. 3 Hurricane Squadron – Squadron Leader S. F. Godden
(to Castletown 7/9/40)

No. 504 Hurricane Squadron – Squadron Leader John
Sample (operating from Castletown Satellite Station; to
Hendon, under Northolt Sector control, 6/9/40)

No. 232 Hurricane Squadron – Squadron Leader M. M.
Stephens (operating from Sumburgh Satellite Station on
half-squadron basis only)

DYCE SECTOR STATION (Coastal Command)
Fighter Section H.Q.: Group Captain F. Crerar

No. 603 Spitfire Squadron – Squadron Leader George
Denholm (operating with one Flight at Montrose (Flying
Training Command); to Hornchurch 27/8/40)

TURNHOUSE SECTOR STATION
Wing Commander the Duke of Hamilton and Brandon

No. 605 Hurricane Squadron – Squadron Leader Walter
Churchill; Flight Lieutenant Archie McKellar (from

11/9/40) (operating from Drem Satellite Station; to Croydon 7/9/40)

No. 602 Spitfire Squadron – Squadron A. V. R. "Sandy" Johnstone (from Drem Satellite Station to Westhampnett, Tangmere Sector, 13/8/40)

No. 253 Hurricane Squadron – Squadron Leader Tom Gleave and Squadron Leader H. M. Starr (until 31/8/40); Squadron Leader Gerry Edge (partially operational from Prestwick (Flying Training Command); to Kenley 30/8/40)

No. 141 Defiant Squadron – Squadron Leader W. A. Richardson

No. 245 Hurricane Squadron (based at Aldergrove, Northern Ireland, station administered from Air Ministry)

Eagle Day: The Luftwaffe

Order of battle – August 13, 1940

AIR FLEET FIVE. Stavanger, Norway
Generaloberst Hans-Jurgen Stumpff

X FLYING CORPS
General Geisler

Long-range bombers

KG 26	*Heinkel 111*	
Staff Flight	Oberstleutnant Fuchs	Stavanger
I	Major Busch	Stavanger
III	Major von Lossberg	Stavanger
KG 30	*Junkers 88*	
Staff Flight	Oberstleutnant Loebel	Aalborg, Denmark
I	Major Doensch	Aalborg, Denmark
III	Hauptmann Kellewe	Aalborg, Denmark

Fighters

ZG 76	*ME 110*	
I	Hauptmann Werner Restemeyer	Stavanger
JG 77	*ME 109*	
II	Hauptmann Hentschel	Stavanger, Drontheim

+ coastal reconnaissance, long-range reconnaissance and
mine-laying units

AIR FLEET TWO. Brussels
Generalfeldmarschall Albert Kesselring

I FLYING CORPS
Generaloberst Grauert

Long-range bombers

KG 1	*HE 111 (except 3rd Wing)*	
Staff Flight	Oberstleutnant Exss	Rosieres-en-Santerre
I	Major Maier	Montdidier-Clairmont
II	Major Kosch	Montdidier-Nijmegen
III	Major Willibald Fanelsa (DO 17 equipped)	Rosieres-en-Santerre
KG 76	*JU 88–DO 17*	
Staff Flight	Oberstleutnant Froehlich	DO 17 Cormeilles-en-Vexin
I	Hauptmann Lindeiner	DO 17 Beauvais
II	Major Moericke	JU 88 Creil
III	Oberstleutnant Genth	DO 17 Cormeilles-en-Vexin

+ long-range reconnaissance units

FLYING CORPS
General Bruno Lorzer

Long-range bombers

KG 2	*DO 17*	
Staff Flight	Oberst Johannes Fink	Arras
I	Major Gutzmann	Epinoy
II	Major Paul Weitkus	Arras
III	Major Wemer Kreipe; Major Adolf Fuchs (from 13/8/40)	Cambrai
KG 3	*DO 17*	
Staff Flight	Oberst von Chamier-Glisczinski	Le Culot

I	Oberstleutnant Gabelmann	Le Culot
II	Hauptmann Pilger	Antwerp/Deurne
III	Hauptmann Rathmann	Saint-Trond

KG 53	*Heinkel 111*	
Staff Flight	Oberst Stahl	Lille-Nord
I	Major Kaufmann	Lille-Nord
II	Major Winkler	Lille-Nord
III	Major Edler von Braun	Lille-Nord

Dive-bombers

II (St)G 1	JU 87	
	Hauptmann Keil	Pas-de-Calais
IV (St) LG 1	Hauptmann von Brauchitsch	Tramecourt

Fighter-bombers

Erpro-bungsgr.	*ME 109–ME 110*	
(Test Group)	Hauptmann Walter Rubensdorffer;	Calais-Marck
210	Oberleutnant Martin Lutz (from 15/8/40)	Monchy-Breton
II/LG 2	Hauptmann Weiss	St. Omar

IX FLYING DIVISION (*later* IX FLYING CORPS)
General Coeler

Long-range bombers

KG 4	*HE 111–JU 88*	
Staff Flight	Oberstleutnant Rath	HE 111 Soesterberg
I	Hauptmann Meissner	HE 111 Soesterberg
II	Major Dr Wolff	HE 111 Eindhoven
III	Hauptmann Bloedorn	JU 88 Amsterdam/Schipol

| KG 100 | *HE 111* | |

| | Hauptmann Friedrich Carol Aschenbrenner (transferred to IV Flying Corps, Air Fleet Three, from 17/8/40) | Vannes, Brittany |

+ mine-laying, coastal reconnaissance, naval co-operation and long-range reconnaissance units

JAFU 2
Regional Fighter Commander: Oberst Theo Osterkamp
Wissant

Fighters

ME 109

JG 3	Oberstleutnant Carl Viek; Major Gunther Lutzow; Hauptmann Hans von Hahn	Samer (from 14/8/40) Colombert (from 21/8/40)
II	Hauptmann Erich von Selle;	Samer (from 14/8/40)
III	Hauptmann Walter Kienitz (from 8/8/40); Hauptmann Wilhelm Balthasar	Desvres

JG 26	**ME 109**	
Staff Flight	Major Gotthard Handrick; Major Adolf Galland (from 21/8/40)	Audembert
I	Hauptmann Fischer; Hauptmann Rolf Pingel (from 21/8/40)	Audembert
II	Hauptmann Karl Ebbighausen; Hauptmann Erich Bode (from 17/8/40)	Marquise

III	Major Adolf Galland; Hauptmann Gerhard Schopfel (from 21/8/40)	Caffiers
	ME 109	
JG 51	Major Werner Molders (from 21/8/40)	Wissant; Pihen
I	Hauptmann Hans–Heinrich Brustellin	Wissant; Pihen
II	Hauptmann Gunther Matthes	Desvres; Marquise
III	Major Hannes Trautloft; Hauptmann Walter Oesau (from 25/8/40)	St. Omer
IV (1/77)	Hauptmann Johannes Janke (from 25/8/40)	St. Omer
JG 52	*ME 109*	
Staff Flight	Major von Merhart; Major Hans Trubenbach	Coquelles
I	Hauptmann Siegfried von Eschwege; Hauptmann Ewald	Coquelles
II	Hauptmann von Kornatzki; Hauptmann Ensslen (to Jever from 18/8/40)	Peuplingne
III	Hauptmann Alex von Winterfeld (withdrawn from Coquelles, 1/8/40)	
I/LGa	Major Hans Trubenbach; Hauptmann Herbert Ihlefeld	Calais–Marck

JG54	*ME 109*	
Staff Flight	Major Martin Mettig; Major Hannes Trautloft (from 25/8/40)	Campagne; Guines
I	Hauptmann Hubertus von Bonin	Guines
II	Hauptmann Winterer; Hauptmann Dietrich Hrabak (from 30/8/40)	Hermalinghen
III	Hauptmann Ultsch; Hauptmann Scholz (from 6/9/40)	Guines
ZG 26	*ME 110*	
Staff Flight	Oberstleutnant Joachim Huth	Lille
I	Hauptmann Macrocki	Yvrench-St. Omer
II	Hauptmann Ralph von Rettberg	Crecy-St. Omer
III	Hauptmann Schalk	Barley-Arques
ZG 76	*ME 110*	
Staff Flight	Major Walter Grabmann	Laval
II	Hauptmann Max Groth	Abbeville-Yvrench
III	Hauptmann Dickore; Hauptmann Kaldrack	Laval

AIR FLEET THREE. Paris
  GeneraIfeldmarschall Hugo Sperrle

VIII FLYING CORPS
General the Baron von Richthofen

Dive-bombers		
St G 1	*JU 87*	
Staff Flight	Major Hagen (incl. DO 17)	Angers
I	Major Paul Hozzel	Angers

III	Hauptmann Mahlke	Angers
St G 2	*JU 87*	
Staff Flight	Major Oscar Dinort (incl. DO 17)	St. Malo
I	Hauptmann Hubertus Hitschold	St. Malo
II	Major Walter Enneccerus	Lannion
St G 77		
Staff Flight	Major Graf Schonborn (incl. DO 17)	Caen
I	Hauptmann Freiherr von Dalwick	Caen
II	Hauptmann Plewig	Caen
III	Hauptmann Bode	Caen

Fighters

V(Z) LG 1	ME 110	
	Hauptmann Liensberger	Caen

+ DO 17 and JU 88 reconnaissance units

V FLYING CORPS
General Ritter von Greim

Long-range bombers

KG 51	*JU 88*	
Staff Flight	Oberstleutnant Fisser	Orly
I	Major Schulz-Hein	Melun
II	Major Winkler	Orly
III	Major Marienfeld	Etampes
KG 54	*JU 88*	
Staff Flight	Oberstleutnant Hoehne	Evreux
I	Hauptmann Heydebreck	Evreux
II	Oberstleutnant Koester	St. Andre-de-L'Eure

KG 55	*HE 111*	
Staff Flight	Oberst Alois Stockl; Major Korte (from 14/8/40)	Villacoublay
I	Major Korte	Dreux
II	Major von Lachemaier	Chartres
III	Major Schlemell	Villacoublay

IV FLYING CORPS
General Pflugbeil

Long-range bombers

LG 1	*JU 88*	
Staff Flight	Oberst Alfred Bulowius	Orleans/Bricy
I	Hauptmann Wilhelm Kern	Orleans/Bricy
II	Major Debratz	Orleans/Bricy
III	Major Bormann	Chateaudun
IV	Hauptmann Hans-Joachim Helbig	Orleans/Bricy

KG 27	*HE 111*	
Staff Flight	Oberst Behrendt	Tours
I	Major Ulbrich	Tours
II	Major Schlichting	Dinard; Bourges
III	Major Freiherr Speck von Sternberg	Rennes

+ naval co-operation and long-range reconnaissance units

JAFU 3
Oberst Werner Junck – Cherbourg, then Wissant from 29/8/40

Fighters (Transferred to Air Fleet Two from 24/8/40)

JG 2	*ME 109*

Staff Flight	Oberstleutnant Harry von Bulow; Major Schellmann	Evreux; Beaumont-le-Roger; Mardyck
I	Major Hennig Strumpell; Major Helmut Wick	Beaumont-le-Roger; Mardyck
II	Major Schellmann; Hauptmann Griesert	Beaumont-le-Roger; Mardyck
III	Hauptmann Dr Erich Mix; Hauptmann Otto Bertram	Le Havre; Oye Plage
JG 27	*ME 109*	
Staff Flight	Major Max Ibel	Cherbourg-West; Guines
I	Hauptmann Eduard Neumann	Plumetot; Guines
II	Hauptmann Werner Andres; Hauptmann Lippert (from 8/8/40)	Crepon; Fiennes
III	Hauptmann Joachim Schlichting; Hauptmann Max Dobislav	Carquebut; Guines
JG 53	*ME 109*	
Staff Flight	Major Hans-Jurgen Cramon-Taubadel; Major Freiherr von Maltzahn	Cherbourg; Etaples
I	Hauptmann Blumensaat; Hauptmann Hans Mayer	Rennes; Le Touquet
II	Major Freiherr von Maltzahn	Dinan, Guernsey
III	Hauptmann Hans-Joachim Harder; Hauptmann Wolf-Dietrich Wilcke	Sempy; Brest; Le Touquet

ZG 2	*ME 110*	
Staff Flight	Oberstleutnant Friedrich Vollbracht	Toussee-le-Noble; St. Aubin
I	Hauptmann Ott; Hauptmann Henlein	Amiens; Berck-sur-Mer
II	Hauptmann Carl; Hauptmann Karlheinz Lessman	Guyancourt; Berck-sur-Mer

Bibliography

Published Sources

Acutt, D. G. F. *Brigade in Action: the History of the St. John Ambulance Brigade in Weymouth, 1939–43*. Weymouth: Sherren & Son, 1945.

Adam, Ronald. *Readiness at Dawn*. London: Victor Gollancz, 1941.

Allingham, Margery. *The Oaken Heart*. London: Hutchinson, 1941.

Among the Few; Canadian Airmen in the Battle of Britain. Ottawa: R.C.A.F. Historical Section, 1948.

Ansel, Walter. *Hitler Confronts England*. Durham, N.C.: Duke University Press, 1960.

Anthony, C. "From Spads to Spitfires," *Air Mail*, n.s., Vol. 5, No. 2, 1953.

Anthony, Gordon, and Macadam, John. *Air Aces*. London: Home and Van Thai, 1944.

Armitage, Squadron Leader Dennis. "The Battle of Britain," *The Elevator*, Journal of the Lancashire Aero Club, Spring-Autumn, 1958.

Austin, A. B. *Fighter Command*. London: Victor Gollancz, 1941.

Baley, Stephen. *Two Septembers*. London: George Allen & Unwin, 1941.

Barker, Felix. "Twenty-four Hours That Saved Britain," *London Evening News*, September 12–17, 1960.

Barrymaine, Norman. *The Story of Peter Townsend*. London: Peter Davies, 1958.

Bartz, Karl. *Swastika in the Air*. London: William Kimber, 1956.

"The Battle of Britain," *The Wire*, Journal of the Royal Signal Corps, Vol. XXI, No. 247.

Baumbach, Werner. "Why We Lost," *The Royal Air Force Review*, Vol. 7, No. 12, 1952–53.

Broken Swastika. London: Robert Hale, 1960.

Beckles, Gordon. *Birth of a Spitfire*. London: William Collins, 1941.

Bekker, Cajus. *Radar-Duell im Dunkel*. Oldenburg-Hamburg: Gerhard Stalling Verlag, 1958.

Angriffshohe 4000. Oldenburg-Hamburg: Gerhard Stalling Verlag, 1964.

Bell, Reginald. *The Bull's Eye*. London: Cassell, 1943.

Bickers, Richard T. *Ginger Lacey, Fighter Pilot*. London: Robert Hale, 1962.

Birkenhead, Lord. *The Prof in Two Worlds*. London: William Collins, 1961.

Bishop, Edward. *The Battle of Britain*. London: George Allen & Unwin, 1960.

Blackstone, Geoffrey. *History of the British Fire Service*. London: Routledge, 1957.

Boebert, Earl. "The Eagle Squadrons," *American Aviation Historical Society Journal*, Spring, 1964.

Bolitho, Hector. *Combat Report*. London: Batsford, 1943.

A Penguin in the Eyrie. London: Hutchinson, 1955.

Bonnell, J. S. *Britons Under Fire*. New York: Harper, 1941.

Boorman, H. R. Pratt. *Hell's Corner, 1940*. Maidstone: Kent Messenger Office, 1942.

Bowman, Gerald. *Jump for It*. London: Evans Bros., 1955.

Braham, Wing Commander J. R. D. *"Scramble!"* London: Frederick Muller, 1961.

Braybrooke, Keith. *Wingspan: a History of R.A.F. Debden.* Saffron Walden: Hart, 1956.

Brickhill, Paul. *Reach for the Sky.* London: William Collins, 1954.

Brittain, Vera. *England's Hour.* London: Macmillan, 1941.

Bryant, Sir Arthur (ed.). *The Alanbrooke Diaries.* London: William Collins, 1957.

Buchan, William. *The R.A.F. at War.* London: John Murray, 1941.

Bullmore, Francis. *The Dark Haven.* London: Jonathan Cape, 1956.

Burt, Kendal, and Leasor, James. *The One That Got Away.* London: Michael Joseph & William Collins, 1956.

Butler, Ewan, and Young, Gordon. *Marshal Without Glory.* London: Hodder & Stoughton, 1951.

Capka, Jo. *Red Sky at Night.* London: Anthony Blond, 1958.

Carne, Daphne. *The Eyes of the Few.* London: P. R. Macmillan, 1960.

Carter, E. *Grim Glory.* London: Humphries, 1941.

Charlton, L. E. O. *Britain at War: The Royal Air Force, September, 1939 – September, 1945.*

Childers, James Saxon. *War Eagles.* New York: D. Appleton-Century Company, Inc., 1943.

Churchill, Sir Winston. *The Second World War, Vol. II: Their Finest Hour.* London: Cassell, 1949.

Clifton, P. "Top-Score Fighter," *The R.A.F. Flying Review*, Vol. 8, No. 12, 1953.

Clout, Charles. "Swastika Over Sussex," *Air Britain Digest*, March, 1965.

Collier, Basil. *The Defence of the United Kingdom.* London: H.M. Stationery Office, 1957.

The Leader of the Few. London: Jarrolds, 1957.

The Battle of Britain. London: Batsford, 1962.

Cook, Raymond. *Shellfire Corner Carries On.* London: Headley Bros., 1942.

Corbell, Peter M. "R.A.F. Station, Hornchurch," *Air Britain Digest*, Vol. Ill, Nos. 9 and 10.

Crook, D. M. *Spitfire Pilot*. London: Faber & Faber, 1942.

Darwin, Bernard. *War on the Line*. London: Southern Railway, 1946.

De Bunsen, Mary. *Mount Up with Wings*. London: Hutchinson, 1960.

Deere, Alan. *Nine Lives*. London: Hodder & Stoughton, 1959.

Dempster, Derek, and Wood, Derek. *The Narrow Margin*. London: Hutchinson, 1961.

"Demu." "Ops Rooms. A Footnote to the History of the R.A.F. in the Battle of Britain," *The Fighting Forces*, October, 1946.

Destiny Can Wait: the Polish Air Force in the Second World War. London: William Heinemann, 1949.

Dickson, Lovat. *Richard Hillary*. London: Macmillan, 1950.

Dietrich, Otto. *The Hitler I Knew*. London: Methuen, 1957.

Dixon, J. L. *In All Things First: a History of No. 1 Squadron*. Orpington: The Orpington Press, 1954.

A Brief History of No. 19 Squadron. Driffield: Registration Record, 1954.

Donahue, A. G. *Tally-Ho! – Yankee in a Spitfire*. London: Macmillan, 1943.

Dowding, Air Chief Marshal the Lord. *The Battle of Britain*, a supplement to the *London Gazette*, September 10,1946.

E. B. B. (ed.). *Winged Words: our airmen speak for themselves*. London: William Heinemann, 1941.

Eeles, Lt.-Col. H. S. *History of the 17th Light Ack-Ack Regt., R.A.* Tunbridge Wells: Courier Co. Ltd., 1946.

Eichelbaum, Dr. (ed.). *Das Jahr Buch von Der Luftwaffe, 1940*, Berlin: Verlaghaus Bong, 1941.

Ellan, Squadron Leader B. J. *Spitfire*. London: John Murray, 1942.

Embry, Sir Basil. *Mission Completed*. London: Methuen, 1957.

Fahrten und Fluge gegen England. Berlin: Zeitesgeschichte-Verlag, 1941.

Faircloth, N. W. *New Zealanders in the Battle of Britain*. Wellington, N. Z.: War History Branch, Dept, of Internal Affairs, 1950.

Farrer, David. *The Sky's the Limit: the Story of Beaverbrook at M.A.P.* London: Hutchinson, 1943.

Farson, Negley. *Bombers Moon*. London: Victor Gollancz, 1941.

Fiedler, Arkady. *Squadron 303: the Story of the Polish Fighter Squadron with the R.A.F.* London: Peter Davies, 1942.

Field, Peter J. *Canada's Wings*. London: John Lane, The Bodley Head, 1942.

"The Fifteenth of August," by a Pilot, *R.A.F. Quarterly*, Vol. 13, No. 4.

Finnie, G. K. "Lessons of the Battle of Britain," *Roundel*, Vol. II, No. 6.

"The First Great Air Battle," *Air Mail*, Vol. 6, No. 5.

Fleming, Peter. *Invasion 1940*. London: Rupert Hart-Davis, 1957.

Forbes, Wing Commander Athol, and Allen, Squadron Leader Hubert. *Ten Fighter Boys*. London: William Collins, 1942.

Forell, Fritz von. *Molders und Seine Manner*. Graz: Steirische Verlagsanstalt, 1941.

Molders. Salzburg: Sirius-Verlag, 1951.

Forrester, Larry. *Fly for Your Life*. London: Frederick Muller, 1956.

Foster, Reginald. *Dover Front*. London: Seeker & Warburg, 1941.

Friedin, Seymour (ed.). *The Fatal Decisions*. New York: William Sloane, 1956.

Front-Line Folkestone. Folkestone: Folkestone, Hythe & District Herald, 1945.

Galland, Adolf. *The First and the Last.* London: Methuen, 1953.

"La Bataille d'Angleterre," *Forces Aeriennes Frangaises*, Nos. 61–65, August–September, 1955.

Gallico, Paul. *The Hurricane Story.* London: Michael Joseph, 1959.

Garnett, David. *War in the Air.* London: Chatto & Windus, 1941.

Gibbs, Air Vice-Marshal Gerald. *A Survivor's Story.* London: Hutchinson, 1956.

"The Battle of Britain," *Journal of the United Services Institution of India*, Vol. LXXXIII, No. 352–53.

Gleave, Group Captain Thomas. *I Had a Row with a German.* London: Macmillan, 1941.

Gleed, Ian. *Arise to Conquer.* London: Victor Gollancz, 1942.

Graves, Charles. *The Home Guard of Britain.* London: Hutchinson, 1943.

The Thin Blue Line. London: Hutchinson, 1941.

Green, Dennis W. *Famous Fighters of the Second World War.* London: MacDonald, 1962.

Gribble, Leonard. *Heroes of the Fighting R.A.F.* London: George G. Harrap, 1941.

Griffith, Hubert. *R.A.F. Occasions.* London: The Cresset Press, 1941.

Gritzbach, Erich. *Hermann Goring: The Man and His Work.* London: Hurst and Blackett, 1939.

Hagedorn, Hermann. *Sunwards I've Climbed.* New York: Macmillan, 1942.

Hanna, A. M. "Fighter Command Communications," *The Post Office Electrical Engineers Journal*, Vol. 38, Part 4.

Harbottle, H. R. "The Network of Telephone Circuits and the Defence Telecommunications Control," *The Post Office Electrical Engineers Journal*, Vol. 38, Part 4.

Hayson, G. D. L. "The Battle of Britain," *South African Air Force Journal*, Vol. II, No. 4.

"How the Few Saved the Many," *Wings*, Vol. 9, No. 10, September, 1950.

Herlin, Hans. *Udet: a Man's Life*. London: MacDonald, 1960.

Hill, Air Marshal Sir Roderic. "The Air Defence of Great Britain," *Journal of the Royal United Services Institution*, May, 1946.

"The Fighters' Greatest Day," *Journal of the Royal Air Forces*, Vol. 3, No. 5.

Hillary, Richard. *The Last Enemy*. London: Macmillan, 1942.

"Hitler's Battle of Britain Plan," *The R.A.F. Flying Review*, Vol. 15, No. 2.

Hockin, John. "The Air Defense of the Port of London," *Port of London Association Monthly*, May, 1945.

Hoffmann, Heinrich. *Hitler Was My Friend*. London: Burke Publishing Co., 1955.

Hollis, Gen. Sir Leslie, and Leasor, James. *War at the Top*. London: Michael Joseph, 1959.

Houart, Capitaine. "Les Aviateurs Belges a la Bataille d'Angleterre," *Vici*, October 17, 1955.

Illingworth, Frank. *Britain Under Shellfire*. London: Hutchinson, 1942.

Ingham, Harold S. (ed.). *Fire and Water: an Anthology*. London: Lindsay Drummond, 1942.

Ismay, Lord. *Memoirs of General the Lord Ismay*. London: Heinemann, 1960.

Johnson, Air Vice-Marshal J. E. *Full Circle*. London: Chatto & Windus, 1964.

Joubert, Air Chief Marshal Sir Philip. "How the Way Was Paved for the Battle of Britain," *The R.A.F. Flying Review*, Vol. 5, No. 2, 1949.

The Forgotten Ones. London: Hutchinson, 1961.

Keeping Them Flying. London: Air Force Publications, 1943.

Kemp, L.-Cdr. P. K. *Victory at Sea*. London: Frederick Muller, 1957.

Kempe, A. B. C. *'Midst Bands and Bombs*. Maidstone: Kent Messenger Office, 1946.

Kennedy, A. Scott. *"Gin Ye Daur": 603 (City of Edinburgh) Fighter Squadron*. Edinburgh: Pillans and Wilson, 1943.

Kent, Group Captain John. "The Battle of Britain: extracts from a personal diary," *The Polish Airmen's Week Review*, June, 1957.

Kesselring, Generalfeldmarschall Albert. *Memoirs*. London: William Kimber, 1953.

Knight, G. *Five Hundred Hours in the Blitz*. (Typescript MS, British Museum Reading Room, London.)

Knoke, Heinz. *I Flew for the Fuhrer*. London: Evan Bros., 1953.

Kohl, Hermann. *Wir fliegen gegen England*. Reutlingen: Ansellin und Laiblin Verlag, 1941.

Lanchbery, Edward. *Against the Sun*. London: Cassell, 1955.

Lecerf, J. L. "La Bataille Aerienne d'Angleterre," *Forces Aeriennes Francaises, 10* Annee, No. 107.

Lee, Asher. *The German Air Force*. London: Duckworth, 1946.

"When Adler Angriff Went Off Half-Cock," *The R.A.F. Flying Review*, Vol. 8, No. 12.

Le Page, M. "Memories of the Luftwaffe in the Channel Islands," *Air Britain Digest*, Vol. II, No. 1.

Lewey, F. R. *Cockney Campaign*. London: Stanley Paul, 1947.

Lewis, J. H. "London Diary, 1940," *Air Britain Digest*, Vol. V, No. 5, 1953.

Lloyd, F. H. M. *Hurricane: the Story of a Great Fighter*. London: Harborough Publishing Co., 1945.

Lowe, Frank. "Twenty Years Ago They Broke the Luftwaffe," *The Montreal Star Weekend Magazine*, September 10, 1960.

Lyall, Gavin, and Knight, Dennis. "The Air War," *The London Sunday Times Magazine*, May 30-June 6, 1965.

M-M S. *Together We Fly*. London: Geoffrey Bles, 1941.

McCrary, John R. (Tex), and Scheman, David E. *First of the Many*. New York: Simon & Schuster, 1944.

McKee, Alexander. *Strike from the Sky*. London: Souvenir Press, 1960.

Mackersey, Ian. "Tally Ho! cried John Peel," *The R.A.F. Flying Review*, Vol. V, No. 2.

Into the Silk. London: Robert Hale, 1956.

Macmillan, Wing Co-Commander Norman. *The Royal Air Force in the World War*, Vol. I–II. London: George Harrap, 1942–44.

Manstein, Field Marshal Erich von. *Lost Victories*. London: Methuen, 1958.

Marchant, Hilde. *Women and Children Last: a Woman Reporter's Account of the Battle of Britain*. London: Victor Gollancz, 1941.

Marchant, P. R., and Heron, K. M. "Post Office Equipment for Radar," *The Post Office Electrical Engineers Journal*, Vol. 38, Part 4.

Marrs, Pilot Officer Eric. "152 Squadron: A Personal Diary of the Battle of Britain," *The Aeroplane*, October 12, 1945.

Marsh, L. G. *Polish Wings Over Britain*. London: Max Love Publishing Co., 1943.

Masters, David. *"So Few"* (8th ed.). London: Eyre and Spottiswoode, 1946.

Mathias, Joachim. *Deutsche Flieger uber England*. Berlin: Steiniger Verlag, 1940.

Mee, Arthur. *1940*. London: Hodder & Stoughton, 1941.

Middleton, Drew. *The Sky Suspended*. London: Seeker & Warburg, 1960.

Milne, Duncan Grinnell. *Silent Victory*. London: The Bodley Head, 1958.

Mitchell, Alan W. *New Zealanders in the Air War.* London: George Harrap, 1945.

Moggridge, "Jackie." *Woman Pilot.* London: Michael Joseph, 1957.

Moller-Witten, Hanns. *Mit den Eichenlaub zum Ritterkreutz.* Rastatt: Erich Pabel Verlag, 1962.

Murrow, Edward R. *This Is London.* London: Cassell, 1941.

Nancarrow, F. E. "The Defence Teleprinter Network," *The Post Office Electrical Engineers Journal,* Vol. 38, Part 4.

Nancarrow, Fred G. *Glasgow Fighter Squadron.* London: William Collins, 1942.

Narracott, A. H. (ed.). In *Praise of the Few: an Anthology.* London: Frederick Muller, 1947.

How the R.A.F. Works. London: Frederick Muller, 1941.

Newton, John H. *The Story of No. 11 Group, R.O.C.* Lincoln: Lincolnshire Chronicle Office, 1946.

"Night Shift." "The Work of A. A. Searchlights in the Last War" *Journal of the Royal Artillery,* Vol. LXXV, No. 11.

Nixon, B. *Bombers Overhead.* London: Lindsay Drummond, 1943.

Nockolds, Harold. *The Magic of a Name.* London: G. T. Foulis, 1950.

Norris, G. McKellar. "Scottish Ace," *The R.A.F. Flying Review,* Vol. XV, No. 8.

O'Brien, T. H. *Civil Defence.* London: H. M. Stationery Office and Longman's Green, 1955.

Offenberg, Jean. *Lonely Warrior.* New York: Taplinger, 1958.

Osterkamp, Theo. *Durch Hohen und Tiefen jagt ein Herz.* Heidelberg: Vowinckel Verlag, 1952.

Parham, H. J., and Belfield, E. M. G. *Unarmed Into Battle.* Winchester: Warrens and Sons, 1956.

Park, Air Chief Marshal Sir Keith. "Background to the Blitz," *The Hawker- Siddeley Review,* December, 1951.

Pawle, Gerald. *The War and Colonel Warden.* London: George Harrap, 1963.

Pile, General Sir Frederick. *Ack-Ack*. London: George Harrap, 1949.

Pollard, Captain A. O. *Epic Deeds of the R.A.F.* London: Hutchinson, 1940.

Postan, Professor M. M. *British War Production*. London: H.M. Stationery Office and Longmans Green, 1952.

Powell, Henry P. *Men With Wings*. London: Allan Wingate, 1957.

Priller, Josef. *Geschichte eines Jagdgeschwaders* (Das JG 26, 1937–45). Heidelberg: Vowinckel Verlag, 1962.

Quednau, Horst. "I Bombed Britain," *The R.A.F. Flying Review*, Vol. VI, No. 12.

R. J. S. *Czechoslovak Wings*. London: Czechoslovak Publications, 1944.

Raeder, Grand-Admiral Erich. *Struggle for the Sea*. London: Willian Kimber, 1959.

Ramsay, L. F. *West Wittering in the Front Line*. Eastbourne: Sussex County Magazine, 1946.

Randle-Ford, J. M. *A Dorset Village's War Effort*. Bournemouth: Roman Press, 1945.

Rawnsley, C. F., and Wright, Robert. *Night Fighter*. London: William Collins, 1957.

Reid, J. P. M. *Some of the Few*. London: MacDonald, 1960.

The Battle of Britain. London: H.M. Stationery Office, 1960.

Reynolds, Quentin. *The Wounded Don't Cry*. London: Cassell, 1941.

Richards, Denis. *Royal Air Force, 1939–45. Vol. 1, The Fight at Odds*. London: H.M. Stationery Office, 1953.

Rieckhoff, Lt.-Gen. H. J. *Trumpf oder Bluff*. Geneva: Interavia S.A., 1945.

Ries, Karl, Jr. *Markierungen und Tarnanstriche der Luftwaffe im 2 Weltkrieg*. Finthen bei Mainz: Verlag Dieter Hoffmann, 1963.

Robbins, Gordon. *Fleet Street Blitzkrieg Diary*. London: Ernest Benn, 1944.

Roberts, L. *Canada's War in the Air.* Montreal: A. M. Beatty Publications, 1943.

Robertson, Ben. *I Saw England.* London: Jarrold, 1941.

Robertson, Bruce. *Spitfire. The Story of a Famous Fighter.* Letchworth: Harleyford Publications, 1960.

Roof Over Britain. London: H.M. Stationery Office, 1943.

Roper, H. R. Trevor. *Hitler's Table Talk.* London: Weidenfeld and Nicolson, 1953.

The Royal Canadian Air Force Overseas. Vol. I. Toronto: O.U.P., 1944.

Rudel, Hans. *Stuka Pilot.* London: Transworld Publications, 1957.

Sands, R. P. D. *Treble One: the Story of No. 111 Squadron.* North Weald: privately printed, 1957.

Sansom, William. *Westminster at War.* London: Faber & Faber, 1947.

Sargent, E. *The Royal Air Force.* London: Sampson, Low and Marston, 1944.

Saundby, Air Marshal Sir Robert. "Preparations for the Battle of Britain," *The Listening Post,* Vol. XXXI, No. 11, March, 1958.

Saunders, Hilary St. George. *The Battle of Britain.* London: H.M. Stationery Office, 1941.

Sayers, W. Berwick (ed.). *Croydon Corporation in the Second World War.* Croydon: Roffey and Clark, for Croydon Corporation, 1949.

Schmidt, Dr Paul. *Hitler's Interpreter.* London: William Heinemann, 1951.

Sheean, Vincent. *Between the Thunder and the Sun.* London: Macmillan, 1943.

Shirer, William. *Berlin Diary.* London: Hamish Hamilton, 1941.

60 Group Radar Bulletin. Welwyn Garden City: Broadwater Press, 1945.

Slessor, Marshall of the R.A.F. Sir John. *The Central Blue*. London: Cassell, 1956.

Smitten City: the Story of Portsmouth Under Blitz. Portsmouth: Evening News, n.d.

Smythe, D. C. "On the Direct Bomber Route," *Our Empire To-Day*, Vol. XXV, No, l-iv.

Spaight, J. M. *The Battle of Britain*. London: Geoffrey Bles, 1941.

The Sky Is the Limit. London: Hodder & Stoughton, 1940.

Sprigg, T. S. "The Battle of Britain," *United Services Review*, July 8, 1946.

The War Story of Fighter Command. London: William Collins, 1941.

Stewart, Oliver. "An Air Battle Over the English Channel," *London Calling*, No. 50.

Student, Gen, Kurt. "Hitler's Secret*s*," *Kommando*, Vol. 3, No. *20*.

Sutton, Barry. *The Way of a Pilot* London: Macmillan, 1942.

Sutton, H. T. *Raider's Approach*. Aldershot: Gale and Polden, 1956.

Taylor, J. W. R., and Allward, M. F. *Spitfire*. London: Harborough Publishing Co., 1946.

Terry, John. "Eleven for Danger," *Air Mail*, Vol. 2, No. 24,1950.

"Their Greatest Day," *Air Mail*, Vol. 3, No. 35,1951.

Thetford, O. G. "No. 600 (City of London) Squadron," *Air Reserve Gazette*, Vol. X, No. 1, 1948.

"No. 603 (City of Edinburgh) Squadron," *Air Reserve Gazette*, Vol. X, No. 4, 1948.

"Twenty-Five Part-Time Years," *The R.A.F. Flying Review*, Vol. VI, No. 4, 1950.

Thomas, R. L. *The Kent Police Centenary: recollections of a hundred years.* Maidstone: privately printed, 1957.

Thompson, Wing Commander H. L. *New Zealanders with the Royal Air Force, Vol. I.* London: Oxford University

Press, for the War History Branch, Department of Internal Affairs, New Zealand, 1953.

Thompson, R. J. *Battle Over Essex*. Walthamstow: Guardian Press, 1944.

Tobin, Eugene, with Low, Robert. "Yankee Eagle Over London," *Liberty Magazine*, March–April, 1941.

Urbanek, Walther. *Fliegerhorst Ostmark*. Innsbruck: Gauverlag und Druckerei, 1941.

Uderstadt, E. R. *Das Jahr VII*. Berlin: Schmidt Verlag, 1941.

"The Victory of Britain," *Faugh-A-Ballagh*, Journal of the Royal Irish Fusiliers, Vol. XXXIV, No. 152.

Walker, Oliver. *Sailor Malan*. London: Cassell, 1953.

Walker, Ronald. *Flight to Victory*. London: Penguin Books, 1941.

Wallace, Graham. *R.A.F. Biggin Hill*. London: Putnam, 1957.

Walwyn, E. H. Sheppeard. *Purleigh in Wartime*. Chelmsford: The Tindal Press, 1946.

War in East Sussex. Lewes: Sussex Express & County Herald, 1945.

Weber, Dr Theo. *Die Luftschlacht um England*. Fraunfeld: Huber, 1956.

Wendel, Else. *Hausfrau at War*. London: Odhams, 1957.

Weymouth, Anthony. *Plague Year*. London: George Harrap, 1942.

Wheatley, Ronald. *Operation Sea Lion*. London: O.U.P., 1958.

Whitty, H. Ramsden (ed.). *An Observer's Tale*. London: Roland, 1950.

Williams, Peter. "The Fateful Fifteenth," *The R.A.F. Flying Review*, Vol. II No. 11.

Williams, R. "Twelve Years Ago," *The R.A.F. Flying Review*, Vol. VII, No. 12 1952–53.

Willis, J. *It Stopped at London*. London: Hurst & Blackett, 1944.

Wilmot, Chester. *The Struggle for Europe*. London: William Collins, 1954.

"Why Hitler Failed to Invade," *Stand-To*, Vol. I, No. 1, January, 1950.

Wilson, A. J. *Sky Sweepers*. London: Jarrold, 1942.

Winslow, T. E. *Forwarned Is Forearmed*. Edinburgh: William Hodge, 1947.

Wooldridge, John de L. *Low Attack*. London: Sampson Low and Marston, 1944.

Woon, Basil. *Hell Came to London*. London: Peter Davies, 1941.

Wykeham, Air Vice-Marshal Peter. *Fighter Command*. London: Putnam, 1960.

Yoxall, John. "No. 65 (East India) Squadron," *Flight*, Vol. 65, 1954.

The Queen's Squadron, London: Iliffe, 1949.

Manuscript sources

Except in the case of public archives, the sources listed here are contemporary, privately prepared accounts, the property of the owners, to whom I am deeply indebted for making them available.

Air Ministry, Directorate of Public Relations. *German Air Force Operations Against Britain: Tactics and Lessons Learned* (Imperial War Museum, London, S.E. 1).

Bailey, Robert. *An Account of Ladwood Farm in the Battle of Britain*.

Beecroft, Pamela. *A Biggin Hill Diary* (Courtesy Mrs. D. H. Grice).

Crossley, Wing Commander Michael. *Diary of 32 Squadron*.

Deacon-Elliott, Air Commodore. *No. 72 Squadron*, a private diary.

Deichmann, General Paul. *Actions of No. II Flying Corps in the Battle of Britain* (Karlsruhe Collection, Hamburg). Translated by Nadia Radowitz.

German Attacks on R.A.F. Ground Targets, 13/8/40–6/9/40: a study (Karlsruhe Collection, Hamburg). Translated by Nadia Radowitz.

Mass Day Attacks on London: a monograph (Karlsruhe Collection, Hamburg). Translated by Nadia Radowitz.

Some Reasons for the Switch to Night Bombing: an appreciation (Karlsruhe Collection, Hamburg). Translated by Nadia Radowitz.

The Struggle for Air Superiority During Phase 1 of the Battle of Britain (Karlsruhe Collection, Hamburg). Translated by Nadia Radowitz.

Donaghue, L. *No. 54 Squadron, R.A.F.* (Air Ministry Public Relations typescript).

No. 19 Squadron, R.A.F. (Air Ministry Public Relations typescript).

No. 65 Squadron, R.A.F. (Air Ministry Public Relations typescript).

Elliott, Donald V. *No. 66 Squadron, a private diary* (Courtesy Christopher Elliott).

Feric, Pilot Officer Miroslaw. *Extracts from the Memoirs of a "Kosciuszko" Pilot: the story of 303 (Polish) Squadron*, unpublished MS. (Courtesy Major L. W. Bienkowski, owner and translator).

First Flying Corps, Luftwaffe: Operational Orders for Attacks "Sea of Light" and "Loge" (Karlsruhe Collection, Hamburg). Translated by Nadia Radowitz.

Gefechtskalendar, Air Fleets Two and Three, 1/8/40–15/9/40 (Karlsruhe Collection, Hamburg). Translated by Nadia Radowitz.

Goring, Reichsmarschall Herman. *Conference Decisions of 21st July, 1st, 3rd, 15th and 19th August* (Karlsruhe Collection, Hamburg). Translated by Nadia Radowitz.

Grabmann, General Walter. *The Fighters' Role in the Battle of Britain*, a study (Karlsruhe Collection, Hamburg). Translated by Nadia Radowitz.

Greiner, Helmuth. *The Battle of Britain*, 4/9/40–7/9/40 (Karlsruhe Collection, Hamburg). Translated by Nadia Radowitz.

Ibel, General Max. *The 27th Fighter Group, Luftwaffe*, a private diary. Translated by Nadia Radowitz.

Jacobs, Squadron Leader Henry. *Jacob's Ladder*, an unpublished autobiography.

Lindemann, Professor Frederick (Lord Cherwell). *The Cherwell Papers* (Courtesy Nuffield College, Oxford).

Mann, E. L. *Recollections of 1940*, an essay.

Matthes, Gunther. *The 2nd Wing, 51st Fighter Group*, a private diary. Translated by Nadia Radowitz.

Milch; Generalfeldmarschall Erhard. *Report of the Inspector General of the Luftwaffe*, 25/8/40 (Karlsruhe Collection, Hamburg). Translated by Nadia Radowitz.

Ministry of Information: Observers' Regional Reports on Morale, 1/8/40–9/9/40 (Courtesy Mass Observation Ltd., London, S.W. 7).

Osterkamp, General Theo. *Experiences as Fighter Leader 2 on the Channel* (Karlsruhe Collection, Hamburg). Translated by Nadia Radowitz.

Page, Wing Commander Geoffrey. *Autobiography*, an unpublished MS.

Richthofen, General the Baron von. *Private Diary* (Karlsruhe Collection, Hamburg). Translated by Nadia Radowitz.

Ring, Hans. *The German Fighter Forces in World War Two*, a study, in preparation. Translated by Nadia Radowitz.

Satchell, Group Captain W. A. J. *The First Polish Fighter Squadron, R.A.F.*, an unpublished history of No. 302 Squadron.

Seidemann, General Hans. *Actions of No. VIII Flying Corps on the Channel Coast* (Karlsruhe Collection, Hamburg). Translated by Nadia Radowitz.

Tobin, Pilot Officer Eugene. *Private diary* (Courtesy Mr. I. Quimby Tobin).

Trautloft, General Hannes. *The 54th Fighter Group*, a private diary.

United States Strategic Bombing Survey Records: including *Record Group 243:* interrogations of General Karl Koller, Professor Messerschmitt, Dr Albert Speer, General Werner Junck, Dr Kurt Tank, Generalfeldmarschall Sperrle, General Werner Kreipe, General Halder, General Goldbeck, Generalfeldmarschall Albert Kesselring, Feld-marschall Wilhelm Keitel, General Adolf Galland (Courtesy David Irving). Microcopy T-321: *Records of H.Q. O.K.L.* (Oberkommando Der Luftwaffe), German Air Force High Command (United States National Archives, Washington, D.C.).

The Eye-Witnesses

The 434 men and women listed below contributed untold help in the preparation of this work – through furnishing specially written accounts, through the loan of contemporary letters and diaries, or by patiently submitting themselves to a detailed question-and-answer interview. To avoid confusion, the ranks and, in some cases, the names given are those that then pertained, followed by the vantage point from which he or she witnessed the Battle.

S/Ldr. Jim Abell, *Fighter Section H.Q., Wick Sector Station.*
S/Ldr. Ronald Adam, *Duty Controller, Hornchurch Sector.*
Delma Addison, *Hurst Green, Surrey.*
Mrs Doris Addison, *Hurst Green, Surrey.*
Frank Addison, *Hurst Green, Surrey.*
Walter "Dick" Addison, *Hurst Green, Surrey.*
John Ainger, *Greatham Farm, Wittering, Sussex.*
P/O Charles Ambrose, *46 Squadron, Stapleford.*
S/Ldr. Gavin Anderson, *Senior Controller, Middle Wallop Sector.*
Hauptmann Werner Andres, *II/ JG 27, Crepon.*
Pte. Ben Angell, *34th Signal Training Regiment, R.A., Swing-gate, Kent.*
F/O Michael Appleby, *609 Squadron, Warmwell.*
P/O Ellis Aries, *602 Squadron, Westhampnett.*
Miss Vera Arlett, *Worthing, Sussex.*
F/Lt. Dennis Armitage, *266 Squadron, Eastchurch–Mansion.*
Sgt. Don Aslin, *32 Squadron, Biggin Hill.*

Tom Aylwin, *Greenwood Farm, Sidlesham, Sussex.*

Sgt. Cyril Babbage, *602 Squadron, Westhampnett.*

F/Lt, the Rev. Leslie Badham, *Chaplain, R.A.F. Station, Leconfield.*

Robert Bailey, *Ladwood Farm, Acrise, Kent.*

P/O Harry "Butch" Baker, *41 Squadron, Hornchurch.*

S/Ldr. John Banham, *264 Squadron, Hornchurch–229 Squadron, Northolt.*

P/O F. H. "Jimmy" Baraldi, *609 Squadron, Warmwell.*

Roy Owen Barnes, *Catford, South London.*

P/O Patrick Barthropp, *602 Squadron, Westhampnett.*

P/O Anthony Bartley, *92 Squadron, Biggin Hill.*

P/O Eric Barwell, *264 Squadron, Hornchurch.*

Oberleutnant Victor Bauer, *III/JG 3, Desvres.*

Casualty Clearing Officer Wallace Beale, *Maidstone, Kent.*

Bill Bear, *Shelvingford Farm, Shelvingford, Kent.*

F/O Eric Beardmore, *No. 1 (R.C.A.F.) Squadron, Northolt.*

Hauptmann Otto Wolfgang Bechtle, *III/KG 2, Cambrai.*

S/O Pamela Beecroft, *R.A.F. Station, Biggin Hill.*

F/O David Beevers, *Operations Room, Tangmere Sector.*

Frederick Bell, *Enfield, Middlesex.*

A.C. Robert Bell, *No, 1 Radio School, Yatesbury, Wilts.*

P/O David Bell-Salter, *253 Squadron, Kenley.*

Feldwebel Karl-Heinz Bendert, *II/JG 27, Crepon–Fiennes.*

P/O Arthur Bennett, *Operations Room, Biggin Hill Sector.*

P/O George Bennions, *41 Squadron, Hornchurch.*

F/O "Razz" Berry, *603 Squadron, Hornchurch.*

Hauptmann Otto Bertram, *III/JG2, La Havre–Oye–Plage.*

F/Lt. Montague Bieber, *Senior Medical Officer, R.A.F. Station, Warmwell.*

F/O Harold Bird-Wilson, *17 Squadron, Debden.*

F/O Robin Birley, *Adjutant, 611 Squadron, Digby.*

P/O John "Bishop" Bisdee, *609 Squadron, Warmwell.*

F/Lt. Francis Blackadder, *607 Squadron, Tangmere.*

Assistant Divisional Officer Geoffrey Blackstone, *LFS, Thameshaven, Essex.*

S/Ldr. Douglas Blackwood, *310 (Czech) Squadron, Duxford.*

F/Lt. Minden Blake, *238 Squadron, Middle Wallop.*

Reginald H. Blunt, *St. Margaret's Bay, Kent.*

Oberleutnant Hans-Ekkehard Bob, *III/JG 54, Guines.*

Hauptmann Erich Bode, *II/JG 26, Marquise.*

Leutnant Erich Bodendiek, *II/JG 53, Dinan, Guernsey–Sempy.*

H. Roy Pratt Boorman, *Editor*, The Kent Messenger, *Maidstone, Kent.*

P/O Peter Boot, *No. 1 (R.A.F.) Squadron, Northolt.*

W/Cdr. Cecil Bouchier, O.C., R.A.F. Station, Hornchurch.

Sgt. Hugh Bowen-Morris, *92 Squadron, Biggin Hill.*

S/Ldr. F. Hugh Bowyer, *Senior Controller, Northolt Sector.*

F/Lt. Finlay Boyd, *602 Squadron, Westhampnett.*

F/Lt. Thomas McMaster Boyle, *Medical Officer, R.A.F. Station, Hendon.*

Miss Gladys Boynton, *St. Marylebone, West London.*

Elizabeth Bradburne, *Higham, Kent.*

Sub-Lt. Kenelm Bramah, *Fleet Air Arm, 213 Squadron, Exeter.*

Frederick Brent, *Frant, Sussex.*

Miss Lilian Bride, *Croydon, Surrey.*

Pte. Alfred Brind, *Stubbington, Hants, Home Guard: Lee-on-Solent airfield.*

F/Lt. Peter Brothers, *32 Squadron, Biggin Hill–257 Squadron, Martlesham Heath.*

P/O R. Clifford Brown, *229 Squadron, Northolt.*

P/O Maurice "Sneezy" Brown, *611 Squadron, Digby–Fowlmere.*

Hauptmann Hans-Heinrich Brustellin, *I/JG 51, Wissant–Pihen.*

F/Lt. John Buckmaster, *Medical Officer, R.A.F. Station, Northolt.*

Oberst Alfred Bulowius, *LG 1, Orleans.*

Sgt. Mike Bush, *504 Squadron, Hendon.*

L.A.C.W. Karen Butler, *Operations Room, Tangmere Sector.*

P/O James Caister, *603 Squadron, Hornchurch.*

Section Officer Alexander Campbell, *Dover Fire Brigade.*

F/Lt. E. W. Campbell-Colquhoun, *264 Squadron, Hornchurch.*

P/O Frank Carey, *43 Squadron, Tangmere.*

P/O Lionel Casson, *616 Squadron, Kenley.*

Mrs Mary Castle, *The Firs Farm, Hawkinge, Kent.*

W/Cdr. George Chamberlain, *Fighter Interceptor Unit, Shoreham.*

S/Ldr. John Cherry, *Senior Controller, North Weald Sector.*

F/Lt. David Clackson, *600 Squadron, Manston.*

Bdr. William Clague, *30th Field Regt. R.A., Runcton, Sussex.*

P/O Douglas Clift, *79 Squadron, Biggin Hill.*

Ernest Collier, *Wittering, Sussex.*

P/O Leon Collingridge, *66 Squadron, Cottishall.*

P/O Bryan Considine, *238 Squadron, Middle Wallop.*

P/O Michael Constable-Maxwell, *56 Squadron, North Weald.*

Gnr. Arthur Cooke, *Operations Room, H.Q. 12 Group, Uxbridge.*

Len Cooke, *Pett, Sussex.*

Mrs Lydia Cooke, *Pett, Sussex.*

Coastguard Reg Cooke, *Pett, Sussex.*

P/O Mike Cooper-Slipper, *605 Squadron, Croydon.*

Sgt. James "Binder" Corbin, *66 Squadron, Kenley.*

F/O Jimmie Coward, *29 Squadron, Duxford.*

Sgt. David Cox, *29 Squadron, Eastchurch–Duxford.*

F/O Dudley Craig, *607 Squadron, Tangmere.*

F/Lt. Michael Crossley, *32 Squadron, Biggin Hill.*

F/Lt. Thomas Cullen, *Medical Officer, R.A.F. Station, Manston.*

P/O Christopher Currant, *605 Squadron, Croydon.*

Michael Currell, *Bembridge, Isle of Wight.*

Police-Constable Tom Dadswell, *Chelsham, Surrey.*

Unteroffizier Hugo Dahmer, *II/JG 26, Marquise.*

S/Ldr. John Dales, *Senior Medical Officer, R.A.F. Station, Manston.*

Mrs Pauline Daniels, *Drellingore, Kent.*

Phil Daniels, *Drellingore, Kent.*

S/Ldr. Horace Darley, *609 Squadron, Middle Wallop.*

William Albert Daw, *Hanns Farm, Bilsington, Kent.*

H. O. Deacon, *Woldingham, Surrey.*

P/O Robert Deacon-Elliott, *72 Squadron, Biggin Hill–Croydon.*

F/Lt. Alan Deere, *54 Squadron, Hornchurch.*

Oberst Paul Deichmann, *Chief of Staff, No. II Flying Corps, Bonningues.*

Cpl. Francis De Vroome, *600 Squadron, Manston.*

F/O Roland Dibnah, *No. 2 (R.A.F.) Squadron, Northolt.*

Hauptmann Bruno Dilley, *I/St G I, Angers.*

Sgt Herbert Dimmer, *No. 2 (R.A.F.) Squadron, Northolt.*

P/O Robert Doe, *234 Squadron, Middle Wallop.*

W/Cdr. Eric Douglas-Jones, *Operations Room, H.Q. 11 Group, Uxbridge.*

Air Chief Marshal Sir Hugh Dowding, *AOC.-in-C., H.Q. Fighter Command, Stanmore.*

Leading Fireman Patrick Duffy, *AFS, R.A.F. Station, Biggin Hill.*

Oberleutnant Ernst Dullberg, *III/JG 27, Carquebut–Guines.*

F/Lt. Roy Dutton, *145 Squadron, Westhampnett.*

Sgt. Richard Earp, *46 Squadron, Stapleford.*

Deputy Chief Officer Arthur Easton, *Hornchurch Fire Brigade.*

Leutnant Hans Ebeling, *III/JG 26, Caffiers.*

P/O Alan Eckford, *32 Squadron, Biggin Hill.*

F/O A. R. "Grandpa" Edge, *609 Squadron, Warmwell.*

S/Ldr. John Ellis, *610 Squadron, Biggin Hill.*

Major Walter Enneccerus, *II/St G 2, Lannion.*

L.A.C. William Eslick, *19 Squadron, Duxford.*

Leading Fireman Herbert Evans, *Margate Fire Brigade.*

Leading Fireman John Evans, *Southampton Fire Brigade.*

Air Vice-Marshal Douglas Evill, *Senior Administrative Staff Officer, H.Q. Fighter Command, Stanmore.*

F/O Scott Farnie, *R.A.F. Kingsdowne, Kent.*

S/Ldr. Harold Fenton, *238 Squadron, Middle Wallop.*

Alfred Finch, *Rotherfield, Sussex.*

Oberst Johannes Fink, *KG 2, Arras.*

S/Ldr. Donald Finlay, *54 Squadron, Hornchurch.*

Leutnant Ernst Fischbach, *III/KG 53, Lille–Nord.*

Denis Fishenden, *Rotherfield, Sussex.*

Lt.-Cdr. John Fordham, LFS, *Thameshaven, Essex.*

P/O Dennis Fox-Male, *152 Squadron, Warmwell.*

Oberleutnant Gert Framm, *I/JG 27, Plumetot–Guinea.*

Mrs Laura Francis, *Waterlooville, Portsmouth, Hampshire.*

S/Ldr. Roger Frankland, *Senior Controller, Biggin Hill Sector.*

Oberleutnant Ludwig Franzisket, *JG 27, Cherbourg-West–Quines.*

Sgt. Frank Freeman, *2/8th Bn. Middlesex Regt., R.A.F. Station, Croydon.*

Arthur B. Fuller, *Tasker's Ltd., Commercial Trailer Manufacturers, Andover, Hampshire.*

W/Cdr. Laurence Fuller-Good, *O.C., R.A.F. Station, Debden.*

Major Adolf Galland, *III/JG 26, Caffiers; Kdre. JG 26, Audembert.*

Sub-Lt. R. E. "Jimmie" Gardner, *Fleet Air Arm, 242 Squadron, Duxford.*

F/Lt. Denys Gillam, *616 Squadron, Kenley.*

F/Lt. George Gilroy, *603 Squadron, Hornchurch.*

F/O David Glaser, *65 Squadron, Mansion.*

S/Ldr. Thomas Gleave, *253 Squadron, Kenley.*

F/Lt. Michael Golovine, *Air Intelligence, Branch 2(g), Ryder Street, London.*

A.C. Geoffrey Gooch, *R.A.F. Station, Duxford.*

Sgt. Geoffrey Goodman, *85 Squadron, Croydon–Debden.*

Station Officer Thomas Goodman, *LFS, attd. Dover Fire Brigade.*

S/Ldr. John Grandy, *249 Squadron, Boscombe Down–North Weald.*

S/Ldr. Robert Grant-Ferris, *R.A.F. Station, Wittering.*

Oberleutnant Hartmann Grasser, *III/JG 52, St. Omer.*

Gunner L. W. Green, *455 Troop, 76th L.A.A. Regt., RA., Poling, Sussex.*

Sgt. Reginald Gretton, *266 Squadron, Eastchurch–Hornchurch.*

CpL Daphne Griffiths, *Air Ministry Experimental Station, Brookland, Rye, Kent.*

John Hacking, *Cadborough Farm, Rye, Sussex.*

Hauptmann Hans "Assi" Hahn, *II/JG 2, Beaumont-le-Roger–Mardyck.*

P/O Peter Hairs, *501 Squadron, Gravesend.*

Sgt Ronnie Hamlyn, *820 Squadron, Biggin Hill.*

Miss Brenda Hancock, *Castle Farm, Hadlow, Kent.*

Major Gotthard Handrick, *Kdre. JG 26, Audembert.*

Oberst Martin Harlinghausen, *Chief of Staff, No. X Flying Corps, Stavanger, Norway.*

Police Sergeant Ernest Harmer, *Chief Executive Officer, Dover Fire Brigade.*

Sgt. Ralph "Titch" Havercroft, *92 Squadron, Biggin Hill.*

Sgt. Peter Hawke, *64 Squadron, Kenley.*

Lifeboatman Jack Hawkes, *Ramsgate Lifeboat.*

Second Officer Edward Hayward, *Southampton Fire Brigade.*

Cpl. Avis Hearn, *Air Ministry Experimental Station, Poling, Sussex.*

F/O Barrie Heath, *611 Squadron, Digby–Fowlmere.*

Patrol Officer "Steve" Heath, *AFS, Hornchurch Fire Brigade.*

Hauptmann Hans-Joachim Helbig, *IV/LG 1, Orleans.*

Alan Henderson, *Hadlow, Kent.*

Cpl. Elspeth Henderson, *Operations Room, Biggin Hill Sector.*

Mrs Martha Henning, *Capel-le-Ferne, Dover, Kent.*

Oberleutnant Karl Hentze, *I/St G 77, Caen.*

Kenneth Heron, *Air Defence Section, G.P.O. H.Q., St. Martins-le-Grand, London.*

F/Sgt. Frederick "Taffy" Higginson, *56 Squadron, North Weald.*

S/Ldr. Johnnie Hill, *222 Squadron, Hornchurch.*

Sgt. Peter Hillwood, *56 Squadron, North Weald.*

A/S/O Violet Hime, *Air Ministry Experimental Station, Brodkland, Rye, Kent.*

Oberleutnant Otto Hintze, *Erprobungsgr. 210, Calais–Marck.*

S/Ldr. Harry Hogan, *501 Squadron, Gravesend.*

Oberleutnant Hermann Hogebach, *III/LG 1, Chateaudun.*

F/O Edward Hogg, *252 Squadron, Warmwell.*

Leutnant Erich Hohagen, *II/JG 51, Desvres–Marquise.*

P/O Ken Holden, *626 Squadron, Kenley.*

Police Constable Ernest Hooper, *Catford, South London.*

F/Lt. Sir Archibald Hope, *Bt., 601 Squadron, Tangmere.*

G/C Frank Hopps, *O.C., R.A.F. Station, Eastchurch.*

S/Ldr. Kelham K. Horn, *Senior Controller, Duxford Sector.*

F/Lt. T. Geoffrey Hovenden, *Medical Officer, R.A.F. Station, Hawkinge.*

Major Paul Hozzel, *I/St G 1, Angers.*

Edward Hubbard, *Addington, Surrey.*

F/Lt. Thomas Hubbard, *662 Squadron, Tangmere.*

F/O Basil Hudson, *Adjutant, 56 Squadron, North Weald.*

P/O Desmond Hughes, *264 Squadron, Hornchurch.*

Sgt. William Hughes, *23 Squadron, Ford.*

Sgt. Ray Hulbert, *601 Squadron, Exeter.*

Sgt Leslie Hunt, *Operations Room, H.Q. 11 Group, Uxbridge.*

Sgt. Fred Hurry, *No. 28 (Essex) Searchlight Regt. R.A., Purleigh, Essex.*

Major Max Ibel, *Kdre. JG 27, Cherbourg-West–Guines.*

P/O Alec Ingle, *605 Squadron, Croydon.*

Mrs Lillian Ivory, *Hotel Mecca, Folkstone, Kent.*

Oberleutnant Hans-Joachim Jabs, *II/ZG 76, Abbeville–Yvrench.*

P/O Henry Jacobs, *600 Squadron, Manston–Hornchurch.*

A.C. Laurence James, *R.A.F. Station, Warmwell.*

Cpl. Albert E. Jessop, *625 Squadron, Kenley.*

F/O Richard Jones, *64 Squadron, Kenley.*

Mrs Rose Jones, *Poling, Sussex.*

Stanley Jordan, *Warehorne, Kent.*

Hauptmann Herbert Kaminski, *II/ZG 26, Crecy–St. Omer.*

S/Ldr. Joseph Kayll, *615 Squadron, Kenley.*

S/Ldr. Ronald Kellett, *303 (Polish) Squadron, Northolt.*

F/Lt. Johnnie Kent, *303 (Polish) Squadron, Northolt.*

Hauptmann Wilhelm Kern, *I/LG 1, Orleans.*

Oberleutnant Karl Kessel, *I/KG 2, Epinoy.*

Hauptmann Walter Kienzle, *Stab. JG 26, Audembert.*

F/Lt, the Rev. Cecil King, *Chaplain, R.A.F. Station, Manston.*

F/Lt. Bryan Kingcome, *92 Squadron, Biggin Hill.*

Oberleutnant Erich Kircheis, *II/JG 51, Desvres–Marquise.*

P/O Julian Kowalski, *302 (Polish) Squadron, Duxford.*

S/Ldr. Zdzislaw Krasnodebski, *303 (Polish) Squadron, Northolt.*

Major Werner Kreipe, *III/KG 2, Cambrai.*

F/O Gregory Krikorian, *Intelligence Officer, 234 Squadron, Middle Wallop.*

Major Ernst Kuhl, *Operations Officer, KG 55, Villacoublay.*

Felbwebel Herbert Kutscha, *III/ZG 76, Laval.*

Assistant Mechanic Alfred Lacey, *Margate Lifeboat.*

W/Cdr. Thomas Lang, *Operations Room, H.Q. 11 Group, Uxbridge.*

P/O Norman Langham-Hobart, *No. 73 Squadron, Debden.*

Miss Molly Langley, *Bermondsey, South London.*

Mess Steward Joseph Lauderdale, *R.A.F. Station, Middle Wallop.*

Chief Officer Robert Leach, *Hornchurch Fire Brigade.*

S/Ldr. James Leathart, *54 Squadron, Hornchurch.*

F/Lt. Jack Leather, *611 Squadron, Digby–Fowlmere.*

Cpl. Clare Legge, *Operations Room, Tangmere Sector.*

S/Ldr. Rupert Leigh, *66 Squadron, Kenley–Gravesend.*

District Warden Ronald Leisk, *Croydon, Surrey.*

F/O Paul Le Rougetel, *600 Squadron, Manston-Hornchurch.*

Fred Lexster, *Abbotsbury Swannery, Dorset.*

Oberfeldwebel Stefan Litjens, *III/JG 53, Brest–Le Touquet.*

Sgt. Reginald Llewellyn, *213 Squadron, Exeter–Tangmere.*

S/Ldr. David Lloyd, *Senior Controller, Tangmere Sector.*

George Lloyd, *Nyetimber, Sussex.*

Miss Emma Lock, *Sevenoaks, Kent.*

Sidney Loweth, *Kent County Architect, Maidstone.*

F/O Robert Lucy, *Engineering Officer, 54 Squadron, Hornchurch.*

Ambulance Officer John Lunt, *St. John Ambulance Brigade, Woldingham, Surrey.*

Feldwebel Johannes Lutter, *III/ZG 76, Laval.*

S/Ldr. James McComb, 611 Squadron, Digby–Fowlmere.

S/Ldr. Aeneas MacDonell, *64 Squadron, Kenley.*

Section Leader Donald McGregor, *AFS, Portsmouth Fire Brigade.*

F/Lt. Gordon McGregor, *No. 1 (R.C.A.F.) Squadron, Northolt.*

A.C. Jock Mackay, *Servicing Flight, R.A.F. Station, Hawkinge.*

F/O Hector MacLean, *602 Squadron, Westhampnett.*

A.C. Thomas McMichael, *603 Squadron, Hornchurch.*

S/Ldr. Ernest McNab, *No. 1 (R.C.A.F.) Squadron, Northolt.*

Area Officer William Manley, *Ministry of Aircraft Production, South and East Areas, Reading, Berks.*

Ernest L. Mann, *Sidcup, Kent.*

Philip Marchant, *Air Defence Section, G.P.O. H.Q., St. Martins-le-Grand, London.*

Anthony Marshall, *Kimmeridge Bay, Dorset.*

Mrs Ivy Marshall, *Kimmeridge Bay, Dorset.*

Mrs Kathleen Marshall, *Kenley, Surrey.*

Tony Marshall, *Kimmeridge Bay, Dorset.*

Hauptmann Gunther Matthes, *II/JG 51 Desvres–Marquise.*

Mrs Diane Maxted, *Ramsgate, Kent.*

Hauptmann Conny Mayer, *I/ZG 26, Yvrench–St. Omer.*

A.C. 1 Harold T. Mead, *610 Squadron, Biggin Hill.*

Herbert Merrett, *Cutmill, Sussex.*

W/O George Merron, *Station Warrant Officer, R.A.F., Biggin Hill.*

Major Martin Mettig, *Kdre. JG 54, Campagne–Guines.*

Sgt. Joseph Mikolajczwk, *Servicing Flight, 303 (Polish) Squadron, Northolt.*

F/Lt. Richard Milne, *151 Squadron, North Weald.*

Oberleutnant Victor Molders, *III/JG 51, St. Omer.*

P/O Hartland De Molson, *No. 1 (R.C.A.F.) Squadron, Northolt.*

Patrol Officer Stanley Money, *Canterbury Fire Brigade.*

Sgt. Roy Moore, *Central Gunnery School, Warmwell.*

Jimmie Murrell, *Hurst Green, Surrey.*

Harry Neave, *Newman's Farm, Udimore, Sussex.*

Pte. Alfred Neill, *5th Bn. King's Shropshire Light Infantry, Deal, Kent.*

P/O George Nelson-Edwards, *79 Squadron, Biggin Hill.*

F/O A. Deane Nesbitt, *No. 1 (R.C.A.F.) Squadron, Northolt.*

Hauptmann Eduard Neumann, *I/JG 27, Plumetot–Guines.*

P/O Glen Niven, *602 Squadron, Westhampnett.*

S/Ldr. Anthony Norman, *Senior Controller, Kenley Sector.*

F/O Keith Ogilvie, *609 Squadron, Warmwell.*

Oberleutnant Hans Ohly, *I/JG 53, Rennes–Le Touquet.*

Oberst Theo Osterkamp, *JAFU 2, Wissant.*

Keith Otterwell, *Rochester, Kent.*

Superintendent Edward Overton, *LFS, Thameshaven, Essex.*

P/O Robert Oxspring, *66 Squadron, Kenley–Gravesend.*

P/O Geoffrey Page, *56 Squadron, North Weald.*

Air Vice-Marshal Keith Park, *AOC, H.Q. 11 Group, Uxbridge.*

P/O Thomas Parker, *79 Squadron, Biggin Hill.*

W/Cdr. Toby Pearson, *Operations Room, H.Q. 11 Group, Uxbridge.*

Oberleutnant Dietrich Peltz, *II/KG 77, Juvaincourt.*

F/Lt Donald Peock, *Medical Officer, 611 Squadron, Digby.*

A.C. George Perry, *attd. 56 Squadron, North Weald.*

F/O Richard Pexton, *615 Squadron, Kenley.*

Hauptmann Rolf Pingel, *I/JG 26, Audembert.*

P/O Paul Pitcher, *No. 1 (R.C.A.F.) Squadron, Northolt.*

Mrs Ethel Powis, *Seaford, Sussex.*

Warden George Powis, *Seaford, Sussex.*

Miss Daphne Prett, *Snodland, Kent.*

Coxswain Dennis "Sinbad" Price, *Margate Lifeboat.*

F/O Philip St. Clere Raymond, *Intelligence Officer, 222 Squadron, Hornchurch.*

P/O Bill "Tannoy" Read, *603 Squadron, Hornchurch.*

Mrs Kay Redpath, *Waterlooville, Portsmouth, Hampshire.*

Hauptmann Ralph von Rettberg, *II/ZG 26, Crecy–St. Omer.*

W/Cdr. David Roberts, *O.C., R.A.F. Station, Middle Wallop.*

P/O Ralph Roberts, *615, 64 Squadrons, Kenley.*

William Robins, *Elmer Sands, Sussex.*

A.C. David Rose, *605 Squadron, Croydon.*

F/Lt. Barrington Royce, *504 Squadron, Hendon.*

F/O Michael Royce, *504 Squadron, Hendon.*

Oberleutnant Walter Rupp, *I/JG 53, Rennes–Le Touquet.*

Assistant Divisional Officer Charles Russell, *Portsmouth Fire Brigade.*

P/O Dal Russel, *No. 1 (R.C.A.F.) Squadron, Northolt.*

P/O Robert Rutter, *73 Squadron, Debden.*

F/Lt. Norman Ryder, *41 Squadron, Hornchurch.*

S/Ldr. Jack Satchell, *302 (Polish) Squadron, Duxford.*

Oberleutnant Kurt Scheffel, *I/St G 77, Caen.*

Oberleutnant Heinz Schlegel, *II/KG 2, Arras.*

Oberleutnant Hans Schmoller-Haldy, *I/JG 54, Guines.*

Oberleutnant Gerhard Schopfel, *III/JG 26, Caffiers.*

Mrs Eva Seabright, *Eastchurch, Kent.*

Oberst Hans Seidemann, *Chief of Staff, No. VIII Flying Corps, Deauville–Cherbourg.*

Hauptmann Erich von Selle, *II/JG 3, Samer.*

Sgt. Raymond Sellers, *111 Squadron, Croydon–Debden.*

Sid Sharvill, *G.P.O. Tunbridge Wells: Biggin Hill.*

Miss Mary Shearburn, *London: 10 Downing Street.*

Mrs Mary Simcox, *St. Mary Cray, Kent.*

P/O Vernon Simmonds, *238 Squadron, Middle Wallop.*

F/Lt. Gordon Sinclair, *310 (Czech) Squadron, Duxford.*

Arthur Smith, *Horsted Keynes, Kent.*

F/Lt. David Smith, *Medical Officer, 607 Squadron, Tangmere.*

F/O Duncan Smith, *600 Squadron, Manston.*

Probationary Nurse Jacqueline Smith, *Chailey Hospital, Sussex.*

Commandant John Robert Smith, *No. 7 Ambulance and Stretcher Party, Croydon, Surrey.*

Sgt. Kathleen Smith, *Operations Room, Filton.*

Sister Margaret Smith, *Cheam, Surrey.*

Miss Eva Smithers, *Knockholt, Kent.*

Norman Smithers, *Knockholt, Kent.*

F/O Derek Smythe, *264 Squadron, Hornchurch.*

Sgt. John Squier, *64 Squadron, Kenley.*

L.A.C. Arthur Standring, *600 Squadron, Manston–Hornchurch.*

Leutnant Johannes Steinhoff, *II/JG 52, Peuplingne.*

F/Lt. Paddy Stephenson, *607 Squadron, Tangmere.*

A.C. George Stokes, *54 Squadron, Hornchurch.*

Len Stone, *G.P.O. Tunbridge Wells: Biggin Hill.*

P/O James Storrar, *145 Squadron, Westhampnett.*

Major Hennig Strumpell, *I/JG 2, Beaumont-le-Roger–Mardyck.*

P/O Freddie Sutton, *264 Squadron, Hornchurch.*

Station Officer Terence Syrett, *LFS, Thameshaven.*

Ronald Tanfield, *Woolwich, South London.*

Cpl. John Tapp, *610 Squadron, Biggin Hill.*

Oberleutnant Paul Temme, *I/JG 2, Beaumont-le-Roger.*

F/Lt. Frederick Thomas, *152 Squadron, Warmwell.*

Mrs Joanna Thompson, *Folkestone, Kent.*

S/Ldr. John Thompson, *111 Squadron, Croydon–Debden.*

Inspector Walter Thompson, *London: 10 Downing Street.*

Inspector Abraham "Jock" Thomson, *G.P.O. Tunbridge Wells: Biggin Hill.*

W/Cdr. Brian Thynne, *O.C., R.A.F. Station, Usworth.*

Leading Fireman Maurice Toomey, *Deal Fire Brigade.*

Major Hannes Trautloft, *Kdre. JG 54, Guines.*

Observer J. H. Troy, *Post J 1, Crowborough, Sussex.*

Major Hans Trubenbach, *Kdre. JG 52, Coquelles.*

F/Lt. Robert Stanford Tuck, *92 Squadron, Pembrey; 257 Squadron, Martlesham Heath.*

Frank Turner, *Folkestone, Kent.*

F/O Stanley Turner, *242 Squadron, Duxford.*

F/Sgt. George Unwin, *19 Squadron, Duxford.*

F/Lt. Dunlop Urie, *602 Squadron, Westhampnett.*

Oberleutnant Werner Ursinus, *II/JG 53, Dinan, Guernsey–Sempy.*

P/O Jack Urwin-Mann, *238 Squadron, Middle Wallop.*

S/Ldr. James Vick, *607 Squadron, Tangmere.*

Oberstleutnant Carl Viek, *Kdre. JG 3, Samer; Chief of Staff JAFU 2, Wissant.*

G/C Stanley Vincent, *O.C., R.A.F. Station, Northolt.*

Oberstleutnant Friedrich Vollbracht, *Kdre. ZG 2, Toussee-le-Noble–St. Aubin.*

Chief Officer Frederick Wain, *Ramsgate Fire Brigade.*

2/Lt. John Walker, *1st Bn. Tower Hamlets Rifles, Duxford.*

F/Lt. Thomas Waterlow, *Adjutant, 601 Squadron, Tangmere.*

P/O Douglas Watkins, *611 Squadron, Digby–Fowlmere.*

P/O Richard Watkins, *Operations Room, Duxford Sector.*

Superintendent Albert Watson, *Margate Fire Brigade.*

F/Lt. John Watson, *Intelligence Officer, 607 Squadron, Tangmere.*

Arthur Weller, *Crockham Hill, Kent.*

Charles Wemban, *Rotherfield, Sussex.*

F/Lt. Innes Westmacott, *56 Squadron, North Weald.*

Sgt. John Whelan, *64 Squadron, Kenley.*

Mrs Beatrice Whitcher, *Shripney, Sussex.*

S/Ldr. Laurie White, *74 Squadron, Hornchurch.*

F/O William Whitty, *607 Squadron, Tangmere.*

Michael Wilcox, *Angmering, Sussex.*

Sgt. Ken Wilkinson, *616 Squadron, Kirton-in-Lindsey.*

F/O Dudley Williams, *152 Squadron, Warmwell.*

Trooper John Williams, *Royal Horse Guards, Knightsbridge Barracks, London.*

P/O Thomas Draper Williams, *611 Squadron, Digby– Fowlmere.*

William A. Williams, *Llandore, Glamorganshire.*

Rev. Cyril Wilson, *Hunsdon, Hertfordshire.*

F/O Douglas Wilson, *610 Squadron, Biggin Hill.*

Cpl. Ernest Wilson, *17 Squadron, Debden.*

Observer Frank Wilson, *Post B 3, Chislet, Kent.*

Sgt. Ralph Wolton, *152 Squadron, Warmwell.*

George W. Woods, *Canterbury, Kent.*

Mrs Gertrude Woods, *Canterbury, Kent.*

P/O Bertie Wootten, *234 Squadron, Middle Wallop.*

S/Ldr. John Worrall, *32 Squadron, Biggin Hill; Operations Room, Biggin Hill Sector.*

F/O Alan Wright, *92 Squadron, Biggin Hill.*

Sgt Eric Wright, *605 Squadron, Croydon.*

F/Sgt. John Wright, *600 Squadron, Manston–Hornchurch.*

P/O Robert Wright, *H.Q. Fighter Command, Stanmore.*

Section Leader Laurence Yates-Smith, *Beckenham (Kent) Civil Defence.*

Cpl. Jerzy Zbrozek, *Servicing Flight, 303 (Polish) Squadron, Northolt.*